ENDGAME

William Reed

TROND BOOKS

TROND BOOKS

ISBN: 978-1-4717-7057-9
Cover design by John Alves

Dedicated to my wife, whose patience and understanding during my mental absences while researching and writing this story were invaluable.

Prologue

The old lady had been very apprehensive when four Muslim students had moved into the house opposite in the small cul-de-sac of twelve redbrick townhouses. Years ago, this had been a respectable neighbourhood, populated by the workers of the steel factory who had built the estate, but gradually, after the factory closed in the late sixties, more and more of the homes had been converted to student accommodation. But she had been pleasantly surprised. They had caused no trouble. On the contrary, sometimes they had even helped her with her groceries. Like her own house, the one across the street was an end unit which had a garage attached in front of a small garden. And it was in their garage that the trouble had started, when they brought an old van there and started to work on it in the evenings. The garage doors were always closed, but the noise of hammering, grinding, and cutting was getting on her nerves. What were they doing in there?

She had mentioned it to Vahid last time he helped her with her shopping bags, and to her great relief, he had assured her that the noise was over and that they just had painting left to do.

Vahid was as good as his word because for the rest of the week, all she could hear was a low humming sound. Then it was over, and all went quiet, except they brought bags and boxes to the house, and they seemed to be heavy, needing two people to carry them.

She had expected the garage doors to open and the renovated vehicle to appear, but that did not happen, and she felt disappointed. She was curious to see what they had done with it. When she asked one of them why they had not taken it for a drive yet, she was told that they were waiting for the registration papers to come through. Two weeks later, they must have done because on a bright Saturday morning, the garage doors opened, and the van backed out into the street. The old lady was in the front garden planting a rose bush next to her front door. When she turned around, she saw a white van accelerating down the road. She could have sworn she saw *BBC News* written on the side of it, but she could not be sure. It was moving too fast.

Sixteen-hundred miles east of London, in a small village southwest of Moscow, an old man was awakened by a noise he had not heard since he was a young man, but he instantly recognised the low rumble and vibration of an articulated vehicle passing through the village. The last time he had heard this noise was in 1986, when a number of nuclear weapons had been mothballed in a storage facility just a few kilometres outside the village in a forested area. The noise had gone on for two weeks and always occurred at night. The villagers had complained to Comrade Ustinov, the town's mayor, who told them that once it was over in a couple of weeks' time, they would never hear that noise again. At the time, it was the result of the nuclear disarmament treaty between Russia and the

US, after the collapse of the Soviet Union, when thousands of nuclear arms were kept in storage facilities around the country. Yet, here was the noise again. Had the relationship between Russia and the US become so poor that the weapons were being reactivated and redeployed for possible future use? Just as well his parents and his wife were not alive to experience this again, he thought. He braced himself for sleepless nights ahead, but they never came, and soon he had forgotten the whole incident.

Chapter 1

He didn't know why he had woken up suddenly in the early hours of the morning or where the idea had come from. The idea, which had come to him, was how to infiltrate al-Qaeda so that the multi-headed monster, which the organisation had become, could be rolled up and put out of action. Killing bin Laden, Zawahiri and a few other al-Qaeda and ISIS leaders since, had not done much to reduce the activity of radical groups around the world. If anything, it had made matters worse. The idea that had taken shape in his head involved a small but very elite group of players: himself, Nathaniel Jameson, deputy chief of mission at the US Embassy in London; Jim Preston, the US ambassador in London; Imam Badawi, head of the largest mosque in Britain; and the vice president and president of the United States of America.

He looked over at his wife, fast asleep, lying next to him. How would he explain this idea to her? Would she think he had lost his mind? No doubt she would tell him that it was too risky and that he had to remember that he had a wife and two children. Sonja was still a beautiful woman at thirty-eight, and she'd been a tremendous support to him over the years. London was his fourth posting in twelve years, but she had never complained. Even when the children started school and had to be uprooted twice, she had taken it in her stride. She told the kids that they were lucky to experience different countries and cultures by living there rather than visiting as tourists. Her positive attitude was infectious, so the children accepted their nomadic lives as an adventure and made new friends easily, working hard at school and at play.

Sonja would be a great help to him if this idea became reality. Both her parents were Jordanian. Her father was a doctor, and her mother, a lawyer. They had left Amman in 1982, having decided that Jordan was not a place where they could secure a good life for themselves and the child they were expecting. Sonja had been born in Washington DC only four months after her parents had entered the country. Her father had built a successful medical practice, and her mother had abandoned law, devoting her life to her husband and children. Sonja's brother, Alan, followed two years later, and the two of them were brought up in a close and loving family setting.

Nat met Sonja at Harvard, where he studied law and economics and she studied history and English. It was love at first sight, at least for him. He'd first met her in the library where, sitting bent over a pile of books on a study table, her corn-blond hair cascading over the books, she had caught his attention. He placed himself at a table opposite so he could take a closer look. It took a while before she looked up, but when she did, his heart stopped. She had high-arching, dark eyebrows framing vividly blue eyes, a perfect nose, and full lips which looked like they wanted to be kissed.

He felt compelled to go over and introduce himself, pulled by a magnetic force. He said something utterly ludicrous: "Are you Nick Carter's sister?" She answered, "No," unsurprisingly, as he did not know anyone named Nick Carter, let alone his sister. But he introduced himself, sat down, and talked about nothing in particular until she told him that she had an essay to finish before tomorrow's tutorial.

He asked her if she would like to go out for dinner and a movie one night, but she said she was "... up to here in work," holding her hand flat under her perfect nose. Yet she gave him her name and phone number and told him to call her in a few weeks' time.

That was seventeen years ago, and here they were in London, in a beautiful, redbrick townhouse in Cadogan Gardens with their two children—Tanya, 12; and Gregory, 10—asleep in their room upstairs.

Sonja was a quiet sleeper. She hardly moved all night. She was lying on her side with one knee tucked up, exposing her slender, golden-brown legs, her hair falling softly over her face leaving only her forehead and long eyelashes showing. He was a lucky man. He had everything a man could possibly want.

He crept out of bed, the clock on the bedside table indicating 5:20 a.m., and deactivated the alarm which was set to go off at 6:30, then proceeded to the bathroom, where he shaved and showered quickly and put on his silk Armani dressing gown, a present from Sonja for his fortieth birthday last August.

The apartment in Cadogan Gardens was a spacious three-storey redbrick townhouse with two large bedrooms, one of which was on the top floor, where the children were fast asleep. The master bedroom suite was on the middle level, and the kitchen, dining room, drawing room, and library were on the first floor, or "ground floor", as the English called it. Grand stairs wound their way up to the children's floor and the attic and then down to the entrance hall which rose through the three levels to an oval skylight at the top of the stairs. Nightlights created just enough illumination to safely negotiate the stairs at night, and Nat descended quietly, entered the kitchen, and switched on the coffee maker which he made ready every night before going to bed.

The coffee would be ready in five minutes. He walked across the hall to the library, which was his favourite room, oak-panelled and lined with bookshelves on three sides and, on the fourth side, opening onto a small garden through a pair of French doors. He switched on his desk lamp from a wall switch as he entered the room and sat down in his comfortable red leather chair.

The question was how to move from idea to reality? The first person to speak to was obviously James Preston, the ambassador. If he did not buy into the idea, it would go no further, and there would be no need to worry Sonja.

He turned on his computer, and started to make a plan of action:

1. Speak to Jim
2. Talk to Sonja
3. Meet with the president and vice president
4. Determine which agencies will be involved
5. Meet with agency heads
6. Prepare operational plan with agency heads for approval by the president and vice president
7. Implement plan

The smell of freshly brewed coffee drifted in, and he went back to the kitchen where Darwin, their comedian dachshund, greeted him in the doorway, wagging his tail and rolling over on his back.

"Hey, boy! What are you doing up so early?" Nat bent down and rubbed his stomach, and Darwin's tail began to slap faster. "Okay, you can have a biscuit but no breakfast until Mommy comes down." He got the milk out of the fridge and a dog biscuit from the container on the counter, which brought the dog up into a perfect *sit* position. Nat placed the biscuit in Darwin's mouth and poured himself a cup of coffee and added the milk. Sonja had tried to convince him that he should drink his coffee black to avoid the fat, but he couldn't get used to the idea, despite some feeble attempts to cut out the milk to please her.

Back at his desk, he took the first sip of coffee, which was always the one that tasted the best, and looked down at the computer screen—*Implement plan—What plan?* He decided that it would be a good idea to set out an action plan, complete with players from both sides and the proposed sequence of events. He was deeply engrossed in this task when the ceiling lights came on.

"What on earth are you doing up at this hour?"

Her hand dropped from the switch, and she raised her eyebrows, waiting for his response. She was a stunning sight to behold, even at six in the morning. With or without makeup, it made no difference. She was a classic, natural beauty—not the kind of person you want to tell lies to.

"I have a meeting with Jim this morning. He wants to go through a draft itinerary for the president's European tour next February, you know, the one that'll bring the rest of Europe on board in the fight against terrorism."

Nat's sarcasm was not lost on Sonja. "And I suppose it's your job to come up with how that is to be accomplished?"

"Of course, darling, and you wonder why I have to get up so early?" He got up and walked over to her, anxious at the thought that she might get a look at his screen, and kissed her soft, waiting lips. At least he was not telling a complete lie; he *was* going to meet with Jim this morning, and maybe Jim could prove to be instrumental in helping to bring an end to international terrorism.

She gave him a long look, then turned and headed for the kitchen. "Have you fed Darwin?"

"No, I told him he had to wait until you came down," he said in response, then returned to his desk and sat down. He just needed another ten minutes or so to finish the plan outline. He would normally find his own breakfast, which, more often than not, consisted of cereal, a banana, orange juice and coffee, but today he needed to buy some time to finish what he had started.

"Darling, could you possibly make me some breakfast? I would like to finish this and get to the office early."

"Your usual?"

"No, it's going to be a tough day; could you make me some eggs and bacon?"

"Sure, darling, but only one egg and two pieces of bacon. You haven't been on the treadmill this morning."

"Thanks."

He got back to work and put the full stop after the final sentence just as Sonja's voice sang out "Come and get it!"

He closed the laptop, put it in its carrying case, and headed for the kitchen, where Sonja was standing in front of the stove with her back towards him. He came up behind her and embraced her, cupping her perfect breasts in his hands. She leaned back against him for an instant and then pulled away laughing. “Not me, you fool, I meant breakfast.”

The table was set for four, but he knew that it would be almost another hour before the children came down at 7:30. Sonja would drive them to school at 8:00, then get on with her own day, always starting with thirty minutes on the treadmill and then moving on to household chores, shopping, and other special weekly events such as tennis twice a week, a book club every two weeks, and sundry impromptu social get-togethers with friends. Nat had suggested, on many occasions, that they should hire a housekeeper, but Sonja refused, except to get some help when they entertained at home.

Pouring a cup of coffee for them both, she said, “I’ll eat with the children.”

They sat down and Nat got on with his breakfast. He’d usually skim the headlines to see which articles he needed to read when he got to the office, but the morning paper hadn’t arrived yet.

“Don’t forget we’re going out for dinner tonight, at 7:00, so you can’t be working very late. You said you had a tough day ahead.”

“We are?” he responded, having had no recollection of the event.

“Remember I called you last week and told you that the Jeffersons had invited us for dinner to meet the new professor of Islamic studies at Exeter University, and you said that that would be very interesting? I took that to be a ‘yes’ and accepted.”

“No, that’s fine. I look forward to it. It had slipped my mind, that’s all. It will be interesting to hear his views on things, like does he think there is anything we can do to defuse the anti-American feelings that seem to permeate the Muslim world? That should provide enough dinner conversation for one evening."

"As long as you behave yourself and listen rather than lecture, which you have a tendency to do after a few glasses of wine," she said, giving him a stern look over the edge of the coffee cup.

"Of course, I will. I shall be on my very best behaviour, just as if we were having dinner with your parents," he said with a grin as he got up from the table and took the dishes over to the sink. "You are going to have to do a lot better than that," Sonja said with a teasing smile. Nat and Sonja's father had, on occasion, heated arguments about how to deal with terrorism and other major world issues, and they often had to end an evening agreeing to disagree, which always seemed easier over the second glass of port.

"Don't worry. I won't embarrass you. I promise."

He disappeared upstairs and then reappeared ten minutes later in a dark blue Brioni suit, white shirt, and red tie. He picked up his briefcase and laptop from the library and headed for the door.

"Stop right there! Have you not forgotten something?" Sonja looked at him sternly, then closed her eyes, tilted her head upwards to him, and puckered her lips. He delivered a cursory token kiss only to find his neck being held firmly and Sonja responding with a kiss that would have stopped any man dead in his tracks. She pulled away slowly.

"There, that's better. Enjoy your day!"

CHAPTER 2

Nat reached the embassy in record time. The traffic was lighter because of the early hour, and he also drove with more urgency. Angela Pemberton, his private secretary, would not be in until nine o'clock, and his wristwatch told him that the time was only twenty past seven. The ambassador normally arrived at half past eight, but Nat decided to leave a message on his voicemail and dialed Preston's internal extension.

"Jim, good morning. This is Nat. Could I see you as soon as you've got a moment this morning? There's something I need to get your input on. Thanks."

He hung up and reached for a small pile of documents on his desk. It was all mundane, routine stuff. Two papers required his signature, and there was an invitation to a grouse shoot in Scotland, but the rest could be dealt with by Angela without further input from him.

He pulled out the laptop and reread the notes he had made earlier. Somehow the whole idea seemed outrageous in the bright light of his embassy office. Maybe Jim would think he had lost his mind, or at least that he was heading for a nervous breakdown, and tell him to go and see somebody. He could erase the notes and talk to Jim about the upcoming presidential visit, and nobody would ever know about his crazy idea, but what if it could be made to work? How many thousands of lives could be saved?

The war on terrorism was not going well. The Taliban were having a revival in Afghanistan. Iraq was still struggling to come to terms with democratic processes, and al-Qaeda had stepped up their attacks in the past few months. Lebanon and Israel enjoyed an uneasy peace, held together by a reluctant multinational force headed by the United Nations.

Hezbollah had not disarmed, as was required by Security Council Resolution 1701, and the Lebanese government showed no sign of attempting to disband the terrorist group. In fact, a large part of the rebuilding effort had been funded by Hezbollah, with the money originating from Iran. This had created a groundswell of support for the terrorist organisation and had weakened the influence of the Lebanese government. This was precisely what Iran was trying to achieve, and it was becoming obvious that the real winner in the region was Iran. They had held fast on their right to develop nuclear technology for peaceful purposes and had successfully avoided the resumption of international monitoring operations. Hamas had gained the upper hand in Palestine and made no secret of their opinion that Israel had no right to exist. And whilst the Caliphate had been destroyed, there was no sign that ISIS had been. In fact, recent US intelligence indicated that the world's major terrorist organisations were now under the umbrella of al-Qaeda, who funnelled funds and identified terrorism targets around the world.

The prospect of nuclear weapons in the hands of a country whose president had publicly expressed the desire to wipe

Israel off the map was a nightmare of unimaginable proportions. There was no doubt in the US president's mind that nuclear weapons in the hands of Iran would spell disaster for the civilised world and that the world's free nations could no longer sit back and argue amongst themselves about how to deal with the issue.

The president's upcoming European tour was to deal with this problem and the real danger of nuclear weapons ending up in terrorist hands, which would threaten the survival of not only Israel but the whole world.

Nat looked around his office, and his eyes fixed on the portrait of the president, which hung on the opposite wall between two tall windows looking out on the park. The president looked back at him with his steely blue eyes under bushy grey eyebrows. He was a strong man, but he was also intelligent and compassionate. He came from Colorado, where his family had been in the cattle business for four generations. His square jaw and broad smile gave the impression of a man of relaxed confidence—a man who was comfortable in his job.

If anybody was equal to the challenges that lay ahead, it was Ted Adams. The buzzer on Nat's desk startled him.

"Morning, Nat. You're up early."

"Good morning, Jim. Yes, I just couldn't stay in bed this morning. Could I come and see you?" Nat asked as he felt his heart beating faster.

"Sure, Nat. You sound like you've got something on your mind. Is Sonja giving you a hard time?" The ambassador chuckled and hung up.

Nat grabbed his laptop and a notepad and headed for Preston's office. Preston rose from his desk and greeted him with a big smile, waving an arm in the direction of his lounge seating area, "Let's sit over here and be comfortable. Would you like a cup of coffee?" Preston had his own coffee machine, capable of producing freshly brewed coffee in ten seconds, and he had a choice of six different blends. He'd already made a cup for himself. Nat didn't really feel like another cup of coffee just yet, as he would normally have a second cup midmorning; nevertheless, he accepted in order to give himself a bit of time to collect his thoughts. "So, what is your pleasure?" Preston gestured to the tray arrayed with plastic cups of various types of coffee.

"Could I have a Newman's Own decaf, please? I've already had two cups this morning."

"Decaf? You pussy! Real men don't drink decaf." Preston shook his head in mock disgust but proceeded to brew a cup of decaf.

Returning to the coffee table, he handed Nat the cup of coffee and sat down opposite in a soft leather armchair. "So, what's on your mind, Nat?" Preston crossed his legs, leaned back in the chair, and took a sip of coffee.

Nat cleared his throat. "Jim, I woke up this morning, and this crazy idea started to take shape in my mind, and the longer I thought about it, the more excited I got that it could work."

"An idea about what? What are you talking about? Spit it out, man!" Preston put his cup down on the table.

Nat opened his laptop. "Jim, promise me you will not have me fired or committed to an asylum; it's just an idea."

"For Christ's sake, Nat, tell me what this is about right now, or I *will* call the doctors."

"It's about getting inside al-Qaeda!" Nat stared straight into Preston's eyes, who stared back, eyebrows raised.

He took another sip of coffee whilst holding Nat in his gaze. "OK, Nat, that sounds like a good idea, but how the hell do we do that? We've tried for years to recruit agents around the world to accomplish this—no takers. It's too risky, and you'd have to kill too many people to prove your worthiness to join, at least at a level which could have a real impact."

"That's right, Jim. My idea is that we have to flush them out!"

"Flush them out?" Preston looked perplexed. "How on earth do we do that?"

"By offering them a prize that is so high they'd want to collect it themselves."

Preston shook his head in disbelief. "So you think they're stupid enough to come out of hiding to collect their own reward money? What did you have in mind—ten billion dollars? What's the price tag?"

Preston glared intently at Nat, who cleared his throat, fixed his eyes on Preston's, and said, "The president of the United States of America."

The two men stared at each other in silence. It was Preston who blinked first, appearing deadly serious. "OK, Nat, I'll call the doctors now. Obviously, you've lost your mind. I must've been working you too hard lately. But to amuse you, while we wait for the ambulance, why don't you tell me all about this idea of yours. It could be your first step back towards sanity, if that is a viable option." He spoke very slowly, as you might speak to a child or an old person to make sure that they understood you.

Nat grinned. "Thanks, Jim. How much time do I have?"

Preston smiled back. "You're OK; I haven't called the ambulance yet."

"Jim, you remember when we invited Imam Badawi here at the time of the hoopla about the Danish cartoons? We told him that whilst the USA was sympathetic to the frustration and anger felt by Muslims worldwide, their response to the cartoons was wholly unacceptable, and we expected Badawi, as head of the largest mosque in Britain, to do everything in his power to use his influence to calm British Muslims and appeal to Muslim clerics around the world to do the same. As you know, Badawi complied, albeit reluctantly, but we also know that he uses his position quietly to promote fundamentalist Muslim ideologies. We suspect that he may have direct links to al-Qaeda, but, so far, we have not been able to prove it. We talked about the meaningless bloodshed and the loss of thousands of innocent lives. He stressed to us that the Muslim faith had no room for violence and that terrorism was a result of injustices that had been perpetrated against the Arab world first by the Jews and then by America supporting the Jews, and, finally, America going to war against Afghanistan and Iraq. He told us that America's reaction to 9/11 and the ISIS Caliphate had improved al-Qaeda's position and made his own position, as a moderate Muslim, more difficult. Knowing what we know about Badawi's real agenda, I would try to get close to him. I would talk to him about the senseless loss of life—innocent women and children, many of them Muslims. As you know, Muslim fanatics have demonised Americans, and enemy number one is the American president. So, the ultimate prize for al-Qaeda, in my mind, would be the opportunity to assassinate the president."

"Yes, Nat, you may well be right on that one, but the president might have some reservations about giving them that opportunity."

"Of course, they would never get anywhere near the president. We would bring them in as soon as we know where they are."

"OK, Nat; that's terrific, but how do we find them? Ever since we got bin Laden, it has become ever more difficult to find top-level al-Qaeda targets."

"Not *we*, Jim—*me*. I would do it by convincing Badawi that I could deliver on creating such an opportunity. First, I would tell him that I'm sick and tired of the way Americans are acting on the world stage, that I am sick and tired of innocent lives being lost and that there is a better way. I would tell him that the Muslim cause would be better served by focusing their fight directly against the American decision-makers rather than the American people. I would explain to him that I, myself, am extremely bitter about the US government's shoddy treatment of war veterans, my father being one of those who came back from the Vietnam War maimed for life, ending up with a pathetic pension that nobody could live on... that he ended up killing himself with a drug overdose. In order to infiltrate al-Qaeda at the highest possible level, I would have to demonstrate that I am sincere and willing and able to get seriously involved myself. To prove that I am sincere and can be trusted, I would offer first to kill you—"

"Hold it right there!" Preston jumped out of his chair, arms raised, "You *have* lost your mind. I better call for that ambulance."

"Please, Jim, hear me out. When I've finished, if you still think I'm crazy, I will call the ambulance myself." Nat raised both arms in a gesture of surrender.

"Hopefully it will make more sense when you see the total picture."

"I certainly hope so, for your sake." Preston sank back in his chair. "This better be good or you will sleep in a straitjacket tonight, and I would not like to have to make the phone call to

Sonja." Preston managed a strained grin. "Continue! You will have no more interruptions from me."

"Thanks, Jim, I'll make it as brief as possible." Nat opened his laptop and scanned through his notes, then shut it again.

"You would 'die' from a fake 'induced heart attack', by something I put in your coffee. You would be rushed to hospital and pronounced dead on arrival. You would be flown back home and 'buried' at the family plot in Colorado. The news media would obviously cover the story so that Badawi and his friends can see for themselves that this is for real. Next, I will be appointed as the new US ambassador in London, which they will know gives me direct access to both the vice president and the president."

"Just a—" Preston started but waved himself off. "Never mind."

"By now, Badawi and his friends should begin to realise that I can deliver, but to bring the point home, and if it became necessary, I would offer to take out the vice president, who would also appear to have died from natural causes," Nat continued. "I'd offer to do this on the basis that al-Qaeda would agree to suspend all attacks on civilian populations worldwide, and I would insist on a written commitment to that effect."

Preston was listening intently. It seemed the idea had caught his imagination. It was an outrageous plan, completely unthinkable, but that was what made it so interesting.

Nat paused and had a sip of coffee. "Of course, the logistics of getting a plan like this to work are challenging, from getting the players involved to agree that they would take part—the legal and political ramifications—to how do you fake two deaths and keep it a secret."

"Yeah, Nat, I couldn't do that to Janet—have her stand over the coffin and cry her eyes out, believing I'm really in there," said Preston, referring to his wife. "She would never forgive me, no matter how good the cause. And, my brother would be heartbroken, but he would forgive me. The other problem is that I could be out of circulation for a long time. My life would be on hold until the operation succeeded or, God help us, it failed. What would I do, where would I go?"

"In my waking hours this morning I had you reentering with a new identity and a new look: a friend of Janet's from the old days. Hell, Jim, these things would have to be worked out by somebody smarter than myself." Nat raised his hands in a defensive gesture. "If you think the whole thing is totally crazy, then we stop it right here. I must say, it seems much more complicated to me now than it did at four this morning." Nat started to get up from his chair.

"Hold it, not so fast!" Preston motioned him to sit down. "It *is* a bloody crazy idea, Nat, but that's what I like about it. Imagine if we could get you inside al-Qaeda, at the top. We might be able to roll up the whole network. We must try and see if we can come up with some answers ourselves and, if we can, take a trip to Washington and talk to the boss and his deputy." Preston got up. "I have two meetings this morning, but I can get with you again this afternoon. Shall we say three o'clock? In the meantime, why don't you try to flesh this idea out some more? Hell, you might have it all worked out by the time we meet again." He reached for his intercom and pressed the button. "Clara, could you please ask George to get the car ready. I have to be at the French Embassy in half an hour."

Nat stood up and turned towards the door.

"Nat, surely you could have thought of an easier way to get my job?" Nat turned and saw Preston grinning from ear to ear. Preston saluted and said, "Carry on!"

CHAPTER 3

Back in his own office, Nat decided to focus first on the problem of how to deal with the life of a person who was supposed to be dead. The vice president was a widower. Betty, his wife, had died from a stroke three years ago, and they had no children. He had no sisters or brothers, so there was no immediate family to be concerned about. He had a number of friends and enemies from his thirty years in the halls of power in Washington, but since Betty's death, he hadn't socialised much. As vice president he'd kept a low profile in public whilst staying close to the president behind the scenes. In fact, the vice president could go undercover and still function as the president's closest adviser. He just couldn't attend any meetings where others were present.

Maybe the biggest problem was the fact that a new vice president would have to be appointed very quickly and be sworn in. Who could it be, and would he or she be let in on the plot and told that this was a temporary position only? Obviously, the fewer people who knew the truth, the better. This seemed to be a question only the president and vice president could answer. The vice president had been plagued with recurring heart problems and might possibly see this as the right time to step down, in any event.

The buzzer on his desk went off. "Good morning."

It was Angela. "Do you want a cup of coffee?"

Nat hesitated. "No thanks. I've had a cup already, with Preston. Angela, could you hold all calls for me this morning unless, of course, it's Sonja or something else which is really urgent?"

"Will do. Can I help you with anything?" Angela's crisp English accent and bright tone brought him back to reality.

"No thanks; just deal with the stuff I left on your desk. Also, could you get me a sandwich later, for lunch, please?"

"What would you like?"

"Make it roast beef with lettuce and tomato, no mayonnaise. Thanks."

Nat returned to his notes. Clearly it would be important to get al-Qaeda's attention as soon as possible. If it could be done after the "murder" of the American ambassador, so much the better. If not, it would be important to follow up quickly with the "assassination of the vice president". The longer the two men had to be kept out of circulation, the greater the risk of something going wrong.

What if they didn't take the bait? The hoax could not be played out indefinitely. Nat figured he would insist that he would not kill the president himself and that he would make it a condition, before "killing" the vice president, that al-Qaeda would strike the final, decisive blow.

Then there was the matter of the staging of the murders themselves. The men would fake their heart attacks, and equally fake emergency response teams would respond and take the victims—where? Preston would, under normal circumstances, be rushed to St. Mary's Hospital or UCH. The call to St. Mary's would be intercepted, and the fake ambulance emergency team would arrive and take Preston to a safe house, for transportation, via a private CIA plane back to the US.

Perhaps the same game plan would work for the vice president? He could be in a meeting with the president and maybe with Nat, as he has just been appointed as the new ambassador in London. Nat's presence at both events would reinforce his position in al-Qaeda and leave no shadow of doubt that he'd upheld his side of the bargain.

In this case, the call to George Washington Hospital Center would be intercepted, and the vice president would be whisked off to a location, perhaps somewhere near Camp David?

What was the likelihood that the two men would agree to be part of a plot like this, and even if they did, could they be part of it without breaking every protocol in Washington's political rule book? These were questions which only the president and vice president could answer, with input from their closest advisers, if it ever got that far. If Preston decided it was too crazy an idea to take any further, that would be the end of it.

If it got past Preston, Nat would have to talk to Sonja. She would be dead set against it, and she would see, at once, that the person who would take the biggest risk would be Nat himself. Infiltrating al-Qaeda was as dangerous as it was difficult. And whether the plan succeeded or failed, would it put their lives in danger forever after? Maybe she could tolerate the risk for Nat and herself, but not for the children. Neither could he. This could be the biggest hurdle to overcome, if it was possible to overcome at all.

Even if the scheme succeeded, and they rolled up the whole organisation, it would be naive to believe that Muslim fundamentalist extremism would cease to exist overnight. The war on terrorism had to be fought and won on many fronts. The winning of hearts and minds was a vital battle which the war in Iraq, and Israel's sortie into Lebanon, had set back a long way. US presence in the Middle East, and its seemingly unconditional backing of Israel, had done nothing to win hearts and minds.

The president was aware of this, and his trip to Europe would be followed up with a trip to the Middle East, despite advice from his security advisers that it posed a logistical security nightmare.

It was rumoured in Washington that the president would unveil a joint American and European plan for the Middle East which would demand that Israel withdraw from all Palestinian-occupied territories and that a separate Palestinian state would be created which recognised Israel's right to exist. No financial assistance would be resumed to the Hamas-led Palestinian government until it denounced violence as a means to resolve conflict and it recognised Israel's right to exist within its 1967 borders.

There was a knock on his door, and Angela came in carrying a tray containing his roast beef sandwich, a bottle of ice-cold Perrier water, and a crystal glass. He looked at his watch and was surprised to see that it was 12:15. He closed his laptop. "Thanks Angela. Could you put it on my coffee table?"

She did and turned towards him. "There were six calls for you. I dealt with three of them, but you need to take care of these." She handed him three pink telephone message slips.

Nat glanced at them and registered that none of them needed immediate attention. “Thanks, I’ll take care of them this afternoon.” Nat got up from his desk and went over to his lounge area which had two soft chairs and a three-seater couch arranged around a heavy glass and chrome coffee table.

“Can I get you anything else?”

Angela was the very essence of an efficient English secretary. She had dark brown hair swept up in a tight bun at the back. She had green eyes behind heavy horn-rimmed glasses, and ruby red, shiny lips. She cut a fine figure in a tan jacket and skirt which showed off her hourglass figure and shapely legs without, in any way, seeming provocative.

“Oh, by the way, Preston said to let you know that he would be back in the office around three o’clock.”

“Thank you, Angela. This is all I need.” He sat down and poured himself a glass of Perrier.

“Very well, sir.” She smiled and left the room, closing the door softly behind her.

Nat started on his sandwich and realised that he didn’t feel at all hungry. Outside, it had turned into a sunny day without him noticing it, and people were sitting in the park enjoying their lunch and the fine weather. He remembered that he’d promised the children a trip to the zoo tomorrow, Saturday. Hopefully, the weather would be like this.

CHAPTER 4

He finished his lunch and returned to the laptop, where he turned his attention to Imam Badawi—how to connect with him, how to win his confidence and draw him into the plot. As he was finishing his narrative on this subject, there was a knock on the door and Preston entered. "Got it all worked out, have you?" he said with a big grin. "The French ambassador is upset because the vice president went on CNN News and lamented the lack of resolve from European nations in the fight against terrorism. I said he needed to understand America's frustration at the lack of a strong, united front, but he would have none of it, telling me that the wars in Iraq and Afghanistan had created more terrorists than had been disposed of. The president will have an uphill battle to convince the French that they should join in, at least until, or unless, they can see that a stable democracy is about to take hold there, just like De Gaulle walking ahead of the allied troops through the Arc de Triomphe after we had beaten the Germans." Preston shook his head in disgust. "So, I hope your idea can be made to work, Nat. With the Brits diddering, it looks like we will be going it alone soon." Preston sat down opposite Nat, who started to go through his notes.

Preston would stop him at times and ask questions and offer suggestions, and between them they cobbled together the outline of a plan which found its way onto Nat's laptop.

"Well, do you know what?" Preston stood up. "It's a wild idea, but I think it's worth at least sharing it with the boss and his deputy. If they don't like it, then it's over."

Nat took a deep breath and exhaled. "Phew. . . I had almost got to the point where I was hoping that you would have said no."

"Not to worry, son." Preston gave Nat a reassuring slap on the back. "We'll take it one step at a time. The president can say no, or his advisers may say no. There probably is a statute that precludes a president from taking part in something like this, and, perhaps, risking his life. The vice president may not like the idea of playing dead, and even if he was OK with it, the legal beagles will probably advise him that he can't do it anyway. So, there are plenty of opportunities for your plot to be shelved. If I were you, I would turn my attention to Sonja. If she says no, the plan is dead, or we would have to find somebody without a wife and children to play your part." Preston gave Nat a long, serious look.

"Yes." Nat nodded. "That's probably the reason I was hoping you would nix the idea right now. I don't know how I can justify this to Sonja; I can't justify it to myself. The thought of placing her and the kids in danger, either from revenge for a successful operation or anger from a failed operation, scares me."

"I don't blame you, Nat, it's a tough one." Preston looked thoughtfully through Nat's window to the park beyond.

"I'm better off than you. At least Janet and I have grown-up children with children of their own. They have their own separate lives and would be unlikely targets for retribution. Of course, the guys at Langley will tell you that they can protect you and your family afterwards by changing your identities and bringing you back to the US, but that is more difficult to do with smaller children. They would probably have to do the same for me, but that would not be so difficult since I'm already *dead*. Maybe we can find somebody else to take your part, Nat?" Preston turned back from the window and faced Nat. His eyebrows were raised, prompting an answer to his question.

"I've been thinking about that, but I can't come up with anybody who I think would have as good a chance of pulling it off. I have established a good relationship with Badawi, my father was a Vietnam vet, and he did commit suicide of sorts, although not intentionally. He died from an accidental drug overdose. My wife is Jordanian. I was, if I may say it myself, a pretty good amateur actor in high school and at Harvard. I don't have to reinvent myself to do this. This part was made for me. That's probably why I dreamt this up in the first place."

There was a knock on the door, and Angela, Nat's secretary poked her head through the door opening. "Is there anything I can do for you before I leave?"

Nat looked at her and then at his watch. It was 5:30. "No, thank you, Angela. Jim and I are doing some work on the president's upcoming European tour. We'll be packing it in soon ourselves."

"Very well. Sonja called, but when I told her you were in with Jim, she told me not to disturb you but just to remind you about dinner at the Jeffersons tonight at seven o'clock. Have a nice evening. Goodbye." She closed the door, and the faint sound of her high-heeled shoes faded as she walked towards the elevators.

Preston got up. “OK, Nat, let’s call it a day. I agree with you. I think you *would* be the best person for this project should it go ahead. But you couldn’t get involved in this without Sonja agreeing, which means you need to talk to her before we go any further.”

“You’re right, Jim.” Nat got out of his chair. “The next step is to talk to her. Give me a couple of days.”

“Hey, take your time. This is not the kind of decision which can be made in a hurry.” Preston headed for the door, opened it, and turned to Nat, who was still standing behind his desk.

“You have to be able to convince yourself that this is worth doing before you can sell it to Sonja. Don’t rush at this one. Take your time, and have a good weekend.” With that, he was gone.

Nat had not moved from the spot behind his desk. How could he ask Sonja to go along with this? Was it even fair to ask her? He looked at his watch. It was almost six o’clock. He had to get going if they were going to make it to the Jeffersons by seven. He closed the laptop and put it in his briefcase, turned off the lights, and left the office. The security guard downstairs gave him a cheerful wave and wished him a good weekend.

CHAPTER 5

When he stopped the car in front of the house, he realised that he couldn't recall which route he'd taken home. The traffic had been heavy and the progress slow, but his mind had been elsewhere, struggling with how to find a way to do this without putting his family at risk.

His thoughts were cut short by Sonja appearing in the front door, fully dressed and ready to go. "Hurry up, darling; we're going to be late. I've called the Jeffersons."

He looked at his watch. It was 6:45. "Sorry honey; the traffic was heavier than I expected. I'll be ready in ten." He gave her a quick peck on the cheek as he passed her and headed into the kitchen where Rachel, the babysitter, was dishing up dinner for the children. "Hello, Rachel, how are you?"

The children interrupted her reply. "Dad!" They jumped out of their chairs and ran towards him.

He set his briefcase on the floor, gathered them up in his arms, and gave them both a big hug and kiss. "How was school today?"

"Good," they replied in unison.

"I've got to go and get ready, but you can tell me all about your day on the way to the zoo tomorrow." He let them down gently, and they resumed their places at the table, where steaming hot sausages and chips were waiting for them.

Sonja appeared in the doorway. "Off you go, Dad! How late do you want us to be?"

Nat took off, taking the steps two at a time, while Sonja gave the babysitter her last instructions. No TV or computer games after 8:30, in bed by 8:45 with a book, and lights out at 9:00.

"Oh, Mom." Gregory decided to try a little negotiation. "Can't I take my computer to bed, instead of reading, just for tonight?"

She tussled his hair and laughed. "Good try, Greg. No, you can't take your computer to bed. Reading makes you sleepy, and the computer does the opposite. Besides, you told me you like to read, didn't you?"

"Yes, Mom," Gregory conceded.

Sonja turned to Rachel, ending any further discussion on the subject. "Please remember to take Darwin out on the lawn around nine thirty, or he may give you a surprise in the house. We will be back around eleven, and here is the Jeffersons' phone number should you need to get hold of us." She handed Rachel a piece of paper. "And help yourself to soft drinks from the fridge, and there's some ice cream if you like."

Rachel was the eighteen-year-old daughter of Sonja's tennis partner. She was in her final year of high school and was working hard preparing to take five A levels. She had brought some study material to work on after the children had been put to bed. Like most young girls, she was concerned about her weight and declined the offer of ice cream, although her tight jeans and black sweater showed that she had nothing to worry about.

Nat reappeared wearing tan slacks, a white shirt, and a navy blazer but no tie. Sonja was wearing a simple champagne-coloured cocktail dress with just a single strand of pearls around her neck. It was seven o'clock. They kissed the children good night and asked Rachel to call if there was anything that she was concerned about.

She said, "Not to worry, we'll be fine," and waved as they drove off.

CHAPTER 6

The Jeffersons lived in a mews house in Queen's Gate Mews, Kensington, opposite the Royal College of Music. It wasn't far away, but the Friday evening traffic was heavy, and Nat decided to cut across town on the smaller streets and head down Cadogan Street towards Draycott Avenue. The clock on the dashboard told him it was 7:10, and he was hoping to get there by 7:30.

Nat turned to Sonja. "How was your day?"

"Good. After I dropped the kids off at school, and I was on my way back to do some serious housework, Pat called and said she needed my opinion on fabric for new curtains and asked if I could please stop off at Conran's. Of course, I couldn't say no, so off I went, and we ended up spending the whole morning looking at fabrics both for the new curtains and upholstery fabric for the living room furniture. What we picked just wouldn't go with the floral pattern brocade she has now. Then we had some lunch, and I didn't get home until 2:30, just enough time to let Darwin out before I fetched the kids. No housework today."

"Damn!" Nat jammed on the brakes and swerved to miss a big black London taxicab that cut in just inches from Nat's bumper. "Can you believe that? Who said the English are civilised drivers?" Nat shook his head in disgust. "You'd think we were in New York!"

"Never mind, darling. He was just testing your reflexes." She gave him a sideways glance with a hint of a smile. "And yours seem to be just fine, thank God."

Nat turned right onto Brompton Road after a long red light, only to be met by another red light at the junction with Cromwell Road where he needed to turn left. The traffic on Cromwell Road was bumper to bumper, as usual.

"So, who is this new professor of Islamic studies that we're going to meet tonight, and what's his connection with the Jeffersons?" They were passing a floodlit Natural History Museum on the right, and Nat was preparing to turn right on Queen's Gate immediately after the museum. The time was 7:20, and he figured they would be there in another five minutes.

"I really don't know much about him other than the fact that he's from Australia—Sydney, I think—and that he's quite young to be a professor, and very good-looking, according to Nancy." Nancy was Andrew Jefferson's very American wife from Springfield, Massachusetts, and Andrew was a highly regarded personal investment banker heading up a Swiss investment bank in London. His investment skills were only matched by his prowess on the golf course, and, being a Scotsman, he had invited Nat to come with him to Glen Eagles and other famous Scottish courses from time to time. "And his connection to the Jeffersons is that professor Harrison and his Swedish wife, Catrin, also have their children in Cottesmore, where the Jeffersons have their son, Daniel. They met at sports day last year and *hit it off,* as they say over here." That's all I know. Sonja turned down the sun visor and studied her hair which was turned up in a relaxed roll at the back. She found some imperceptible imperfection and corrected it, and turned the visor back to the ceiling.

"OK, here we are." Nat took a sharp left turn followed by an almost immediate right turn, and there they were in front of the Jefferson's elegant two-storey town house. Stone steps led up to a massive oak front door which was framed by a Georgian porch. Nat drove past the door and parked in front of the double garage which was set far enough back from the road to allow for two visitors' cars to be parked off the street. There was no other car there. Maybe they were not the last to arrive after all?

Nat had just reached for the polished brass bell pull when the front door opened, and a smiling Mr. Jefferson stood framed in the warm light from the entrance hall. His red cardigan, white shirt, and blue and white cravat gave him the look of the archetypal Englishman rather than the Scot he was so proud to be.

"Welcome, welcome." He reached out for Sonja's hands, gave her a kiss on both cheeks, and turned to Nat. "Working too hard again, are we? With all the staff you have at the embassy, you shouldn't have to work at all." He ushered them in. "The Harrisons are here. They had the good sense to take a taxi. Shall I take your jacket?" He held a hand out to Nat, who was glad to give the jacket up.

Nancy Jefferson and Sonja were embracing in the doorway to the drawing room. She waved them in. "Come and meet the Harrisons, our friends from Cottesmore." She gestured them towards the lounge seating arranged in front of a massive soapstone fireplace where a cosy fire was throwing warm, flickering light across the faces of the Harrisons as they rose from their chairs and greeted the new arrivals.

Nat conceded, in his mind, that Bob Harrison wasn't a bad-looking man, although most of his face was covered by a full medium-brown beard. He was Nat's height—six feet two inches—or perhaps half an inch taller, broad shouldered, and heavyset. A mop of unruly, not quite curly, hair gave the impression of a Robinson Crusoe who had just been rescued from his island retreat.

"Pleased to meet you." Bob took Nat's hand and shook it vigorously and gave Sonja the same treatment.

Catrin Harrison was quite the opposite, with short cropped black hair; perfect, pure white skin; and a slender body. She wore a simple low-cut, sleeveless black cocktail dress and spoke very softly as she introduced herself.

After a short exchange of pleasantries, Andrew went to the cocktail trolley and asked Nat and Sonja what they'd like to drink. Sonja asked for a sherry and Nat for a scotch and Perrier which were produced with a deftness that could've made a seasoned bartender envious. Andrew asked everybody to be seated and raised his glass in a toast: "Here's to a better world! We need it!" They drank to a better world.

Nancy looked at her husband and frowned. "How about toasting our guests first and thanking our lucky stars that we can get together like this without worrying that a rocket might land on our house while we're having dinner?"

Nancy and Andrew raised their glasses again. "...To our guests." Andrew did the honours.

The women launched into a conversation about the children, their health, school, their behaviour, and the men listened attentively for a while, making sporadic, polite comments.

When Andrew felt they'd stayed on the topic long enough, he leaned forward towards Nat and Bob and said in a low voice, so as not to disturb the women, "I wanted to get the two of you together. I've had interesting dinner conversations with both of you separately on the subject of terrorism and how best to fight it. You both come at it from different vantage points, but I believe, having listened to both of you, that the best way forward may be found in combining your ideas. Bob, why don't you start by telling Nat how you ended up being a professor of Islamic studies? It is not immediately obvious that a brawny Aussie should be in that position." Andrew smiled disarmingly at Bob.

"Well, to make a long story short..." Bob cleared his throat. "It stems from the fact that I spent seven years in Bahrain between the ages of seven and fourteen. My father was posted there by Cable and Wireless and managed the station there until he retired and we moved to England. I went to an English-speaking school there, but quite a few of my schoolmates were Bahrainis. I enjoyed my years there, and there was many a time, particularly in winter, on a cold and wet rugby pitch at boarding school, that I longed back to the brilliant, shimmering heat of the Arabian archipelago. I'd learned a bit of the language and kept up correspondence with a Bahraini schoolmate of mine—in English, mind you. After two years at Bryanston, I was invited back by my friend to stay with him and his family at their summer retreat on a small island in the archipelago. I had a fabulous time there, fishing and sailing and driving dune buggies in the desert. I fell in love for the first time, with my friend's sister, but she never knew that I had a crush on her. My friend ended up coming to my school for the last three years of his secondary education, and I got him to teach me both to write and speak Arabic. I was far from fluent, but it stood me in good stead when I applied to Nottingham University to study history and philosophy."

Bob paused and took a sip of his drink before he continued.

"I spent a year there, but the Middle East was in my blood. I looked into it, but Nottingham did not offer any courses on Islamic studies or the Middle East, except as small parts of geography, so I ended up at Exeter, where I took Arab and Islamic studies, which brought me to Alexandria for my year out. That got me hooked. The culture, the history, the people, the contrast between the modern world of oil, and those who were part of that, and those who continued to live as people did when the pyramids were built—the outrageous wealth of some and the abject poverty of others. The contrasts were, and are, mind-blowing. I came back home, finished my undergraduate degree and went for the master's degree, and finished up doing a doctorate. The title of my thesis was 'Complexity and Contradiction in the Arab World.' My tutor advised me that he thought it was too big a subject, and there were times when I thought he might have been right, but I persevered and ended up with a piece of work which was well received. I was offered a teaching post at Exeter and taught for ten years. Last year, I was offered a professorship which I was very pleased to accept, and that was the short version." Bob shrugged his shoulders apologetically and took another sip of his drink.

"Well, there we have it. A professor and a madman!" Andrew gave Nat a teasing smile, and Nat thought, *You don't know how right you are*.

"Anybody who goes to work at seven in the morning, comes home at seven, and takes work home is mad," added Andrew.

"Come on, Andrew, those are the exceptions, not the rule."

"No, it's your American work ethic. Careful, old boy, it could shorten your life." Andrew raised his glass and toasted them both.

"Nat is second in command at the US Embassy, so I guess he's working to become number one. Mind you, he does carry the weight of the world on his shoulders and seems to think it's his personal responsibility to sort the world out. You should hear him on the subject of world terrorism. He gets quite excited and emotional about it."

Nat looked at Sonja, who, although apparently in deep conversation with Bob's wife, found the time to give him a warning glance. Her eyes said, *Don't get carried away! Behave yourself!*

Nancy had disappeared to the kitchen, and Sonja and Catrin were on the subject of shopping for clothes in New York, talking about the unlimited choices offered by designers from around the globe.

Nat drained his glass and placed it on the table in front of him and declined Andrew's offer of another. He turned to Bob and said, "I just wish there was a way to stop the madness that plagues the world today. It seems to me that we are engaged in a war that we are reluctant to fight yet can't afford to lose. Some people say that if we can sort out the Israeli/Palestinian conflict, our problems will be over, but that is wishful thinking at its most extreme. It seems to me that Islamic fundamentalists are at odds with the modern world and want to pull us back into the dark ages. We have a clash of cultures which goes way beyond any issue specific to the Middle East."

CHAPTER 7

"Dinner is ready!"

Nancy appeared from the kitchen and gestured towards the dining room, where the table was set with deep blue and gold plates on a dark red tablecloth. The silverware and the crystal glasses sparkled in the light from two silver candlesticks. A warm glow permeated the space from a fireplace that cast a flickering light on the linen-fold oak panelling and the paintings on the walls.

Nancy placed Bob on her right and Nat on her left so that they were sitting opposite each other. Andrew occupied the head seat at the other end of the table, with the fireplace behind him, Catrin to his right and Sonja on his left. Their Polish maid, Flora, appeared from the kitchen with a large tray of soup bowls. She carefully set the tray down on the sideboard and served the dishes two at a time. "The dinner tonight is entirely Middle Eastern," Nancy announced, "starting with soup avgolemono, egg and lemon soup, followed by a lamb dish called *lana um*; and for dessert, we shall have *badmen kayos*, which is baked apricots stuffed with almond paste."

Bob's face lit up. "Nancy, that is fantastic. Lana um is a favourite of mine. Do you know what it means?" Nancy shook her head. "It means: 'his mother's milk' and implies that the young animal is cooked in his own mother's milk."

Nancy frowned. "How cruel. Anyway, this isn't. Bon appétit!"

They got on with the starter and, in the momentary silence which ensued, the crackling of the wood fire seemed to fill the room.

Catrin broke the silence. "The soup is delicious, Nancy. Isn't it difficult to make? How do you stop the eggs from curdling?"

"I didn't; Andrew did. He is the soup specialist in our family. I cannot take any credit for the soup, but I agree it does taste very good."

"Well, of course, it's very complicated." Andrew looked at them all with a serious expression. "It has taken me years to perfect this recipe."

"Oh, stop it, Andrew!" Nancy laughed at her husband. "Tell the truth!"

Andrew shrugged and sighed. "Well, if I have to. The trick is to make sure that you don't let it boil when you stir in the lemon and eggs. I've had some spectacular failures with this dish before I got it right, but practice makes perfect, and modesty is not my strongest suit."

"Oh, I don't know about that?" Nat came to life. "Last time we were at Glen Eagles together and you got that hole-in-one, you said it was pure luck?"

"Pooh, what choice did I have after three bogeys? Golf is a very humbling game. If I wasn't Scottish I would give it up."

They all laughed. The conversation continued in a light vein until they had finished the soup. Flora appeared and collected the empty bowls, and Andrew and Nancy excused themselves, got up, and disappeared into the kitchen.

"Do you play golf?" Nat looked across at Bob who shook his head.

"Not really. I have a set of clubs, but my efforts on the golf course are limited to Rotary Club fundraising tournaments and the occasional twosome best ball fun tournament at the university. I enjoy it every time and promise myself that I'll make a point of getting out there more often, but I haven't made good on it yet."

"I'm not much better," Nat conceded. "Andrew has just about given up on me. Maybe the three of us could have a round some time?"

"That sounds like a great idea. I'll get my practice balls out and do some practicing; otherwise, you'd be doing a lot of waiting around." Bob chuckled and gave his wife a quick glance. "And Catrin would be glad to get me out of the house for a while."

"Absolutely." Catrin nodded energetically. "Bob is sitting down too much. I've a hard time getting him to turn his computer off."

The door from the kitchen swung open, and Andrew appeared carrying a steaming serving dish with the lamb followed by Nancy with the rice and Flora with a bowl of dried mint. As the food was passed around, Andrew returned to the kitchen and reappeared with three bottles of red wine on a tray. As he poured it out, he announced, "The wine is not Middle Eastern, it's Middle European—French, to be specific. I'm not into New World wines, although I admit that both Americans and Australians have come up with some very good *white* wines." Andrew took his place at the head of the table and raised his glass. "Here's to a better world—new and old!"

Silence fell over the table as they concentrated on the steaming hot lana um. The silence was broken by Bob, who looked up from his plate with a beaming smile. "That is just the way I remember it from my time in Egypt. To Nancy!" He raised his glass, and the others followed suit. Putting his glass back down, Bob switched his attention to Andrew, "And Andrew, the wine is excellent, but next time you have this dish you should try it with a bottle of wine from the vineyards of Chateau Kefraya."

"Chateau Kefraya?" Andrew looked puzzled. "Never heard of it. French?"

"No, Lebanese. Chateau Kefraya is a vineyard in the heart of the Bekka Valley, on the steep slopes of Mount Bark. The soil is chalky and stony, and with a six-month dry and sunny season, the conditions are near perfect for the growing of vines, which, by the way, come from French root stock. I can email you some names of specific wines, if you are interested."

"Well, what do you know, I had no idea. Sure, I'm interested." Looking around the table, Andrew added, "It's hard to believe that anything good can come out of the Middle East these days. Western news media have painted a very lopsided picture of the region."

"So, they have," Nat put his knife and fork down. "They are ignoring all the good news from the region, to the point where American public opinion has been turned against our continued involvement there. When free elections, held in countries which have been run by tyrannical rulers for twenty-five years or more, become a minor blip on the news firmament, what possible chance do we have of changing the world for the better?" Sonja gave him a warning stare which said, *This better not be one of your half-hour monologues on world affairs.*

Nat continued undeterred: "Billions of dollars have gone into reconstruction works in Iraq and Afghanistan. Electricity, water, sewer, schools, hospitals, roads, bridges, the oil industry—you name it, and it's being worked on, but you hardly see or hear mention of it in the news media. A lot of the money which was earmarked for reconstruction has gone into bolstering security: the police, security forces, prisons, and so on. To some extent this is understandable, because it's obviously difficult to rebuild a country's infrastructure while it's still at war. Insurgents have been attacking Iraq's and Afghanistan's infrastructure, from oil fields to the small corner store, anything to try to prevent the new governments from succeeding in creating a better life for their citizens. So, if Iraq and Afghanistan are to become the success stories that we all hope for, then the rebuilding effort must proceed with the same priority and commitment as the fight against the terrorist." Nat finished his point with a sip of wine.

CHAPTER 8

They finished the main course, and Flora cleared the table and brought the baked apricot dessert. Nancy, who brought a jug of cream, stressed that the cream was optional and not authentic. Andrew explained that he had "improved on" the ancient recipe to make it more agreeable to his Scottish palate. When Nancy passed the jug to Nat, he poured himself some cream before looking over to Sonja, who gave him a mock stern look and shook her head.

Catrin complimented Nancy on the dessert and asked for the recipe, and it was agreed, by general consensus, that Middle Eastern cooking was delicious, at least as performed by the Jeffersons.

As they were finishing the dessert, Andrew tapped his spoon on his wine glass to get everyone's attention. "Don't worry, I'm not going to launch into a long, or even short, speech. I just have a suggestion, and that is that the men retire to my study for a coffee and brandy, while you ladies have your coffee and after-dinner drinks in the drawing room. I would like to hear more from Bob and Nat on the situation in Iraq and Afghanistan and the whole question of international terrorism.

My guess is that you ladies have other things that you would like to talk about?"

Nancy looked at Sonja and Catrin. "I vote for the drawing room. Important as it is, there's more to life than world terrorism. What do you say?" They agreed, and the men retired to Andrew's study where two couches and a glass table were arranged in front of another lit soapstone fireplace. The fire reflected in the glass tabletop which, in turn, made a dancing pattern of yellow and orange on the white ceiling. Between the seating area and Andrew's desk stood a trolley with Remy Martin cognac and three brandy snifters. Andrew went to the trolley, while Nat and Bob took a seat, opposite each other, nearest the fire. There was a light knock on the door, and Flora appeared with the coffee tray and placed it on the glass table. The coffee pot was sterling silver in the shape of an elephant. Flora poured the coffee out through the raised elephant trunk and invited them to help themselves to milk and sugar, as Andrew returned with two brandy snifters.

"Thank you, Flora, leave the rest to me." She disappeared as quietly as she had arrived, and Andrew returned with his own glass of cognac, the golden liquid sparkling in the reflections of the fire.

Andrew sat down next to Nat. "I hope you don't mind; I thought the girls might have had enough war talk." He raised his glass. "And I feel we have only just started. Cheers!"

They sipped the cognac and washed it down with some coffee.

"Uhm, good! This is the life!" Nat closed his eyes and sank back in the couch.

"Ditto," said Bob, "the only thing missing is the cigar."

"Sorry," Andrew said, "but I gave that up seven years ago. That is, I gave up smoking ten years ago, but I hung on to the cigars for another three years. That was until Nancy told me that the filthy stench of cigar smoke was worse than the cigarettes, and could I please return to cigarette smoking? She said that even if it killed me, it would be better. I know she was practicing elemental child psychology 101, but it had the desired effect."

"No, no, I was just kidding." Bob smiled. "I've never smoked anything, not even weed. I would've had to turn down your very best Havana."

"What about you, did you ever smoke?" Andrew turned to Nat.

"Yes, I did—started with a pipe in my last year at College and progressed to cigarettes at university, quit at the end of university and, after some relapses during the next twelve months, I've never smoked since." Nat twirled the brandy snifter in his hand. "But there are some things I'm not willing to give up, and this is one of them." They all took another sip.

Andrew stood up and put another log on the fire. "It's all very well to talk about the past and what has gone wrong in our fight against terrorism; there's plenty of blame to go around, to be sure, but my question to the two of you is, given the current situation, where should we go from here?" Andrew took his place on the couch again. "Nat, I know you have some very strong feelings on the subject."

"I do. Let's go back a bit because where we are today has a lot to do with what took place many years ago. Take for example all the so-called mistakes which, allegedly, were made in Iraq, starting with the reasons for going to war in the first place.

First of all, the decision to go into Iraq was based on intelligence which suggested Saddam was in possession of weapons of mass destruction. The mere fact that none were found does not prove that these weapons did not exist. He had plenty of time to hide them, and my guess is that, if we could have taken out a search warrant against Syria and done a thorough search there, we might well have found them. We knew, from the mountain of disclosure documents produced for the UN inspectors, that there was no accounting for what had happened to these weapons. If he had destroyed them, why not say so and avoid a certain invasion?"

"Perhaps he never thought the Western powers would have the balls to invade?" Bob volunteered. "Don't forget the French, the Germans, Russia, and China had made it clear that they wanted no part in an attack on Iraq. Saddam probably thought the Americans and the Brits would not be prepared to go in alone. Don't forget, Saddam claimed victory when the old man Bush didn't finish the job in 1991. In the Gulf War, he had a large international coalition backed by a UN resolution against him. They threw him out of Kuwait, but they left him in power. As for weapons of mass destruction, the Americans knew he had them because they sold them to him, in copious amounts, during the Iran–Iraq War. Saddam was using these weapons against Iran already in the early 1980s, with American blessing. Anything to stop the spread of Muslim fundamentalism from Iran to the rest of the Middle East." Bob paused to take a sip of his cognac and coffee.

"OK," said Andrew. "So we know he had stacks of chemical weapons. Could he have run out after the attack on the Kurds?"

"Highly unlikely," Nat jumped in. "We also sold him the technology to manufacture these things."

"OK, so let's say the war was justified." Andrew wanted to move the discussion forward to the question of what to do next. "We were totally bogged down in Iraq for a long time, and we are starting from scratch in Afghanistan after the Taliban took over. Thousands of soldiers have lost their lives, and *hundreds* of thousands of civilians have lost theirs. There's relative calm on the surface, but the insurgents have not given up."

Bob put his glass of cognac on the table and jumped in. "Well, first of all, it must be made quite clear to the Iraqi and the Afghan governments that they must get their acts together. Militias must be outlawed and their weapons taken away from them. No easy task, but it is possible if the will to do it is there. Secondly, measures must be put in place to rout out corruption and waste. This goes for the US involvement as well. Hundreds of millions of reconstruction dollars, for example, weren't accounted for when we left Iraq, and they still aren't to this day. The same goes for Afghanistan, where, again, we left too early, for political reasons. Since security had to take priority over reconstruction, we lost the battle for the 'hearts and minds' and left an opening for the Taliban and al-Qaeda to re-establish themselves. This is already happening, and we believe most of it is based on al-Qaeda–sponsored initiatives. They would like the world to think that the fight is all about getting the coalition forces and, especially, the Americans off Arabian soil, but if that were so, all they would have to do is stop their terrorist activities, let Afghanistan's and Iraq's democracies take hold, and we would be out of there in a heartbeat. We will not succeed in our fight against terrorism by sticking our tail between our legs and heading home before the time is right. 9/11 only happened because we allowed bin Laden and his followers to think they could attack us with impunity. We haven't had an attack on American soil since we took the fight to them in Afghanistan and Iraq. We must hold firm in both places, and we must redouble our efforts to roll up the al-Qaeda networks and bring the people in them to face trial as the criminals they are, in an international court. We must extract al-Qaeda's backbone to the point where we can get back to dealing with disorganised, individual groups of fanatics, poorly funded, which is where we were forty years ago. We must also learn from our battle with ISIS. We dismantled their caliphate, but we did not eliminate ISIS; instead, we scared them into the fold of al-Qaeda." Bob drained his glass and coffee, and Andrew asked if he would have a refill. Bob declined, saying he needed to keep a clear head and focused on Nat. "Finding al-Qaeda leaders, even after our success with bin Laden, has proven to be a difficult task. Why? Because there are so many people out there who are prepared to hide them. This goes from people in high places to a poor peasant family in the countryside. In the case of bin Laden, he was seen as invincible and a hero for standing up to the decadent West. He had almost become a mythical figure in the Islamic world. Al-Qaeda has given many a sense of pride and purpose. They've been able to feed on inequalities and injustices which have existed for years in the Arab world. Undemocratic, oppressive regimes, like Saudi Arabia, Egypt, and Syria, have enjoyed Western and, in particular, American support for a very long time. It was easy for bin Laden to demonise America in the eyes of poor, disenfranchised Arabs, and it has been convenient for Arab leaders to let the Americans take the heat. I doubt very much that there would've been a push for the democratisation of Arab countries had it not been for 9/11. But the penny has finally dropped that the terrorists' recruiting grounds are the countries where the social injustices are the greatest. The Arab Spring, was a step in the right direction, but that process has been sabotaged by Islamic militants who see the instability as an opportunity to hijack the process and replace a secular dictatorship with a religious one."

Bob paused briefly, collecting his thoughts before continuing: "We cannot win the war against terrorism by bullets alone. We have to find ways to stem the flow of new recruits. We must find ways to connect with the Middle East, in a sincere and meaningful way, and support the formation of modern, forward-looking democracies. We also need to insist—and I mean *insist*, not *suggest*—that Israel, over a period of time, withdraws to its original pre-'67 boundaries in return for full recognition from all Arab nations of Israel's right to exist. The 'occupied territories' are just that, and all these years later, they are still occupied. It's going to be difficult. The occupied territories have been developed extensively by the Israelis over the years, and the Israelis who live and work there aren't going to want to move. But this land grab is costing the Israelis *and the world* dearly, and it cannot be allowed to continue." Bob exhaled as if exhausted from his monologue.

"Wait a minute! Can I come in here?" Andrew raised a hand, "Israel fought four wars, starting with the War of Independence in 1948, so called because it started the *day after* Israel became an independent state. Egypt, Syria, Transjordan, Lebanon, and Iraq invaded Israel but were repelled despite the numerical superiority of the Arab armies. If I remember correctly, the war lasted for fifteen months and claimed some six thousand Jewish lives which, at the time, represented nearly one percent of the population. A UN-brokered peace plan was negotiated with each country except Iraq which, to this day, has refused to consider any kind of accommodation with Israel. In this peace plan,

Israel relinquished almost all territories which they had conquered and were left with half of Jerusalem. The Arabs broke all the terms of the agreement, including blockading access to Israeli ports. Eight years later, in 1956, the Sinai War broke out. The same adversaries struck at Israel again and were repelled. As before, Israel gave up most of the conquered territories only to be hit again in 1967 in the so-called Six Day War, followed, in 1973, by the Yom Kippur War. Can anybody really blame the Israelis now for not wanting to return to the pre-1967 borders? The Arabs still want to wipe them off the map. The Palestinian Covenant of 1969 makes that very clear."

"Wow! I didn't know you were a history buff." Nat gave Andrew a broad smile.

"I'm not, but the Jewish–Palestinian conflict has fascinated me and bothered me for a long time. I've done some reading to try to understand why these people can't find it in their hearts to live peacefully together. Jews have lived in this part of the world for 3,300 years, and for most of those years, Arabs and Jews *did* live side by side peacefully. It's all very well to blame it on the British, but I don't buy it." Andrew got up and walked over to the drinks trolley and poured himself another cognac and waved the bottle invitingly at Nat and Bob, who both shook their heads. "Well, I can tell you don't drink like a Scot." He took his seat on the couch and continued: "In the Balfour Declaration of 1917, England envisaged a *homeland* for the Jews, not a state. They wanted to create an area for the Jews within Palestine where Jews and Arabs could live peacefully together, but the Jews wanted more. They wanted their own independent country, and, after the Second World War, they forced the issue. The British refused to lift the ban on immigration to allow a hundred thousand displaced Jews into Palestine after the war, and the Jewish underground forces carried out several attacks against the British. In 1946, the Irgun blew up the King David Hotel in Jerusalem, killing ninety-two people. The hotel was only the headquarters of the British administration, for Christ's sake! Realising that they were losing control, the British announced that they would terminate their mandate by May 1948. So, don't tell me the mess we now have in the Middle East is the fault of the British." Andrew finished his point with a generous sip of cognac and leaned back on the sofa.

"Well, well. What do you say, Nat, shall we let the Brits off the hook?" Bob gave Andrew a teasing wink.

"Yeah, let's do that. At least for tonight," Nat added, then continued. "In fact, I think if we should blame anyone for the continued conflict in the Middle East, it should be Yasser Arafat, who turned *down* the offer of a separate Palestinian state. What was he thinking?"

"He was staying true to the Palestinian Covenant of 1969 which does not recognise the state of Israel," Andrew replied, and added, "at the same time as he was playing along with the Western 'peaceniks' and collecting hundreds of millions of dollars in international aid for the Palestinians, most of which would seem to have found its way to his own bank accounts. I read somewhere, that he had a personal wealth of 1.5 billion dollars when he died! He had turned the Middle East conflict into a thriving business—Middle East Conflict, Inc. What do you think, Bob?"

Bob took a deep breath and exhaled slowly. "I think we need to step back and look at the bigger picture. The most fundamental problem stems from the Muslim faith itself. First, in the view of a devout Muslim, there is only one true religion. If you do not believe in Allah and pray to him, you are an 'infidel'.

So, there is a mandated intolerance of other religions. Secondly, and it follows from this, every Muslim should strive throughout his/her life to convert infidels to true believers—i.e., a fundamental objective of the Muslim faith is that it should dominate the world. Therefore, the peace-loving aspects of the Muslim faith, which is often stressed by 'moderate Muslims', really apply to the brotherhood of Muslims only. The Arab world is out of step with the modern world, where freedom of expression, association, and religious beliefs are enshrined in the constitutions of most countries. The Catholic Church exercised this kind of absolute power in the Western world for some time until its excesses caused a rebellion which resulted in the *separation* of state and church which is the backbone of Western democracy today. In the Muslim world, there's no such separation. Even in a country like Turkey, which prides itself on its secular government, religious leaders have considerable influence on the decision-making process because they actively pursue political power as a natural extension of their religious power. So, we have a serious clash of cultures and of values."

CHAPTER 9

As the discussion continued, Nat found his mind drifting to Sonja. How was he going to tell her of his wild plan to get inside al-Qaeda, and when? It would have to be soon. Jim, despite what he had said, would expect an answer on Monday morning. Nat could hear him now: "So, Nat, do I request a meeting with the president or don't I? What did Sonja say?"

What *would* Sonja *say*? She'd probably tell him that he'd lost his mind, that he was overworked and needed a holiday in the South of France. She would stress the risks and question the rewards. What were the chances of the plot succeeding? What were the downsides if it failed or, for that matter, if it succeeded? Was it reasonable for him, as a family man, to put himself in harm's way? Why couldn't somebody else do it? Somebody who was trained in intelligence operations? He would need to have good answers to all these questions and, right now, he wasn't sure that he could answer any of them.

He was listening, with one ear, to Bob and Andrew, while in his mind, he started to prepare for his talk with Sonja. He decided that he'd bring it up tomorrow night after they had put the children to bed. That would give him all of Sunday to try to convince her of the merit of at least exploring it with the powers that be.

"What do you think, Nat?" Andrew's voice jolted him back to the present.

"Huh, what do I think?" Nat tried desperately to recall what they had just been talking about, but he drew a blank. "I, I—"

"Nat, are you all right?" Andrew looked concerned. "You don't seem your usual argumentative self tonight. Is something wrong?"

"No, no I'm fine. I was thinking we found bin Laden, and we had hoped that this would've enabled us to roll up his whole organisation, but it hasn't. If anything, it has made it more difficult to get to al-Qaeda itself. What were you saying?"

"Bob was saying that Western media don't seem to have grasped the role that Iran is playing in Iraq. They fear that a democratically elected, secular government would succeed and turn Iraq into the economic powerhouse that it could be, hence their support for the Taliban in Afghanistan and al-Qaeda in Iraq."

"I agree. We have intelligence which supports that theory," Nat replied. "And it's one of the reasons we are convinced that Iran's nuclear programme isn't primarily for peaceful purposes," he added.

"It took years to find bin Laden." Bob left Iran alone and focused on Nat's observation. "He had time to perfect his hiding places, his movements, and methods of communication. Since we killed him, his lieutenants have become even more careful. We are groping in the dark again."

"Unless al-Qaeda could be infiltrated at the highest possible level?" Nat asked.

Bob replied, "That is even more difficult. To prove yourself worthy, you would have had to kill a lot of people before you could get anywhere up the ladder in that organisation. Even the most clandestine US intelligence operatives don't have a license to kill on that scale."

There was a knock on the door, and Flora entered and walked over to Andrew and spoke in a very low voice: "Mrs. Jefferson would like you to join the ladies in the drawing room."

Andrew looked at his watch. It was quarter past eleven. He knew that Nancy was playing in a tennis tournament tomorrow morning, and she had told him that she did not want a very late night. He nodded to Flora and asked her to remove the coffee tray.

Nat looked at his watch. "Good Lord, look at the time! We're taking the kids to the zoo tomorrow, which means they'll get up really early with tea in bed for Sonja and me. Time to hit the road." He got up and stretched a hand out to Bob. "Nice to have met you, Bob. We must get together again and continue the conversation at our place." And turning to his host: "Thank you, Andrew, for a very enjoyable evening."

They joined the ladies in the living room, where Sonja was already standing making her goodbyes: "And I hope you can both join me for lunch next Wednesday?" Nancy and Catrin said they would love to come, and Sonja said she would call them with the venue. There were thank-yous, kisses on cheeks, goodbyes, and they were off.

CHAPTER 10

Nat tried to focus on the traffic while his mind was grappling with the task of how to approach Sonja. Tonight was not a good time. The discussion would likely go into the early hours of the morning and prevent them both from having a good night's sleep.

It was Sonja who broke the silence. "Do you think we'll ever win the war on terrorism?"

It startled him. Could she read his mind? "What was that apropos of?" He gave her a quick sideways glance.

"We were talking about our children's future. What kind of world they will inherit, and Catrin said that there cannot be a draw in the battle against Islamic fundamentalists; we have to win decisively." She was staring ahead, where a light drizzle of rain was just starting to coat the windscreen.

He started the wipers. "Catrin is right, but it is becoming very clear that, to win decisively, we have to get inside al-Qaeda." The light went green. The rain was coming down heavier as he turned the car onto Draycott Avenue. Fortunately, there was very little traffic to worry about. Should he take this opportunity to broach the subject of his plan or at least plant a seed? She'd given him the perfect opening. His gut told him that he could not afford to miss this opportunity. "What would you say if I told you that a plan is being hatched to do just that? Not by scouring the mountains and caves of Pakistan and Afghanistan but by luring them out of their hiding places. I shouldn't really be telling you this—it's highly confidential—but I know I can trust you to keep a secret. It is early days yet."

"Luring them out of their hiding places; surely that's impossible?" She gave him the wide-blue-eyes treatment.

It occurred to him that, if he gave her the outline of the plan, without going into specifics, including his own involvement, and she were to buy into it, this would give him an advantage when it came time to explain his *own* involvement. "It might be possible if we created an opportunity for them to win a prize which was so desirable, from their point of view, that they would find it irresistible."

"Yeah, right! Like the president's head on a platter?" She gave him a mocking look.

"My god, you are good. That's it, precisely."

"Come on, Nat, how many did you have tonight?"

"No more than you; listen!" He gave her the plan, leaving out the part about the "killing" of the London ambassador to make sure she didn't get the scent of his own role in the plot.

"That is the most unbelievable and outrageous idea I have ever heard! I can't see the president and the vice president agreeing to something like that. What a crazy plan! Who on earth dreamt up this one?"

"I can't tell you. I shouldn't have mentioned it." He turned into Cadogan Street and parked the car in front of their townhouse. The rain was drumming on the roof of the car and quickly obscured the view out when he turned the windscreen wipers and the engine off.

"I'll call Rachel and ask her to come out with a couple of umbrellas."

Nat was glad to change the subject. He got his cell phone out and dialled their number. Rachel responded on the second ring. "Hello, Jameson residence."

"Hi, Rachel; it's us—"

She broke in. "Everything OK?"

"Yes, we're fine. We're outside. Forgot to bring any rain gear. Could you please bring out two umbrellas from the stand in the hall?"

"I'm on the way." She hung up and they could see the light come on in the hallway. The front door opened, and Rachel's figure, distorted by the rain, appeared in the doorway, where she struggled to open one of the umbrellas. She succeeded and came down the front steps, carefully holding the folded umbrella in her left hand. She opened the door for Sonja and passed her the folded umbrella to give to Nat.

They reached the house with their shoes soaking wet. The dripping umbrellas were left next to the front door, and Sonja headed straight for the kitchen. "This calls for a hot cup of chocolate," she said, to no one in particular and then to Rachel, "Children all right?"

"Yes, they went to bed like little angels. They were both fast asleep when I checked on them half an hour after they went to bed, and I haven't heard a peep out of them since."

Nat paid her twenty-five pounds, based on their agreed hourly rate of five pounds, and asked her, "Will you be OK to drive home in this weather?"

Rachel had borrowed her mother's car for the evening. "Absolutely! But could you lend me an umbrella? I didn't bring any rain gear either."

Nat found her a dry umbrella from the stand in the hallway. They thanked her for her help, and Rachel disappeared into the rainy night.

Chapter 11

Back in the kitchen, Sonja made up two mugs of steaming hot chocolate, and they sat down at the kitchen table. A sleepy Darwin appeared in the doorway wagging his tail. He always slept in the children's room when Nat and Sonja were out in the evening but always returned to his own basket in their bedroom when they came to bed. Sonja got up and gave him a dog biscuit from a glass jar on top of the fridge.

"Here, Darwin; a bonus biscuit for looking after Tanya and Gregory." She came back to her chocolate and sat down. "Now, tell me who came up with this crazy idea for dismantling al-Qaeda?"

"I did." The words just fell out of Nat's mouth. He had not meant to go any further with this conversation tonight, but somehow he felt relief that it was out on the table.

"You!" She stared at him in disbelief. "You must be out of your mind! Does anybody else know about this? How did you dream this up?"

"You're right, I *did* dream it up, literally. I woke up in the early hours this morning with this idea in my head. I couldn't shake it, so I got up and put it down on paper—electronic 'paper', that is—then I shared it with Jim and worked on it some more in the office."

"What did Jim say? He must've thought you'd lost your marbles." Sonja put the cup down heavily and stared at him intently.

"At first he did, but as we talked about it, he came around, to the point where he said he, or I should say *we*, would take the idea to the president, if you would agree with it." Nat held her gaze but blinked first and took a sip of chocolate. Sonja sat absolutely still, looking straight at him, but he could see that her mind was working furiously to take it all in so that she could come up with the right response. She looked down, took a deep breath, and raised her head again. "I can see that this is so totally wild that it just might work. But what I don't like is *you* putting *your* life on the line. Couldn't somebody with intelligence training and field experience do your part?"

"Not easily. With someone like that you have to *create* a person with a believable past history which will stand up to scrutiny from al-Qaeda's leadership. It would have very little chance of succeeding. I am what I am. I have developed a relationship with Imam Badawi over the past couple of years. Everything they would look into in terms of my background would check out. As the plan unfolds, as the new ambassador to the Court of St. James, I would naturally have access to the vice president and the president to continue the operation. Al-Qaeda would have a trusted man with access to the top."

"It would be one thing if it was just you and me." Sonja put a hand on his arm. "But we have the children to think about. How would we explain to them if we needed to change our names and become a different family altogether? Would they even be able to keep it secret? It is a lot to ask and to expect from them. And you—" She faltered. "You would be guaranteed to have a *Fatwa* issued against you."

"No, darling, that would not happen." He smiled and gave her hand a squeeze. "Bringing al-Qaeda to face justice in an international court, or being responsible for their destruction, would not be an offence against Allah; in fact, it should not offend any moderate Muslim. No doubt the fanatics would want revenge, but they would not be able to find us."

"Where would we go?"

"I don't know. We could go anywhere. If this succeeds or even if it failed, I don't think early retirement with a good pension would be out of the question. On the other hand, a job back in Washington, with a new name, a grey beard, and horn-rimmed glasses might not be a bad idea."

Sonja gave him a long look. "You make it sound so simple, but what about the children?"

"I don't know, Sonja. We have to see if we can work that one out somehow. I wonder what kind of life they will have if we *don't* win the war on terror. We obviously can't discuss this with them, but I wonder what their reactions would be if we could."

Sonja took her empty mug over to the sink. "Oh, I know what they'd say. Greg would say: 'Go for it, Dad!' And see you as the new James Bond. He would be so proud of you; he would want to tell all his schoolmates. And Tanya, well, Tanya would have a more calm and measured response like: 'al-Qaeda are bad, bad men. They kill women and children. I would like you to stop them doing that, but I don't want them to kill you, Daddy,'" Sonja mimicked Tanya's soft, sweet voice.

"They would want you to do it without understanding the consequences." Sonja took his empty mug from the table, rinsed it under the tap, and put it in the dishwasher.

Nat stood up, picked up his blazer, which hung on the back of the chair, and walked over to Sonja and put his free arm around her shoulders. "Let's sleep on it, darling. We can't make a decision about this tonight, nor do we need to. Let's give it some time. I don't expect you to give me an answer just like that." She leaned against him, and he guided her up the staircase with his arm still around her shoulders.

They paused briefly on the first-floor landing before continuing up to the children's bedroom on the top floor. The door to their room was half open, and the glow from the nightlight was throwing a faint light across the landing. The children were fast asleep. Sonja went to Tanya first, and Nat to Gregory. Gregory was lying on his stomach with both hands under his chest and the bed covers thrown off. Nat covered him up and gave him a light kiss on the neck. He looked so innocent and so vulnerable. *What will give him a better life?* Nat thought. *I forget this crazy idea, and we continue to live with the threat of terrorism escalating, or we make an outrageously bold move which could tip the balance in favour of a safer and saner world in the future?* There was no simple answer. Sonja came up next to him for her turn to say good night, and he went over to Tanya, who was lying on her back with one arm stretched back over her head and the other across her chest. She reminded him of the Statue of Liberty, with her curly blond hair spread out on the pillow like a halo. Her face was peaceful. He bent down and kissed her forehead. Liberty, peace, and prosperity, the pursuit of happiness. These were all ideals that had been fought for through the ages in different parts of the world, but not even in the two, so-called, world wars had the conflict been truly global as the war against international terrorism had now become.

Sonja came up behind him, put her arms around him, and said into his back, "I know what you're thinking. Can I afford *not* to take this chance if it can produce a better world for our children?"

"Yes, something like that." He turned around and took her into his arms. "We'll talk about it some more over the weekend; I need to get back to Jim with our decision on Monday morning." Sonja did not reply; she just held him tighter, and his heart swelled with love.

Back in their own bedroom, Nat had finished in the bathroom first and was lying in bed thinking about how blessed he was. Sonja came out of the bathroom in a pale pink silk nightgown, her blond hair, turned to gold by the bathroom light, fell softly against her shoulders. She covered the distance to the bed in long strides and placed one knee on the bed and her left hand flat against his chest. "You are *my* James Bond, darling." She tipped forward and fell into his arms.

CHAPTER 12

Sonja woke up from the light knocking on the door. The clock on her bedside table showed 7:30. She gave Nat a gentle nudge. "Wake up! Tea is here." The door opened, and Gregory stepped inside holding the door for Tanya, who followed gingerly, holding a tray with two cups of tea and nothing else.

"Good morning." They spoke in unison.

Greg said, "You haven't forgotten what day it is, have you?" Not waiting for an answer, he jumped onto the bed. "It's zoo-day! Hurray, for zoo-day!"

Nat opened one eye. "Save us the early morning poetry, will you?" But he stretched an arm out and pulled Gregory to him for a morning hug. "Good morning, son. Did you sleep well?"

No reply. Gregory turned around and pointed to Tanya, who was putting the tray down on her mother's bedside table. "Tea is served," he said, finishing with a grand gesture of both arms outstretched towards his sister.

"Thank you very much. That is just what we needed." Sonja passed a cup over to Nat and left her own on the bedside table. "Up you come, young lady. You're not too old for a Saturday morning cuddle in bed yet." She stretched her hand out to Tanya, who did not need to be asked twice.

The children sat between them, Tanya next to her mother and Gregory next to his father. Once the hugging and kissing was done and they'd had the first sip of tea, Nat gave the children a serious look and said, "You don't really want to go to the zoo, do you?"

"YEEES!" A loud, choral response.

"But you've seen it all before, *many times*."

"Daddy—" Tanya was about to give him a lecture. "There is always something different to see there, always something new to learn about. I want to bring my sketch pad along so I can draw the antelopes."

"And *I* want to see the lions and the pandas," Gregory added. "Besides, you promised, Daddy, and you have told us we must always keep a promise." Tanya gave him her version of a strict school-mam's look.

"Now, now." Sonja put her teacup back on the bedside table. "Daddy is teasing. He's been looking forward to this all week, and so have I," she added, leaving no doubt in anybody's mind where they would be going.

"OK. You win. We'll go to the zoo. Maybe I can get a ride on an elephant?" Nat gave them a teasing look.

There was a scratching sound on the side of the bed, and up peered Darwin, tail wagging, wanting to join the party. "No, Darwin, we're getting up," said Sonja. "We'll have a quick breakfast and then we'll take you for a walk." *Walk!* Darwin's tail speeded up, and he started to bounce around on the carpet. "Darwin may not be highly literate, but he certainly understands what the word *walk* means. Look at him," said Sonja. She got out of bed and headed for the bathroom. She turned around in the doorway and addressed the bed sitters: "Breakfast will be ready in twenty minutes. Everybody, get washed and dressed and ready. Let's take Darwin to Hyde Park. We've got plenty of time; the zoo doesn't open until ten o'clock."

Breakfast was a noisy affair. The children were discussing which was the best exhibit, and it was clear, from their level of agitation, that they were excited about the visit to the zoo. Nat was trying to concentrate on the *Telegraph*, with little success. They drove to the park. Darwin was in the front seat, standing on Sonja's lap with his short front legs on the dashboard. He stared intently at the road ahead, tail wagging slowly in anticipation.

Nat had put on his jogging suit to have a run around the park, while Sonja and the kids walked and played with Darwin. Gregory had brought his soccer ball which Darwin was a master at controlling, nosing it around at breakneck speed. It was a sunny, crisp September morning, perfect for a day at the zoo and a walk in the park. Tanya had put on her "roller shoes" she'd gotten for her birthday three weeks ago. She was practising hard to catch up with a friend at school who had gotten her shoes two months earlier. "And it wasn't even her birthday," Tanya had observed, suggesting a certain mean streak in her parents, who had made her wait until it was hers.

Nat parked the car on Rotten Row, relying on his US Embassy sticker to avoid being ticketed. They agreed to meet up at the bandstand in thirty minutes and set off in opposite directions. Sonja, Darwin, and the children headed down the Flower Walk, and Nat set off towards the Lido, determined to do a few laps around the Serpentine Lake. It was 8:30 and the park was almost empty except for some walkers and joggers and the occasional person heading to work. Nat felt remarkably well, considering the late night he and Sonja had had the night before. He felt a tingle at the thought of the way it had ended, the soft curves of her body pressing urgently against his, and the love-making which erased the tension brought on by his revelations about the al-Qaeda plot.

He sent a thought heavenward, looked up into a pale blue autumn sky, and thanked God for Sonja.

He reached the Lido and headed west towards the bridge. He was overtaken by two young girls, both with headphones and armband heart rate and pulse monitors. They were out of sight in seconds, and he thought they were probably professional marathon runners or triathletes who travelled around the world from one major event to the other. His own speed was sedate by comparison, and yet he could feel his heart pumping fast as he passed the Serpentine Gallery.

His thoughts wandered back to his meeting the previous afternoon with Jim Preston, the US ambassador. Jim had, in the end, seemed excited about his crazy idea to infiltrate al-Qaeda. Nat dreaded the prospect of having to tell him that he had been unable to convince Sonja, or worse, convince himself that it was worth pursuing. But right now, he felt it would not be fair to Sonja or the children to put them at risk in any way. He loved them too much for that. He realised that nothing in this world mattered more to him than Sonja and the children. He worked hard at his job, and sometimes he would come home late, and sometimes he had to travel, and he would be away from them for two or three days at a time, sometimes longer. He had not thought much of it. It was just part of the job, and there was nothing he could do about it. But now he realised why he always had a sense of unease when he was away from them. He missed them and felt complete only when he was with them. And he thought, *What am I doing here, jogging by myself?*

I should be with them right now, kicking the ball with Gregory, or just be there.

Nat took a left turn towards Temple Lodge and headed in the direction of the Flower Walk. He speeded up. It was suddenly very important to catch up with them as soon as possible. He passed the Serpentine Gallery breathing heavily, and he overtook a middle-aged man in a purple track suit and a white sweatband. He thought, *Maybe he thinks I'm a marathon runner.* He ran down the Flower Walk, and thought, *What if I can't find them?* He looked at his watch. It was ten minutes until they were to meet at the bandstand. *The bandstand!* There were *two* bandstands in Hyde Park, one at the west end near the Round Pond and the other towards the east end of Serpentine Road. To which would they go? He decided to head for the nearest one by the pond and cranked the speed up another notch.

He was gasping for air as he saw them in the distance. He felt a surge of relief. Darwin was tearing around on the grass with the ball seemingly attached to his nose, chased by a laughing Gregory, and Sonja was in the bandstand with Tanya, who was showing her some new moves on the roller shoes.

He stopped a distance away to catch his breath. My God, was he glad to see them. Sonja saw him first and waved, and he set off again, at full speed towards them.

"Goodness gracious, I thought you were going for a jog, not a sprint? Have you been twice around the lake already?" Sonja gave him a concerned pat on the arm, accompanied by a warm smile. She had the bluest eyes.

"No, I, I—" Nat tried to catch his breath. "I haven't even been around once. I got to the fountains when I realized that I hadn't told you *which* bandstand we were to meet at, so I came here first since this was the nearest." His heart was racing, but his breathing was improving.

"We realised the same thing," said Sonja. "So we decided to come here and wait for you, knowing that if we were not at the bandstand you had in mind on the allotted hour, you would look for us at the other."

"Hi Dad. Look at me!" Tanya did a figure eight on the bandstand floor.

"That's very nice, sweetheart. Does this mean you will pick up with the figure-skating again this winter? You have lots of talent." Nat picked her up and swung her around a full circle before putting her down gently. She slid backwards on one shoe with the other leg outstretched behind her.

"Like that, Dad?" She gave him a bright smile as she came to a stop at the railing.

"Yes, honey. Just like that."

A winded Gregory appeared with the ball held high over his head and Darwin dancing circles around his feet, his tongue hanging down almost to the ground and his shiny black eyes fixed on the ball.

"He won't stop, Dad; he'll play till he drops. Won't let me have a kick, even."

"Don't complain, Gregory. You'll be able to charge admission to the greatest dog soccer show on Earth." Nat looked at his watch, "Anyway, we should be heading back. By the time we have cleaned up and watered Darwin, it will be time to head for the zoo."

Nobody needed to be asked twice. They headed back to the car at a brisk pace, with Darwin still dancing around Gregory's feet. Back at the house, Nat had a shower, and Sonja filled Darwin's dish with dry dog food and recharged his water bowl which he had emptied the minute they got in the house.

"Everybody ready?" Sonja was in the hallway having changed into a pair of light blue jeans and a three-quarter-length brown leather jacket over a white blouse. She had a red scarf around her neck and a white headscarf showing a fringe of combed-back blond hair.

The children came rushing down the steps, taking them two at a time.

"Slow down, slow down!" Nat came out on the middle, landing behind them. "You won't make it to the zoo if you break a leg." But he also took the steps two at a time, and they were out the door in record time.

"Wait a minute!" Sonja turned around as Nat was locking the door. "My camera. I left it on the table in the hallway."

"I'll get it." Nat unlocked the door, disappeared inside, and reappeared with Sonja's digital Canon camera.

"If Daddy is going for a ride on an elephant today, then we must get a picture of it, don't you think?" She looked at the children.

"Huh? They won't let him ride no elephant," Gregory scoffed at the idea.

"That's wrong," said Tanya. "You can't say *no* elephant; it's not good English."

Gregory mumbled something as he got into the car, and when Tanya got in next to him in the back seat, he said, "I speak American, not English, so there."

"Well, it's not good American either." Tanya was not going to let it go.

"OK, you two. That's enough of that. Tanya is right, Gregory, what you said was not grammatically correct. We speak English with an American accent, and we write just with a few words spelled differently."

"Yes." Tanya picked it up. "Like *colour* spelled *o-u-r* rather than *o-r* and *harbour* spelled the same way." She sat back in her seat and gave her brother a superior sideways glance. Her brother was proof positive of what the girls at school knew, that all boys are stupid.

CHAPTER 13

They arrived at the car park a few minutes after ten o'clock. Judging by the number of cars already parked, it was going to be a busy day at the zoo. By the time they had walked to the entrance, it was quarter past ten, and there was a large group of parents and children queuing for tickets.

A BBC TV van was parked next to the entrance, prompting Gregory to say that maybe they would be watching themselves on the TV news tonight.

After much discussion in the car, it had been agreed that they would look at the Gorilla Kingdom exhibit first, which housed the western lowland gorilla in an area designed to reproduce their natural African open-forested environment.

They entered the exhibit via the African aviary, but the children hurried them through. "We've seen it many times before," said Gregory and tugged at his mother's arm when she stopped to look at one of the exotic birds which shares the lowlands with the gorillas. Leaving the aviary, they followed a pathway through the forest which soon opened into a large clearing edged by water. There, on a grassy knoll, sat what appeared to be a gorilla family. The male was much bigger and darker than the female, and the two little ones were lighter still. They were the first gorillas born in captivity and taken as proof that the new environment that had been created for them, at a whopping cost of č3.5 million, was one in which they felt totally at home. As they moved closer to them, the male got up and placed himself between his family and the Jamesons.

"Look at him," said Sonja. "He's protecting his family." There was no aggressive or threatening behaviour by the gorilla dad, but he stood there, calmly looking at them with kind, intelligent, and steadfast eyes. "Look," said Sonja. "I remember him from last year. He used to always wear a deep frown on his face. He looks happy and content in his new home. He can live a normal life, or close to a normal life. The way he looks at us, I'm beginning to feel that *we* are the exhibit."

As they moved through the area, they saw more groups of gorillas. They were always together; nobody was sitting around alone. What looked like an elderly couple sat close together, and she was looking for fleas in his thick, mangy-looking coat.

"There is devotion for you," said Nat. "How come I never get treated like that?"

Sonja looked at him in mock surprise. "I didn't know you had fleas, darling." They all laughed.

"Look!" Tanya exclaimed and pointed. "They're holding hands!" A pair of gorillas were walking away from them in the distance, heading for the shade of a large tree, holding hands like two young lovers.

"Can there be any doubt where we originated from?" Nat pointed to the gorillas who were settling down under the tree. "They're just like us, only with fur coats."

"Wait a minute! I have a fur coat," said Sonja, "Do you think I look like a gorilla when I'm wearing it?"

"Yes, sweetheart, but a very pretty one."

"I think gorillas are ugly," said Gregory.

"Well," said Tanya. "They probably think we are ugly too. Especially you," she added, poking her brother in the ribs.

He swiped her hand away. "And you look like a, a—" He couldn't think of an animal ugly enough to compare her to.

"I know one thing," said Sonja. "That gorilla family over there *behaves* better than we do."

"Not at the dinner table," said Gregory.

After the Gorilla Kingdom, Tanya reminded them that she wanted to draw the antelopes, so they went through the tunnel next to the zoo entrance on the other side of the outer circle road and headed left, to the African Exhibit.

They saw tigers and lions, giraffes and wildebeest, and, eventually, the antelopes, which Tanya attempted to sketch but gave up after a while, complaining that they did not stand still long enough. Gregory suggested she could go to the Reptile House and draw the old crocodile there. "It never moves," he said. Nat suggested that they head back towards the cafe through the rain forest exhibit, after which they would take another tunnel back under the road that would take them straight to the cafe where they would have lunch and rest their legs.

They ended up spending an hour in the rain forest. There were so many creatures to see, from the marmosets and tamarinds doing acrobatics in the rain forest canopy to the malagasy, a giant jumping rat, and the long-nosed Potoo, which used its long, skinny tail to grip and carry twigs. Both lived in the Night-zone, a permanently moonlit area inhabited by the nocturnal animals of the rain forest. Gregory's favourite was the Roderigues fruit bat. "It looks like a dog with wings," he said.

"That's why they're called flying foxes," said Tanya, who'd taken the time to read the plaque just in front of them.

"How do you know that?" Gregory sounded impressed.

"Because I'm a very smart girl."

"No, you're not, but you can read," said Gregory, who had just seen the plaque himself.

"Time for lunch," said Sonja. "My feet are killing me."

They arrived at the Oasis Cafe, a bright, cheerful place, five minutes later. Gregory could not be persuaded to have a sandwich; it was a hamburger and fries or nothing. Tanya had a pizza, and Nat and Sonja both ordered caesar salads with chicken. They were halfway through lunch when it happened.

A loud noise, like a clap of thunder close by, shattered the sunny afternoon.

"Good God! What was that?" Sonja looked alarmed. They all looked at each other. "That sounded like an explosion."

Nat had hardly finished the sentence when a plume of black smoke rose up from the direction of the zoo entrance. "My God!" Nat got up from the table. "Something's gone very wrong." They all started to get up from the table, but Nat waved at them to sit down again. "You stay here! I'll go and investigate. Don't move from this spot." He set off in the direction of the zoo entrance. When he was out of view from the cafe, he broke into a fast run.

The scene that greeted him was one of utter chaos. Some people were running towards him, away from the entrance area. One man, with his little daughter in his arms, ran straight into him, almost knocking him over, and carried on in the direction of the cafe.

When he reached the gate, a security guard, who appeared from nowhere, blocked his way, shouting, "Stop! Go back! Don't come this way; there has been an explosion!" Two more guards came running from the outside, and Nat could see through the gate more security guards on the scene against the backdrop of black smoke billowing up from an area just on the other side of the ticket office. Nat could not see the origin of the smoke.

"Can I be of some help?" he shouted at the guard who was still just a few feet away stopping other visitors heading towards the entrance.

"Are you a doctor? We have badly injured people out there!"

Nat's answer was drowned out by the siren from a police motorcycle which came to a screeching halt just out of Nat's line of vision. Seconds later, he could hear many sirens approaching from different directions, then different sounds from ambulances, police cars, and fire trucks. *A terrorist attack!* The thought struck him with certainty. He ran back to the cafe where two security guards and a policeman had everybody sitting down at the tables where they'd been eating lunch. Nobody was eating. Sonja saw him approaching and started to get up. Nat gestured to her to stay put as he took the last few steps in long leaps and sat down next to his family.

"What's happening, Dad?" asked Sonja.

"I'm not sure," said Nat, addressing them all. "It looks like a car has exploded near the entrance."

As he finished his sentence, the policeman raised a megaphone to his mouth. "You are not in any danger. Stay calm! You will be escorted back to the car park via a different exit. Those of you who came here by public transport or by taxi will be escorted to Baker Street tube station. Alternatively, if you have somebody who can pick you up, call them now. We have cell phones available if you should need to borrow one. Ask the person you are calling to pick you up at the car park entrance.

A van has exploded near the ticket office, and there have been some injuries."

Nat stood up and walked over to the policeman, who was now talking on his radio. He finished his conversation, and Nat introduced himself and showed him his embassy ID. "Could you please tell me what has happened so I can brief the ambassador?"

The policeman, a tall muscular man in cycle-squad gear, looked like he was going to dismiss Nat's question, then thought better of it and replied, "Sir, a BBC TV van, which was parked right outside the entrance, has exploded; people are wounded, some badly; some may be dead—women, children, parents, grandparents."

"The bastards!" His voice trembled with pent-up anger. "So, it looks like it was a terrorist attack?" Nat knew the answer but felt he had to ask the question anyway.

"That is for certain, sir. The only question is: who's going to take the credit this time?" As he spoke, the wailing sirens died down as the emergency vehicles arrived at the scene. Flashing blue and red lights were visible through the trees. Then more sirens started up in the distance.

Nat went back to the table where Sonja was sitting between Tanya and Gregory with an arm around them both. She looked up at him, shaking her head. She seemed almost unnaturally calm. He went up behind them and put his arms around them. He thought, *That could have been us out there*. He had a great urge to take them away immediately but knew that he had to wait for further instructions from the people in charge.

Ambulances were heard leaving the scene as others were arriving. The bellowing smoke had disappeared. Voices of rescue workers could be heard, occasionally, between the noise from the emergency vehicles. It was pandemonium on a grand scale.

Nat could feel the anger rising from the pit of his stomach, up through his chest, and exploding in his head. He wanted to scream out loud, curse the murderous savages who had done this, but he sat very still with his arms tightly around his family. "We will be home soon," he said quietly.

Names, addresses, and telephone numbers were taken down by a female police officer before they were escorted away by two armed and flak-jacketed police officers who took them out through a small service gate to the Outer Circle Road and back to the car park where other groups, like their own, of twenty to thirty people, mostly families, were being delivered by armed security guards and police.

Nat's only thought was to get his family home. As they drove off, Tanya started to sob quietly. "Oh, oh, that was horrible!" She covered her face in her hands.

Sonja put her arms around her. "Now, now, sweetheart; we're OK. Everything is all right. You'll be home soon." Tanya turned her head into her mother's bosom, wrapped her arms around her neck, and cried uncontrollably. Sonja rocked her back and forth, comforting her as best she could.

Gregory sat silently in the front seat looking out the window. He turned and caught his father's eyes and said, "Dad, was it al-Qaeda who planted the bomb?"

Nat decided it was no point beating around the bush with this, so he said, "Nobody knows yet, but it certainly looks like it could be. The police will find out who did it and bring them to justice." Nat's cell phone rang, and he scrambled to get it out of his pocket. "Yes? Oh, hi. Yes, we're OK. Thank God. But we were only four hundred yards away. No, we're all a bit shook up. We're on our way home for a cup of tea. How did you hear about it? Oh. That was quick. Has anybody claimed responsibility for it? No. I guess it's too early for that. Thank you, Jim. I'll tell her." Nat closed his cell phone and said to Sonja over his shoulder, "That was Preston. He was worried. I must have told him we were going to the zoo today. He was watching a BBC program on the Middle East when they broke in with a special news bulletin. They—" He saw Sonja shaking her head in the mirror and looking down at Tanya, who was still sobbing quietly in her mother's lap.

"They have no details yet," he continued. "He sends his love to us all."

CHAPTER 14

They arrived at the house and were greeted by a tail-wagging Darwin, who was happily oblivious of their ordeal. His cheerful greeting had a beneficial impact on Tanya, who got down on the floor with him and gave him a big cuddle.

Sonja went to the kitchen and put the kettle on. Nat tussled Gregory's hair. "Us boys will wait for our tea in the living room." He put his arm around the boy's shoulder and walked him into the living room. "How are you doing, big fellow? Do you want to talk about it? Come and sit on my lap." Nat patted his knee as he sat down in his favourite armchair by the fireplace. Gregory did not need a second invitation. Nat put his arms around him and gave him a tight squeeze. They remained still for a moment, neither of them knowing what to say.

Then Gregory broke the silence. "Dad, why do people kill each other?"

Nat hesitated. It was not an easy question to answer. "Well, son..." He was groping for the right words. "...People don't normally kill each other except when countries are at war, like in the Second World war, when America and her allies fought a German dictator called Adolph Hitler after he had attacked and conquered most of Europe. Millions of people died in that war so that we can live a life in freedom today."

"Are we at war, Dad?" Gregory leaned back and looked straight at his father.

"In a way, we are at war, but it is a different kind of war from those we have had before. It is not a war between countries but a war of cultures. It's hard for me to explain it to you, but there are people out there who hate our way of life, and they fear that we will try to impose our way of life on them. So, they see us as evil, and they feel justified in fighting against us."

Gregory frowned. "Can't we let them live the way they want to so they'll not fight us anymore?"

"We aren't really trying to tell them how to live, but television, computers, and cell phones are changing their world, as they have changed ours, and challenging their beliefs and customs, and all these gadgets come from the Western world. Muslim fundamentalists, as we call them, don't want any part of our Western way of life, and yet they use all the modern gadgets we have invented to their advantage, such as the internet, for example."

Gregory twisted around on Nat's knee, "Jamal, at school, has a cell phone already, and I don't. He's Muslim and I'm not." Gregory gave his father an accusing look.

Nat smiled back. "That's not going to work, Greg. You'll get a cell phone on your twelfth birthday, just as your sister did. But good try!" He prodded his son in the ribs.

"Tea is ready!" Sonja appeared with the tea, followed by Tanya carrying a plate of biscuits. Darwin stayed close to Tanya, his eyes fixed on the plate in her hand.

Sonja poured the tea and sat down in the couch opposite Nat and Gregory. Tanya put the biscuits on the coffee table and climbed up on the couch close to her mother, legs tucked under and carefully balancing her cup of tea in one hand and a biscuit in the other.

“Tanya and I have talked in the kitchen about what happened at the zoo.” Sonja took a sip of tea. “We have all seen these things on television many times, but it is quite different to be right there when it happens. Thank God we are all unhurt. I think we all are in a state of shock, whether we know it or not, and we need to take it very easy and be very kind to ourselves and each other. After tea, we should all have a warm bath or shower and then a rest before dinner. I’ve got a chicken stew started in the crockpot, so dinner will cook itself while we have a lie-down. And I suggest we give the evening news a miss tonight. We can get all the facts from the morning paper.” She looked across the table at Nat and Gregory and waited for a reaction.

“I think Mom’s right,” said Nat. “We need to take it easy and let ourselves recover. A hearty stew will help, followed by an early night, and we’ll wake up feeling much better in the morning.”

So, they followed the plan, and half an hour later they were all in bed. Darwin was confused by this sudden change in routine, but after three unsuccessful attempts at getting up in bed with Nat and Sonja, he settled down in his basket, his head hanging out over the edge, and his forlorn dachshund eyes staring into space. What was the matter with these people?

Nat had tried to start a conversation with Sonja, but she had put a finger over his lips. “Not now, darling. I know what you want to talk about. We’ll talk about it tomorrow.” And with that, she had turned over, and five minutes later he could hear from her breathing that she was fast asleep.

Nat could not sleep. He laid there with his hands folded behind his neck and stared at the ceiling. Maybe he was too angry to think straight, but what had happened today had convinced him that he had to pursue his plan of infiltrating al-Qaeda. Sitting back and doing nothing was not an option anymore. He could not be sure, but he had a sense that Sonja might feel the same way, but she wanted more time to think about it, and she wanted *him* to have more time to think about it before they made a decision.

The phone rang next to him. *Damn!* He grabbed it quickly after the first ring and whispered into the phone, "Hold on, I can't talk here. Sonja is asleep." He took the phone from his ear and headed for the bathroom. He closed the door quietly and leaned against it. "Who is it?" Oh, hi Andrew." Of course, he had mentioned at the Jeffersons last night that they were taking the kids to the zoo today.

"Thank God you're all right, Nat. Sonja and the kids too?"

"Yes, we're all OK. Just a bit shook up. They're all asleep."

"Oh, sorry, I didn't mean to wake you up."

"You, didn't, I couldn't sleep anyway." Nat switched the phone to his other ear.

"Nancy and I just came back from a rather long and tedious lunch with some clients who are over from Zurich. I turned on the TV, and there it was. We just had to make sure you were OK. Nasty business. Three people are dead, twelve are seriously injured, and another twenty are wounded but not in critical condition. Police have not given any details, but eyewitnesses believe that perhaps two of the dead are children and many of the wounded are also children. Of all the diabolical things these bloody lunatics have come up with, this takes the prize. Targeting children! May they all burn in hell! What kind of warriors do they think they are? Killing children in the name of Muhammad? Fucking cowards! Thank God you are all unhurt. Where were you when it happened?"

"We were at the cafe having lunch. Just a stone's throw away. It was an almighty big bang, like a clap of thunder straight above our heads. But, of course, it was a clear blue sky, and then we saw the black smoke billowing up behind the trees. Sonja and the kids were great. They kept calm and followed instructions from the police and zoo security personnel, who, by the way, did a good job. It was a nasty experience, though. We're having a quiet evening, early supper, and no TV and an early night. Thank you for a nice evening last night, Andrew. And please convey our appreciation and thanks to Nancy."

Nat looked at himself in the mirror. He looked pale and drawn, and the crease between his eyebrows was deeper than he remembered. He wanted to say to Andrew, *We will find them, and bring them to justice*. But he thought better of it, and he felt too tired to continue the conversation.

As if Andrew had read his last thought, he said to Nat, "I'm not going to keep you. You must be exhausted. Try and get some sleep. We'll see you soon, old chap."

Nat went back to bed and realised he must have fallen asleep when Sonja woke him with a light kiss on the cheek. "Dinner is ready. It's just you and me. The kids are fast asleep, and I don't see the point in disturbing them. I think they'll sleep through till morning."

Nat went to the bathroom and splashed his face with cold water, brushed his teeth, and put on a pair of jeans and a sweater over the shirt he had slept in. He felt cold, yet the thermostat read twenty-two degrees Celsius.

A candlelit dinner for two was set at the kitchen table, soft music playing in the background. "This will soothe our frazzled nerves," said Sonja, as she poured him a glass of ice-cold Chardonnay. She raised her glass to him. "Thank you for being you. I couldn't have made it through today without you." They both took a long sip of wine. The smooth, cool liquid turned to warmth in the pit of his stomach.

"And you were marvelous." He leaned back in the chair. "You were calm as a cucumber through the whole ordeal, and you handled the children beautifully."

Sonja dished out the steaming chicken, and sat down opposite him. "Bon appetit," she said. "You probably aren't very hungry."

"I'm not, but we'll sleep better with something warm in our stomachs."

Much to their surprise, after a slow start, they both finished a respectable portion of stew while the conversation had focused on today's event and the impact it might have on the children. They agreed that it was important to make sure that the children knew that it was OK to talk about it and that Sonja and Nat were prepared to answer any questions they might have.

Nat was loading the dishwasher when Sonja came up behind him and put a hand on his shoulder. "Nat, I've been thinking.... What happened at the zoo today, it changed things for me. I mean, we can't protect the kids from random attacks like this. There is no way of knowing where or when it will happen again. This situation will not get any better until we all get serious about fighting and winning the battle against terrorism. Somehow, your idea, which seemed so crazy to me this morning, doesn't feel that way tonight."

Nat straightened up and turned towards her. "I've been thinking the same thing. I feel like fighting back. We must stop this madness. These people want to destroy our way of life. They want to destroy us. I have felt helpless and angry at myself for feeling that way. Maybe that's why I woke up with this idea. I want to *do* something! I want to help make this a better world for our children. . . . And for us," he added. He put his arms around her and pulled her close.

She looked up at him and said simply, "You can tell Jim I'm OK with it."

Nat cupped her face in his hands. "I love you, darling. Maybe nothing will come of it. If the president says no, it's over. But at least we gave it a shot."

He kissed her gently, and they held each other tightly. More words were not needed. The oneness he felt with Sonja was stronger than ever. She was a part of him. She made him whole.

CHAPTER 15

The headline in the *Sunday Telegraph* the next morning was "MAYHEM AT THE ZOO" and was accompanied by a picture of the burning van and people being taken into ambulances on stretchers. The death toll so far was three, but another fifteen people were listed in critical condition in hospital. Nine were in hospital in 'stable condition', and another fourteen people had been treated for minor injuries and sent home.

Nobody had claimed responsibility for the attack, but it was thought that this was the work of al-Qaeda or a group linked to, or inspired by, al-Qaeda. The British prime minister, the US president and heads of state in Europe, South America, and the Far East, had condemned the attack as the most heinous and cowardly act of violence since 9/11. Russia and China had also joined in the condemnation. The targeting of innocent women and children on a day's outing to the zoo was described as terrorism having reached a new level of depravity and lunacy.

Sonja and Nat had agreed that Sunday should proceed as planned, which meant that the children had friends coming over to spend the day, Sonja had a game of tennis in the afternoon, and Nat would spend some time with his stamp collection while keeping an eye on the children.

The phone rang twice in the morning. The first call was from Nat's mother, who had been watching CNN news with her early morning breakfast.

Nat told her they were all fine and did not mention that they'd been anywhere near the zoo. Half an hour later, Sonja's father called, concerned about what he had seen in his morning paper. Sonja told him the whole story but assured him they were all fine.

"I think you and Nat should think seriously about coming home," he said to Sonja. "It's just too dangerous over there. Let me speak to Nat." Sonja handed the phone over.

"Hey, Raul. . . . Yes, it was a bit too close for comfort. . . . We're all a bit shook up, but we're doing fine. . . . No, they're OK. They've got friends over. Gregory is playing computer games with Thomas, his best buddy from school, and Tanya and her friend Daisy are poring over the fashion pages in the weekend supplement. We're back to normal. . . . Well, you know. . . . Getting a transfer isn't that easy, but I'll look into it. I might be coming to Washington next week. Jim Preston, my boss, the ambassador, believes we will be required for some high-level talks relating to the president's planned tour of Europe next year. I'm sure this incident, and others, will be discussed. I hope to get a chance to drive down and see you. Yes. . . . Of course, put her on. All the best, and don't worry about us." Sonja's mother came on, and Nat went through the same discussion with her before he handed the phone back to Sonja. "Your mother wants to come over and look after the children."

"No, the kids are coping well; we're coping well. Mother, there's no need. Besides, . . . who'd be looking after Dad? Listen, why don't you and Pap come over for Christmas? . . . We'll talk it over. We'd love to have you here with us. . . . Yes, Mom.

. . . Don't you worry. . . . I will. . . . Bye, bye. We'll call you soon. Love you!" She hung up and turned to Nat, "They're as concerned about their children as we are about ours."

"Yes," said Nat. "They want us home so they can keep an eye on us."

Lunch was hot dogs, a special treat. The typical American diet of junk food was not the norm in the Jameson household. Gregory and Tanya had told their friends about their visit to the zoo, and it was clear from the conversation over lunch that they had acquired a certain heroic status in the minds of Daisy and Thomas. Gregory was basking in the glory of it all.

"I wasn't really scared, not really," he said, through a mouthful of hot dog.

"Mind your manners, young man," said Sonja. "We don't speak with food in our mouths, and we don't tell lies."

"I was scared," said Tanya. "But I'm OK now."

"We were all frightened," said Nat. "But we managed to control our feelings so that we did not panic. That's the only difference between a brave person and a coward. One can control his or her fear; the other cannot."

After lunch, the kids watched a movie on the DVD player. Sonja went to her tennis game, and Nat retired to his study, intending to install some new stamps in his collection. Somehow, he could not focus on his stamps. He reached for the phone on his desk and speed-dialled a number.

"Ambassador Preston's residence," the clipped voice of Jim's butler announced at the other end.

"Good afternoon, Harold; this is Jameson. Could I have a word with Mr. Preston?"

"Pardon me, sir. The ambassador told me about your ordeal at the zoo yesterday. Bad luck, sir!"

"You mean, 'good luck', Harold; we got away unhurt," Nat corrected him.

"My mistake, sir. Mr. Preston has luncheon guests, but I am sure he would want to speak to you. Just a moment, sir."

Silence ensued, then broke moments later. "Hi, Nat, how are you doing?"

"Good, Jim. We're doing fine. Sorry to disturb your luncheon party; I can call back later."

"No, no, not at all. What can I do for you?"

Nat hesitated a moment, then said, "Sonja and I have talked, Jim. She's on board."

"That's my girl." Preston sounded relieved.

"Strange as it may sound, it was our visit to the zoo that brought her around," Nat continued. "And I wanted you to know sooner rather than later. The next move is yours, if you still think it's a good idea, that is?"

"*Good idea?* I think it's a bloody brilliant idea—crazy, but brilliant. I'm prepared to stick my neck out for it, which either means that you are really on to something, or I'm as nuts as you are. Look, I'll call the president tonight. He's at Camp David for the weekend, just relaxing, no visitors. I'll call him eleven o'clock our time which will be six over there. He'll be having his Jack Daniel's before dinner and in a good mood. Timing is important."

"Are you sure you want to go through with this?" Nat felt he had to give Jim a way out.

"You better believe it, Nat. We can't sit back and do nothing. These lunatics will stop at nothing—women and children, for Christ's sake! We've gotta fight back with everything we've got. Leave it to me. I'll see you in the morning." Preston hung up—no goodbye or goodnight.

Jim is excited, Nat thought.

CHAPTER 16

Nat arrived at the embassy early, beating the rush-hour traffic through a grey, drizzly morning. He arrived in his office to find a handwritten note on his desk: *Please, come and see me in my office. Jim.*

Nat put his briefcase down on the desk and pulled out his laptop, hung his coat and umbrella in his closet, and headed for the ambassador's office. He found Preston deeply engrossed in the morning papers which were spread out across his desk—all featured headlines and photographs from Saturday's bomb attack at the zoo.

Preston looked up as Nat entered. "Listen to this! Police say they have two suspects in custody—one masquerading as a cameraman and the other as a reporter for BBC News—admitted to the zoo early Saturday morning, allegedly, to do a story on the gorilla baby. They were not apprehended at the zoo, but police arrested two suspects based on a phone call from a lady who gave them a tip that she thought her two neighbours had something to do with it, and matched descriptions given by the zoo official who received them and admitted them. They presented fake BBC TV identity cards—a carefully planned, diabolical plot conceived to create maximum fear. The police say they believe the two belong to a larger group which has been under surveillance for some time. More arrests are expected to follow." Preston looked up. "But that's not what I wanted you in here for. Have a seat." He cleared the papers off his desk, folded his hands in front of him, and looked at Nat. "You and I have an appointment on Wednesday morning with the president and vice president. How's that?" Preston grinned.

"I, I… Wow, that's great! What did he say? What did *you* say?" Nat leaned forward across the desk, his heart beating faster.

"I told him I had a lunatic working with me who had come up with this harebrained idea to get inside al-Qaeda. No, I didn't put it quite like that. When I called, he thought it was to fill him in on the attack at the zoo, so we talked about that first. Of course, it was the perfect segue into what I wanted to tell him. I told him about your idea, and I've got to hand it to him; he didn't interrupt me once. When I finished, he simply said, 'Well, Jim, I think you boys should get yourselves over the pond so we can talk about it. I'll tell my folks here I want you fellers back so I can get a firsthand account of what happened at the zoo. They'll wonder why that is necessary. Jack will tell me he can get me all the info we need, without going through the embassy, but I'll tell him I want to meet your man who was there on the spot, and I want to meet with you to work out the strategy for how we respond to this. You boys be in my office first thing Wednesday morning. Would seven be OK? I start early.'" Preston sat back and took a deep breath. "That's it. Almost word for word what he said. No 'Are you crazy? I'm the president, Jack's vice, we couldn't possibly even contemplate something like that.' I think he's fired up about the idea, and he wants to take a serious look at it. Arrangements are being made to get us out on a plane Tuesday afternoon. Are you OK with that?" Preston gave Nat a serious look, as if to say: *Don't chicken out on me now*.

"You bet I'm OK with that! I can't sit back and do nothing anymore. It would drive me crazy. Sonja feels the same way."

"Good." Preston got up from his desk. "Let's run through the plan outline you've put together one more time. We should make it as complete as possible to give it our best shot."

Nat fetched his laptop, and they spent most of the day filling in as many gaps as they could, from the initial approach to Imam Badawi to the "assassination" of the vice -president. They spent a lot of time trying to come up with ways to keep the "dead" ambassador and vice president under cover whilst at the same time enabling them to live, under these unusual circumstances, relatively normal lives. How to deal with close family and friends was also explored. The issue of what to do if Nat was successful in gaining al-Qaeda's confidence, and getting inside their organisation, was left to the professionals. They imagined that if they got that far, Nat would be fitted out with a locater which would tell Special Ops where to go.

They were having lunch in Preston's office when his secretary buzzed him on the intercom. "Imam Badawi, returning your call, sir."

Preston shot Nat a quick glance. "I placed a call this morning. He was in prayer, so I asked him to call me back as soon as possible."

Preston lifted the receiver, held his hand over the mouthpiece, and said to Nat, "Pick up the phone on my coffee table—line three."

"Hello Mr. Badawi. . . . Yes, thank you, I am well, or should I say as well as can be expected under the circumstances. I am sure you know why I called you. ... That's right. ... No, of course I don't blame you; I called to ask for your help. I have been asked to provide a full report to our president, and he asked me, specifically, to ascertain the sentiment of Muslim leaders in Britain. I read in this morning's papers that one of the two who have been arrested is an English Muslim convert, and the other a Moroccan Muslim with British nationality." Preston looked at Nat across the room. "He was?" Preston shouted into the mouthpiece. "A student at your mosque? Expelled, you say?" He gave Nat a knowing nod and covered the mouthpiece with his hand. "This could play nicely into our hands, Nat."

Then back to Badawi. "Good, the president will be pleased to hear that. I am leaving for Washington, and Mr. Jameson is coming with me. He was there with his family on Saturday. ... No, they're all fine. ... Yes, I'll extend to him your words of sympathy and good wishes. We expect that you and your fellow Imams around the country will strongly condemn this heinous attack on innocent people. Targeting children brings terrorism to a different level of depravity. There will be a tremendous reaction to this event, which is likely to make life for all Muslims increasingly difficult, not only in Britain, but in the whole Western world. Condemning these acts is no longer going to be enough; we need to see action from the Muslim community that shows you want to be part of the solution. ... Yes, that's good, let's get together when we get back. Mr. Jameson or I will be contacting you to set up a meeting. ... And to you. Goodbye." Preston replaced the receiver and looked at Nat, "So what do you think of that, then?"

Nat's face was flushed with anger. "I think he's a bloody murderer! He might as well have planted the bomb himself."

"You're right," said Preston. "The investigators will be all over him and his congregation. He will have to be seen to co-operate and come out strongly against terrorism, which could make him an even better candidate for participation in your plot."

They were interrupted by Preston's secretary's voice on the intercom: "Sir, shall I clear the lunch dishes?"

"Yes, please, Clara, we're done. Thanks."

She appeared moments later with a tray, placed the remnants of their lunch on it, and disappeared as quickly as she had appeared.

"You're right, Jim, being at the zoo with my family makes my plea to Badawi more real; stop killing innocent people, women and children, and go straight for the people who have the power to fight you. I can help The Cause if you can convince your leaders to do it my way." Nat gave Preston a puzzled stare. "It makes sense, doesn't it? Ordinary people are not their enemy. The Western superpower, USA, who is fighting them on their own turf, is the *real* enemy, and the man in charge is the president. Do this my way, and you can have the ultimate victory. Hey, I have to be careful I don't start believing it myself," Nat added.

"Yeah, right." Preston looked at the picture of Ted Adams hanging on the wall opposite. "The president would certainly have second thoughts if he thought you could turn into a double agent."

They spent the rest of the afternoon fleshing out the plan. Clara called to say that arrangements had been made for their departure from Biggin Hill Airport tomorrow afternoon at 2:00 p.m.

Back in his own office, Nat called Sonja and gave her the news. When he told her where he was going, she knew what it meant, but all she said was "Good," and then she told him about her day. The children had both seen the school psychologists at their schools, but apart from that, they'd had a normal school day until Sonja picked them up. Gregory was surrounded by admiring fans when she arrived for him, and he was in the middle of telling his story for the umpteenth time when she beeped her horn to catch his attention. He had waved at her and moved towards the car, still talking to his friends, who followed him as if he were a movie star. Tanya, who was in the front seat next to her mother, had turned to him when he got in the car and scolded him for being such a show-off, an accusation which he did not accept.

Sonja had spent the afternoon with them, supervising their homework and giving them afternoon tea with chocolate biscuits as a special treat. Nat promised her that he would be home early so that they could all have supper together.

As he hung up the phone, Angela appeared with some papers for him to sign. Among them was a letter to Imam Badawi, condemning Saturday's terrorist attack at the zoo and expressing concern at the negative impact it would have on the Muslim population in Britain. Nat was asking for a meeting with Badawi on his return from Washington. He and Preston had agreed that this was necessary, whether they went ahead with the plot or not.

Angela pointed out that he had three appointments scheduled for later in the week which needed to be postponed, and he asked her to reschedule them, leaving Monday free for a meeting with Badawi on their return.

He left the embassy at five and was home by five thirty. The children had finished their homework and were sitting on the kitchen floor working on a gigantic puzzle laid out on a sheet of heavy cardboard so that it could be moved around. Tanya had started the puzzle two weeks earlier. It consisted of one thousand pieces of a photographic image of Trafalgar Square, and the completed image would be two meters squared. "If we ever get it completed—" as Gregory had said, when he finally joined his sister after she had struggled with it for a week. They jumped to their feet when Nat came through the front door and ran into the hall to greet him with Darwin, tail wagging, following close behind. Nat scooped them up and gave them a big hug.

Sonja appeared from the kitchen wearing the apron he had given her last Christmas. It was burgundy coloured and read:

Sophisticated

Seductive

Complex

And

Full-Bodied

(...And the wine is not bad, either)

She walked into his arms and gave him a big kiss which lasted a bit longer than the average hallway kiss. "We have prepared your favourite dinner. Gregory peeled the potatoes, Tanya did the beans and the carrots, and I did the rest. What is it?" Nat made a big thing of sniffing the air, like Darwin would do when something good was cooking.

And, with a broad smile, he gave his answer: "Roast beef and Yorkshire pudding?"

"Wow, Daddy, you and Darwin have really good noses," said Tanya. She took his hand and guided him to the kitchen, where the oak table in the middle of the room was set for the feast.

"Wait a minute, Tanya, Dad needs to have a shower and put on some casual clothes, to relax," said Sonja, "and then we'll have a drink while the roast is resting."

"Resting?" said Gregory. "It's stone dead. It doesn't need to rest."

Sonja laughed. "It means the roast has to come out of the oven and sit on the counter for a while before your father carves it."

Nat disappeared to have his shower while the discussion on the finer points of preparing roast beef continued downstairs. When he reappeared fifteen minutes later, the children had returned to the puzzle, and Sonja had poured him a scotch and Perrier which sat on the kitchen counter waiting for him.

She lifted her own glass of gin and tonic and said, "Cheers! We wish you a safe and successful journey." She held his eyes with hers as their glasses touched. "I have told the children that you are going to Washington with Ambassador Preston to finalise the plans for the president's upcoming European tour and that you may be meeting with the president himself."

"Dad, if you do meet the president..." Gregory looked up from the puzzle. "...could you ask him to please stop these terrorists?"

"Sure, Greg, if I get the chance, I'll tell him that you said that. You know we have lots of people out there trying to do just that, but it's not easy."

"I think they should give themselves up," said Tanya. She got up from the floor and joined the others at the table. "They must be miserable people to create so much misery around the world. How can killing people make anybody happy? What do they want?"

"That's a good question, Tanya," said Nat. "They have not come out and said, 'If you, meaning *us*, do so-and-so-and-so, we will stop killing innocent people.' It is not at all clear what they are trying to achieve, but it would seem that world domination may be one of their objectives."

"OK, that's enough of that," Sonja broke in. "The roast is ready. Let's eat."

Sonja made a point of keeping the conversation off the topic of terrorism during dinner. They talked about their plans for Christmas, which would be spent in Switzerland this year. Sonja had found them a lovely chalet in Zermatt, and they would be there for Christmas and New Year's.

Gregory was the only snowboarder among them, and the rest were all competent downhill skiers. Nat was the only one who would do a black diamond run, but he would spend most of the time with the rest of them on the easier slopes.

Sonja had also found a spa in one of the resort hotels and had booked a whole day there. "To make sure I stay young and beautiful for you, my darling," she had answered when Nat had questioned the sense of spending a whole day in a spa.

The children were sent to bed at nine thirty, and Nat and Sonja cleared the table and retired to the living room with their coffee. They settled down on the couch in front of the fire, and Sonja snuggled up in the crook of his arm.

"Promise me something." She rubbed her forehead against his chin. "Whatever happens in Washington, you need to keep me in the loop. I need to know what's going on. We're in this together. And if the president says no, don't try to talk him into it! I know how persuasive you can be."

Nat chuckled and pulled her closer. "I promise, darling. I've never lied to you except that time in the library when I 'mistook' you for Nick Carter's sister. But you have to remember; I was desperate to get to know you." He lifted her face gently towards him and kissed her softly. "I'll never ever lie to you again, sweetheart."

Her eyes were moist, but she smiled at him through the mist. "I love you, Nathaniel Jameson."

CHAPTER 17

George, Preston's driver, moved the Bentley deftly through the London afternoon traffic. He estimated that the drive to Biggin Hill Airport would take them about forty-five minutes. Nat looked at his watch. The time was twelve-forty-five, which meant that they should reach the airport around one – thirty, half an hour before the scheduled departure.

"Relax, they're not going to leave without us," Preston pointed out when Nat suggested that they had not given themselves enough time. A Gulfstream G5, private jet, was waiting for them at Biggin Hill. The president had insisted that they travel that way.

"Gives you fellers a chance to do some more homework, should you need to, and keeps you in better shape for our 7:00 a.m. meeting on Wednesday morning," he had told Preston when they had spoken on Sunday night.

They reached the airport in just under forty minutes, went through security and immigration, and were told that George could drive them straight out to the plane, where they were greeted by the pilot and co-pilot, at the bottom of the steps. Hank, the captain, who was from Idaho, stood about six foot four inches tall. His bushy blond hair had a touch of grey at the temples. Nat estimated that he'd be in his mid- to late forties. Travis, the co-pilot looked quite a bit younger but looked less fit, judging by the stomach which was straining his belt. They shook hands, and Travis helped George put the suitcases in the hold. Preston thanked George for his excellent driving and warned him, with a twinkle in his eye, not to waste any money on the horses this afternoon.

They proceeded up the steps followed by Hank and Travis. At the top of the steps, they were greeted by Caroline, the stewardess, who welcomed them on board, took their overcoats, and gestured them towards the cabin. "Gentlemen, make yourselves comfortable." The front half of the cabin had four wide leather seats, two and two opposite each other, with a glossy wood table between each pair. The back half of the cabin was laid out with a side table, and across the aisle was a larger table in the same highly polished wood, with two three-seater leather couches. Preston and Nat elected to sit next to each other across the aisle in the front section.

Caroline reappeared from the cockpit. "Could I offer you a cocktail before lunch—a glass of champagne or a mimosa—or something?" The crow's feet around her blue eyes suggested to Nat she was in her early to mid-forties, but she was well preserved and cut a fine figure in her pale blue uniform which, somehow, made her curly bleach-blond hair look even brighter.

Preston led the way. "What a wonderful idea; a glass of champagne would be just the ticket." Nat asked for a mimosa to give himself the illusion that he was just having a glass of orange juice.

Caroline returned with their drinks and an assortment of snacks which they both declined, wanting to save their appetites for lunch.

"Gentlemen, I hope Caroline has got you comfortable." It was the pilot's voice over the loudspeaker. "We have been cleared for take-off in ten minutes and will be pushing off in a couple of minutes. Please make sure your seatbelts are fastened. We'll be climbing to a cruising altitude of forty-five thousand feet, and we expect a very smooth seven-hour flight to Washington. Enjoy your flight."

Caroline returned after a few minutes and collected their glasses, tidied them away, and took one of the seats behind Nat and Preston as they taxied down to the runway.

"Have you ever flown *private* before?" asked Preston, as the pilot lined them up on the runway.

"No, never," admitted Nat, "but I like it already."

The engines roared into life, and the plane surged forward and almost immediately lifted off at a very steep angle and banked to the right after less than a minute in the air. The steep climb continued, and Preston commented that he thought the pilot was anxious to get to cruising height so that he could hand the plane over to the computer. Soon the plane levelled off, and Caroline unstrapped herself. She addressed Preston as she came by: "Shall I serve lunch at the table in the back, or would you prefer to have it where you are?"

Preston did not hesitate. "Thank you. We'll have it back there in the 'dining room'. It's nice to move around a little."

"Very well." Caroline got busy in the galley, and, in less than ten minutes, the table was set for lunch with linen tablecloth and napkins—silver and crystal. The side table was laid out with fresh shrimp, smoked salmon, and caviar, all beautifully garnished. There were ingredients to make their own salad—three different kinds of lettuce, ordinary tomatoes, cherry tomatoes, asparagus, heart of palm, black olives, and three different kinds of beans. Arranged at the far end of the table were an array of fruit and a large cheese platter.

"Gentlemen, lunch is served. Help yourselves to a starter, and I'll take your orders for the main course when you are seated." Caroline held a bottle of champagne in one hand and a bottle of white wine in the other.

"My goodness; I could get used to this!" said Nat, as he gave himself a healthy helping of the starters.

"Enjoy it while you can," said Preston. "I don't think this will become the standard for diplomatic travel for quite some time." They sat down, and Caroline offered them more drinks. Nat declined, but Preston went for another glass of champagne. "Hell, I have to take the opportunity when Janet is not around. She read somewhere that more than two drinks a day is bad for you."

Caroline reappeared to take their orders for the main course. "Your choice of main course is grilled halibut with julienned vegetables, saffron rice with a mushroom velouté sauce, or beef Bourguignon."

Preston ordered the fish, and Nat the meat, saying, "I never eat fish when I'm out. Sonja insists that we eat fish at least twice a week, sometimes three times a week, and I'm not really a great fan of fish, except the trout we used to catch when I went dry fly-fishing with my father. That was twenty-five years ago."

"Sonja is just trying to keep you alive, Nat; all that red meat is not good for you."

"Oh yes, it is," said Nat. "You just have to make sure you have enough red wine to go with it."

A short discussion ensued on the medicinal merits of alcohol in general and red wine in particular. Preston argued that the "French Paradox" had not been conclusively proven to be the result of wine consumption. Some researchers had drawn the conclusion that the relatively low incidence of heart decease in France, despite the French's love of food and heavy sauces, was a result of the generous use of olive oil in their cooking.

"Well," said Nat, "that's why I use both. Why take any chances?"

They finished their starters, and Caroline appeared instantly and cleared the empty dishes away, saying she would return in a moment with the main course. True to her word, she returned, carrying a tray holding two plates with silver covers, placing one in front of each of them.

"Voilà!" She removed both covers, simultaneously, with great flourish. "Bon appetit! Would you care for some wine with your meal? We have a Chardonnay, Cuvaison 99, Napa Valley, and for the red, a French Pauillac, Grand-Puy-Lacoste, 1996."

"Well, now you've done it. I was going to be good, but I can't resist a glass of the Pauillac. Ninety-six was a very good year for Bordeaux wines. It would be a crime to miss it."

"Very good." Caroline gave him a brilliant smile.

"And what about you, Mr. Ambassador?"

"I'll stick with the champagne. I think it will go very well with my fish."

She brought the champagne in an ice bucket in one hand and the bottle of red wine in the other. She poured the champagne first. It was Dom Perignon, 1998. Preston declined the invitation to taste it before she poured him a full glass. "No need," he said. "I can tell from the bubbles."

Nat, on the other hand, made a big production of tasting the red, swilling it around in his glass first and then holding it to his nose, breathing deeply he closed his eyes. "Ah, absolutely lovely! First class! It just needs to breathe a little. When it opens up, it will be fantastic."

Caroline looked concerned. "Shall I decant it for you?"

"No, no, just pour it in the glass," replied Nat. "It can breathe in there."

She left the wine and the champagne on the table, and, as she turned to leave, she pointed to a small button on the bulkhead next to Preston. "Push the button when you need me. I'll leave you in peace to enjoy your lunch."

Once she was out of earshot, Preston raised his glass to Nat. "Here's to you and your crazy plot; may it bear fruit! The world needs it to succeed."

"Thank you, Jim, but maybe it is just a little *too* crazy to get off the ground?" They drank to the crazy idea.

"Well, Nat, we'll have to see what the president has to say, but I'll tell you one thing, we wouldn't be sitting here eating caviar and drinking champagne if he didn't at least like the *idea* of it."

Preston dug into his fish. "Eat your boeuf Bourguignon before it goes cold." They ate in silence. The steady whine of the jet engines was the only indication that they were going somewhere. The plane was moving smoothly through the still air; not a bump or a jolt or any vibration could be felt.

It was Nat who broke the silence as he poured himself a second glass of wine. "I wonder where al-Qaeda's headquarters might be. I have a feeling they might be masquerading as totally legitimate businessmen with offices in a gleaming new office tower in Dubai."

Preston stopped his fork in midair and returned it to its plate. "Yes, that is a possibility, although all our intelligence sources seem to agree that they are pinned down somewhere in the mountains between Pakistan and Afghanistan. Mind you, these are the same people who told us that Saddam had weapons of mass destruction. They could be wrong again."

"They weren't wrong," said Nat. "Saddam had plenty of time to get rid of them before the UN inspectors were let in." He took a large swig of red wine.

"You may be right, but I don't think we'll ever know the answer to that one." Preston finished his fish and leaned back in his seat. "Unless, we got a search warrant for Syria, that is," he added.

"And not even the president of the United States of America can arrange that one," said Nat.

"Well," said Preston, "we could go in without one, like we did in Iraq."

"I don't think so, Jim; how many more soldiers are we prepared to sacrifice on wild goose chases?"

"No, you are right, of course; besides, we have proven by now that we can't win the war on terror just with superior firepower and hi-tech gadgets. Our involvement in Iraq and Afghanistan seems to have created more terrorists than it has eliminated." Preston took a thoughtful sip of champagne.

"That is hard to say," said Nat. "We have no idea how many of them there were before. What we *do* know is that there is now a concentration of them in those countries and in Pakistan, which is not a bad thing. It has kept them away from our shores at least."

"True, but how many sleeper cells in America are hatching plans as we speak?" Preston sighed heavily and poured himself another glass of champagne.

"Maybe it would all come to an end if we followed bin Laden's recommendations from 1998," said Nat.

"Oh yeah?" Preston looked sceptical. "And could you please remind me what those recommendations were?"

"He issued his second fatwa which declared that Muslims should kill civilians and military personnel from the US and allied countries until they withdraw support for Israel and withdraw military forces from Islamic countries. Seems like a reasonable request, don't you think?"

"Certainly, would save us a lot of money—" said Preston. "But I'm not so sure it would work."

"And why not?" came Nat's mock challenge.

"Well, two reasons, really—" Preston studied the bubbles in his glass. "For one, we could not leave our Jewish friends in the lurch, and, secondly, you must have forgotten Osama's words of 2006, when he declared that 'Death is better than living on this Earth with Unbelievers among us.' "

Nat could feel the red wine beginning to take effect. He decided to keep the "argument" going. "Exactly, he meant us unbelievers having military bases in Muslim countries."

"Christ, Nat, I'm glad you decided not to practice law. What did I just say?"

Preston did not wait for an answer. "Death is better than living on this Earth with unbelievers among us—on this EARTH—that's the whole ball, Nat!" Preston's voice was raised a few decibels in fake agitation. His face was flushed with the glow from the champagne, and he was happy to continue the argument. "The *unbelievers* among us, Nat; you know who that is, don't you? That is anybody on the face of this earth who is not a devout Muslim, people like you and me but also any Muslim who is not a Sunni fundamentalist, which, hopefully, is the vast majority of Muslims who are peace-loving, ordinary people who just want to live a normal life like the rest of us. So, you can go and suck up to al-Qaeda and tell them we'll pull our troops out of the Middle East and we'll throw the Israelis to the wolves, but don't come crying to me when some crazed Mullah stands in Times Square with a small nuclear bomb in his backpack and threatens to blow himself up unless we all convert to Islam and trash our military capabilities."

"OK... OK," Nat raised his hands in surrender. "I get your point. You're saying this is not about the Middle East; this is about world domination."

"Bingo! My God, I think he's got it." Preston mimicked Rex Harrison's English accent from *My Fair Lady*. Then he continued in a more serious tone. "You must understand that what Islamic extremists are aiming for is a totalitarian Islamic empire encompassing all current and former Muslim lands. This means territory stretching from Europe to North Africa, the Middle East, and Southeast Asia. ISIS made a small start before we stopped them. They have rejected the possibility of peaceful coexistence with the free world. They hate freedom in any form. They are the Goldfingers and the Blofelds of the real world. We are living in the midst of a James Bond drama, the only difference being that the crazy baddies who crave world domination are not figments of a writer's imagination; they are real flesh-and-blood madmen led by a deadly organisation called al-Qaeda."

They had finished their main course, and Preston pressed the button next to him. Caroline was there in an instant to clear the table.

"I hope you enjoyed your meal?" she said, showing her perfect and brilliantly white teeth in a big smile.

"Yes, thank you," Preston leaned back and emptied his glass of champagne. "My fish was delicious."

"So was my beef," added Nat. "And the Pauillac was the perfect choice to go with it." Caroline looked at his near empty glass and motioned to pour him another. Nat covered the glass with his hand. "No thank you, Caroline. Half a bottle is my normal limit, and I can see that I have made it a generous half."

Caroline turned to Preston. "How about you, Mr. Ambassador. Can I refill your glass?"

Preston hesitated, then answered. "No thanks, Caroline. We've got a big day tomorrow. I better not."

"Very well, gentlemen. Please, help yourselves to some fruit and cheese."

Caroline gestured towards the buffet table. They both declined but accepted the offer of coffee.

"We have some work to do," said Preston to Caroline as she returned with the coffee tray. "So, if you could clear the table, we'll do it right here."

With the table cleared, and Caroline back in the galley, Preston suggested that they take a run through the plan outline on Nat's computer.

Nat brought it back to the table and sat down next to him.

"I've been thinking," said Preston. "About what to do when I'm 'dead'. Not the kind of problem I thought I'd ever have to face," he added with a chuckle. "And this is what I've come up with: I'll come back as Janet's friend from the past, as you suggested, and I'll invite her to join me on a three-month world cruise, to take her mind off the terrible loss she has suffered."

"What if she doesn't agree?" said Nat.

"What do you mean?" Preston had a wicked glint in his eyes. ". . . doesn't agree that she has suffered a terrible loss or doesn't agree to come on a cruise?"

Nat laughed. "Dare I say both?"

"She has always wanted to do a world cruise," Preston continued. "She would jump at the opportunity. It would be the one thing that would entice her to go along with this crazy affair. You have to understand, Janet would have to be in on this. I couldn't possibly let her believe I was dead."

"Of course not, Jim. I know you couldn't do that. A world cruise is a brilliant idea. Keeps you out of reach of family and friends for three months so you won't have to lie and act and cheat to keep the thing going."

"And before the cruise," continued Preston, "she could spend some time at our summer house in Brittany, alone with her paints. Everybody will understand her desire to be alone for a while. The last time she took a painting holiday by herself was while we were in Madrid. I was very busy at the embassy, so, one day, she just said she'd had enough, packed her easel and paints, and took off to France. It was Janet who found our place in Brittany, just outside Pampol. She was very excited when she called me. I joined her for a long weekend, and six months later the place was ours. She spent the whole of the next summer there, painting up a storm—oils and watercolours. I joined her when I could. She told me that she was having an affair with François, which didn't bother me too much, for he was the farmer next door—seventy-some years old, with a toothless grin. Perhaps I should have worried; he was French, after all, but he also chewed tobacco. We always had fresh vegetables and fruit in the summer. He and his wife are both gone now, and the farm, such as it was, is owned by an English couple who modernised the farmhouse, added a swimming pool, and rented the farmland to a neighbour." Preston poured himself some more coffee. "I'll grow a beard," he continued, "and wear some horn-rimmed glasses, and I could add a toupée and colour my receding grey hair slightly less grey. Nobody will recognise me."

"Hey, you've got it all worked out!" Nat sounded impressed.

"Not really," said Preston, as he started to get up from the table, "Any idea where the bathroom might be?"

"There's no room for it up front, so my guess is it must be back there." Nat pointed at a wood panelled wall with a door in the middle at the back of the plane.

Preston disappeared, and, when he came back, he commented on the abject luxury of the toilet accommodation, and continued, "I thought I could take off to Paris in my new life, and Janet could meet up with her 'old friend' there, by chance. After a few months of his occasional visits to Janet's summer residence, it would not seem out of place that he should invite her for a world cruise. This way, we would be together but nowhere near our normal circle of friends for five to six months. And if you haven't rolled up al-Qaeda by then, maybe Janet will have to get married to her 'old friend,' and they'll end up living between Paris and Pampol for a while. It wouldn't be so bad." Preston was trying to convince himself.

"No, that doesn't sound like such a bad life at all, Jim. Sounds like what you would end up doing in any case, when you retire. Sonja and I can come and visit from time to time. Nobody would think it odd that we would go and visit my ex-boss's widow from time to time. This way I can also keep you briefed on our progress. Wow! Here I go, talking as if this is already happening." Nat stared at his computer screen. "And all it is right now is a bunch of words on a laptop."

"Now, you listen to me, old chap." Preston put on a mock English accent. "Those words might just turn the tide in our fight against terrorism. We have been swimming against it for many years now. Despite the loss of lives and the hundreds of billions of dollars thrown into the battle, we are not winning this war. We *have to* come up with something else, something new and innovative. We have to—to use a worn-out phrase—think outside the box. And your idea, my friend, is as far out of the box as it can get, and that's why the president likes it. Now, the vice president, he may not be so enthusiastic. Playing dead is nobody's idea of fun. It takes both commitment and sacrifice. Ask the people who have tried it for insurance fraud purposes over the years. They all get caught, eventually, which is why this operation will have a limited window of opportunity, should it get off the ground. It's wrong to call it an advantage, but Jack is a widower, and his only brother has Alzheimer's and has forgotten who Jack is. They have no children, so in Jack's case, it's his friends at the country club, and people he's working with, who are going to be the problem. Despite his low public profile as vice president, his face is known well enough around the world that he would be recognised wherever he might go, where somebody has a television. But changing your appearance is not a big problem, and it does not have to be permanent."

"Maybe the vice president could take a world cruise as well?" suggested Nat.

"I don't think so." Preston smiled. "He hates boats—got seasick as a child crossing the Atlantic with his parents on the *Queen Mary*. A cruise for Jack would be worse than death. We have to come up with something different. He told me once that his favourite place on earth was Venice. In fact, he told me that his idea of heaven would be to go there, write his memoirs, and drink Veneto wines."

"So, do you think we could talk him into taking early retirement and live there anonymously for a while?" Nat, made some notes on his laptop.

"Who knows? We'll see if we get that far." Preston yawned. "I need to take a nap. The champagne is taking its toll."

"Good idea." Nat closed his laptop. "There is nothing more we can do until we meet tomorrow."

CHAPTER 18

They landed at Reagan International Airport at 3:50 p.m., ten minutes ahead of schedule, and Nat recognised the white corrugated roof line and cylindrical shape of the control tower. In the distance, across the Potomac River, he could see the Washington Monument and the Jefferson Memorial. When the plane stopped and the doors opened, two immigration officers entered and checked their passports. It was done in two minutes.

"Welcome home." The big, burly officer, who seemed to be in charge, gave them a friendly smile as he passed back their passports.

When they had left, Caroline gave Preston and Nat their jackets and overcoats. "It's been a real pleasure, gentlemen. Have an enjoyable stay in Washington. We hope you'll be flying with us again soon."

"So do I," said Nat. They thanked the captain and co-pilot, then descended the steps where the deputy assistant to the president for appointments and scheduling was standing with a driver next to a Lincoln Town Car.

She stretched her hand out to Preston. "Welcome to Washington, Mr. Ambassador. My name is Melinda Jackson, and I am under strict orders from the president to take good care of you," she added, as she shook hands with Nat.

Melinda was a tall, slender redhead dressed in a pale grey suit—skirt just below the knee, and she wore a simple white blouse with a colourful silk scarf around her neck. Her curly hair was on fire from the low sun. *Less than thirty years old,* Nat thought.

They were ushered to the back seats, and Melinda got in next to the driver. She turned halfway towards them, her emerald green eyes sparkling in the sunset. "We've booked rooms for you at the Hay-Adams Hotel, two suites on the top floor, with views to the White House. I hope that suits you?" She gave them a warm smile showing off a perfect set of white teeth.

"Thank you, that's great. I've stayed there a couple of times before," said Preston. "Have you, Nat?" Preston gave Nat a sideways glance.

"No, but I've had dinner at The Lafayette restaurant, and that was very good, as I recall." Nat settled into the soft leather seat.

They arrived at the hotel in less than ten minutes and were installed in their rooms ten minutes later. Melinda had explained that she would pick them up at 6:45 a.m. tomorrow morning and take them to the White House for their 7:00 a.m. meeting with the president. When Nat protested and said they could walk it in ten minutes, she explained that it would greatly simplify the entry procedures if they came with her. "Besides," she said, giving the driver a teasing wink. "Harry, here, needs the work."

They checked in and were taken to their rooms on the eighth floor. The suites were adjacent to each other but without a connecting door. Both had magnificent views of the White

House across Lafayette Square. The Washington Monument, in the background, looked like a large chimney growing out of the White House roof.

Nat and Preston had agreed to meet in the bar at 7:00 p.m., and dinner had been booked for 7:30 p.m. Nat looked at his watch as the porter placed his suitcase on the luggage rack. It was 4:30—time to call Sonja and tell her that they had arrived safely. He tipped the porter and made the call. Sonja picked up after the second ring. "Jameson residence."

"Hi, darling, it's me." Nat stretched out on the bed.

"Hey YOU! God, I miss you already!" She sounded relieved to hear from him. "How was your flight?" Nat filled her in on the benefits of private air travel, leaving out any mention of the vintage champagne and wine. "Well, darling, you owe me one," she concluded. She reported that the children were fine and were fast asleep after a busy day. Nat promised that he would call earlier tomorrow, before the children's bedtime. She reminded him that he should call his mother, and her parents, sooner rather than later. "If the president goes for it, you probably won't have time later." He promised her that he would call before he went down for dinner.

"Have a shower and get some rest. I love you very much, and I'm very proud of you. Good luck tomorrow."

"Love you too," Nat replied, and they hung up.

Nat took the clothes out of his bag and put them away carefully. All he had was his suit-bag which had room for one suit, half a dozen shirts, some underwear and socks, and his toilet bag. He had travelled in a navy blazer and tan pants and had worn the only tie he had brought for the trip; nothing like travelling light. He showered and shaved, put on a luxuriously soft bathrobe, and threw himself on the bed. *Ah, that's better.* He could feel the stress and tension of the last few days melting away, assisted, no doubt, by the wine at lunch.

He woke up by the phone ringing next to his bed.

"Fell asleep, did you?" It was Preston's voice. "It's seven fifteen. I'm calling from the bar. Are you going to join me for dinner?"

Nat struggled to clear his foggy mind. The digital clock radio on his bedside table confirmed the time. He struggled to get the words out. "Yes, sure, Jim. Sorry. I lay down on the bed and passed out before I had a chance to set the alarm. I'll be down in fifteen."

"Take your time," Preston offered. "I guess you're too young to take the strain." He chuckled and hung up.

Nat got up, went to the bathroom, and splashed cold water in his face, then brushed his teeth, pulled a neatly folded, fresh shirt from a drawer and put it on. He frowned at the faint creases left from the folds but knew he neither had the time nor the inclination to do any ironing. He pulled on the tan slacks and his black shoes. Debating with himself for a moment, he decided to wear a jacket and retrieved the blazer from the closet. He grabbed the key card and headed for the door. He stopped dead, remembering he had promised to call his mother, and Sonja's parents, before he went for dinner. He looked at his watch. He had told Preston *fifteen minutes* and realised that he had five minutes to spare.

"Hello, Mother; it's Nat. How are you? ... No, it's not the middle of the night. I'm calling you from Washington. ... Yes, REALLY! I'm here with Ambassador Preston for a meeting with the president, to do with his upcoming trip to Europe. ... No, Sonja and the kids are fine. I spoke to her a little while ago. ... Yes, of course I will try to come down to see you. I'll have a better idea of our schedule after our meeting with the president tomorrow morning. I've got to go; Preston is waiting for me downstairs for dinner. . . . I love you too."

He looked at his watch as he was dialling Sonja's parents. The phone rang six times before the answering machine cut in, and he left a message telling them where he was and what he was doing in Washington. He was surprised how easy it was to lie about this. He promised to call them tomorrow, then hung up.

Preston was waiting for him, seated in a large easy chair in front of the fireplace in the bar. The cosy room was almost full of people, but the atmosphere was quiet and relaxed.

"Very punctual," said Preston, looking at his watch. "At least about the fifteen minutes."

Nat took a chair next to him. He had no sooner sat down when a waitress was at his side, asking him if he would like a drink. Nat looked at Preston, who was nursing a martini. "I'll have a scotch and Perrier in a tall glass, please, meaning: lots of Perrier," said Nat, and turning to Preston, "I apologise for my tardiness, Jim—not used to alcohol at lunchtime; don't touch it usually, because I know it puts me to sleep."

"No harm done," said Preston. "It gave me a chance to catch up on the local news." He pointed to a folded *Washington Post* on the coffee table next to him.

"Anything interesting?"

"Nah, the usual nonsense. The Democrats are calling the Republicans names, and the Republicans are saying that the Democrats would relinquish world power to Muslim fundamentalists if they only knew how to word the apology for being American."

The waitress appeared with Nat's drink and bowls of black olives and macadamia nuts. She poured a small amount of Perrier water on top of the scotch and withdrew, leaving the bottle. Nat topped up with Perrier, leaving only a pale hint of there being anything else in the glass. Preston raised his glass. "Here's to showing them all how it's done!"

They drank in silence, both staring pensively into the flames flickering in the fireplace. Preston broke the silence as he leaned forward placing his glass on the table. "Did you know? I was a Democrat once, back in university days. I marched on the White House, objecting to the Vietnam War, to the atom bomb, to nuclear power plants, to fur coats, to—you name it—I objected to it, hair down to my shoulders. I even started taking guitar lessons. But somewhere along the line, something happened to me. Maybe it was LBJ trying to run the Vietnam War from the White House, expecting our armed forces to fight a war with both hands tied behind their backs. Or maybe it was when they ridiculed Ronald Reagan for being America's stupidest president ever and not apologising when his politics dismantled the Soviet Union, giving all the credit to Gorbachev instead. The final straw was when Mr. Popular himself, 'Slick Willy' Clinton, ignored the rise of world terrorism until it was too late. Mind you, I was a card-carrying Republican by then." He reached for his drink and took a sip. "Anyway, all that doesn't matter now; it's history. But we sure as hell can't afford to let another Democrat back in the White House, with the world we have today. They're still talking like world terrorism was George W.'s fault. He planned the Twin Towers bombing for Christ's sake, or at the very least, he knew all about it and did nothing to stop it. Can you believe these people?" Preston was working up a head of steam.

Nat thought he might be on his second martini. He looked at his watch. "Shall we have something to eat? I would like to make it an early night; it's getting on for three o'clock in the morning in London."

"Sorry, Nat. Of course, we should eat. Getting carried away. It's not good for my blood pressure."

"You have high blood pressure?" Nat looked concerned.

"No, just a turn of phrase. I'm as healthy as can be, for an old feller." Preston got up, steady on his feet, and they headed for the dining room. They were seated by the maître d', Anton, a dapper young man from Austria. He sailed between the tables as if he were a slalom champion.

They were seated at a corner table. Nat explained that they had come across the Atlantic this afternoon and were in jet lag and asked if they could have dinner as quickly as possible so that they could get to bed.

"No problem, sir."

Anton handed them the leather-bound menus. Preston said he could not eat very much at this "late hour", and just ordered the lobster bisque.

Nat felt hungry but decided it was more important to get to bed than to eat. So, he followed Preston's example and asked for the Icelandic shrimp starter only. They declined the wine list and ordered some still water.

"Did you know," said Preston, after the waiter had poured their water, "that bottled water is the biggest gimmick foisted on mankind?"

"I'm not so sure," said Nat. "It sure beats the chlorinated water in London, New York, and Washington."

Nat looked around the room. The restaurant was almost full, mainly with business people, but a few tables had families, probably people visiting the Capitol City to give the children a history lesson.

The waiter arrived with their food, and they ate quietly for a while, until Preston broke the silence. "Have you met the president before?"

"No, never."

"You're in for a treat. Ted Adams is very direct—goes straight for the essence of things, has no time for political gamesmanship—always speaks his mind. Besides, he's got a good sense of humour."

"You sound like you know him well?" Nat looked up from the shrimp and took a swig of water.

"Not really, but I have met him a few times. The last time was when we had the second train bombings in London. I didn't meet him, but he called me in the middle of the night. I couldn't tell him any more than he could have learned from watching the news, but he wanted to hear my take on it. I don't trust the news hawks to get it right," he said. "They jump to conclusions too fast sometimes. He was furious, and I remember he called the prime minister and had a private talk before he issued his public condemnation and words of sympathy. Ted Adams doesn't get bogged down with protocol, much to the despair of his cabinet and White House staff. For example, he refuses to go about town in a motorcade with sirens blaring. He has a bulletproof limousine with a driver and two bodyguards. He refuses to travel in a manner that is designed to draw attention to himself so that he needs an army of security people to keep him safe."

They finished their meal. Preston asked for the check but was told that it had been taken care of. "Well," said Preston, looking around the room, "whether it goes on my expense account or is paid for by the White House, it's the taxpayer's treat."

CHAPTER 19

The man in front of him looked remarkably like bin Laden, except he was dressed in a dark blue pinstriped business suit. He sat behind a massive desk, and the wall behind him was covered by a luminous map of the world. He got up from the desk and gestured to Nat that he should come closer. Nat hesitated. What did he want—to show him something on the map? Nat moved closer. The man turned to the map and put a finger on London. Rings of light poured across the map from the end of his finger. When he turned again, Nat realised that it was bin Laden. When he spoke, blood was running out of his mouth. Nat wanted to run, but his feet were like lead. Bin Laden laughed, but it sounded more like a death rattle. He was trying to say something: "Sonja... Sonja... Sonja, and the kids. . ." Nat tried to grab him, but he could not reach. He screamed, but there was no sound. "No, no, no! You're dead, you're dead!"

Nat woke up—his heart racing—drenched in sweat. God! What a nightmare! He looked at the digital clock radio on his side table. It was only 2:30 in the morning, but he was wide awake. He felt a sudden urge to call Sonja and the kids. With the five-hour time difference, they would just be getting up. He turned on the bedside light, grabbed the telephone, and dialled—nothing, no dial tone, and no ring tone. Then he realised he had forgotten to dial nine, for an outside line, and tried again. This time, the phone rang, and it kept ringing and ringing. What was wrong? Where could she be at this hour? Nat sensed a feeling of panic rising through his body.

"Jameson residence." Sonja's voice came through loud and clear, and the breath he had been holding escaped like a gust of wind.

Nat tried to sound calm. "Good morning, baby. It's just me. I hope I didn't wake you up?"

"Goodness, no. I was in the shower. What on earth are you doing calling at this hour? It's the middle of the night over there. Are you OK?"

"Yes, yes I'm fine. I woke up and realised that, if I called now, I would catch the kids before they go to school." Nat could feel his heart settling back to a normal pace.

"Tanya is in the bathroom, and Greg is already downstairs in the kitchen with Darwin; I'll call them."

"Wait a minute! I want to talk to you first. I've been lying here thinking. . . " He lied. ". . . Are you still OK with this? I mean, if the president says yes, I guess it will be full steam ahead. Have you had any second thoughts?"

"Yes darling, I have." She sounded very calm and resolute. "I've had *many* second thoughts, but I always come back to the same conclusion: Your crazy idea is brilliant because it is so, well—crazy, and, to win the war against terrorism, we must do the unexpected as well as continue with what we have been doing. We *have to* try something different. I worry about you and us, but I worry even more about what will happen if we don't win this war. You are doing the right thing, Nat, and I am very proud of you. Ah, here's Tanya. It's Daddy on the phone, sweetheart. . . " Her voice trailed off.

"Hi, Daddy! I miss you already. How was the flight?"

Nat told her that the trip had been very pleasant. "Maybe one day we'll all take a trip in a private jet."

"Mrs. Burton asked me if I would like to write an essay about what happened at the zoo," said Tanya. "Do you think I should, Daddy?"

"I think that would be good, if you feel up to it, sweetheart."

"I do, Daddy." Tanya's firm reply left no doubt in Nat's mind that his daughter was on a mission and welcomed the opportunity to tell her story. Knowing Tanya, she would write a thoughtful and thought-provoking essay, much beyond her years. "I'll let you read it before I give it in to Mrs. Burton. OK, Dad? Oh, here's Gregory. Bye, Daddy, I love you!"

"Hi, Dad, how was the Gulfstream?" No pleasantries from Gregory—straight to what was on his mind.

"Hi son; how are you?" Nat deliberately ignored his son's question.

"Fine, Dad, fine. What was it like?"

Nat laughed. "It was marvellous—very smooth, very fast—takes all the hassles out of traveling. Maybe we'll all do it together some day?"

"That would be cool, Dad. I looked up Gulfstreams on the internet." Gregory raced ahead. "They have a much bigger plane now—the G650—with a range of seven thousand nautical miles and a cruising altitude of fifty-one thousand feet. Can we go on it?"

Nat laughed. "Not so fast! I can't promise anything like that. We'll just have to wait and see. I hope you are looking after your sister and your mother while I'm away? You're the man of the house while I'm over here."

"Huh," said Gregory. "They're both telling me what to do."

"Cheer up, Greg, welcome to the real world. Never mind, you *are* the only man in the house now, and they need your help, so be helpful."

"Yes, Dad." Gregory sounded like a man who had just received a death sentence.

"Could you put Mommy back on? I need a word with her. Have a nice day."

"Bye, Dad. Don't forget to ask the president to get the terrorists. You promised."

"I won't forget; I promise."

"Hi, darling." Nat could see her and smell her just by hearing her voice. He felt a sudden urge to hold her tight and to reassure her that everything would be all right. He choked up for a moment and cleared his throat.

"You're not getting a cold, are you?" Sonja's voice sounded concerned.

"No, honey, I'm fine—just a bit of travel sinus trouble. I just wanted to say that I love you, and I miss you, and that sounds like *The Young and the Restless*, but I can't help that. That's how I feel, and I've got to say it like it is. And you know I wouldn't be doing this without your blessing. Thank you for giving it."

There was a pause while Sonja waited for the children to be out of earshot. She lowered her voice. "And I love you, darling. Very much. But you know, I don't think I would have gone along with this had it not been for our trip to the zoo, and I think that is important. Things happen for a reason. I really believe that, and that means that you are meant to be in Washington right now. I will be there right next to you when you meet with the president in the morning. I must get the children their breakfast, so I'll hang up now. Please call me, as soon as you can, after the meeting. Good luck, darling. I love you."

"I love you t—" *Click*. She had hung up before he could finish his sentence.

CHAPTER 20

He woke up by the telephone ringing next to his ear. He fumbled for the receiver, groggy with sleep.

"This is your six o'clock wake-up call. Have a nice day."

"Thank you, you too."

Nat had not finished his sentence when the voice started again. "This is your six o'clo—"

He replaced the receiver, feeling foolish that he had talked to a machine. The digital display on his bedside clock radio showed 6:01 in big red numerals.

He must have dropped off after all. He had lay staring at the ceiling, after the call to Sonja, going through in his mind endless versions of the meeting the next morning. Last time he looked at the clock it had said 4:45. *I must have passed out*, he thought. He got out of bed, showered and shaved, then dressed quickly. The pale grey suit, white shirt, and red tie with small, pale blue flecks made him at least *look* like a sane person, he thought, as he gave himself an inspection in the full-length, dressing room mirror. He returned to the bedroom and called Preston, who answered on the second ring. They agreed to meet downstairs at 6:30 for coffee and a Danish. Nat looked at his watch; it was twenty after six. He went to the living room, where his laptop had been sitting on charge overnight, put it in its carrying case, and checked that the notepad he had put in the outside pocket was there. Then a final check in the bathroom mirror—he straightened his hair, and, looking at the red eyes staring back at him, found some eye drops in his overnight bag, squirted some in his eyes, and put the bottle in his pocket.

It was 6:27. He picked up his room key and laptop, turned the main switch off, and left. A black bag, with the *Washington Post* in it, was hanging on the doorknob outside. He grabbed the bag and pulled the paper out enough to look at the headline while he waited for the elevator.

"NUCLEAR WARHEAD MISSING FROM RUSSIAN ARSENAL"

The elevator doors opened, and he folded the paper and returned it to the black bag. There were two Japanese men and a woman in the elevator engaged in what appeared to be a heated discussion. *Perhaps the newspaper headlines?* Nat thought. The elevator doors opened at the lobby level, and the Japanese party headed for the restaurant gesticulating wildly and talking to each other simultaneously. Nat hesitated and looked around the lobby area. Preston was sitting in the lobby lounge, reading his paper. In front of him were two cups of coffee and two plates, one with a Danish on it. Nat smiled as he approached. Good old Jim—always thoughtful, always calm, always cool and collected.

"Ah, there you are." Preston looked up from his paper. "And a very good morning to you. Did you have a good sleep?"

"Good morning, Jim," Nat said, as he sat down opposite Preston. "To be honest, I didn't sleep all that well. How about you?"

"Like a rock," said Preston, folding the paper. "Have some coffee and a Danish; it'll perk you up." He looked at his watch. "Melinda will be here in ten minutes."

Nat took a sip of coffee. He noticed that Preston's cup was empty like his plate. *He must have been down here a while,* Nat thought, reading the paper. *How come he didn't say anything about the headline?* He pulled out his own paper and pretended to see it for the first time. "Bloody hell! Have you seen this?" He turned the paper towards Preston. "It's happened! They've got their nuclear weapon!"

"Not so fast," said Preston. "I've read the article. There is a vital piece missing from the device, without which it cannot be detonated. Apparently, atomic stockpiles are kept this way for added security. Still, it is a scary thought that somebody has been able to breach the security of a lethal weapons store. The man in charge of it, Colonel Sergei Ivanovitch, has been relieved of his command, and an investigation is underway. Our president has offered to help the investigation, and so has Britain, France, and Germany. So far, the Russians have declined any outside help. In fact, they thought they had the whole story under wraps, but an anonymous source tipped off a reporter at the *Washington Post*, and when they went to verify, the Russians admitted it immediately, saying that they had only kept it quiet to aid their own internal investigations. It's going to be interesting to hear what the president has to say about it."

Melinda entered the lobby as Preston finished his sentence. She wore navy blue slacks and a tan jacket over a simple tan blouse. She came towards them with an energetic stride, flashing a bright smile. "Good morning, gentlemen; how are you? I hope you had a pleasant evening and a good night's sleep?"

They said: "Thank you," and that they'd had a pleasant evening, then got up from the table.

"Harry is waiting for us outside."

Nat looked at his watch, which read 6:46. Melinda was a good timekeeper. They went outside under the large colonnaded porte cochere, where Harry stood behind the opened rear door. The polished shade of his cap glowed orange under the porch lights. It was still dark, but the sky was clear. It was going to be a beautiful day. They got in, and Harry closed the door behind them. Melinda was already in the front seat and turned around, asking, "Have you got your passports with you?"

"Yes," they both confirmed.

"Could I have them, please?"

They handed them to her.

Harry took them down Pennsylvania Avenue. The traffic was light, and they soon stopped in front of the West Gate. Melinda showed her own ID and their passports to the guard, who took a long look into the car. He handed the documents back to Melinda and spoke into the microphone, which was projecting out from the side of his helmet. There was a short pause, then he nodded and spoke into his microphone. The wrought-iron gate in front of them opened slowly, and the guard waved them on. They proceeded up a long, wooded drive, which continued to the north portico main entrance, but Harry made a right turn, and soon they stopped in front of the more modest entrance to the West Wing. Melinda and Harry held the car doors open, and Preston and Nat got out. Melinda led the way to the entrance and guided them through a mantrap, using her proximity card, while a guard kept a watchful eye. Once through the mantrap, she went up to the guard and stated their business. When he heard that they were there for a meeting with the president and the vice president he looked at them with renewed interest before picking up a telephone and speaking in a low voice. Nat looked at his watch. It said 6:58. Melinda had timed it perfectly. A door opened and in came a man which Nat judged to be in his late forties, early fifties. His brown hair was thinning at the top and greying at the temples, but he looked trim and fit in a dark blue suit. Melinda made the introductions: "This is Hal Masters; secretary to the president, and this is James Preston, ambassador to The Court of St. James, and his deputy chief of mission, Nathaniel Jameson."

They shook hands, and Masters gestured towards the open door. "This way, gentlemen; the president will see you in his office." He led the way down a wide, well-lit hallway at the end of which was a curved wall with a large, panelled door. He opened the door and followed in closely behind them. They stopped, and he passed them and walked towards the desk.

"Mr. President, let me—" The president waved his secretary off as he rose from his desk.

"OK, Hal. Cut formalities; we're all friends here. Leave the rest to me." Hal withdrew.

The president was taller than Nat had imagined: . . . *Six foot two or three*, Nat thought, and he had a firm handshake.

"Good morning, Jim." He shook Preston's hand. "Good to see you again." And, turning to Nat, "And you're the young man with the plot to kill me? Nice to meet you!" He shook Nat's hand vigorously. The bright blue eyes under the bushy grey eyebrows had a mischievous look in them.

"No, sir," Nat spluttered out nervously. "That would be the *failed* plot."

The president threw his head back and laughed. "It sure would be, from my point of view. Let's sit over there." He pointed to a seating area in front of the fireplace. "Jack will join us shortly. Seven o'clock is a bit early for him."

Nat took a deep breath. Here he was in the office of the most powerful man on Earth, and what a magnificent place it was, but the relaxed and friendly manner of the man who occupied it made it seem like an ordinary office—a place to work, and work hard. Nat looked down and saw that he was standing in the centre of the president's seal, which was embroidered in a dark blue carpet covering most of the room. The room was well lit by diffused cove lighting which shone up into the white ceiling, where a plaster medallion repeated *The Presidential Seal*. There were two big sofas, opposite each other, either side of the fireplace and at right angles to it. In the middle was a coffee table with an intricately inlaid top, on which stood a silver coffee service. A chair, with its back to the fireplace, stood between the two couches, and President Adams headed for it but turned around as he passed the coffee table.

"Would anybody like a cup of coffee?" He picked up the silver mug.

My God, thought Nat. *The president is going to pour the coffee himself!* And so he did; he poured three cups and passed two to Preston and Nat.

"Help yourselves to milk and sugar, if you take that stuff," he said. "I take mine black." He sat down in the chair and waited while Preston and Nat took some milk. They sat down, opposite each other, on the couches before President Adams started the conversation. "So, Nat... Jim tells me you've come up with a humdinger of an idea for infiltrating al-Qaeda? He gave me the gist of it over the phone, and I must tell you that

I was—I *am*—intrigued. How on earth did you come up with such an outrageous idea?"

"Well, Mr. President, I—"

The president cut him off. "Hold it right there, son! If we're gonna get anywhere with this, you're gonna have to call me by my name. Ted's my name."

"Yes, sir." Nat could feel himself blushing. The president looked at him and smiled. "OK, that's better. It takes a bit of getting used to, don't it? Anyway, you were saying?"

"Sir, it came to me out of nowhere, in the middle of the night. I don't know how or why. . . it just appeared."

"Are you superstitious?" The president looked at Nat over the edge of his coffee cup.

"No, sir, I'm not."

"Well, *I* am." The president set his cup down on the saucer forcefully, as if to reinforce his statement. "Nothing comes from 'nowhere', as *you* put it. Our thoughts and our actions are just a small part of the overall energy in the Universe. It is part of an overall logic which we cannot see, particularly when things go against us. So, who knows; maybe you're on to something—something really big and important for all of us. Who knows? Besides. . . " he continued. "Do you think it was pure coincidence that you and your family should find yourselves at the London Zoo last Saturday? Would you be sitting here this morning if that hadn't happened?"

Nat thought of Sonja and what she had told him. "No, sir," he said. "I probably wouldn't."

There was a knock on the door, and in walked a thin, grey-haired man with an equally grey moustache.

"Good morning, Jack." The president rose from his chair and introduced his vice president. "I want you to meet our London ambassador, James Preston, and his deputy, Nat Jameson. Sorry to get you out of bed so early, but you can see from the headlines that we're gonna have a busy day."

"Yes, Mr. President; it has finally happened," said Jack, as he eyed the coffee tray.

"Help yourself," said the president, "and cut the formalities; we're all on first-name terms here."

They discussed the missing nuclear warhead, concluding that, even if this was a harmless piece of hardware without the trigger mechanism, it was clear that a nuclear threat from terrorists was getting closer to becoming reality.

"And let's make no mistake about it," said the president. "They won't hold a nuclear weapon as a tactical negotiating tool. They'll just blow us up—New York, Washington, Boston—who knows where, or maybe all of them together, depending on the size of the device. The world would never be the same again. We must not forget the words of Khalid Sheikh Mohammed at Gitmo, that, if bin Laden was captured or killed, an al-Qaeda sleeper cell will detonate a weapon of mass destruction. We thought that since it didn't happen within four years of us getting him, it was just a boastful threat. Now I'm not so sure."

"It seems for every step we take forward in our battle against terrorism, we end up taking two back," Jack commented.

"Well," said the president, "we're running out of time. All we're doing is scratching the surface of this problem when we need to get to the core of it." Turning to Jim and Nat, he continued: "But that's why I invited you to meet Jim and Nat here. They have come up with an idea that I thought we should take a look at. Now, Jack, I warn you; the stuff you're gonna hear will take your breath away. Don't have a heart attack." He looked at Nat and winked. "Why don't you give us a complete run-through, son."

The vice president sat down next to Preston, while Nat got his laptop out and placed it on his lap. "First, I want to thank you both for letting me do this in the first place," said Nat as he pulled up the file. "I woke up last Friday morning with this idea in my head. I have no idea where it came from, but I felt compelled to pursue it, so I mentioned it to Jim, knowing that, if he said no, it would go no further." He looked at Preston. "At first, Jim was ready to have me committed, but something brought him around, and he agreed that my wild plan was worth, at least, exploring."

"OK, son," said the president. "Let's have your plan. Jack is dying to hear what this is all about, and I'm curious to hear the details you've come up with as to how you think this could be pulled off." He turned to his vice president, "Jack, what you are about to hear is an idea for how we get inside al-Qaeda and demolish the organisation from the inside—the endgame on world terrorism. You and Jim here, and Nat, are the main actors, and I'm the bait."

"I'm intrigued," said the vice president, turning to Nat. "Let's have it, Nat."

Nat took them through explaining the relationship he had developed with Imam Badawi, and how, if he could get his confidence, he thought he could infiltrate al-Qaeda at the highest level. When he got to the part about "killing" the ambassador, Jack shot Preston an alarmed glance.

"I can live with that," said Preston, and they laughed. Nat then explained about the "heart attacks", supposedly induced by him, and how he would take over as the new ambassador while Preston changed his identity and moved to Europe and met up with his "widowed" wife.

Having shown Badawi that Nat was as good as his word, he went on to explain that he thought it might be necessary to pull off the second "assassination" and that the person he had in mind was no lesser a figure than the vice president himself. The president gave his second in command a long look.

"What do you think, Jack? Too crazy for you?"

"Wow, give me a minute." The vice president drew a long breath. "I've got to let that one sink in a little." All eyes were on Jack, who was staring intently at the wood grain in the coffee table. The room was dead quiet.

Jack looked up. "The country can't be without a vice president for any length of time, and we couldn't swear in a make-believe vice president.

I'd have to resign—-secretly, that is—since, officially, I'd be dead." He looked around the table, and his eyes rested on the president, "Well Ted, funny isn't it, that I told you just the other day about my desire to live in Venice when I retire?"

Preston shot Nat a quick look that said: "What did I tell you?"

"I've got you at a disadvantage, Jack," said the president. "I've known about this idea since Sunday evening, when Jim gave me a call at Camp David. I was intrigued. I realise that there are many legal, practical, and technical obstacles that would have to be overcome for this to be set in motion, but I thought it would be worth exploring. Obviously, if you and I can't be convinced of the merit of it, then it stays within these four walls—one wall," he corrected himself, looking around the Oval Office.

"I could do with a cup of coffee," said the vice president. He got up and poured himself a cup, then asked the others if they wanted a refill. They all declined.

"Ok, Nat, carry on," said the president.

Nat described how the vice president's "assassination" could be accomplished following the format of the London ambassador's "death", emergency response, and burial, and it was Jack himself who volunteered that early retirement in Venice did not sound so bad. "If you can call retiring at seventy-two 'early retirement'," he added. Nat took this as an indication that the vice president was warming to the *idea* of it, at least.

When Nat came to the end of the plan narrative twenty minutes later, a deep silence filled the room. The grandfather clock against the wall showed five past eight.

It was the vice president who broke the silence. "That's one hell of a plot, son! You're sure putting your life on the line. Is your wife OK with this?"

"Yes, sir," said Nat. "Since Saturday at the London Zoo, she is."

The president got up from his chair, walked over to his desk, and sat down. "The question, Jack, is do I call the people who would need to get involved and take this to the next level, or do we just thank Nat and Jim for their effort and send them back to London?"

Jack gave the president a long look. "I say we give it our best shot, Ted. Looking at this morning's headlines, we are running out of time."

"My thought, entirely," said the president. He picked up the house phone. "Hal, could you please call Charlie Benson and Bob Rosen, and tell them I need their presence asap. They're expecting your call." He put the receiver down.

Nat knew that Benson was the director of the CIA, but he had not read, nor had he heard, of Rosen. He had not completed the thought when the president remarked, “In case you didn’t know, Bob is my chief counsel. He can tell us what we can and can’t do with this thing, from a legal point of view. Is deceiving the public, in this case, the same as covering up the Watergate break-in? I’ll be darned if I know.”

“I can see *one* problem right away,” said Jack. “Jim and I would have to resign from our posts before we could be replaced. There is no such thing as a make-believe vice president or ambassador, so, technically, our replacements cannot be appointed while we are still alive, unless we have resigned.”

“Yeah, tricky business,” said the president. “Those resignations would have to be kept secret. Besides,” he added, “I would need to have the continued benefit of your wise counsel from time to time. And the same goes for you.” He turned to Preston.

“You’d be sacrificing your careers, gentlemen.” The president folded his hands in front of him on the desk. “Is that something you are prepared to do?”

The vice-president replied first. “Retirement wouldn’t be so bad. Let’s face it, at seventy-two, I’m past my ‘use by’ date in any case.” He chuckled.

“No offence, Ted, but I have to tell you, apart from playing dead, which I don’t relish the idea of, the thought of retirement is not abhorrent to me.”

The president nodded and turned to Preston. “And what about you, Jim; are you ready to be put out to pasture?”

“I’ll be sixty-five before the year is out. I have had a long and interesting career, and finishing off taking part in a plot that might strike a fatal blow to terrorism would be the icing on the cake, as far as I'm concerned. And Nat's idea is so outrageous, I think it might work."

"Well then," the president turned to Nat. "It would seem you have two of the main players on board. That leaves me. What do *I* think? What do *I* think?" He tapped his fingers on the desk. There was a look of serious concentration on his face. He looked straight at Nat and raised his voice. "I think this is the most preposterous suggestion I have ever heard! Involving the president and vice president of the United States of America in a sting operation like this is absolutely *unthinkable*!"

He paused. Nat thought, *It's over*, and he felt disappointment and relief at the same time.

"But *that*," continued the president, "is precisely what makes it so fascinating."

Nat let out a long stream of air, which he had been holding on to without realising it.

"I really like your idea, son," said the president. "This is outside-the-box stuff, all right." He gave Nat a big smile. "I still can't understand how on earth you came up with it, but it's very clever. That's what it is—clever. Shall we have another cup of coffee while we wait for the—"

There was a knock on the door, and the president's secretary appeared in the doorway. "Benson and Rosen to see you, Mr. President."

"Thanks, Hal." The president rose from his desk and walked over to greet the newcomers.

The CIA director was a tall, square-jawed, athletic-looking man with dark, receding hair. He wore a navy blue suit, crisp white shirt, and red tie. He spoke with a booming voice: "Good morning, Mr. President; it's good to see you."

"Thanks for coming over, Charlie."

The president shook his hand and turned to his chief counsel. "And you too, Bob." Rosen was a short, skinny man with the looks of a young Albert Einstein. They shook hands, and the president introduced them to Nat and Preston. "I suggest we all sit down over there."

The president gestured to the seating in front of the fireplace. "You need to be seated when you hear what Nat here has cooked up for us."

The president reclaimed his seat in front of the fireplace, and the others sat down opposite him on the two couches and two chairs facing the president.

"Let me give Nat a little lead-in so you can absorb what he is telling you with the knowledge of what Jack and I think." The president cleared his throat. "What you are about to hear is a plot—let me say, an *ingenious* plot—to get inside al-Qaeda at the top. What you are about to hear may shock you, but I want you to keep an open mind, and I want you to hear Nat out before you respond to what he has to say. I also want you both to know that Jack and I agree, in principle. In fact—correct me if I'm wrong, Jack—it is true to say that the vice president and I are keen to see this plan through to execution. OK, Nat; please run through it again, and don't skim over anything just because Jack and I have heard it before."

Nat took them through the plan again, step by step, and was careful to follow the same sequence of events and place emphasis on the parts he had before. The CIA director sat motionless through the whole presentation and did not reveal any response by facial expression or body language. Rosen, on the other hand, raised his eyebrows, bit his lip, shot furtive glances at the president from time to time, whilst constantly fidgeting in his chair. He looked like he had a difficult time not interrupting Nat's narrative.

When Nat came to the end, Rosen was the first to speak. "Mr. President, with all due respect—"

"Bob," the president broke in, "when people say that, they always come out with strong objections to something."

"Yes, Mr. President; I don't think this idea, clever as it may sound, can be made to work." Rosen stopped.

"And why is that, Bob? We are all ears," said the president. "This is what you are here for, to give me all the legal, and perhaps constitutional, reasons why this cannot be done." He gave them all a serious look.

"Thank you, Mr. President."

The president's counsel drew a deep breath. "First of all, Mr. President, as you know, covert actions are normally recommended by the National Security Council. Then, if you agree, you task the CIA, and, once they have received your instructions, the Intelligence Oversight Committee must be notified."

"Bob, I'm well aware of the *normal* procedure," said the president. "But we are not talking about a *normal* covert action. We have had only limited success with normal covert actions since we caught bin Laden. Terrorists have become even more careful and difficult to find. Is there any reason why the initiative for a covert action could not come from the president himself?"

Rosen squirmed in his chair. "No, sir, there is no reason."

"Well then," said the president. "I didn't think so. In fact, Bob, and correct me if I'm wrong, only the president can direct the CIA to undertake a covert action. The only difference in this case is that the action would not first have been recommended by the NSC."

Rosen cleared his throat. “That is correct, sir.”

“OK. Now we’re getting somewhere.” The president got up from his chair and strolled over to the coffee table. “Anybody else for a cup of coffee?”

They all declined, and the president poured himself a cup and returned to his seat. “Now then, what do you think of having an ambassador and a vice president play dead, Bob, apart from the obvious practical problems, some of which Nat here has already addressed? Are we running into any legal or ethical obstacles here?”

Rosen hesitated. “That is a difficult one, Mr. President. I imagine that the fewer people know about the plot, the better chance it would have of succeeding. This would involve a degree of deception, which is, to say the least, unprecedented.” Rosen paused, and straightened in his chair. “I think,” he continued, “that you would be taking a big risk politically, even assuming that they would get nowhere near you. But if they did, you would have put your own life in danger, which is obviously completely unacceptable.”

“Quite so,” said the president. “But in this scenario, neither the vice president nor I would be in danger. The man who would be taking the greatest risk is Nat here.” The president gave Nat a serious look.

“You’d be right there in the lion’s den if this worked out, son. They’d cut your head off if something went wrong. Are you ready for that?”

“No, sir, can’t say I am, but I hope I would be, should it come to that.”

“Then there is the issue of succession,” Rosen broke in. “When a vice president dies, the mantle passes to the speaker of the House. Fortunately, the speaker is Republican presently, but that could change next year. As you know, Mr. President, we do not have a comfortable majority in the House at this time."

The president took a sip of coffee. "All the more reason to get cracking with this thing as soon as possible, Bob. I sure as hell wouldn't want to end up with a Democrat for vice president. Any problem with a secret resignation of a vice president?" The president stared intently at his legal counsel.

Rosen twisted in his chair. "Apart from the fact that it must be kept secret, which of course is unprecedented, I do not believe that it would break any laws. I will need some time to research this, though."

"OK, you do that. Use the office next door, and do what you have to do."

Rosen disappeared and the president turned his attention to the CIA director. "What do you think, Charlie? Could you make this work or what?"

"We could make it work all right." Benson's deep voice exuded confidence. "The big question is: would al-Qaeda take the bait? Why disrupt lives and careers on this scale if we are not sure of success?"

"OK, Charlie." The president got up from his chair and walked over to the coffee table, changed his mind and returned to his chair. "How many covert actions have you canned because you were not sure of their success?"

There was a pregnant pause while Benson did a mental scan of his projects. "None, Mr. President, but they were all worked out with professionals along normal covert action principles. This is not in our manual." He gave them all a big grin. "Which means," he added," that it's not in *their* manual either, and that is what fascinates me, the idea of mounting an *unthinkable* operation."

The president returned to his seat in front of the fireplace. He sat down and gave Benson an intense stare. "So are you telling me that you're on board, Charlie?"

Benson did not hesitate. "Yes, sir, I am, in principle."

"In *principle*? Now you sound like a politician." The president glanced at his watch.

"I mean, sir," said Benson, "that there are a lot of details to be worked out relative to the 'deaths' and disappearance of the ambassador and the vice president. Nat will need to undergo some basic training in covert activity, and we will need to implant a locater device, probably in one of his molars. Protocols will need to be put in place for lines of communication, and so on."

"OK, now we're talking," said the president. "I would like you to start working on those details right away, while Jim and Nat are here, which means over the next couple of days. Can you do it?"

"Can do," said Benson. "If they can come back to Langley with me after this meeting, we can start this morning."

The president turned to Jim and Nat. "Is that OK with you fellas?"

Jim gave Nat a quick wink. "That it is, Mr. President."

Nat felt his heart do a somersault and pick up pace. They were on their way. His crazy plan was going to become reality. He felt a mixture of elation and apprehension. His mouth suddenly felt dry, and he swallowed hard.

"Any second thoughts, son?" The president leaned forward and gave Nat a concerned look. "If you want to change your mind, now's the time. Maybe Benson can find a replacement for you—one of his own agents?"

"No, sir," said Nat. "This part is made for me. I *want* to do this, and I think Mr. Benson would agree that putting a new player on the scene would arouse suspicion."

"That is absolutely right," Benson confirmed. "With Nat, we don't have to make up anything; he is what he is, except a murderer and a traitor."

"Very good, gentlemen!" The president rose, walked over to his desk, and pressed a button. "Hal, could you please ask Mr. Rosen to rejoin us."

"Yes, Mr. President."

Rosen reentered the Oval Office moments later. He had a yellow pad in one hand and a pen in the other, and he looked flustered.

"How are you doing, Bob," asked the president. "Have you found the reason we can't go ahead with this plan?"

"No, sir, there would appear to be no *legal* reason preventing it." Rosen gave an exasperated sigh. "But I would like to go through, with you, some of the risks and pitfalls I feel are associated with doing this thing."

"Such as. . . ?" said the president.

Rosen referred to his notes. "As you know, you're obliged to notify the Intelligence Oversight Committee once you have tasked the CIA. When you do, it would raise a lot of eyebrows if you did not make any reference to the National Security Council. I think it would get out if you tried to bypass the NSC, and it would cost you a lot of political capital and potentially jeopardise the project."

"OK," said the president. "I hear you, and you're right, so I will sit down with the NSC *first,* and I'll brief them. I don't need their permission, do I?"

"No, sir, you don't."

"OK. I'll get them on board. They're good people; I think they'll see the merit of it." The president left no room for argument.

"The other problems, as I see it. . . " Rosen adjusted his horn-rimmed glasses. ". . . is the degree of deception that is involved in this scheme. Faking your death is *illegal*—if your widow goes to collect your life insurance, for example. There is also the issue of wills—the execution of wills—which is the inevitable result of a death." Rosen looked up. "And I assume, gentlemen, that you both *have* wills?" he said, addressing the vice president and Preston.

"I do," said the vice president. "It is very simple. Everything I leave behind goes to cancer research. It was Betty's last wish."

"It all goes to my wife," said Preston.

"And what about life insurance?"

They both shook their heads.

"Well, that makes it a bit easier, at least in your case, Mr. Ambassador. As long as you trust your wife, we could work something out." Rosen focused his attention on the vice president, who spoke first. "I know what you're going to say, Bob; it's not very simple at all. What will I live on if my inheritance goes to cancer research *before* I'm gone?"

"Precisely," said Rosen. "That is a very good question."

Nat could feel his heart sinking. This was getting very complicated, perhaps too complicated?

Rosen interrupted his thoughts. "Of course, you could *change* your will, observing the spirit of your wife's wishes. You could establish a trust and a trust fund and instruct your trustees to manage the fund to grow it by prudent measures and pay a specified amount per annum to cancer research. However. . . " Rosen hesitated. ". . . your trustees would have to be in on it. Funds would have to be channelled to you, also, to live on." He removed his glasses. "I guess..." he said, wiping his glasses with a handkerchief. "...I could be one of those, and you need a minimum of two."

"Heck, Jack," said the president. "We've been friends for forty years! You wouldn't mind having me for a trustee, now, would you?"

Rosen replaced his glasses. "Mr. President, I don't think—"

"Hold it, Bob!" The president waved him off. "Don't tell me I can't act as a trustee for my friend Jack because I happen to be the president right now! It's not against the law, is it?"

"No, sir. It's not against the law; I just think you will be in for a lot of criticism when it all eventually comes out, which it will, whether the plan succeeds or fails."

"Criticism!" The president scoffed. "Now, there is something I'm used to, and if we wind up al-Qaeda, do you think I—we all—would be forgiven for our little deception?" Not waiting for an answer, the president stood up and walked over to his desk. He turned around, facing them, and sat down on the edge of the desk. "I think I have heard enough, gentlemen. You are all telling me that this is doable. The rest is in the details. I give you two weeks to work it out and get back to me. I want to be able to sit down with the NSC before we break for Christmas." He turned his attention to Nat. "As for you, son; that's a hell of a plot you've come up with. Maybe you're in the wrong profession? Anyhow, Charlie, here, will teach you some tricks over at Langley and get you ready for your journey to the snake pit." The president stood up and addressed the room. "That's what all these people are—cowards who kill innocent people, then slither back in their holes to wait for the next opportunity. We can't win this war as long as they hide among ordinary people and use them as human shields. Terrorists have no respect for human lives or normal human values; they are like a cancer growing inside you. You either remove it or you die. Let's remove it! Thank you all for coming, and Godspeed."

CHAPTER 21

The drive to CIA headquarters, in the CIA director's limousine, took less than fifteen minutes. On the way, Benson explained that, although the CIA headquarters is often referred to as Langley, it is not located in Langley itself but in the Langley suburb of McLean. He also told them that they had a college-campus-like atmosphere, with the buildings set on 258 acres of land, which provided a secure and secluded environment for the facility. Nat was stunned when Benson told them that there was 1.4 million square feet of space in all. Somehow, Nat had always thought of 'Langley' as a much smaller place. When he asked Benson how many people worked there, Benson gave him a smile and said, "I can't tell you; it's a secret." He also told them that visitors were not allowed but added, "You'll be allowed in because you're with me."

Preston asked him if anybody had broken the code of the *Kryptos*, the sculpture by James Sandborn of coded messages cut out in an S-shaped copper screen in the courtyard of the New Headquarters Building.

Benson laughed and told them that many of his staff had spent their lunch hours in the courtyard trying to break the code, but that, so far, its secret remained intact.

They pulled up under a large concrete canopy in front of the Old Headquarters Building, and Benson led them into the lobby, which was brightly lit, highlighting the CIA seal depicting the eagle, the shield, and the sixteen-point compass set in the floor. Preston and Nat were issued guest tags, and Benson headed for a bank of elevators which took them past the Memorial Wall where 139 stars were chiselled into the stone in memory of those CIA agents who had made the ultimate sacrifice for their country. Below the stars was the glass encased Book of Honour, naming ninety-four of the agents who had lost their lives. The other forty-five officers remained secret, even in death.

Benson did not introduce them to his secretary as they passed her on the way to his office, and Nat thought this a little odd. As if he had read Nat's mind, Benson explained that Wendy was used to him not letting her know the identity of some of his guests.

Benson sat down behind his desk and gestured Preston and Nat to take the two chairs in front of him. On the wall behind him was a picture of President Adams, flanked by two large American flags.

Benson pushed a button on his desk and asked Wendy to send in coffee. He leaned forward in his chair, reached for a picture on his desk, and turned it around towards them.

"When you told us about your experience at the zoo, I couldn't help thinking what I would have felt like if it had been my family."

The photograph showed a dark-haired woman in her late thirties to mid-forties flanked by two boys, both in their early teens. The backdrop was Big Ben in London.

"As you can see," Benson continued, "this picture was taken in London. We were there on vacation two years ago. The day before this picture was taken, we had been to the zoo and had a wonderful time there. Anyhow..." He turned the picture back to face himself and set it back in its place. "Let me walk you through what we need to accomplish while you are here." Benson explained to Preston that he would be rehearsed in how to fake a heart attack. "It's not so hard to do," he said. "Actors do it all the time." He pressed the button on his desk. "Wendy, could you please ask Leonard Cook and Robert Martin to come to my office? Thanks. Lenny is our theatrical expert, and Robbie is our gadgets man. I don't think you'll need any props, Jim. But Nat, here, he'll need to be fitted with an indetectable locater, one you'll activate should you get an audience with al-Qaeda." He gave Nat an encouraging smile.

There was a knock on the door, and a young girl brought in a tray with coffee and doughnuts. She placed the tray on Benson's coffee table and asked him if she should pour it for them. "No thanks, Mollie," said Benson. "If the president can do it, so can I." Mollie left, and Benson poured the coffee and offered them each a doughnut. "Brain food," he said, as he took a big bite.

They had just taken the first sip of coffee when the buzzer sounded on Benson's desk. Wendy announced that Cook and Martin were waiting outside.

"Send them in." Benson leaned forward and polished off the last bit of his doughnut.

The door opened and two young men, both in jeans and sport shirts, entered. Benson introduced them. "This is Lenny, our theatrical expert. They say he's so good he could teach a dog to masquerade as a butler."

Lenny was tall and skinny with a mop of red curls which flowed down to his shoulders. "And this is Robbie, our gadget man; James Bond would be glad to have him." Robbie was built like an American football player, the fast, muscular type who got the touchdowns.

He was a light-skinned African American with short-cropped hair and intelligent eyes behind steel-rimmed glasses.

Benson introduced Preston and Nat by their first names only, as two people who would be involved in a special operation—nothing about their backgrounds or the nature of the operation. He explained that Preston needed to be able to pull off a convincing heart attack and asked Lenny to escort Preston back to Benson's office when he was satisfied that his pupil had mastered the skill. They left, and Benson turned to Nat. "And Nat needs to be fitted with an indetectable locator—I imagine an implant of some description—but it must be capable of being activated by Nat without anybody realising he is doing it. The range must be worldwide."

"Sounds like a job for our Molarfix," said Robbie.

Benson chuckled. "That's a good idea, provided Nat is not scared of the dentist?" He explained that Robbie was suggesting a transmitter which could be implanted in one of Nat's teeth, preferably under an existing filling.

"I have two fillings," said Nat. "And, provided your dentist is like mine, generous with the anaesthetic, I'll be fine."

"Good," said Benson. "Advise Dr. Carpontier of your preference for pain-free dentistry. Good luck. I'll see you back here in about half an hour."

Dr. Carpontier was a distinguished-looking, grey-haired man in his early to mid-sixties. Luckily, his equipment was state of the art, to the point where his office looked like it came out of *Star Wars*.

A flat-screen television was mounted on the ceiling over the chair, and Nat was fitted with earphones and a remote. Much to Nat's relief, Dr. Carpontier was a soft-spoken French Canadian, who quite agreed that dentistry should be a painless experience. It was determined that the filling on the lower right was the best choice. It was easier to reach and larger than the one on the other side. First, the anaesthetic cream, followed by two needles and a five-minute wait, and Dr. Carpontier went to work, while Nat tuned in to CNN news. The missing Russian nuclear warhead was the top story, and the news anchorwoman, who was talking to a US security expert, made the point that if a nuclear warhead could be stolen, so could the trigger-mechanism that was needed to activate it.

He agreed that it was possible but that the Russians had assured the world that all trigger mechanisms were accounted for and now under heightened security. She asked him if it was known who had stolen the warhead, and he answered that the Russians thought it was an inside job, saying that security was simply too tight for it to be breached from the outside. The security expert did not necessarily agree with this statement, saying that lack of proper security for Russia's nuclear arsenal had been a major concern since the collapse of the Soviet Union.

"Perhaps," he said, "this incident would make the Russians more open to assistance from the US when it came to securing their nuclear weapons. A fully functional warhead of the type, stolen, in the hands of terrorists could. . . " he pointed out, ". . . obliterate New York City and create a nightmare scenario that so far had been limited to Hollywood productions."

"OK, we're done," said Dr. Carpontier. He pushed the lamp up out of the way so that it partially blocked the television screen. It startled Nat, who had been so absorbed by the news program that he had forgotten that he was sitting in a dentist's chair. He had not noticed the little steel pellet, no larger than a buckshot, which was carefully placed and covered so that it looked no different to when they started. "You have a fine set of teeth, young man. Continue to take good care of them." Dr. Carpontier eased himself off his stool. "Robbie is waiting for you outside. I guess I will see you again when your mission is accomplished. That's the most expensive filling you'll ever have, and they're not going to let you keep it. Good luck, young man! Whatever it is you are embarking on, I wish you all the best."

Robbie sat outside in the corridor and sprang to his feet the moment Nat opened the door. "Are you OK?"

"Yes, I—" Nat's tongue felt like it filled his mouth. It was difficult to talk. "I have a mouthful of tongue. I can't talk very well." He rubbed his cheek and could not feel anything.

"Never mind," said Robbie, "follow me."

They walked along the corridor for a while until they came to a bank of elevators—not the ones they had come down in—and Robbie pressed the button for the second floor. He turned to Nat. "I know you can't tell me, but I sure as hell would love to know what this is all about. You're not one of us, yet you get one of the most expensive pieces of hardware installed in your mouth, a piece of equipment which suggests that you are going deep undercover, in serious enemy territory. You are going to find somebody or something and lead us to it. I hope you know what you're doing?"

"So do I," muttered Nat, as best he could with his uncooperative tongue.

Robbie took Nat to a room, adjacent to his own office, which looked like a storeroom for props in a Broadway theatre—hats, belts, suspenders walking sticks, cigarette lighters, ladies' handbags, briefcases, suitcases, umbrellas, an assortment of watches and digital clocks, ties, cufflinks, wheelchairs, golf clubs, and banks of drawers below the open shelves.

Robbie opened one of the drawers and pulled out what appeared to be a tray of jewellery. He picked out a small box and opened it. It contained four small steel pellets. He picked one up and showed it to Nat. "This is what you now have under your filling. When you switch it on, it will transmit a signal, via satellite, back to us, here, which will enable us to pinpoint your location anywhere in the world within a radius of ten feet. You will activate it using a watch; I notice you are wearing a Rolex, which is lucky for me because I think I've got one here which will be almost a perfect match."

He pulled out another tray with a dozen Rolex watches for men and women in different styles and finishes. He picked up a Rolex Oyster with a ceramic bezel and white-gold wristband. It matched Nat's watch perfectly.

"This is my lucky day," said Robbie. "Not even the most suspicious mind would think your watch, which you have had for... how many years?"

Nat thought for a moment. "Exactly ten years."

"...that a watch you have had for ten years is anything other than what it seems to be. But here's the difference." He held it up to Nat's eyes. "You pull the crown out in the normal way to adjust the time and date, but you push the crown *in,* a minuscule amount, to activate the locater. You have to give it a *hard* push. This is to avoid accidental activation. I will keep your own watch here so that when you leave, there will be only three persons in the world who know that this is a special timepiece that you are wearing." Robbie saw the expression of concern on Nat's face and added, "Of course, when this is all over, we will swap watches again. If you think yours was expensive, I've got news for you; you've got the best deal in this swap."

"Thanks. It was an anniversary present from my wife, so whilst yours may be more expensive, mine has greater sentimental value, for me that is."

Nat removed his watch, gave it to Robbie, and put the other watch on. Apart from the coolness of the metal, it felt like his own.

"Try it," said Robbie. He turned to a telephone on the wall and dialled a number. "Hi Charlie; give me a check on locater L3." Nat pressed the crown in. Robbie waited. "Good stuff, Charlie; we're in business. Thanks."

Robbie escorted Nat back to Benson's office, where a man was standing opposite Benson's desk, looking like he had just arrived. He turned around, and Benson introduced him as communications expert Walter Farley. "Farley will run through some communication protocols with you. In the beginning, it will be you reporting your progress back to us, until you're ready to stage the first event. We'll be planning that, starting now, so that we're ready to move when you are. It is important that everything happens as smoothly and as naturally as possible."

Nat spent another half hour with Farley in his office. It was determined that Nat would report to Langley, always via a secure line in the embassy. No cell phone, email, or fax communications would be allowed. Nat was given two numbers to call—one for regular communications and another for situations where an immediate response was required. Farley explained that a team of people at Langley would be assigned to the project which would give Nat the best support a field agent could wish for. *Field agent.* Nat felt a chill run down his spine. He was entering a different world—a world full of lies, deception, and danger—a world he was not trained for, and yet he felt a strange sense of confidence that he would be equal to the challenges that lay ahead. In fact, he realized that he felt better than he had in a long time. He felt a surge of satisfaction from knowing that he was going to be part of something that could change the world for the better. No longer was he going to be a powerless spectator to a world being torn apart by religious fanatics and opportunists. He was going to do something about it—he was entering the fight for a saner and safer world.

Farley took Nat to the communications centre, which would receive his calls. It looked like a large open-plan trading office with lots of people with earphones and microphones on their heads, sitting in front of multiple monitors and a bank of telephones. Farley explained that the operation Nat was about to embark on had been code-named "ENDGAME" and that, when Nat started his calls with that word, the call would automatically be channelled to the right people at Langley. All calls would also be recorded and added to the electronic file which would be built up as the project progressed.

CHAPTER 22

When Nat got back to Benson's office, it was 12:30, and Preston was there with Benson, who was speaking on the telephone.

"Yes, sir. We have had a very productive morning here. Ambassador Preston's skill at faking a heart attack should get him an Oscar nomination, and Nat, who has just rejoined us, has been kitted out and fully briefed on the communications protocols. . . . Put you on the speaker? . . . Certainly, sir."

Benson held his hand over the receiver.

"The president wants to have a word with you." He pressed a button. "Can you hear us ok, Mr. President?"

"Sure can." The president's gravelly voice came through loud and clear. "I just wanted to wish you all good luck with the project and to thank you, in particular, Nat, for having hatched the idea in the first place, and you, Jim, for not killing it at birth but having the balls to bring it to my attention. I have a good feeling about this. Maybe we can outsmart them after all? God knows we've had enough failures, expensive failures at that. Anyway, Charlie, please keep me posted on this one, step by step, and don't leave anything out. You won't be boring me with the details."

"In that case, I will send you a full report on what has been done here this morning," said Benson.

"Please do." There was a slight pause, and the president continued: "How did you boys like your transportation?"

Preston got the point first. "Mr. President, Nat will not contradict me when I say it was the most comfortable flight we've ever had."

"Good," said the president. "Then you won't mind going back the same way. And, please, Jim, call me Ted, would you? I can't stand all this formal bullshit. We're in this thing together up to our asses. Let's be friends. Safe journey, and good luck." He hung up before any of them could reply.

They had lunch with Benson at CIA Headquarters and discussed the next steps, from Nat gaining Imam Badawi's confidence, the "murders" of Preston and the vice president, to how to best set the scene for a face-to-face meeting with the head of al-Qaeda. Benson thought that gaining the al-Qaeda leader's confidence would be the biggest challenge. To have avoided capture for so long, it was very clear that there could be only a handful of people, at any one time, who knew of his whereabouts, and those people were his closest advisers, most of whom had been with him from the beginning.

But Benson said that he was sure that he would be tempted to meet the man who had killed two prominent Americans, to prove that he meant what he said, and that he would be curious to meet the man who said he could hand him the president of the United States of America, ready for the kill. And, after all, was it not curiosity that killed the cat?

After lunch, Benson's chauffeur drove them back to the hotel, where a note was waiting in reception for Preston from Melinda, the president's secretary for appointments and scheduling.

Dear Mr. Ambassador,

Please let me know when you wish to return to London so that I can make sure your plane will be ready for you. The president indicated that, given the recent tragic events in London, you might be anxious to return as soon as possible. Please give me a call, any time, at your convenience.

She had left her cell phone and office numbers.

Preston looked at his watch—it was 3:30 p.m.—and then at Nat, "I don't know about you, but I could do with a little lie-down before we head back to London. This is a note, from Melinda, asking us when we wish to return."

Nat had hoped that there would have been time for him to visit his mother and his in-laws, but he knew that it was more important for Preston and him to be back in London as soon as possible. The terrorist attack on the zoo meant that they had a number of issues to be dealt with, one of which was the meeting with Imam Badawi, which would also be the start of the plot to infiltrate al-Qaeda. Nat was anxious to get back and get started.

"I'm ready to go when you are, Jim. I just need to make some calls—first to Sonja, then to my mother and my in-laws—and I'll be set to go."

"OK," said Preston. "I suggest we leave at eight tonight; that way, with the time difference, we'll arrive in London around eight in the morning, hopefully after a good night's sleep so we're ready for a full day in the office."

They agreed to meet in the lobby at seven, ready to go. Preston said he would call Melinda so that she could make the flight arrangements.

Back in his suite, Nat headed straight for the telephone, on the desk in the living room, and dialled Sonja. The phone rang only twice before she picked up. "Jameson residence—"

"Hi sweetheart, it's me." Nat felt short of breath.

"Oh, Nat! I've been pacing around here waiting for your call. How are you? How did it go with the president?"

Nat swallowed and tried to sound calm. "He went for it, Sonja! They ALL went for it! We're going ahead!"

"That is wonderful news, Nat! Congratulations!"

"I can't go into the details on the phone," said Nat, "but we are flying back tonight, so I'll be home tomorrow evening, about six, and I can give you a full report."

"That's wonderful," said Sonja. "We miss you, darling. Having you away right now just feels worse than usual. I guess we're not quite ourselves, yet, since Saturday. The kids are asleep, so I won't wake them up to talk to you. They asked me when I thought you would come home, and I said, '. . . probably not until the end of the week.' They'll be glad to hear you're getting back so soon."

Nat told her that he had spoken to his mother on the phone and had called her parents and got no reply. He promised her that he would try again before they left for the airport. She was disappointed when he told her that he would be going straight to work the next morning but felt better when he suggested that she join him for lunch so that he could fill her in on what had taken place in Washington.

They said goodbye, and Nat hung up and dialled his in-laws.

"Mahabir residence." Sonja's father's deep, gravelly voice seemed to fill Nat's earpiece.

"Hello, Raoul; this is Nat. How are you?"

"Hi, Nat. I'm fine; we're both fine. How are you? How did your meeting go this morning?"

"It went really well. We met with the president and vice president to go over the details of his upcoming European tour. . . . Yes, he wanted to hear all about our experience at the zoo. He's a hell of a nice guy—very direct, very straightforward, and very determined to win the war on terrorism. He likened the terrorists to a cancer which we either remove or succumb to."

"Yes," said Raoul. "And it is important to get the whole cancer, in order to have a complete cure."

"Unfortunately, I won't be able to come for a visit. We are going back to London tonight," said Nat.

"We understand," said Raoul. "Have a word with Fatima; she's standing right next to me. Safe journey." Raoul handed the phone to his wife. Nat assured her that they were all fine, that he had just spoken to Sonja, and that he hoped they would join them for Christmas in Switzerland.

She promised that they would consider it and get back to them with an answer shortly. They said goodbye, and Nat hung up and dialled his mother, who was very disappointed when he told her that he would not be able to drive down to see her in Harrisonburg, where she had lived since her husband died. She told him she thought he ought to ask for a transfer to a safer country like Norway or Sweden, or, better still, get a job back in Washington. Nat laughed and told her that his father-in-law had suggested the same thing, and he promised her that he would be looking into it. He assured her that they were all doing very well, and he told her that Tanya was writing an essay on the day at the zoo. He gave her the official version of his visit to the White House and told her how impressed he was with President Adams.

"But how are you doing, Mom? Last time we spoke, I never asked how *you* were."

"Except for worrying about you folks over there, I'm just fine," she said. But there was something in her voice that caught Nat's attention.

"Are you sure, Mom? Tell me the truth."

"No, really, I'm OK; my last medical checkup gave me a clean bill of health, except for a bit more bone loss. Dr. Wainwright says I have the heart of a thirty-year-old, which is not bad for a seventy-three-year-old and yet—" She hesitated. "It's my heart which is aching the most. You know, I read a lot, and I watch the news, and I despair at much of what I read and see. The attack at the zoo, for example, an attack targeting women and children is horrendous, but look at the number of innocent men, women, and children who were killed by the Israelis in Lebanon and Gaza some years ago. Is that justified? Is it any better? A dead child is a dead child whether it is Arab or Israeli. We have gone back to a world where it's an eye for an eye and a tooth for a tooth, and yet we pretend that we live in a civilised world! It doesn't make any sense to me! The waging of war against the Palestinian *people* to get the terrorists is, I think, insane."

My God, thought Nat, *how right you are*. Aloud he said, "The problem is that some terrorists are operating from highly populated areas, often using private homes, schools, and churches as their bases, including sites for launching rockets into Israel. The Israelis are protecting their people; they are defending themselves."

"Defending themselves by killing women and children on the other side is not self-defence in the long term, and you know it, Nat. It breeds more hatred and more terrorists, as *we* call them. As far as *they* are concerned, we and the Israelis are the terrorists. We, and, when I say 'we', I mean the Western powers who gave the Palestinians' land to the Israelis and are helping to kill their women and children. So, are *we* any better than the terrorists?"

Nat realised he had no short answer to that question. "I don't know. All I know is that the killing on both sides needs to stop because it has been proven, beyond any doubt, that it is not going to solve the problem. The Middle East conflict can only be solved if Israel agrees to go back to the 1967 boundaries and dismantles all the settlements which fall outside those boundaries. This is not going to be easy, but I think that, by now, if all the surrounding Arab states, including Syria and Iran, and also Hamas and Hezbollah, recognised Israel's right to exist, then the Israelis might be convinced that it is the only way to secure a lasting peace."

Before retiring eight years ago, Nat's mother had been a reporter for the *Washington Post*, and her interest in, and knowledge of, world affairs had not diminished. He wished he could tell her what he was about to get involved in and let her know that he would be fighting to help stop the senseless killing of innocent people, but he knew that was not possible. Instead, he told her that President Adams was determined to achieve a lasting peace in the Middle East and that he was prepared to think and act "outside the box" to achieve this goal.

"That is good," said Nat's mother. "But I hope you realise that, even if lasting peace is achieved, it is not going to stop al-Qaeda from pursuing their aim of Muslim fundamentalist world domination. Peace in the Middle East will shrink their pool of recruits, but it will not put them out of business. Anyway, son, I didn't mean to bend your ear on world affairs. I'm sure you must be tired after your meeting with the president. I hope you'll be able to get some sleep on the trip back."

Nat told her that they were flying private and assured her that he would get a good night's sleep.

"Well, darling, I must close now," she said. "I'm hosting our weekly bridge evening, which means—making dinner. We eat early and chat and then we play until we get tired. Tell Sonja I will be very glad to join you in Switzerland for Christmas, but I won't be able to get there until the twenty-fourth. I'm throwing a Christmas party for the children's home on the twenty-second."

"Great, Mom. We look forward to seeing you. I'll call you when I'm back in London. There's a lot to do, more so because of the zoo episode."

They said goodbye, and Nat hung up. Nat looked at his new watch; the time was only 4:15. He realized, suddenly, that his mother had been right. He felt tired and decided to have a soak in the bathtub and then a lie-down. He was about to step into the steaming hot water when the thought came to him that he did not know if the new watch was waterproof. He debated whether to call Langley to find out, when it occurred to him that it was probably not a good idea to call on the hotel phone, where the call would be logged on the hotel computer and printed out on his bill. He decided to use his cell phone, when he remembered that Farley had told him cell phones could not be used to communicate with Langley. He took a deep breath and said to himself, "Slow down; don't screw up before you even start." He removed the watch, placed it on the marble vanity, and sank into the hot water. The first call to Langley would have to wait until he got the secure line installed in his office.

The hot water felt soothing, and he could feel the tension melting out of his body. He sank as deeply into the tub as he could, leaving only his nose and eyes out of the water. He wondered whether he would ever get to al-Qaeda's headquarters. As far as he knew, no Western reporter, or Western person in any capacity, had achieved a meeting with a top al-Qaeda general since Peter Bergen's audience with bin Laden in 1998. Could he, a Western "infidel", gain the organisation's trust to the point where he would be granted an audience? And, if so, where would he be taken?

Would it be to a remote village in the Afghan mountains, a semi-detached dwelling in Dollis Hill in North London, a suite at the Ritz Paris, or to corporate headquarters in Dubai?

Somehow, Nat found it difficult to believe that the al-Qaeda executive was hiding out somewhere in a cave in Afghanistan or Pakistan. Would they not have found them by now if that were the case? Nat could feel his eyes wanting to close, and he realised that he'd better get out of the tub before he fell asleep and drowned.

He got out, towelled himself off, and put on a soft bathrobe. Back in the bedroom, he decided to pack his carry-on and left a fresh shirt, socks, and underwear out ready for later. He called reception and requested a wake-up call for 6:30, crawled into bed, and fell asleep as soon as his head hit the pillow.

CHAPTER 23

The flight back to London was every bit as pleasant as the one coming over. They had the same aircraft and crew, and after a light supper, Caroline made up two beds in the rear of the cabin so that Preston and Nat could sleep their way across the Atlantic. Preston did, but Nat was too excited. In his mind, he kept going through how to make that first approach to Badawi. It would be a critical moment. He needed to convince Badawi that he was sincere, that he was stable and sane, and that he was doing this to stop the senseless killing of innocent people. His own experience at the zoo, where he and his family could have been among the dead or wounded, would help make his offer to Badawi more believable. He resolved to call Badawi first thing, when he was back in the office tomorrow morning, and request a meeting for Monday. That would give him Thursday and Friday to clear his desk and go over things with Preston and the weekend to polish up the plan for his first approach to Badawi.

Caroline woke them up one hour before landing. She had set a breakfast table with fresh fruit, bread, cereal, tea, and coffee, and she asked if they wanted a cooked breakfast. She offered scrambled, fried, or boiled eggs.

Preston opted for a boiled egg, and Nat went the same route, to keep things simple. Caroline stripped the beds and put everything away, while Nat and Preston had their breakfast. As if he had read Nat's mind, Preston suggested that Nat set up a meeting with Badawi for Monday morning. "... so we can clear our desks and get ready for your meeting with Badawi," he said.

"Aren't you going to join us?"

"I will to start, but then I'll leave it to you. You couldn't make any overtures to Badawi with me hanging around."

Preston smiled and got up from the table. Nat followed him back to their seats upfront. Caroline cleared the table and returned with their jackets and overcoats.

"You'll be glad to have these; it's only six degrees centigrade in London this morning. We'll be landing in about twenty minutes."

They landed into a golden sunrise. It was going to be a beautiful day. George, Preston's driver, stood next to the car at the bottom of the steps, and by the time Nat and Preston had said their thank-yous and farewells, their luggage was in the car.

"Home or to the office, sir?" George looked at Preston in the mirror.

"Home would be nice, George, but the office it is."

"Very well, sir."

They sank into the soft leather back seat as George navigated the Bentley out of the airport. Nat looked at his watch. *His watch?* He realised that he had not told Preston about the watch and what it could do. Now was not the time; it would have to wait until they got back to the embassy. The watch said

3:38. He needed to reset it for the local time—8:38. He loosened the strap, placed the watch in his left hand, and pulled the crown out, making sure he exerted no inward pressure. He adjusted the watch and pressed the crown back carefully. There was a faint click. Nat realised he was holding his breath and exhaled slowly as he returned the watch to his wrist. "Good idea," said Preston. He took his watch off and reset it in half the time it had taken Nat.

They were caught up in the morning rush-hour traffic, heading towards the city, but George knew a network of back roads which got them to the embassy in just over an hour.

"Well done, George," said Preston, when they were delivered to the front door. "You sure know your way in and around London."

"Thank you, sir; that I do. Have a nice day." He brought his right hand to his chauffeur's cap, in a military-style salute.

Back in his office, Nat asked Angela to set up a meeting with Imam Badawi for Monday morning. On his desk were a stack of newspapers with reports and photographs of the zoo bombing. Among the headlines was one which read *Muslim cleric condemns zoo bombing*. Badawi was quoted saying that he hoped the perpetrators would be caught quickly and brought to justice.

Angela called back a few minutes later and told Nat that the meeting with Badawi was confirmed for 10 a.m. Monday morning. Nat went through the mail on his desk and made some notes to Angela, for letters that needed a response or action of some kind. Despite six hours of sleep on the plane, he felt drowsy, so he asked Angela to bring him a cup of coffee. When it arrived, he asked her to make a luncheon reservation for two at the Boxwood Café, a Gordon Ramsay hotspot in The Berkley

Hotel in Knightsbridge. Angela called back moments later to confirm the reservation. Nat dialled his home number, and the answering machine kicked in after the fourth ring. He left a message for Sonja to meet him at the Boxwood at 12:30, put the phone down, and immediately lifted it back to his ear and dialled his wife's mobile phone.

"Hello, darling! Welcome home." Sonja's voice came through after the second ring. "I've been waiting for your call. How are you?"

"I'm fine, but I'll be much better when I see you, sweetheart. I've booked us a table at the Boxwood for 12:30."

"Wonderful, I'll see you there. I'm so proud of you! I'm at Harrods getting the ingredients for your surprise dinner. The children went wild when they heard you were back already. Be prepared for a lot of questions about the president and the Gulfstream jet; Gregory has been glued to his computer studying private planes. He said you had promised him we'd all fly in one someday."

"I did no such thing, but I tell you, it takes all the hassles out of travelling. I hope we *can* all do it together one day. Oh, honey, take a taxi to the restaurant. I think we should have a glass of champagne, don't you?"

"Sounds lovely, but only one glass. I have to pick the children up at three. See you, darling."

There was a knock on the door, and Preston entered. "Just to let you know, I'll talk to Janet tonight. I think she might like the idea of my early retirement, but—" Preston paused. "I don't suppose she will be too happy about going to my 'funeral.' "

"No, she might put her foot down and say no way."

"I don't think so. Not when she hears that the whole affair has been approved by the president. That's why I did it this way. She probably would have shot it down otherwise. Have you set up the meeting with Badawi?" Nat confirmed that he had. "Good," said Preston. "I'll poke my head in briefly and then leave you to it. Are you nervous?"

"A bit, but I'm also anxious to get on with it." Nat looked at the portrait of the president. "Besides, we can't let *him* down. He's really sticking his neck out on this one. To be honest with you, I didn't really think he would go for it."

"I did," said Preston. "But then I know the president a little better than you do. This is right up Ted's alley, doing something no other president has ever done or would ever do."

Nat's phone rang. It was Preston's secretary. "Could you please tell the ambassador that the Chinese ambassador is here?"

"Will do." Nat looked at Preston, who looked at his watch.

"That's my ten o'clock with Chang. His bosses want to renegotiate trade agreements with us. We're not buying enough, and they keep buying our debt to keep the dollar strong and keep us going. We can't afford to rough the Chinese up right now. I'll see you later."

Preston left, and Nat sat back in his chair. *What a world we live in,* he thought. Terrorism on land, piracy at sea, and America running out of money, fighting back with little help from the rest of the free world. And where were the United Nations? They seemed to be incapable of mounting any kind of concerted effort to stop criminals operating internationally. Wasn't this precisely one of the main roles they were mandated to play when they were created? The UN had lost its way. It had turned into an unwieldy juggernaut, incapable of timely and relevant decision-making. Even its aid programs were often too little, too late.

Nat spent the next hour ploughing through his emails—some he responded to directly, and others he forwarded to Angela for her to deal with. It was ten past twelve (time to go) when he finished the emails.

He reached the restaurant at 12:25. Sonja had not arrived yet, but he asked to be seated and got a table so that he would see her when she arrived. The place was busy, mainly with businesspeople, but with a few tourists who gave themselves away with their cameras and maps of London folded on the table. An elderly Japanese couple had two cameras and a camcorder and looked like they should be working for a travel magazine.

Maybe they do? Nat thought. Nat had just opened his menu when Sonja entered. She looked painfully beautiful, and Nat could feel his heart beating faster. She was wearing a simple just-below-the-knee pale blue suit with wide lapels, a white silk blouse, and light grey high-heeled shoes. The suit accentuated her narrow waist and curvaceous body. Her blond hair lay in gentle waves down to her shoulders, and her eyes were hidden behind a pair of dark sunglasses. Nat realised that he was not the only man in the room who was staring towards the entrance. He rose as the maître d' turned to escort her to the table. Sonja caught sight of Nat, dismissed the waiter with a wave, and came towards Nat with a big smile that said everything. Nat moved around the table and met her halfway across the floor. She walked right into his arms and kissed him, not a restaurant kiss—on both cheeks—but the real thing. The familiar feeling of her body, and her scent, made Nat forget where he was, and he kissed her back unreservedly.

"Welcome home, my darling!" She leaned back and looked up at him as she removed her sunglasses. Her blue eyes were twinkling with mischief and made him think of all kinds of things other than lunch. As if she had read his mind, she leaned forward and whispered in his ear, "Later, darling. Later." All of a sudden, the room was filled with spontaneous applause, and the people around them were all smiles. Nat could feel his face warming as he helped Sonja to her seat.

"Wow," he said, quietly, under his breath. "You are getting me into a lot of trouble, here, you know. I feel like I did on our first date."

"Good. So do I," she said. "I had no idea I could miss you so much in just two days."

"Would you care for a drink to start?" A waiter had materialised without them noticing.

Sonja looked at him. "Yes, thank you; we would." She looked at Nat. "We would like two glasses of champagne—Pol Roger—if you've got it?"

"Very well, madame." The waiter disappeared.

She took Nat's hands in hers and leaned forward across the table. "Now, darling, tell me all about it!"

Nat had only gotten to describing the trip over, and their arrival at the Hay-Adams Hotel, when the waiter returned with the champagne.

"Here's to you, darling; I am so very, very proud of you." Sonja held her glass towards him. "Here's to us."

Nat touched his glass to hers. "I can't do it without you. And thank you for going along with it. I know it was a tough decision to make."

"It was, but it was the right decision. So, tell me about your meeting with the president."

Nat was halfway through the meeting in the Oval Office when the waiter returned to take their order. Sonja ordered the duck salad and Nat went for the vale of beef. Nat continued his narrative, telling her about the reactions from the vice president, the CIA director, and the president's chief counsel.

"I must say that Rosen seemed like he really came around," said Sonja, "offering to be one of the vice president's trustees like that. He sounded like he was dead set against the whole idea in the beginning."

Nat agreed and told her that the worst moment, for himself, when he thought it was all over, was when he had finished his presentation and the president responded that it was the most preposterous idea he had ever heard.

"I thought that was the end of it," said Nat. "And I felt relief and disappointment at the same time. When he then continued to say that that's why he liked it, I was totally blown away."

"He sounds like a real character," said Sonja, as the waiter returned with their lunch. He asked if he could get them anything else, and Sonja ordered a bottle of Perrier water. Nat asked if she would like another glass of champagne, but she declined.

"I have to be back at the house by two thirty, to pick the kids up at three." Sonja lifted his sleeve to check the time. It was ten past one. Nat looked at his watch. *His watch? . . . Should he tell her?* He had promised her that she would be in the loop.

"Lovely watch, isn't it?" He looked at it admiringly.

"I'm glad you like it, darling. I don't think you've taken it off since I gave it to you." Sonja gave his hand a pat.

"Well, honey, that's not true," said Nat. "I *have* taken it off."

"You have? When?"

"I promised you I would share everything with you if this wild idea were to become reality, so that starts right now."

Nat told her about the watch and what it could do, and he told her about his visit to the dentist, at CIA headquarters, to have the locater device installed.

Sonja glanced cautiously at the tables near them. "Not so loud," she whispered, bringing an index finger to her lips. "Somebody could hear you."

Nat smiled. "Nobody can hear us, with all the chatter in this place. Let's eat! My beef is getting cold."

They ate for a while, in silence, until Sonja broke it. "Tanya has finished her essay about the zoo. She wants you to read it before she hands it in. I've read it, and it bowled me over. It is hard to believe it was written by a twelve-year-old girl. When you read it, you will know that you're doing the right thing for all of us. It brought tears to my eyes."

"That's my girl," said Nat. "She'll go a long way, that one. In the meantime, you and I have to do our best to ensure that the zoo episode does not rob them of their childhood. We have to bring their lives back to normal as best we can—try and take their minds off what happened. It won't be easy. The media will feast on this incident for some time."

"When will you start the operation?" Sonja looked at him over the edge of her champagne glass.

"I meet with Imam Badawi Monday morning, to discuss the attack at the zoo and the consequences it will have. I plan to drop the first hint that I'm sympathetic to the Islamic cause and, hopefully, start the process of gaining his confidence."

Sonja raised her glass. "Let's drink to the success of your plan. Good luck!" They took a sip of champagne, and Nat could see in Sonja's blue eyes the love, the pride, and the apprehension she felt for him. He took another gulp of champagne, to remove the lump that had formed in his throat.

The waiter returned with the water, and they continued their lunch while Nat finished his account of the trip to Washington. "By the way," he said, "Mother promised she would join us for Christmas, and I spoke to your parents, and they promised to get back to us soon. They both sounded OK on the phone."

"I hope they *will* join us," said Sonja. "I feel that this is *one* Christmas when we should all be together."

They finished the meal, and the waiter appeared immediately and cleared the table. He returned with the dessert menus, which they declined in favour of two cappuccinos.

Nat forgot to ask for the decaf version, so Sonja asked, "Could you make one of those *decaf*?"

"Certainly, madame."

The waiter returned with their coffees, and Nat started to tell Sonja how they intended to make Preston and the vice president disappear after they had been "killed". Sonja listened intently, for a while, when, all of a sudden, she stopped him abruptly.

"Sorry, darling, what's the time? I don't want to be late for the children."

Nat looked at 'his' watch. "It's five past two."

She finished her coffee. "I must go, darling. Let me hear the rest after dinner, when the children have gone to bed." She stood up and, before Nat could get up, kissed him on the cheek, turned on her heels, and headed for the door. She exchanged some words with the maître d', who followed her outside and hailed a taxi, which must have been waiting outside because it arrived immediately.

Nat finished his coffee, paid the bill, and headed back towards the office. Halfway there, he hesitated; he didn't feel like going back to work. He had an urge to be with his family, to hold Sonja and the children in his arms. He took his cell phone out. "Hello, Jim. It's Nat. Look, if it's OK with you, I'd like to take the afternoon off and be with Sonja and the kids. I've just had lunch with her, and she's picking the children up from school at three. I have this great urge to be home when they get back to the house."

"Nat, I think that is a splendid idea," said Preston. "I'll see you in the morning."

CHAPTER 24

He arrived home just after three and got a hero's welcome from Darwin, who was waiting for him in the hall when he opened the front door.

"There's my boy!" Nat put his travel case on the floor and roughed him up around the ears with both hands. Darwin returned his attention to the front door, which Nat had closed behind himself. "They'll be home soon," said Nat. Darwin wagged his tail and sat down facing the door. "OK, we'll both wait." Nat decided he would open the door for them when he heard the car outside.

Nat was hanging up his overcoat in the cloakroom under the stair when Darwin announced that something was happening. Nat ran to the front door and opened it just as Sonja pulled in to the curb.

"DAD!" The passenger-side front door opened, and Gregory tumbled out. He had only taken a few running leaps towards the front porch when the back door opened, and Tanya jumped out, chasing Gregory up the front steps.

Nat opened his arms wide and caught them both in a big double hug. Darwin was dancing around their feet, and Sonja was leaning against her car, smiling at the scene in front of her. Nat carried the children into the entrance hall.

"Hey, did you miss me, or something?"

"Yes!" They hugged him tighter.

"I missed you too, but my arms are going to drop off." He lowered them, gently, and Darwin took over welcoming them home.

"Well, you are a man full of surprises," said Sonja. "I thought you had work to do?"

"It can wait. I just had to get home."

Sonja walked into his arms and kissed him. "Sorry, I forgot to say goodbye and thank you for lunch. It was a lovely lunch; we must do that more often."

She turned to the children. "Run upstairs, and put your things away, and wash your hands *and* faces, and come right back, and we'll have a cup of tea, and Daddy can tell us about the trip to Washington." They set off at a gallop. Nat followed Sonja to the kitchen, where she filled the kettle, and as she put it on the jet, he came up behind her and put his arms around her.

She turned around, and they kissed as if the world was about to come to an end. Sonja pulled away gently. "Goodness, you *did* miss me!" Her voice sounded hoarse.

They had tea around the kitchen table, and Nat told them what little he could about the trip to Washington. Luckily, Gregory focused on the private jet, and Tanya wanted to know what the Oval Office looked like. Nat did tell Gregory that the topic of how to end terrorism had been discussed.

"What did he say?" Gregory had not forgotten that he had asked his father to ask the president to stop terrorists killing people.

"He said that he would do everything in his power to make that happen."

Nat decided to leave it there.

Tanya pulled a notebook out from behind her back. "Here's my essay, about our trip to the zoo, Dad. Would you like to read it?"

Nat shot Sonja a quick glance, as if to say, "Is this the time?"

Sonja gave him a wink and an imperceptible nod and said, "Read it, Dad; Tanya wants to submit it tomorrow." Tanya passed him the notebook, opened to the right page.

A Day at the Zoo

Last Saturday, my brother and I went with Mom and Dad to the zoo. It was a beautiful day. The sun was shining, and the zoo was full of happy grownups and children. We had a lovely time wandering around and seeing all the animals. We had been looking forward to this all week, and, I am sure, so had all the other people who were there with us.

We had just sat down to have some lunch (it was nice to sit down after we had been walking around for two hours) when all of a sudden, there was, like, a big bang of thunder. It seemed right over our heads, but the sky was still blue, so we knew, right away, that something else had happened. Daddy said it sounded like an explosion, and he told us to stay put and went off to find out what was going on. We could see clouds of black smoke coming up from behind the trees, and then we heard the sound of sirens in the distance. Soon there were many sirens, and they were getting closer and closer, and we heard people shouting and yelling, and then two security guards and a policeman came running and told us to stay calm and remain seated.

Soon Dad came running back, and he said that there had been some kind of explosion by the main entrance. The policeman spoke to us and told us to stay calm, which we did. And then he took us out of the zoo through a small gate which I have not seen before, even though I have been to the zoo many times. I was pretty scared. By this time a lot of ambulances had stopped outside, so I knew that a lot of people must be hurt. With all the shouting and yelling, and the sirens coming and going, it sounded like there was a war going on out there.

When we got back to the car and we were driving home, Dad said that it looked like this could have been a bomb that was set off at the entrance to the zoo. My brother asked if it was al-Qaeda who did it, and Dad said nobody knew who had done what yet, but he said he was sure the police would find out what had happened and who was responsible.

I felt really sad, and I cried on Mommy all the way home. I knew that lots of people had been hurt, and maybe some were dead, and I thought of all the children holding their mom's and dad's hands and being happy together, and the next moment, they were dead or lying on the sidewalk badly hurt, not knowing what had happened to them.

And I thought how can people be so cruel? How can anybody want to kill another human being? We are not animals; we do not have to kill each other to eat! Dad says that all life is a gift from God and that we must respect all living things, large and small. I know this is true because I see it every day in the little ant carrying a leaf, the bee visiting a beautiful flower to collect honey, the little lamb suckling its mother, and the baby elephant hiding under its mommy's tummy. The flowers, the trees, the rivers, the oceans, and all life on earth, big and small, is one great big miracle. We should all just enjoy being part of the miracle.

I hope that one day all human beings will live in peace with each other. There will be no more wars of any kind, anywhere. Only when this happens, and we respect each other and nature, will we achieve the true happiness, which God has intended for us all.

Nat swallowed hard. Tanya looked at him, waiting for his comments.

"What do you think, Dad? Should I change something? Should I write some more about what I saw at the zoo?"

Nat pulled her to him and lifted her chin so he could look straight into her bright blue eyes. "Honey, I wouldn't change a thing!"

"Oh, good." She grabbed the notebook. "I'll hand it in to Mrs. Buxton tomorrow, after I've typed it up on my computer." She excused herself and disappeared up the stairs to get working on it.

CHAPTER 25

"Imam Badawi is here, sir." Nat's secretary's voice came over the intercom. Nat looked at Preston across his desk. He could feel his heart beating faster.

"OK," said Preston. "Here we go! I'll spend five minutes or so with you and give him the president's reaction to the zoo bombing, and then I'll excuse myself and let you get on with it."

They both rose and turned to the door as it opened, and Angela beckoned Badawi to enter. He seemed to fill the whole door opening, dressed in a flowing white robe and a white headscarf held in place by a black and gold ropelike cord. Dark brown, almost black, eyes shone out from behind round gold-rimmed glasses. The rest of his face was covered by a black and grey beard which flowed down to his chest.

"Good morning, gentlemen."

Preston's hand seemed to disappear in Badawi's massive paws.

"Thank you for coming," said Preston. "You know my colleague, Mr. Jameson. He was at the zoo with his family Saturday before last, as you know. We have just returned from a meeting with President Adams."

Nat shook hands with Badawi, and gave him an encouraging smile. "We have a lot to talk about, Mr. Badawi. We must work together to stop this madness."

"Yes, Mr. Jameson. I am deeply sorry for what happened to you and your family."

"We were the lucky ones, getting away unhurt, but many were not so lucky."

"Would you like a coffee?" Preston broke in.

Badawi declined. Preston ushered them to the seating area opposite Nat's desk and launched into a doctored account of their meeting with the president.

"The president strongly condemned the zoo attack as the most cowardly and senseless act of murder of innocent people, and he asked that Muslim leaders around the world redouble their efforts to show the world that moderate Muslims condemn terrorism in all its forms and that they will help the West in the fight against the fundamentalist fanatics who were killing Christians, Muslims, and Jews indiscriminately."

Preston finished his account of the meeting and stood up. "And now, if you will excuse me, I shall leave you to work out the details of how we can accomplish this with Mr. Jameson here. He will be reporting back to me, and I to the president, with any progress made on this subject. The eradication of terrorism around the world is a top priority for our president, and he will do everything in his power to stop it." Preston said his goodbyes and left.

"So, Mr. Badawi, where do we go from here? The president is of the opinion that moderate Muslims are not doing enough to fight the scourge of terrorism. In fact, he feels that mosques, such as your own, are breeding grounds for terrorists, and since one of the persons apprehended was a regular in your own mosque, he is inclined to hold you personally responsible for what happened at the zoo."

"No, no, no, Mr. Jameson, that is not so." Badawi's black eyes sparkled behind his glasses. "We teach the Quran. The Quran does not permit the killing of women and children. The Quran does not condone violence. I thought Mustafa and Vahid were good boys. They studied hard and prayed well. We are shocked, and their mothers are heartbroken. Vahid's father died many years ago fighting the Russians in Afghanistan."

"Was he one of bin Laden's Jihad soldiers?"

Badawi was taken by surprise. "I don't know; I don't think so, but he could have been." Badawi looked down, and then up again, staring defiantly at Nat. "It was a good fight, and we defeated the Russians."

"We?" Nat stared back with lifted eyebrows. "You were there, too?"

"No, I mean we, the Muslims, threw the nonbelievers out of Afghanistan, with God's help."

"And ours," added Nat. "Don't forget the hundreds of millions of dollars and the weaponry you received, in aid, from America. That was quickly forgotten by both bin Laden and the Taliban. You would have lost that war were it not for our support. We helped your cause in Afghanistan; now we are asking for your help. What are you proposing to do?"

Badawi looked down and stroked his beard. "I have spread the word to all my fellow imams in Britain that we must mount a concerted effort to condemn the zoo incident, in particular, and terrorist acts in general." He paused. "But you must understand, Mr. Jameson, that, for many Muslims, there is no difference between Israelis killing our women and children in Palestine and what happened at the zoo."

"The difference, Mr. Badawi, is that civilians in Palestine are caught in the crossfire between Hamas and Israel. Often women and children are used as human shields. If Muslims would all agree that Israel has a right to exist, there would be no aggression from the Israeli side."

Badawi looked away. "I know that is true, but it is a hard sell. There is too much history, too much hatred, and too many broken promises."

"On both sides," added Nat.

Badawi looked at Nat. "I will do my best, Mr. Jameson. I will mount a campaign throughout the Muslim community in Britain to condemn violence in the name of the prophet. We will organise special meetings and invite everybody to come, Muslims and Christians. We will speak out against the violence with one voice."

Nat thought Badawi sounded like a politician on the campaign trail. "That is an excellent idea, Mr. Badawi. Please understand—I have a lot of sympathy with Muslims who feel abused by the Western powers." Nat felt it was time to start the process of gaining Badawi's confidence. "I believe it was a big mistake to allow the creation of Israel, as a separate state, in the middle of Palestine. That is off the record, of course; my country and the country we both now live in are loyal supporters of the state of Israel, and that is not going to change any time soon—and, please, don't get me wrong—I do not for a moment believe that the killing of innocent people is going to help the Palestinian cause at all. The people who are to blame, on both sides, are the politicians, the policymakers, the people at the top. The decision-makers, who have the real power to effect change, seem to live in a vacuum, seemingly oblivious to the pain and suffering that is the result of their political posturing. My father fought in the Vietnam War. He was a conscripted soldier, fought a war he didn't believe in, was wounded and became an invalid, only to come home and be ignored by Uncle Sam, who gave him no real support to get his life back together. He died in his wheelchair from an overdose of heroin."

Nat could see he had Badawi's attention. He had stopped fidgeting with his beard, and was staring, perhaps in disbelief, Nat thought, as Nat continued his pitch. "Your idea of special meetings, bringing everybody together, is a good one, and I hope you will move forward with that, immediately. I also believe that the Muslim-Christian dialogue should be exported beyond Britain's borders and become an international phenomenon; after all, terrorism is an international problem needing an international solution. Therefore, I ask that you do your best to contact your fellow clerics, in other countries, and ask them to join you in this effort."

Badawi seemed to slump in his chair, disappointed, perhaps, that Nat's declaration of sympathy and support for the Muslim cause had come to naught, that it was just empty words spoken by a smooth-talking, career diplomat. Nat thought, *Now's the time!*

He leaned forward in his chair and looked straight into Badawi's black eyes. "But we have to go beyond *condemning* the violence." Nat's heart was thumping in his chest. He hoped Badawi could not hear it. "You and I must come up with something more, something that begins to tackle the issues from the top. The experience at the zoo changed a lot of things for me, Mr. Badawi, and I've been doing a lot of thinking and soul-searching. The time has come to focus on the guilty so that the innocent can be saved. This is not the time or the place to go into this, but I have an idea that I want to share with you in the near future. You are going to think that it is outrageous and unbelievable, and you might even think that it is a trap, but I can assure you that what I will suggest to you is meant sincerely, and I believe it to be achievable."

"Why do we not talk of it now?"

Nat could see that Badawi was curious to hear what he had in mind, and he debated with himself whether he should continue but dismissed it. Better to let him wait and realise that this was very serious business for both of them. "I would like for you to go ahead and implement your plans for engaging the world's imams in an international dialogue between Muslims and Christians. When this is underway, and I hope it will be soon—it needs to be soon—you and I will get together, and I will share with you my idea for how to build a better world. I want you to think about what I have said. I want you to prepare yourself to hear and accept the unthinkable. I am prepared to make a leap of faith. The question will be: are you?"

Nat stood and extended his hand. "I thank you for coming. I will give you a call next week, assuming that you have set the wheels in motion to condemn the violence. Together we can make a difference." Badawi's handshake was weak and clammy.

He was nervous, too, thought Nat, as he followed Badawi to the elevator.

Preston was seated at Nat's desk when he returned to his office.

"How did it go?"

"I planted a seed." Nat recounted his conversation with Badawi, and Preston did not interrupt once.

When Nat finished, Preston got up and shook his hand. "Excellent start! You have got him thinking, and you have prepared him for the fact that what you will tell him is going to seem unbelievable, and that gives it more credibility. I've got to hand it to you; you've made a good start. I would expect to see some headlines soon, with Badawi coming out and making good on his promises. Good work, Nat; if I didn't know better, I would start to worry that you were the better diplomat of the two of us. Of course, if this works out, you'll have my job soon enough anyway." He was grinning from ear to ear.

"Better report your meeting to Langley right away. At this rate, I could be 'dead' in a couple of weeks, and they need time to prepare, and so do I. I was going to talk to Janet over the weekend, but I chickened out. She was too busy preparing for our upcoming thirtieth anniversary. I'll do it tomorrow night. We're having a quiet night to ourselves, the only night this week. That is one thing you will not like about being the ambassador—you'll be entertaining and dining out a lot more. Sonja will have to get a full-time housekeeper, whether she likes it or not."

CHAPTER 26

It was three days later before the city papers had headlines showing that Badawi was doing what he had promised to do. the *Telegraph*, the *Times*, the *Daily Mirror*, and the *Daily Mail* had given Badawi front-page coverage, with headlines in bold, large print:

IMAM CONDEMNS ZOO BOMBINGS

MUSLIM CLERIC CHALLENGES MUSLIMS AND CHRISTIANS TO COME TOGETHER IN FIGHT AGAINST TERRORISM

BRITISH IMAM ASKS MUSLIM CLERICS AROUND THE WORLD TO JOIN HIM IN THE FIGHT AGAINST TERRORISM

All papers carried a file photograph of Badawi talking to a large crowd in front of the Regent's Park Mosque.

Nat had reported his meeting with Badawi to "Tom", his contact at CIA headquarters, who had told him that they would be ready to execute Preston's "heart-attack", emergency response and funeral in two weeks and that Nat should proceed to the next step with Badawi when he felt the time was right. Preston was taken aback with this timeline, saying that he needed more time to get things organised at his end. Nat assured him that even if he got back with Badawi tomorrow, which he was not about to do, and assuming that Badawi went for the plan, he would surely have to go up the chain of command before any decision was made to accept Nat's offer.

No doubt, a decision to put their trust in Nat on this scale would be made at the very highest level of al-Qaeda and would probably take weeks rather than days.

They would, undoubtedly, do a thorough background check on Nat and find that everything he had told Badawi about himself, and his background, was supported by the facts. They would discover that his wife and in-laws were Jordanian which would help to make his pro-Muslim sentiments more credible. Nat reassured Preston that even if all went well and they swallowed the bait in record time, "I control when I consider the time is right to 'kill' you."

"That is very kind of you," said Preston.

"Which means," said Nat, "that you'll have to tell me when *you* are ready."

They agreed that Nat's next approach would be made the following Monday. Nat would call Badawi today, congratulate and thank him for making good on his commitments, and suggest that he pick him up next Monday at 10:00 a.m. so that they could go for a drive and have a chat in total privacy. Badawi would realise that this was something special, something that Nat wanted to keep away from the prying eyes and ears of the embassy. Nat made the call shortly before the end of the day, to find that Badawi was not available, so he left a message asking him to call him back on his cell phone.

They had just finished dinner when Nat's phone rang.

Sonja gave him a stern look. "Since when did you start to bring your mobile phone to the dinner table?"

"Sorry, darling, but I've been waiting for a very important call. Please excuse me." He got up from the table, headed for his study, and closed the door behind himself.

"Hello, Mr. Jameson." Badawi's gravelly voice was at the other end. "I am sorry to call at this hour, but since you left me your cell phone number, I don't think your intention was to leave this conversation until tomorrow?"

"That's right, Mr. Badawi. Thank you for getting back to me, and thank you for the actions you have taken so far, regarding to our last meeting. The ambassador and I were pleased to read the papers this morning, and so was the president. So, I feel it is now my turn to continue where we left off and tell you what I am prepared to do to make the world a better place. However, the nature of what I wish to discuss with you is such that it cannot be done over the phone or even in my office; therefore, I would like to invite you to come for a drive with me next Monday morning, should we say, ten o'clock, outside your office?"

There was a moment's silence, and Nat thought that maybe Badawi had been warned not to set himself up for walking into a trap. "I shall be there at ten, Mr. Jameson, and you will be pleased to know that I have been getting a good response from fellow clerics both here and overseas."

"That is excellent news. I look forward to seeing you on Monday morning. Good night."

"What was that all about?" The children were in bed, and Sonja and Nat were washing the dishes together. Sonja refused to use the dishwasher unless it was a full load. "Imagine the millions of gallons of water that are wasted every day by these machines," she would say when anybody complained about doing a few dishes by hand.

"That was about the beginning of Operation Endgame. We met with Badawi last Monday and started the ball rolling. Now he and I are meeting again next Monday. I am taking him for a drive, and I'll offer my services to al-Qaeda."

Sonja looked stunned. "So soon? You've only just got back from Washington!"

"Yes, honey; we've got to get going with this while my anger at the zoo incident is fresh and palpable. This is the experience which is driving me to do what, under normal circumstances, nobody would think me capable of doing. It's now or never."

"I know." Sonja dried the last dish. "But it is all happening so quickly. I can't help being worried about you."

Nat took her in his arms, her eyes filled with tears as she attempted a smile. "Don't worry, baby; I have the best cover possible. I am who I am, and you can rest assured that the CIA will uphold their end of the bargain." He kissed her lightly on the forehead.

Sonja looked up at him. "Promise me that you will always tell me what is going on. I couldn't bear to be left out."

He drew her close. "I promise, darling."

CHAPTER 27

When Nat pulled up in front of the Regents Park Mosque Monday morning just after ten o'clock, he thought that Badawi had changed his mind. There was no sign of the cleric, that is, until Nat realised that the tall man in a black business suit was not a city banker but Badawi, dressed entirely in Western clothes. Nat reached over and opened the passenger-side door.

"Good morning, Mr. Badawi. I didn't recognise you for a moment. . . . Thought maybe you had changed your mind?"

Badawi smiled as he squeezed his big frame into the passenger seat. He removed his dark sunglasses, placed them in his breast pocket, and buckled his seat belt. "Mr. Jameson, I have thought of nothing else since we last spoke. I am very curious to learn what you have in mind."

Nat pulled out from the curb, thinking how ironic it was that Winfield House, the ambassador's residence, was just a stone's throw down the road. The thought felt unsettling somehow. He headed down Park Road, in the direction of Madame Tussaud's Wax Museum, having no idea where to go other than to let the traffic take him.

"I am so glad you came, Mr. Badawi. The experience I had with my family at the zoo, was, as we Americans call it, a defining moment. The loss of innocent lives has always bothered me, and in this conflict, the targets are more often than not in this category. It has to stop! And I have an idea which I would like to share with you, an idea which I believe could stop the senseless killing of innocent people and bring the battle to those who are guilty. I shall be going out on a limb, and the route back, should you decide to cut it off, would be difficult, but I would say that it was the beginning of a failed sting operation and hope to get away with it." Nat gave Badawi a quick glance before returning his attention to the traffic. It was clear that he had Badawi's full attention.

OK, he thought. *Here goes!* "What would you say if I told you I could help you win the war against Western oppression without sacrificing more innocent lives on both sides? You are losing the hearts and minds of your own people by the indiscriminate killing of women and children. There is a better way."

"And which way is that, Mr. Jameson?"

Nat kept his eyes on the road and said quietly, "Kill the president of the United States of America." They stopped at a red light, and Nat turned slowly and looked calmly into Badawi's eyes which were staring back at him in shock and disbelief.

"How—. How do I know that you are sincere?" Badawi cleared his throat. "That this is not a trap?"

Without blinking, and without taking his eyes away from Badawi's bulging, watery eyes, Nat replied, "If you wish to achieve the objective I stated, I will prove to you that I can be trusted."

"You will? How?" Badawi licked his lips and brought a handkerchief out to wipe sweat off his forehead.

"I will kill the US ambassador, here in London, if you arrange for an ad to be taken out in the *Daily Telegraph* saying

Stop the senseless killing of innocent people! Let us work together for a better world! . . . signed by yourself and appearing for one day only, two weeks from today. Within one week, or so, of the ad appearing, you will discover that the ambassador has died from a massive heart attack."

The traffic was moving again, and Nat returned his attention to the street, leaving Badawi to struggle with the processing of the information he had just received. Badawi also seemed to focus on the traffic whilst mopping his brow. There was no response, but Nat decided he had to wait for Badawi to make the next move. The chess game had started, and Nat had made his first move. It was Badawi's turn.

"I. . . I. . . I do not know what to say." Badawi's voice was shaking, and he was wheezing as if he was having an asthma attack. "It is so unthinkable, so unimaginable! Killing the president of the United States of America? You would kill your own president?"

"No, that I would not do, but I would make it possible for his arch enemy, al-Qaeda, to strike that blow." Nat gave Badawi a quick, sideways glance. "Do you think they would be interested in getting such an opportunity?"

Badawi was clearly struggling with his response. Sweat was running down his face, but he seemed not to notice. "How would I know, Mr. Jameson? I have never met any of them. I do not know what they might—or might not—want."

"But you do know that they are fighting to free the Muslim world from the tyranny of American world aggression, and you do know that the Israeli oppression of the Palestinians would not be possible were it not for the unwavering support of America, and, when I say 'America,' I don't mean the American people. I mean successive American governments, led by American presidents, from 1948 until today. It is easy to make these decisions from the safety of the Oval Office." Nat paused to let Badawi digest what he had just said. "But I can imagine," he continued, "that the blind political support for Israel, from future presidents and US governments, would evaporate if what I just told you were to take place. And if this event is combined with a commitment to stop the random killing of civilians, I am convinced that the Muslim cause will be greatly advanced around the world. The champions of the Muslim cause will no longer be hiding like cowards in a cave and sending children and women on suicide missions; they will have taken the battle to the real enemy, leading the fight from the front rather than the rear."

Nat could see that Badawi was struggling to come up with a response. He was sweating profusely, licking his lips and staring blindly at the traffic. "What do you think, Mr. Badawi? Do you think al-Qaeda would welcome such an opportunity?"

"I don't know what to think." Badawi looked down at his hands, which were squeezing his soaked handkerchief. "It is blowing the mind, to hear what you are saying."

Nat noticed that his command of the English language seemed to have taken a turn for the worse. Clearly, the man was under extreme pressure. Nat started to feel that it might all be over before it got started. *I have to help him come up with a reply*, Nat thought.

"You are probably thinking that I have lost my mind, that the episode at the zoo has caused me to have a nervous breakdown, but I can assure you that my mind has never been clearer. Is it crazy to kill an ambassador and a president if it will save thousands of people and give the Palestinians their country back? Do you think that is crazy, Mr. Badawi?"

"No, that is not crazy, but to think that it could be done might be." Badawi gave Nat a quick look before he refocused on his hands.

"I believe it can be done." Nat stopped behind a red double-decker bus, which was belching smoke. "With Ambassador Preston out of the way, I am confident that I will be appointed to the job, and, in that position, I will have direct access to the president. With direct access, it will be possible for me to arrange a meeting with him and an al-Qaeda assassin disguised, say, as a Middle Eastern businessman. The precise cover would have to be worked out closer to the time." Nat paused as he pulled up alongside the bus and turned left on Maryellen Street. "I don't blame you for doubting my sincerity. That is why I am offering to prove to you that I mean what I say and that I can deliver on what I say."

"I don't know how to think about this." Badawi was tugging at his seat belt as if he was planning to make a quick exit. "If I say yes, you will believe that I am a terrorist, no?"

"No, I will believe you are as sick and tired of the deaths of innocent people as I am. I don't expect you to give me an answer here and now. How could you? There is no point doing any of this unless al-Qaeda likes the idea, and I know you can't speak for them."

"I don't know them. I have never even met any of them, and I have no idea where to find them. I don't know how to get a message to them." Badawi looked dejected. He shook his head. "You are talking to the wrong man, Mr. Jameson."

"I don't think so. I didn't bring this idea to you because I think you are a terrorist, Mr. Badawi. I decided to share this idea with you because I think you also want the madness to stop."

"That I do; that I do." The last words died in a whisper, as Badawi nodded his head and closed his eyes.

"So, here my friend," said Nat, "is where I suggest we should leave it for now." Nat handed him a piece of paper. "Here is the wording for the advertisement which, if you place it as I suggested, will trigger the death of the US ambassador, and we will be on our way to helping the Muslim cause and the cause of world peace. I said that the ad must appear two weeks from today, but I take that back. I know this must be very difficult for you. I will start looking for the ad two weeks from now, and if I see it, I see it, and if not, then two weeks later, I will take it that this is a no-go, and we will both forget we ever had this conversation. If you try to use it against me, it will be your word against mine. Producing the piece of paper, which I just gave you, will not compromise me because of the wording, which is, under the circumstances, very reasonable. The words work for both of us either way we go from here."

Badawi looked up and sighed a sigh of relief, Nat thought.

"I will think about this very hard," said Badawi. "I can see that what you are offering could make a very big difference for all of us. Please forgive me for being so vague."

"Not at all, Mr. Badawi. It is a lot to digest, and there are many complications to unravel. Say no more; I will be looking out for the ad two weeks from now. Shall I take you back to your office?"

"No, thank you. Drop me off anywhere you can; I need to do some walking. I think best when I walk." Badawi attempted a smile which did not reach his eyes.

"Very well." Nat pulled over, and Badawi got out at a speed which seemed impossible for such a large man. He waved goodbye as Nat drove off.

Nat took a deep breath and realised how tense he had been throughout the journey. In fact, he had no idea where he was until he came to the next junction, which showed that he was on Oxford Road at the junction of Davis Street. He started to run through the conversation with Badawi. The man was hard to read, but there again, what could he have said? Clearly, a decision of this magnitude was not for him to make, nor did he want it to seem that he had any connection with al-Qaeda. No wonder he had been sweating. At least he had not told Nat to stop the car and jumped out. The line was overboard; the bait was on the hook.

Chapter 28

"How did you make out?" Preston got up from Nat's chair and came over to the other side of the desk. "You look bushed. Want a drink?"

"Yes, but no thank you. Angela is getting me a cup of coffee."

Nat went over his conversation with Badawi, trying his best to leave nothing out. "All we can do now is wait for the ad."

"And prepare for my heart attack," added Preston, with a grin. "By the way, I have spoken to Janet. I must say, she took it very well. I think she sees that it could be the early retirement she's been after me to take. She loves the idea of the cruise and spending a lot more time at our summer house in Brittany. She is concerned that we will be deceiving my sons, our two daughters-in-law, and our grandchildren, but when I told her that it would be for a short period, she agreed, albeit very reluctantly. She has a lot of admiration for the president, and I think his endorsement and participation in the plan is what swayed her."

There was a knock on the door, and Angela appeared with Nat's coffee and, seeing Preston there, said, "Would you like a cup of coffee also, Mr. Ambassador?"

"No, thank you, Angela. I had copious amounts of some very fancy Arabian coffee with the ambassador of Egypt this morning. The only thing that made it drinkable was the sugar—lots of it."

Angela left, and Preston turned to Nat. "I'll leave you to report back to Langley. I guess they'll have to organise the emergency response team which will rush to my assistance when I have my 'heart attack'." He stood up and headed for the door. "I'll be in my office practicing, should you need me." He shook his head, rolled his eyes, and muttered under his breath, "I must have been crazy to go along with this nonsense." He closed the door behind himself.

Nat reached for the new telephone on his desk which gave him a secure line direct to Langley. He dialled and waited. . . .

"Code name?"

"Endgame."

There was a short silence.

"Start report now."

Nat recounted his meeting with Badawi, being careful not to leave anything out, and ended with the words "End of Report" and hung up. He looked at his watch. It was only 6:30 in the morning, Washington time, so he figured he would not hear anything back for a couple of hours. Angela had left some telephone messages, and when he spread them out on his desk, the one that caught his eye was from Dr. Robert Harrison, the professor of Islamic studies who he and Sonja had met for dinner at the Jeffersons'. The message read, *Would like to have lunch with you sometime this week. Please call.* Nat remembered their discussions on the Middle East, Islamic fundamentalism and terrorism and remembered that he had been impressed, not only with Bob's depth of knowledge on these topics but also with his ability to look at the issues from many points of view. They had not got on to the subject in any detail at the Jeffersons', but Nat thought it was very likely that Bob was also an authority on al-Qaeda. *He can help me*, Nat thought. *The more I can learn about al-Qaeda, the more likely it is that I will succeed in infiltrating their organisation.*

Nat had barely finished the thought, when he dialled the number.

"Hello. Dr. Harrison's office; how may I assist you?" The female voice spoke with an accent which Nat could not quite place, but the voice sounded familiar.

"Good morning; this is Nat Jameson returning Dr. Harrison's call."

"Hello again, Nat; this is Catrin." It was Bob's Swedish wife.

"Catrin, hello! I thought your voice sounded familiar, but I had no idea you were Bob's secretary. How are you?"

"Very well, thank you." She chuckled. "And I am not Bob's secretary, except when she goes on holiday. Just a moment, and I'll put you through to Bob. Say hello to Sonja for me; we had a lovely lunch together last week."

Nat remembered that Sonja had asked Catrin and Nancy for lunch as they were leaving the Jeffersons'. Somehow that seemed a long time ago.

"Hi, Nat; thanks for calling back." Bob's Australian accent sounded stronger on the telephone. "If the girls can have lunch together, why can't we? I've asked Andrew as well, and he is OK for tomorrow. Can you make it?"

"Hey, Bob, that sounds great. Let me just check my appointment calendar." Nat brought it up on his screen and saw that Tuesday was clear. "Yes, Bob, thank you. Where and when?"

"Stef's at one o'clock. I look forward to seeing you again, Nat. Andrew tells me you have been to see the president? Was that about your diabolical experience at the zoo?"

"That and his upcoming visit to Europe in February next year. I'll tell you all about it tomorrow." *Not ALL*, Nat thought, *but I will bring up the subject of al-Qaeda*. They said goodbye and hung up.

Nat dealt with the remaining phone messages and was just about to leave the office for his luncheon appointment with the Italian chargé d'affaires, when the secure phone rang. Nat picked up on the second ring.

"Hi, Nat. Tom here. It would seem you have made a good start with your friend Badawi. Here's what we want you to do. If Badawi takes the bait—and please, do not write anything down, commit it to memory only—when you see the ad, notify us immediately. Do not contact Badawi—the less said the better—let action speak for itself. We think it is best that you are in Preston's office when he has his heart attack and that you make the 999 call before you run out to your secretary and tell her you've made the call and ask for help to loosen the ambassador's clothing, to make him as comfortable as possible while you wait for the ambulance. The 999 call will be intercepted by us, working together with MI6, and the emergency response team will be a joint team of undercover agents. You should insist that you accompany Preston to the hospital, which will be St. Mary's. The emergency team includes a nurse and a doctor who will pronounce the ambassador 'dead on arrival', and, having presented his medical credentials to the head of ER at St. Mary's, he will explain that, rather than have the postmortem carried out there, the US authorities wish to have the body sent back to Washington Hospital Centre for the post-mortem to be carried out there. The ambulance will proceed to an 'undertaker', who is part of our response team, to have the 'body' prepared for the journey home. The ambassador's death will be on St. Mary's records, and you return to the embassy, report the tragic news to the staff, and do what you would normally do under the circumstances, which will include a press release reporting the tragic, sudden death of the ambassador. Mr. Preston will be flown out in a private jet and accommodated in one of our safe houses near Washington." Tom paused and drew a deep breath. "OK so far?"

"Yes, I'm with you so far." Nat cleared his throat and tried to sound calm. "What happens next?"

"Preston's 'funeral' will take place about one week later, and you will obviously attend. Mrs. Preston will decide that there will be no viewing of the body. While you are in Washington, you will be appointed ambassador at the insistence of the president, and you will return to London as the new ambassador to the Court of St. James. Your deputy chief of mission will be Anthony Burville."

Burville! Nat had met Burville on a few occasions and had not liked the man. He had struck him as the kind of man who would sell his own grandmother if he thought it would be in his own interest. He decided there was no need for him to share this with the CIA.

"I am curious about the funeral," said Nat. "What if members of the family insist that they want to see the body?"

"It is unlikely that anybody would go against the 'widow's' wishes, but, obviously, if his sons, say, were to insist, it would seem very strange for Mrs. Preston to refuse them; so, the body will be a real body of approximately Ambassador Preston's build, and a makeup artist will create a plausible likeness of Preston's face."

Nat decided not to ask where the body would come from. It was none of his business. Washington had its share of indigents, many with no family or friends who could identify them or arrange for their burial. They had probably already found a candidate in the morgue which received a steady stream of these poor, unfortunate beings. Nat shivered at the thought. *This whole thing was my idea,* he thought. *Don't get squeamish now.*

Aloud, he said, "Will I have an opportunity to see Jim before I return to London?"

"No, I'm afraid not. He is dead, remember? Until we change his appearance and identity and he resurfaces in a new form, you will not be able to see him. We will be working with Mr. and Mrs. Preston on their future lives together, and we will inform you, in due course, of what we have come up with."

Nat shared with Tom the idea of Preston reappearing as an old school friend of Janet's, the summer house in France, and the idea that the old school friend would invite the "widow" on a world cruise.

"Not bad, Nat. That sounds very workable. We will explore that idea. It certainly is a good way for the Prestons to carry on as natural a life as possible under the circumstances. So, sit tight; go over, with Mr. Preston, the drill for his heart attack, and wait for the ad to appear."

Nat could tell that Tom had come to the end of this conversation. Nat had many questions he would like to ask about the next steps beyond the first "murder" but decided not to. Clearly, Tom wanted to take it one step at a time. Why worry about the next step before you took the first?

Nat could see the logic in his method, and, as if Tom had read his mind, he said, "We'll take it one step at a time. And, Nat, chances are al-Qaeda will, assuming they take your offer seriously, attempt to install listening devices in your home. Typically, this is accomplished by tapping into your phone and/or sending a team of gas technicians looking for a reported gas leak. We will check on the former and let you know if your phone is being tapped, but you must let your wife know that she must play along and let the "gas people" do their job. Whatever they do, if anything, we must let them do, and act and behave accordingly. We'll run daily checks on your telephone, and please let us know if workmen arrive at your house on the pretext of fixing or checking anything. That's it for now. Stay sharp." Tom hung up.

Nat replaced the receiver just as his normal phone rang. It was Angela. "The ambassador would like to see you in his office at your earliest convenience, Mr. Preston."

"Thank you. I'll be right over. Oh, Angela, could you make sure we are not disturbed? Thank you."

Nat walked across the hallway and knocked on Preston's door, which was normally left open, but today it was closed.

"Enter!" Preston's voice even sounded different.

Nat entered and closed the door. "Hi Jim, 'enter'? What happened to 'come in'?"

Preston gave Nat an awkward smile as he rose from his desk. "I've been practicing my 'heart attack', and in my theatrical state of mind, 'enter' just sounded better. I need some help! There are many ways to fake a heart attack. For example, should they find me slumped over my desk or on the floor?"

They sat down in Preston's easy chairs, and Nat recounted his conversation with Tom and his suggestion that Nat would be in Preston's office when he had his "heart attack" and that Nat would make the 999 call.

"I'm your supporting actor, so we have to practice this scene together, Jim. We'll be like Starsky and Hutch."

"Oh, that's better. I thought I might be out there on my own." Jim seemed relieved.

Nat recognised the excitement, which rose in his chest, from his acting days in college and at Harvard. "I think you should be standing right over here with a cup of coffee when the attack occurs, and you collapse onto the floor, spilling the coffee all over the place. I call 999 and shout for help, and our girls will, no doubt, be the first through the door. You'll be lying on the floor, breathing heavily, clutching at the pain in your chest, your face contorted in agony. The girls will help, loosening your tie and clothing, while we wait for the ambulance, and maybe you should slip into unconsciousness before it arrives? This way it will look like you've had a massive event, which makes the 'dead on arrival' that much more believable. My presence will support the 'fact' that it was I who 'killed' you."

Preston smiled. "Hey, Nat; that's very good. You have lost your calling. Sounds to me like you should have become a movie producer and actor."

"Well, I came close," said Nat. "I became a diplomat."

They laughed, and the tension they had felt left them both.

"So then," said Preston, "all we can do is wait for the ad. I shall be disappointed if it does not materialise. I am looking forward to an early retirement. The more I think about it, the more I like it."

When Nat was on his way back to his own office, Angela looked up at him. "I have called Mr. Perroni to say you will be a bit late for lunch."

"Oh heck! It totally slipped my mind!" Nat ran into his office, picked up his jacket, and headed for the elevator. In all the excitement of the morning, Nat had forgotten about his luncheon engagement with the Italian chargé d'affaires. *I better not forget my day job here at the embassy*, he thought, as he headed for the elevator.

"George is waiting for you downstairs." Angela's voice reached him just as the elevator doors were beginning to close.

When Nat arrived home, he asked Sonja to look out for any workmen who might come to the house on the pretext of checking or fixing something, and filled her in on Tom's instructions if this were to happen. She confirmed that nobody had showed up so far.

That evening, after the children were in bed, Nat told Sonja what was happening with Operation Endgame. She listened quietly and did not interrupt. When Nat came to the end of his account, she said simply, "I feel sorry for Janet and even more sorry for the rest of Jim's family. At least Janet will know that Jim is alive and well, but the rest of them won't." She poured Nat a cup of chamomile tea and sat down on his lap. "You know, Nat, there will be a lot of pain and suffering coming out of this. How long do you think this can go on for?"

"That is hard to say. Remember, it has not even started yet. If the ad does not appear, nobody will have to play dead, and nobody will grieve. If the ad does appear, then I think things will happen fairly quickly. I will carry out my promise to 'kill' the ambassador within two weeks of the ad appearing, and then it depends on whether this gets me the 'entry form' to al-Qaeda that we're looking for. If not, I will have to 'kill' the vice president also, which is where I stop. The rest is up to al-Qaeda. If they want to take out the president, they will have to meet me, and I want to meet with all the top brass. If all goes well, I think we could be done inside six months. Certainly, no longer than twelve."

Sonja put her arms around his neck and leaned into him. "The thought of you going inside al-Qaeda worries me a great deal. What if they find out the truth, the fact that you didn't kill anybody, but they pretend to accept you into their organisation just so that they can mete out the appropriate punishment?"

Nat could feel her tremble and pulled her closer. "Darling, I have complete faith in Langley's ability to do their part. And, guess what?" He smiled at her. "I have complete confidence in my ability to do mine."

"I know, darling, but please, please, please—be very, very careful." She rubbed her nose in the crook of his neck and stood up; still holding his hand, she gave him a teasing smile. "I have never doubted your ability to do your part, darling. Time for bed."

Chapter 29

When Nat's taxi pulled up in front of Stef's large red awning, the smell of garlic left no doubt that this was an Italian restaurant. Judging by the crowd inside, it was also a *popular* Italian restaurant. The maître d' guided him towards a raised banquet stall where Bob and Andrew were sitting, sipping the house red and talking animatedly. They stopped talking, stood up, and shook Nat's hand.

Bob gestured to the empty seat opposite himself. "So pleased you could come! What's your pleasure?"

Nat saw the bottle of Pellegrino water, which stood unopened on the table. "That will do for me at the moment, thank you." Bob got a waiter's attention and asked for a tall glass with ice.

Then Bob asked if Andrew would like a glass of water also, Andrew declined, saying that the health benefits of water had not been proven, whilst the health benefits of wine were beyond any reasonable doubt.

"So, I see the Russians have charged Colonel Ivanovitch with the theft of the atomic warhead," said Bob. "Apparently he has confessed to having it removed and shipped to Iran. IRAN, of all places! Of course, the Iranians are denying everything, just like they denied enriching uranium for military purposes. The Israelis knocked out their enrichment facilities, bless them, so now the Iranians are trying to do a shortcut and get their hands on atomic weapons without having to make their own."

"Thank God all the trigger mechanisms are accounted for," said Andrew.

"So, they say. . . ." Nat jumped in. "But since when could we trust anything the Russians tell us?"

The waiter returned with Nat's glass of ice and poured some Pellegrino water. No one spoke until he was out of earshot.

"Nat, you might be right," said Andrew. "But this is one time when even the Russians can't afford to lie; or could they?"

"They could," said Nat, "if they are stupid enough to believe that Iran is an ally and, therefore, not a potential threat to Russia. For all we know, the Russian government could be behind the whole affair and poor colonel what's-his-name became the fall guy when Western intelligence discovered the 'theft' of the warhead. The Russians may have forged a strategic alliance with Iran to enhance their influence in the Middle East. Imagine an Iran with nuclear capability, backed by Russia. They could look to take control of the supply of oil to the West. It would change the playing field completely. It would give the Russians an opportunity to pay us back for our role in hastening the collapse of communism." Nat drained half of his Pellegrino water and gave Bob and Andrew a challenging look.

"Interesting theory," said Bob. "But it is unlikely that the Russians would be that stupid. A nuclear-weapons capability in Iran would be a threat to us all, including Russia. Don't forget, the Russians have a very uncomfortable relationship not only with Islamic extremists but with mainstream Islam."

The waiter returned to take their order, and conversation ceased as they focused on what to have for lunch. They ordered, and the waiter asked if garlic bread should be brought for the table.

"Yes, please," said Bob. "Let's have some garlic bread *and* some bruschetta for the table." Then, turning to Nat he said, "How about a glass of wine with your meal, Nat? The house red is very respectable."

Nat declined; alcohol at lunchtime made him feel like sleeping rather than working in the afternoon. "The ambassador would not be very impressed if he found me snoozing right now; we're in the middle of preparing for the president's European tour in February next year."

"He's a brave man," said Andrew. "I'm sure al-Qaeda would like nothing better than to find a way to bump him off. The security measures must be phenomenal."

The waiter returned with their garlic bread and bruschetta.

"The security arrangements for this trip are mind-boggling," said Nat. "And the cost, too, is mind-blowing, but President Adams is not the kind of man to be easily intimidated." Nat thought that this would be a good time to lead the conversation onto the topic of al-Qaeda. "In fact, he told me he would welcome the opportunity to meet the al-Qaeda leaders face to face and have it out with them. He called them cowardly murderers, fanatics and lunatics. I wouldn't want to be in their shoes if they were to meet on equal terms. The president would tear them to shreds with his bare hands."

"That is a fight I think they would relish," said Bob. "They may be many things, but cowards is not one of them. Take bin Laden for example; the accounts of him joining the *mujahideen*, 'holy warriors', battling the Soviets in Afghanistan are legendary. His bravery in battle is well documented, such as the Battle of Jaji, where bin Laden had established his own military force consisting of Arab fighters only. Strategically, it made no sense at all; the Arab 'force' was counted in the hundreds against the Soviets' 175,000 to 250,000 troops, but it worked wonders as a publicity stunt. The Arab fighters held out against Soviet attacks for a while after the Afghan mujahideen had fled, and the Afghans started talking about the bravery of the Arabs defending Jaji."

"I must admit that I know very little about the man," said Nat. "But it seems to me that we—when I say 'we', I mean we Americans—helped turn bin Laden into the 'hero' that he was to many in the Arab world. I have heard it said that he was a very shy, soft-spoken individual."

"Well, he was." Bob helped himself to another piece of bruschetta. "Until he became the number-one enemy of the United States after 9/11. The attack on Afghanistan that followed propelled bin Laden to fame. You might remember his television interview at the beginning of the Afghan War? Bin Laden was cool and calm, while the bombs were raining down from American bombers. These images were seen throughout the Muslim world, and I hate to say it, but they turned him into a hero. Bin Laden stood up and took the bow for 9/11, and the reserved, soft-spoken man from Riyadh, who drew his first breath on the tenth of March, 1957, ceased to exist. I guess, like most celebrities, the success and the fame that it brought went to his head?"

"I must admit," said Andrew, "when I have seen pictures or film clips of the man, he just didn't come over as a fanatic. He was handsome. He had a calm, serene face, and he spoke softly. He reminded me more of Jesus than of Hitler."

"In looks and mannerisms, you're right," said Nat. "But there the similarity stops. Jesus came from a relatively poor background; bin Laden grew up in the construction empire of his father and was said to be worth hundreds of millions of dollars in his own right. With a background like that, how did he turn out to be the most wanted terrorist the world has ever known?"

Nat directed his question to Bob, who put down his utensils and cleared his throat, clearly in preparation for a major lecture. "Well, of course, bin Laden, thankfully, is no longer with us, so he is no longer central to the situation we find ourselves in now, but to understand al-Qaeda, I think it is important to have some understanding of the man who created the organisation." Bob took a swig of wine and settled back in his chair.

"I don't profess to be an authority on the subject, but what I can do is give you some background and history which may be helpful." Bob broke off and looked at Andrew. "That's provided it's not going to bore Andrew to death?"

"Not at all," said Andrew. "Please go on. I am as curious as anybody to know what turns a human being from being ... well ... from being 'human' to becoming a monster."

"OK." Bob took a sip of wine and cleared his throat. "Let's go back to the beginning: Osama bin Laden was born in 1957 in Riyadh. His mother was a young and very beautiful Syrian woman, one of four wives of Mohammed bin Awad bin Laden, Osama's father, who was born in Hadramawt, in south Yemen. He came from a labouring class but founded his contracting firm in 1931, and, from its humble beginnings, it grew with the growth and prosperity of Saudi Arabia to a multibillion-dollar conglomerate, branching out from the construction business to petroleum, mining and chemicals, telecommunications, power projects, manufacturing, and trading."

"That's 'The American Dream', isn't it?" said Andrew. "From 'rags to riches'. How on earth did he do it, in Saudi Arabia of all places?"

"You're right," said Bob. "It really is quite impressive. Awad bin Laden emigrated from Hadramawt to Jeddah, before World War I, to what was to become the Kingdom of Saudi Arabia. Remember, this was before the oil bonanza. He worked as a porter before he started a small construction company building houses for ordinary folks and villas for the well-to-do. But he was building his business steadily and, come the 1950s, he won a contract to work on the king's palaces, the king being King Saud. Later, when Saud's brother Faisal took over, old bin Laden had played a role in getting Saud to step down and was appointed minister of public works. So, his company became the company of choice for the king and for anybody who was anybody in the fast-expanding economy of the now oil-rich Saudi Arabia."

"He sounds like your regular hard-nosed mercenary American entrepreneur," said Andrew.

"He might well have had some of those attributes," said Bob. "But he was also a devout Muslim, and his children were brought up strictly in the Muslim faith and with great respect for the family business. Osama took great pride in the fact that his father helped to rebuild the al-Aqsa mosque in Jerusalem and that the family company also renovated the holy mosques of Mecca and Medina."

Two waiters approached with their food, and conversation ceased while they tasted their lunch. Bob offered Nat a glass of white wine to go with his frutti di mare risotto, and Nat accepted, thinking he wanted to extend this luncheon as long as possible and learn as much as he possibly could about the organisation he hoped to join in the not-too-distant future.

After a while, Nat broke the silence. "What I don't understand is why bin Laden did not follow what, presumably, would have been a very secure and profitable career in the family business."

"That is a very good question," said Bob. "I believe that is what probably would have happened had it not been for two events that occurred in 1967. One, which I am sure you know about, is the 1967 War or the Six-Day War, so-called because that is how long it took the Israelis to defeat the attackers—Egypt, Syria, and Jordan. The second event was the death of his father in a plane crash later that year. Osama was only ten years old at this point, and he worshipped his father. The 1967 War was a major humiliation for the Arab world. The Egyptian government, led by President Gamal Nasser, had promised a quick victory. The spectacular defeat called into question Nasser's regime, a regime which was based on secular Arab socialism and nationalism. The defeat became a catalyst for the growth of Islamist movements throughout the Arab world." Bob paused while he ate some of his lunch.

"Do you think Osama blamed his father's death on the Israelis?" Nat was anxious to keep the conversation on topic.

"No," Bob continued. "The old man died when his company Beechcraft crash-landed at Usran in southwest Saudi Arabia. However, I am sure Osama was well aware of his father's very strong anti-Israel, anti-Jewish feelings. In fact, he recounted, to a Pakistani journalist, the story of his father, after the 1967 War, asking his engineers how many bulldozers he had, and when he was told that they had more than two hundred and fifty bulldozers, he asked if they could be converted to tanks. When he was asked why, he said, "I want to use them against the Jews because they have captured our land.' Osama bin Laden never wavered from his position that the Israeli state is illegitimate and that the Jews must be thrown out of Palestine—not just the occupied territories but from the whole Arabian Peninsula. I am sure his father would have agreed."

Bob took a sip of wine, followed by some bites of his avocado royal salad.

"So, are you saying that the Six-Day War, and his father's death, turned bin Laden into a terrorist?" asked Andrew, who had finished his lunch. He poured himself another glass of the house wine, seeing that his host was too busy to notice his empty glass.

"No." Bob put down his knife and fork, indicating he was finished with his meal even though his plate was half-full. He wiped his mouth on the napkin and continued. "I am saying that the two events of 1967 sent bin Laden in a certain direction. They started him on a path which led him to where he ended up. Osama was only ten years old when his father died and, therefore, much too young to take over the running of his father's business empire. And given the fact that he was the seventeenth son of Mohammed, his claim to any significant role in the family business, even in the long term, was tenuous. In the end, Salem, Osama's eldest brother, took control of the business in the early seventies. The company had been put into trust by King Faisal when the old man died. Educated in England, Salem spoke fluent English, and he had a lot of Western friends. The links to the royal family, which his father had worked so hard to cultivate, had diminished, but Salem was able to rekindle that relationship and assure the continued success of the family business."

"So, what happened to Osama after his father died?"

"Starting in 1968, a year after his father's death, Osama attended the elite secular Al-Thager Model School, where he remained until 1976. He was an average student, but considering that this was one of the two most academic schools in the country, he certainly was way above average in terms of academic ability. There, he was one of thirty students, but he stood out because he was taller than everybody else. His English teacher remembers him as an exceptionally courteous young boy, shyer than his classmates. He sat quietly but with a confident smile. He was not pushy and did not put his hand up to get the teacher's attention, but when asked, he would, more often than not, come up with the right answer."

Bob paused for a sip of wine before continuing. "After Al-Thager Model School, he enrolled at King Abdulaziz University, where he studied economics and business administration."

"So, he was being educated to enter the family business," observed Andrew.

"I am sure that was the plan," said Bob. "But Osama's main interest was religion, and it was here that he first became associated with the Muslim Brotherhood."

"So, did Osama ever join the family business after he finished university?"

Andrew posed the question as he scooped up the last bits of his lunch.

"Yes," said Bob. "He did spend some time there and became something of a demolition expert. It would appear that his brother Salem got him started on the ground floor, as it were, a long way from a desk job or any management position within the firm."

"This must have been pretty demoralising for him," observed Nat.

"Perhaps," said Bob. "But Osama was already set on another course. At university, he came under the influence of two well-known teachers of Islamic studies, Muhammad Qutb and Abdullah Azzam. Muhammad's brother, Sayyid, was the author of *Signposts*, which became the 'bible' of the Jihadist movement. Qutb's writing had a fundamental effect on bin Laden. Qutb argued that most modern societies—Muslim societies included—are in a state of ignorance, *Jahiliyyah*, which was the state of Arab nations before the revelations of the Quran. He argued that only through jihad can this state of ignorance be eradicated. He was talking about an offensive jihad against all enemies of Islam—non-Islamic and Muslim societies. It is from this precept that bin Laden's cadres feel justified to target not only the West but also Muslim regimes such as Saudi Arabia."

"So, what you are saying is that bin Laden felt he had a solid ideological basis for his actions," said Nat.

"Absolutely," said Bob. "And now consider this: 1979 was the start of a new century in the Muslim calendar, and it was a very turbulent start. The Shah of Iran was overthrown in January. In March, Israel and Egypt signed a peace treaty. Then, in November, we had Islamist militants seize the Grand Mosque in Mecca, which resulted in a bloody battle, leaving hundreds of people dead. And finally, that year in December, the Soviets invaded Afghanistan."

The waiter appeared to remove their plates and take their orders for dessert. Nat passed but asked for a decaf cappuccino. Bob picked a chocolate mousse and Andrew a cheesecake. They both ordered a regular coffee. When the waiter left, Bob apologised for his monologue, and for a while, the conversation drifted onto other topics. Nat was determined to get the conversation back to al-Qaeda and after a while, decided to plunge back in.

"Bob, tell me this: if the Soviets had not attacked Afghanistan, would we still have had an al-Qaeda to deal with?"

Bob paused for a moment. "That is a good question. I think not, but there are many who disagree with me. I think not because I believe that without that war, which was a just war, bin Laden would never have attained the status and following that he did. On the other hand, I do believe that bin Laden would have ended up an Islamic extremist in any event, but I think his sphere of influence would have been limited to the Middle East. He was always highly critical of the Saudi royal family and their close ties to America. I think the focus of his effort would have been against them and against the secular government of Egypt, the 'traitors' who signed a treaty with Israel. Afghanistan was Osama's opportunity to fight a fight that he believed his father had always wanted him to fight—the fight against the enemies of Islam. In this, he believed he was the only son who had acted according to the wishes of his father."

The waiter returned with the desserts and the coffee. Andrew stood up and excused himself. "Must make room for the coffee. I'll be right back."

Bob looked at his watch; it was two fifteen. "I have a three o'clock meeting with a colleague from university," he observed. "Too bad; I could keep going for the rest of the afternoon on this topic. Bin Laden is a fascinating individual, well worth a study in his own right."

"It has always intrigued me," said Nat, "that here was a man who had everything going for him, born into an immensely wealthy family; the world could have been his oyster. He could obviously have played a major role in the many family businesses. The sky was the limit, and instead he chose a path of self-sacrifice and strict piety. Why?"

"Well, this may sound strange," said Bob, "but I think Osama ended up the way he did because he was a man of principle."

"PRINCIPLE?" Andrew had just rejoined them and caught the end of Bob's sentence. "A man murdering innocent people is a man of principle? I know we live in a fucked-up world, Bob, but that takes some explaining." Andrew sat down and attacked his cheesecake.

"OK, let me try," said Bob, his chocolate mousse remaining untouched. "It goes back to 1948 with the creation of the state of Israel. You would be hard-pressed to find a Muslim anywhere who agrees that taking land from the Palestinians to create the state of Israel was a reasonable thing to do."

"And yet, Jewish presence in Israel dates back 3,400 years," Andrew jumped in.

"That's right," said Bob. "OK, let's step back a bit. Here's a quick history lesson. The Israelites are believed to date back to 1400 to 1100 BC. They established an independent kingdom around 1050 BC which split in two—the Kingdom of Judea and the Kingdom of Israel—around 950 BC. The Assyrians exiled the Israelites about 720 BC, and they became the 'Lost Tribes of Israel'. Then came centuries of Babylonian, Persian, and Greek rule, until Jewish rule was restored around 174 BC. Jewish rule then lasted until 64 BC. Then followed four centuries of Roman rule, ending with Byzantine Christian Roman rule from AD 330 to 631. This was followed by Arab rule from 636 to 1099 and then came the Crusaders who ruled the area from 1099 to 1291." Bob paused and tried his chocolate mousse, then glanced at his watch. "Heck, I'm running out of time." He gulped down some coffee and continued. "So, I think you can see that it is not easy to say who Palestine belongs to. Anyway, during the latter part of the Crusaders' rule, Israel became the frontier between Mongol invaders and the Mamluks, who won and ruled until 1517."

"Excuse me," said Nat. "My grasp of history is not quite up to your standard. Who were the Mamluks?"

"A Mamluk was a soldier of slave origin who had been converted to Islam. Mamluks rose to become a powerful military cast who, among other amazing feats, seized the sultanates of Egypt and Syria. So, Palestine was under Egyptian Islamic rule until 1517, when the Ottomans took over, and it switched to Turkish Islamic rule, and Israel became part of the province of Syria. The Ottomans were in charge for four hundred years, until 1917, when the British conquered the area, named it Palestine, and defined boundaries, including Gaza, Jordan, the West Bank and, what is today, modern Israel. You would think, with all these years of Muslim rule, that Israel would have turned completely Muslim, but that is not the case. By the nineteenth century, Israel or, I should say The Land of Israel, was largely populated by Muslim and Christian Arabs, as well as Jews, Greeks, Druze, Bedouin, and other minority groups. Jews were the largest population group in Jerusalem, and by 1890, they were the absolute majority in the city even though, as a whole, they were less than 10 percent of the region."

"So, the idea that the Jews came from the outside, pushed the Palestinians aside, and created their own country, is not entirely accurate," observed Andrew.

"That is not how it began," said Bob. "The success of the British invasion, led by General Allenby, resulted in Israel's independence from the Ottoman Empire and the establishment of a sovereign state of the British Empire. Prior to this event, and as a result mainly of the persecution of Jews in Europe, a Zionist movement had taken root there, and the First Zionist Congress in 1887 proclaimed the decision to establish a home for the Jewish people in Palestine."

"And a 'home' for the Jews was not to say that they wanted to establish a separate country?" Nat asked.

"Well..." Bob paused and stared thoughtfully at his uneaten chocolate mousse. "...that's not what the Brits had in mind. They saw the sovereign state that they had established, comprising Israel, the West Bank, Gaza, and Jordan, as a country where Muslims, Christian Arabs, and Jews could live peacefully together. And maybe it could have worked, but the Second World War put paid to that dream. When the persecution of Jews became the *annihilation* of Jews by the millions, the demand for a separate Jewish state got louder and louder, and the migration of Jews from Europe to Palestine grew at a rate which was alarming to the Arab population. The British tried to resist but lost, and the State of Israel, as a separate entity, became a reality, as you know, in 1948. Jordan had gained its sovereignty back in 1920, so what remained after 1948 was the West Bank and Gaza, a 'de facto' 'country' for the Palestinians, consisting of two pieces of land hopelessly divided by Israel and with a combined land mass that runs contrary to the population split between Jews and Arabs in the area. The upheaval and disruption to the Palestinian population was devastating, and, as you know, their struggle continues to this day."

"So, you were saying that bin Laden was a man of principle." Nat felt the time was right to bring the conversation back to where they had started. "What did you mean by that?"

"The injustices against the Palestinians have never been put right," said Bob. "In fact, insult and *more* injury were added to injury when the Arabs lost the Six-Day War in 1967. This was a war led by Egypt and joined by Syria, Lebanon, Jordan, and Iraq. The plan was to expel the Jews from Israel and reclaim the land for the Arab Muslims. This Arab coalition mobilised and encircled Israel for an imminent, coordinated attack. Except the Israeli Air Force struck first and destroyed the Egyptian Air Force, then turned east to destroy the Syrian, Iraqi, and Jordanian Air Forces. At the end of the war, Israel had gained control of the Sinai Peninsula, the West Bank, the Gaza Strip, the Golan Heights, and eastern Jerusalem. It was a humiliating defeat for the Arabs and, in my opinion, a contributing factor to the upsurge in Islamic militancy. The turmoil in the region today is a legacy of the Six-Day War—"

". . . which never would have happened if the Arabs had left Israel alone within their original boundaries," Nat observed.

"That is very true," replied Bob. "But the fight, to this day, is about Israel's right to exist. The Palestinians are saying 'You have no right; you never had any right to the land you were "given" by the British.' It is our land, and we want it back. The Israelis are saying 'We have every right to that land and to the land we won in the Six-Day War. If we go back to the prewar boundaries, you will probably attack us again.' Of course, the Israelis have handed back some sections of the conquered land but not all of it. Some has been kept for reasons of national security, and giving it all back is not likely to satisfy the Palestinians in any event, so why do it? That is the Israeli point of view, and given the number of times they have been attacked by their neighbours, it's no wonder they feel that way."

"So, are you saying that if Israel agreed to give back all the occupied territories, it would make no difference to their conflict with the Palestinians?" asked Andrew.

"If the Israelis really believed it would solve the conflict, they would have bitten the bullet and withdrawn from the occupied territories, but they don't believe it, and for good reason. As far as the Palestinians are concerned, the Israelis are occupying *their* land."

"So, what are you saying, Bob? Bin Laden was a man of principle because he wanted to throw the Jews out of Palestine?" Andrew polished off the last of his cheesecake and washed it down with some lukewarm coffee.

Bob looked at his watch. "I've got to run, but let me leave you with this thought: In al-Qaeda's collective mind, there are no grey areas; it's all black or white, right or wrong, and there is no room for doubt. Doubt is weakness. Walking the narrow path of righteousness is their way. The 'principle' they live by is simple: The Western world, in their view, is threatening to destroy the Islamic world. This is clearly demonstrated, as they see it, by the Israeli occupation of Palestinian lands, which started back in 1948 and continues to this day supported by the world superpower, America. Al-Qaeda's goal is to right this 'wrong' and to restore the Nations of Islam to their rightful place in the world, to make up for the humiliation and defeat suffered at the hands of Israel and to establish the dominance of Islam worldwide. The victory over the infidels in Afghanistan was the beginning of this quest." Bob stood up. "I've got to run. I apologise for monopolising the conversation. It's your fault, Nat, for getting me going on al-Qaeda."

They thanked him for lunch. He said goodbye and headed for the door at great speed, stopped abruptly, and headed back to the head waiter and paid for their lunch.

"Wow! It would appear the professor of Islamic studies knows his stuff." Andrew was clearly impressed.

"That he does," Nat agreed. "But I am not sure I agree with him calling bin Laden 'a man of principle'. If he had been, he would have found a peaceful way to further the cause of the Palestinians and Muslims worldwide. There is no equation between a just fight against Communist aggression in Afghanistan and the killing of innocent people around the world. How did he get from one to the other?"

"Would he not have gone further, setting up an international organisation, promoting a peaceful coexistence between Jews and Arabs based on the premise that both groups have, as history shows, a right to live in this area? I am sure there would have been a groundswell of support for such a movement, a movement which recognised that people can live peacefully together, whatever their religious background. A movement which recognised that man's spiritual side should be a unifying factor, not a divisive one. We are all equal under God, whatever we have chosen to call him."

"That is a wonderful thought, but unfortunately, just so much wishful thinking," said Andrew. "But hey, why don't you write al-Qaeda a letter and suggest it?"

"I would," said Nat. "If I knew where to send it."

They finished their coffees. Nat looked at his watch. It was almost three o'clock—time to get back to work.

CHAPTER 30

Imam Badawi walked the streets of London for two hours, trying to digest what the deputy ambassador had told him on their drive. His first thought had been that this was a trap to expose him and what was going on behind the scenes at the mosque. But, as Mr. Jameson had continued his reasoning for proposing what he had, Badawi had started to feel that the man was sincere and that this could be an opportunity of vast proportions for the Islamist movement, of which he was, at the moment, just a small player. Mr. Jameson's offer could change that. It could place Badawi centre stage in an organisation where, until the zoo plot, he had been a minor figure. In fact, he had told Mr. Jameson the truth—he had never met bin Laden or any of the top figures who followed in his footsteps. Badawi's role in the zoo bombing plot had been one of encouragement only. He had not been involved in the planning nor its execution; that had been left to his most brainwashed pupils at the mosque. He had not instructed anyone to do anything, but he had talked extensively about the loss of innocent Palestinian lives, the murder of women and children at the hands of the Israelis, and the need to seek retribution. He had planted a seed and nurtured it carefully. He had obtained a video with footage from Gaza showing bombed-out homes and crying children rummaging through the rubble. To this he had added a promotional video from the London Zoo showing happy families enjoying themselves on a sunny summer afternoon. The finished product had the desired effect. Even his ordinarily peaceful students were upset, and his more militant students were outraged. Badawi knew that the seed had taken root, and all he needed to do was to wait and encourage the seed to grow.

Allah works in mysterious ways, Imam Badawi thought as he picked his way through the crowded sidewalks of London in the general direction of the Central Mosque. The man who, with his family, could have been killed in the zoo bombing had been inspired by that experience and had been delivered to Badawi with a proposal which could change the course of history. *Allah be praised!* Badawi lifted his gaze to the heavens. What to do next: that was the question. He had no direct links to al-Qaeda, but it was his friend, Iqbal Mahoud, who had written him a note thanking him for Badawi's 'inspiration' for the zoo bombing. Mahoud had a small barbershop in Manchester, but he was a regular visitor to the Central Mosque on his frequent trips to London. Badawi had always thought that Mahoud had some connection with an al-Qaeda sleeper cell, but they had never talked about it. Badawi resolved to write a letter to his friend in Manchester and ask for his advice. He would have one of his students drive up and hand-deliver it. Having made that decision, his next thought was to get back to his office as soon as possible. He hailed a cab and was back at his desk twenty minutes later composing a letter to his friend in Manchester.

My Brother,

In the name of God, the merciful.

God works in mysterious ways. Praise be to Allah!

Today I have had a most extraordinary conversation, with the most extraordinary offer being given to me by the deputy US ambassador in London. You will have seen his name in the papers recently in connection with the zoo bombing. He was there with his family, and I believe it may be so that God sent him there that day to prepare him for the great task of helping Muslims in our Jihad against the Western aggressors. His name is Nathaniel Jameson. He is married, with two children. His wife is Jordanian.

His father, who was a Vietnam War veteran, committed suicide after getting ignored by the authorities when returning seriously wounded from that war. Mr. Jameson is very bitter about his father's experience with the US authorities. He told me that his father's experience, and his own recent experience at the zoo, has made him realise that he can no longer continue to sit back and watch innocent people take the brunt for decisions made by callous world leaders. He is very sympathetic to the plight of the Palestinians and believes that the arrogance and aggression displayed by Israel is made possible only by the endless support of successive American presidents. He believes that this support would evaporate if those who make the decisions are made to pay for them.

He says he is prepared to help make that happen. He is offering to create the opportunity for al-Qaeda to kill the president of the United States of America! Yes, to kill our arch-enemy. Mr. Jameson is right when he says that it is not the American people who are our enemy; it is the American decision-makers, headed by the American president, who are the real enemy. He says that, to prove his sincerity, he is prepared to assassinate the US ambassador, his own boss, in London.

It sounds too good to be true, but having known Mr. Jameson for some time, he strikes me as being a man of great compassion.

The killing of innocent people in the name of power politics is what he is seeking to stop by making this offer. He is offering the ultimate prize to stop the senseless killing, as he calls it.

Is this something that could be of interest to us? I do not know, but I do know that we are all prepared to lay down our lives for the glory of Islam and our people.

So, I am asking for your advice. Do you think this is something that might be worth pursuing?

I look forward to your response.

God is great!

Your servant,
Imam Badawi

Badawi printed the letter and signed it and then rummaged around for a plain envelope on which he wrote the name and address by hand. He placed the letter in the envelope and was about to seal it, when he hesitated. He pulled the letter back out. Did he really want to get involved at this level?

Badawi had come from a simple background. His father was a poor farmer in a mountain village near Peshawar, and Badawi's education had taken place in a madrasa in Peshawar which, like all madrasas, provided free education and room and board for its students. Badawi had been a model student who had dedicated himself not only to the study of the Quran but also to the sayings of the Prophet Mohammad (*hadith*), jurisprudence (*fiqh*), and law. His teachers had realised that he was a young man of great potential, and one cleric in particular had taken him under his wing.

It was under this man that Badawi had gradually become radicalised, and it was he who had encouraged Badawi to emigrate to England to, as he put it: "...further the cause of Islam in Europe." Badawi had spent the first five years in Manchester teaching in a madrasa, then followed another four years as Imam in a small regional mosque in Birmingham before he was appointed to head up the London Central Mosque, home of the Islamic Cultural Centre in Great Britain. He was now in his fourth year at the Central Mosque, where he was more like the CEO of a major corporation than a cleric, although he had, at his own insistence, maintained four hours of teaching per week. He had perfected the art of brainwashing and took pride in his ability to identify students who could most easily be radicalised. He had never uttered the words *kill* or *destroy* to his pupils, and yet he had sent many out into the world to join the jihad against the Western oppressors.

Badawi placed the letter back in the envelope and sealed it. What was he afraid of? Would it not be a sin to ignore this amazing offer? Was it not for the leaders of al-Qaeda to decide what to do with this? Nobody had the right to make this decision for them. He deleted the letter from his computer and got a wax stick and a seal from his desk drawer, together with a box of matches, and applied a seal to the envelope. He reached for the telephone on his desk and dialled an internal number, "Hassan. ... Badawi here; sorry to disturb your class, but I have a most urgent message I need to get hand delivered to Manchester; could you spare Aariz for the afternoon?" "Certainly, Imam Badawi; as you will." Hassan new that hand-deliveries and ordinary mail through the postal service was reserved mostly for matters of a sensitive nature, something that needed to be kept from the prying eyes and ears of the authorities.

A lanky eighteen-year-old boy stood before Badawi's desk in less than two minutes. He looked ill at ease, rocking from left to right, his big brown eyes darting around the room. "No, Aariz; you are not in trouble. I have a job for you to do, and I know I can trust you to do it right. Here," Badawi held out the envelope, "I want you to take this letter to Manchester right away. It is a matter of great urgency that it gets there today, but do *not* speed. You do not want to be stopped by the police who would ask you all kinds of questions." Badawi turned to his computer, Googled Manchester, and found a map of the city which he printed out and marked Mahoud's barbershop. "Here you are. Drive carefully, and don't get lost!" Aariz bowed courteously and turned to leave. "Wait!" Badawi's booming voice filled the space. "Come back!" Badawi pulled a twenty pound note out of his pocket, "Here, take this to help with the petrol and a bite to eat on the way back."

"Thank you, Sir." Aariz's voice was just a whisper. He backed to the door, fumbled behind himself to find the door knob, opened the door, and bowed again on his way out.

Badawi looked at his watch. It was 2 p.m. He hoped to hear back from his friend in Manchester before the day was out.

CHAPTER 31

Badawi had turned the light off in his office and was about to shut the door when his phone rang. He switched the light back on and hurried back to his desk and lifted the receiver.

"My friend, how are you? I received your message, and I thank you for your kind invitation."

Badawi recognised the voice as Mahoud's. *Invitation? What was he talking about?* Suddenly, Badawi realised that Mahoud was being careful not to give anything away over the phone.

"Yes, Mahoud, you are welcome. Are you interested?"

"I am. I will be in London tomorrow, and I will come and see you, and I may bring a friend, if that is OK with you?"

"Of course." Badawi could feel his heart beating faster.

"I look forward to seeing you. Do you know when you might get here?"

"I plan to leave here around nine in the morning, so I should be with you around midday, if that is OK with you?"

"That is perfect. I have two classes in the morning, but they finish at 11:30."

"Very well. I'll see you tomorrow."

Mahoud hung up, and Badawi was left holding on to the receiver. There was excitement in Mahoud's voice, he could tell.

He replaced the receiver slowly. Who was the mystery guest? He decided to put it all out of his mind. He looked at his watch. It was almost time for the sunset (*Maghrib*) prayer. He would pray in the mosque this evening and ask the prophet and Allah for their divine guidance in the awesome challenge which had presented itself to him. He turned out the light and closed and locked his office door.

Badawi was unable to focus on his classes the next morning. Rather than getting his students to read segments of the Quran and then having a discussion of their meaning in class, he had given them reading to do and asked them to write down their own interpretations which were to be handed to him at the next session. He pretended to be reading the good book himself, but his mind was on the upcoming meeting with Mahoud.

He kept looking at the clock on the back wall of the classroom, and it seemed to him that time was almost standing still. He looked at the dark heads of his pupils bent over their books in deep concentration. Their devotion to religious studies never ceased to amaze him. Yet he knew that for many it was an escape from reality, from poverty, uncertainty, fear, and frustration. He remembered his own early schooling at the madrasa in Peshawar. It had not been an extremist madrasa. Religion was only one of many subjects taught at the school. What had drawn Badawi into the extremist Islamist camp was the American drone which had killed his mother and father when their village was attacked for allegedly harbouring Taliban fighters. This was the event that had made it possible for him to accept that attacks on innocent civilians were acceptable.

Over the years he had discovered how easy it was to steer young people in the direction of violence without them knowing. He had never picked a young man and coaxed him to become a suicide bomber, nor would he ever do that. He led his students down a path where revenge and retaliation seemed like a reasonable choice—a noble struggle in the name of Islam—creating a false reality, where not to fight seemed wrong and cowardly. Yet Mr. Jameson had struck a nerve when he had said, "Let's get to the people at the top who carry the ultimate responsibility for these abuses of power." Badawi sensed that Jameson was right when he said that the killing of innocent people would not further the cause of Islam in the long run, nor had it done so in the short term. The failure of ISIS to sustain and grow the caliphate had shown this to be so.

Badawi's thoughts were interrupted by the bell which rang to mark the end of the lesson. The clock said 11:30. Badawi dismissed the class and hurried back to his office.

His secretary had left some papers on his desk, and he flicked through them quickly to see whether anything required his immediate attention. There were two letters from imams in response to his call for condemnation of the zoo bombings. They wholeheartedly supported his call. Then there was a new lease to be signed for the operator of the halal cafe downstairs. It could wait. Badawi was about to open another envelope when the phone rang on his desk. It was his secretary.

"Imam Badawi, I have two men out here who will not give their names. They say to tell you that your visitors from Manchester are here."

Badawi's heart made a jolt. "Send them in." He stood up from his desk and moved towards the door as it opened. The man who came first was a stranger, tall, dark curly hair, and dressed in a grey, pinstriped suit. *He looked like a city lawyer*, Badawi thought. He was followed closely by Mahoud, who looked like the barber that he was, in baggy black trousers and a worn tweed jacket over a white shirt. He drew level with the stranger to make the introductions.

"This is my friend Omar... Imam Badawi." They shook hands.

Omar was not likely his real name, Badawi thought. He offered them the two chairs in front of his desk and retook his own behind it.

After a few pleasantries about family and the weather, Mahoud came to the reason for their visit. "I was intrigued to receive your letter yesterday, so much so that I called my friend Omar to ask his advice on the matter."

"Omar" had kept his eyes focused on Badawi since he sat down. He gave Mahoud a quick sideways glance, cleared his throat and returned his attention to Badawi.

"Your friend, Mr. Jameson, has made a most amazing proposition." He spoke with a perfect Oxford English accent.

Maybe he really is a lawyer? Badawi thought.

"Of course, it is so amazing that it is hard to believe," Omar continued. "How long have you known Mr. Jameson?"

Badawi thought for a moment. "Almost four years—since shortly after I was posted to the Central Mosque."

"Did you ever feel, in your interactions with the man, that he was erratic, unpredictable, or unstable?"

"No. On the contrary, he has always struck me as being a very sincere and reliable person—a man of integrity."

"A man of integrity?" Omar raised his eyebrows. "Would you say that a man who proposes to kill his boss and betray his own president is a man of integrity?"

Badawi struggled to find an answer. "I feel he is sympathetic to our cause, particularly to the Palestinian cause. He sees the creation of Israel as a mistake and the continued occupation by Israel of the territories captured in the Sixty-Seven War as a gross injustice."

Omar stopped him. "Yes, very well. Perhaps you could go through your meeting with Mr. Jameson for us so that we can get a better understanding of where the man is coming from?"

Badawi did his best to paraphrase his meetings with Jameson, going back to the first meeting at the embassy and then the drive through the streets of London, when Jameson had made his amazing offer. He did his best to leave nothing out.

When he finished, there was a long silence. The distant sound of the London traffic seeped through the closed windows. Nobody moved.

Omar stared intently at Badawi, who did his best not to avert his eyes.

"So, you are telling me that we should take your friend seriously?"

Badawi swallowed hard. "I believe we should, yes."

Omar looked sideways. "And what do *you* think, Mahoud; is this for real?"

Mahoud picked some imaginary fluff off his sleeve while pondering his answer. "Well, the way I see it, the only way to find out is to put the ad in the paper and see if it causes the ambassador to have a heart attack and die. If that happens, I would say Jameson is for real, yes." Mahoud looked nervously at Omar, as if he were expecting rebuke for his response.

A faint smile spread across Omar's face. "Those are my thoughts, precisely. Mr. Jameson has set this up so that we can make the next move without risk. The wording of Imam Badawi's ad, calling for peace and unity, does not expose us in any way. It is diabolically perfect, and it is this perfection on Mr. Jameson's part that makes me think that it is worth taking this to al-Qaeda for their consideration. Bin Laden told me once, when we were pinned down in the Tora Bora mountains and the American bombs were raining down on us, that he looked forward to the day when he would repay the Satan who was visiting this upon us. The 'Satan' he was referring to was the president of the United States of America." Omar paused, and looked at the other two men in turn. "Gentlemen, I think if there is an opportunity to rid the world of this Satan, then in the name of our blessed departed leader, it is our responsibility to bring it to al-Qaeda's attention."

Badawi could feel his heart beating faster. *Omar had been with bin Laden in Afghanistan!* Badawi realised that this could bring himself centre stage in the struggle against the oppressors of Islam. He felt that this was the reason Allah had sent him to London.

"Very well, my friends." Omar rose, closely followed by Mahoud. "I shall take the next step and get back to you..." He looked at Badawi. "...with an answer. In the meantime, none of this must go any further; this stays among the three of us." Omar stretched his hand out to say goodbye.

"Will you not join me for lunch downstairs in our cafe?" Badawi asked as he took Omar's hand.

Omar looked at his watch, then at Mahoud. "What do you say, Mahoud; do we have time for lunch?" Omar seemed to ask for permission.

Who is in charge here? Badawi thought.

Mahoud smiled. "I always like to have a meal with my friend when I come to London, and today is, I think, a special day—a day that we may all remember for the rest of our lives. Thank you, Imam Badawi; we shall be pleased to take lunch with you."

CHAPTER 32

Nat had kept an eye on the classified ads in the *Daily Telegraph* every morning since his meeting with Imam Badawi. Ten days had gone by, and no ad had appeared. He put the paper down and looked at Sonja across the breakfast table. He had not told her about the ad and how, if it appeared, it would trigger the start of Operation Endgame. He had decided there was no need to get her stressed out about something that might not happen. He had told her about his meeting with Badawi and that he was waiting to hear back from him; that was all.

Sonja got up and started to clear the table just as the children stormed into the kitchen in mid-argument.

"That's not true." Tanya gave her brother a withering look. "*All* Muslim women are not terrorists."

"Oh yeah? Why do they wear masks then?" Gregory poured himself some cereal while he waited for his sister's response.

Tanya rolled her eyes and shook her head. "They're not masks, stupid! They're religious veils."

"OK, that's enough of that," Sonja broke in. "Get your breakfast. We're leaving in ten minutes."

They sat down opposite each other.

"They look like gangsters," said Gregory, his cheeks bulging with cereal. "I saw a film about a bank robbery, and the robbers wore ski masks," he continued. "And they looked just like the Muslim women in their veils."

Nat thought he should come to his son's rescue. "Greg has a point. The burqa and niqab, which cover the whole of a woman's head except her eyes, do create problems sometimes, especially for security people at airports where photo IDs are often required. A woman covered from head to foot in religious dress with just her eyes exposed is more difficult to identify than a bank robber in a ski mask. Fortunately, most women who dress this way are ordinary peace-loving Muslims, but there have been some notable exceptions such as women suicide bombers with suicide vests hidden under their black dress and terrorist men disguised as women to avoid detection." Nat looked at his watch. "I must be on my way. Have a great day." He kissed them goodbye and went over to Sonja, who was washing the dishes, and kissed her on the neck.

Sonja turned and smiled up at him. "Have a nice day, darling."

"Come in!" Preston looked up from his newspaper as Nat entered his office. "Good morning, Nat. Nothing there, is it?" Preston folded his paper and put it down on his desk.

"Nothing," said Nat. "Waiting like this is driving me crazy. I guess al-Qaeda's intelligence service is checking me out."

"All they have to do is go on our website and read your CV. The only fact missing from it is that you own a dachshund called Darwin." Preston chuckled. "Whatever they do, you will pass their scrutiny. Then, it's my guess that your offer will go to the al-Qaeda leader, who will solicit advice from his Shura

Council. It's going to take some time. We have to be patient." Nat sat down, and Preston gave him a questioning look.

"Does Sonja know what is going on?"

"Just that we are waiting to hear from Badawi. I have not gone into the details of how that is to happen. It is enough that one of us plough through the classifieds every morning."

Preston stood up and went over to his coffee machine. "Care for a cup?"

Nat, shook his head. "No thanks. I've had my quota for the day already."

Preston made his coffee and walked back to his desk. "You know," he said, "I think al-Qaeda is going to take a serious look at your offer. They have been losing hearts and minds in the Muslim world big time, killing Muslims in Muslim countries, especially in Iraq, Afghanistan, and Pakistan. Al-Qaeda's approval rating in Saudi Arabia is only 10 percent, and the support for suicide bombings in countries like Bangladesh, Lebanon, and Indonesia has dropped by half over the past five years. Support for al-Qaeda is dropping around the Muslim world."

"That must be why they are now focusing their propaganda campaign on Palestine," said Nat. ". . . the cauldron of Muslim discontent, fuelled by the Israelis' refusal to give the Palestinians a fair shake," he added.

"Maybe." Preston stirred the sugar in his coffee. "You can't blame them. The situation in Palestine for the Palestinians is beginning to resemble what the Jews themselves experienced in the ghettos."

"How strange they can't see that themselves." said Nat. This was a question he had asked himself many times. How could a people, who had suffered oppression on an unprecedented scale under the Nazis, subjugate another group with a heavy, sometimes ruthless, hand?

It was as if Preston had read Nat's mind. "I think it could be that, despite their superior strength, they still see themselves as the underdog. They have made themselves believe that everything they are doing, they are doing in self-defence."

"Building illegal new settlements, bulldozing Palestinian homes, and shutting off water, electricity, and fuel supplies is self-defence?" Nat's question hung in the air.

Preston took a sip of his coffee and stared out at the last autumn leaves hanging on stubbornly to the oak tree outside his window. "The Palestinians are hanging on like the leaves on the trees out there. The policy of closure, which the Israelis have adopted, has caused untold hardship for the Palestinians. The Great Wall of Palestine is not built to keep the Palestinians out of Israel; it cuts Palestine in half—north-south. It is built on Palestinian land and runs far east of the original Green Line. The Israelis are effectively making Israel bigger. The policy of closure, which has created the ghettos of Gaza and the West Bank, are themselves divided internally by barricades, checkpoints, and roadblocks that prevent Palestinians from moving freely around, even in their own areas. Normal economic activity is impossible under these conditions. Raw materials, parts, and machinery all have to come from Israel, and the Israelis have shut down the supply lines. Manufacturing is dead." Preston pushed his empty coffee cup away. "Anyhow, that's enough of that. We aren't going to solve the Middle East conflict this morning. Have you read the article about the missing Russian warhead?"

Nat shook his head.

"Colonel Ivanovitch has confessed to selling the warhead to Iran. The Iranians say they have no warhead and claim the whole affair is a Western plot designed to justify military intervention into Iran. So far there is no sign of the warhead. A Security Council resolution has been passed, mandating a UN-sponsored inspection team to carry out a search for it. As usual, China abstained, content to sit on the fence. The stakes are getting higher in the war on terrorism. We cannot allow nuclear weapons to fall into the wrong hands."

"No," said Nat. "But do we really have the moral authority to tell other nations that they cannot develop nuclear capabilities? We have more lethal nuclear power than anybody. The nonproliferation treaty is just a way for us to ensure that we have the upper hand. If we were really serious about nonproliferation, we would start a concerted effort to eradicate nuclear weapons, including our own. The small gestures we have made in that direction with the Russians are symbolic, to say the least. Have the Iranians agreed to allow the UN inspectors unfettered access for a meaningful search?"

"Not yet. They're thinking about it," said Preston.

". . . just like Saddam did while he was spiriting his WMDs away to Syria?" asked Nat. He had long held the belief that Saddam had fooled the international community into believing that he did not have weapons of mass destruction, simply because none were found. The Western media had been quick to condemn the military action against Iraq for that reason, handing Saddam a "moral" victory. As far as Nat was concerned, this demonstrated an almost childlike naivety on the part of the media and lulled the populations in the western hemisphere into a false sense of security—a false sense of security which could prove fatal for Western civilisation given al-Qaeda's commitment to what amounted to Islamic world domination. Nat rose. "I better get back to my own office. I am being interviewed on BBC this afternoon, answering questions about the zoo bombings, if you recall?"

"Of course I do." Preston stood also. "It may be an opportunity to reinforce your proposal to Badawi if you are really clever—anger at the perpetrators but also a subtle hint of repressed anger at the situation in the Middle East. You have to be careful not to cross the diplomatic line; after all, Israel *is* our ally. I have the utmost confidence in your diplomatic skills." Preston started to focus on a stack of papers on his desk.

"Thanks for the vote of confidence." Nat smiled and headed for the door. "I'll stop by after the interview. It will be on the four o'clock news; you can give me your verdict then."

CHAPTER 33

Nat arrived at the BBC studios at 2:30 and was greeted by Carol, a short brunette in tight blue jeans and a baggy, black sweater. Carol escorted him first to a room marked Makeup, where a young man with a ponytail and very pale, long, narrow hands went to work on Nat's face. When Nat noted his displeasure at being made up, Richard assured him that it would be very light. "... just enough to take out any reflections and to enhance your very fine features, sir," as he put it, with a faint cockney lisp.

"There!" Richard stood back and admired his handiwork. "That does it. You're good to go, mate!"

He removed the protective cape, while Nat looked with horror at his own reflection in the mirror. *I look like I could be Richard's date,* he thought.

Carol reappeared and took him to an empty office. They sat down in front of a stylish chrome and glass desk, and Nat gave Carol a quizzical look. "Ms. Tolaram should be along shortly."

As Carol finished the sentence, a very attractive, bronze-skinned young woman burst into the office. Her jet-black hair was carefully styled to frame her oval face, which provided the setting for the most stunningly beautiful dark brown eyes Nat had ever seen. They looked even better in real life. "Sorry I'm late. My name is Natalia Tolaram."

She had a firm, confident handshake, and she needed no introduction. Nat had seen her on TV many times doing special reports focused mainly on the Far and Middle East.

"Thank you very much for agreeing to do this interview, Mr. Jameson. As you know, the print media have had extensive coverage of the zoo bombing, but we have not done anything since the initial news pieces. When I asked my boss why that was, he could not come up with a good answer. When I asked him if it had something to do with the fact that the perpetrators masqueraded as BBC TV reporters, he gave me a, 'Definitely not,' and said, 'Why don't you do a follow-up story'; so, here we are."

She spoke with a typical BBC English accent—pronouncing every word precisely.

"I saw an article in the paper stating that the US ambassador was going to Washington to brief the president on the incident and that you were going along since you were there visiting with your family and experienced the tragic event first-hand. That got me thinking that you were the perfect person to do this follow-up interview with. You can talk about it from a personal point of view, as well as putting it in a larger context in your capacity as deputy ambassador. So, if you don't mind, I'll start asking some personal questions about what you and your family experienced that day and then some more general questions about the problem of terrorism in the UK and worldwide. Does that sound OK to you?"

Nat nodded. "Yes, that will be fine."

Natalia looked at her watch. "All right then, let's go to the studio." She stood up, and Nat and Carol followed.

Carol stopped at the studio door. "This is where I leave. Good luck, Mr. Jameson." She turned and disappeared down the corridor.

The studio was smaller than he had imagined it would be. There was a podium with two easy chairs and a small glass coffee table, on which stood two glasses and a carafe of water. The chairs were arranged so that a white backdrop, about six feet wide, would be clearly visible between them. There were two cameras and an array of movable lights and reflectors.

Natalia asked Nat to take the chair on the right, and she sat down opposite, with a small, electronic notepad on her knee.

A young woman appeared from behind the intense glare of the lamps and attached microphones under their lapels. Natalia gave him a reassuring smile. "Please say something so they can balance the microphones, Mr. Jameson."

Nat felt awkward. *What to say?* "It... it's very hot from those lamps," he stuttered.

Natalia looked out beyond the darkness of the flood lights, turned back towards him, and gave him a big smile and the figure "O" with her thumb and index finger. "OK, Mr. Jameson. We are all set. Are you ready?"

Nat nodded. He could feel his heart picking up the pace; he took a deep breath.

Natalia delivered a brief introduction, recapping the events of the zoo bombing, the current state of the investigation into those who were responsible, and finished her review by introducing her guest:

Natalia: *With me, today, is the deputy chief of missions at the US Embassy, Mr. Nathaniel Jameson, who was at the zoo with his family the morning of the attack. Thank you for taking the time out of your busy schedule to come on the program and talk with us.*

Nat: *It is my pleasure.*

Natalia: *Mr. Jameson, three weeks ago you and your family were at the London Zoo when it was attacked by terrorists. Could you tell our viewers what you and your family experienced that morning?*

Nat: *We had been walking around for a couple of hours and had just sat down at the restaurant to have some lunch, when we heard what sounded like a loud clap of thunder. It was a clear, crisp day, so I first thought that it must be a traffic accident. I went to investigate, having told my family to remain in their seats at the restaurant, and I ran outside and saw a cloud of black smoke rising from the main entrance area.*

Natalia: *You told your family to stay in the restaurant. Does that mean you already suspected foul play?*

Nat: *It did occur to me; in fact, as I ran outside, I thought what I had heard sounded more like an explosion than a collision. And in the world we live in today, I think we are almost conditioned to think "bombs and terrorists" when we hear a very loud noise.*

Natalia: *What happened next?*

Nat: *I ran towards the entrance and met people, clearly in a state of panic, running towards me, away from the entrance area. One man, with his daughter in his arms, ran straight into me. He had terror written all over his face. When I got closer to the entrance, a policeman stopped me. He told me it had been an explosion and told me to go back and stay with my family until we received further instructions.*

Not long after that, we started to hear the sirens of ambulances and fire engines approaching, and there was a lot of commotion and shouting coming from the zoo entrance area.

Natalia: *When you got back to the restaurant, what were your wife and children doing?*

Nat: *They were sitting at the table where I had left them. They were calm and collected. I was very proud of them. By this time, a policeman and two zoo security officers were on the scene telling us what had happened and advising us that we would be escorted out of the zoo through alternative exits once the police gave the clearance to do so.*

Natalia: *How would you describe the response from the zoo officials and the police?*

Nat: *They were excellent—very efficient and firm—but also caring. There must have been hundreds of people there, yet we were out in just over an hour, taken back to the car park via one of the small service gates. I don't think the emergency response could have been any better.*

Natalia: *Can you tell us a little about how you and your family are dealing with this now? I imagine that life can't be quite the same after an experience like this?*

Nat: *Well, it is amazing how well everybody has taken it. It was a dreadful experience, and we all admitted to each other that we were frightened. But the children went back to school the following Monday, and both of them have been receiving counselling at their respective schools. My daughter, Tanya, wrote an essay about it, and, I tell you, it was a story well worth reading. The final paragraph took my breath away.*

Natalia: *Can you remember what it says?*

Nat: *Yes; I most certainly can. That paragraph is etched in my mind. It goes like this:*

"I hope one day all human beings will live in peace with each other. There will be no more wars of any kind, anywhere. Only when this happens, and we respect each other and nature, will we achieve the true happiness which God has intended for us all."

(Pause)

Natalia: *How old is your daughter, Mr. Jameson?*

Nat could see that her eyes looked shinier.

Nat: *She is twelve.*

Natalia: *Remarkable! ... A world without wars and people caring for each other and nature.*

(Pause)

I would like to hear your thoughts on the bigger picture, Mr. Jameson. You have experienced the effects of terrorism first-hand. Thankfully, you and your family were not injured, but many were, and some died. What would you like to say to the people who did this?

Nat: *Stop the madness! Killing innocent people? It will achieve nothing except fuel further division and hatred. Look at the Middle East, where Jews and Arabs lived peacefully together for centuries. Negotiation after negotiation has failed, and people's lives are pure misery. Hamas fire rockets into Israel, and Israel responds with heavy artillery and air strikes.*

The people on both sides are suffering, and nobody in a position of power seems to be able to do anything about it. Yet it was Western political leaders who created Israel. It was Arab political leaders who decided to attack Israel in 1956, 1967, and 1973, and who lost their lives? ... Ordinary, everyday citizens from both sides, and there is no end in sight.

In 2005 Israel removed 8,500 settlers from the Gaza Strip, along with its military bases, and what happened? ... Palestinian militants, Hamas-sponsored militants have been pounding southern Israel with rockets ever since. And, of course, the Israelis fight back with stupendously superior firepower, and the killing machine grinds on.

Natalia: *You travelled with the US ambassador to Washington and met with the president. Can you tell us how your meeting went?*

Nat: *The president is very upset. He feels that the zoo attack represents a serious turn for the worse in that this was an attack that focused on children and families. That, he said, brings terrorism to a new level of depravity. He is committed to fighting terrorism on all fronts, and his upcoming trip to Europe is about getting all Western nations to come together in an all-out effort to stamp out what he calls "the evil cancer in our midst". He has promised that he will do everything in his power to stop the madness.*

Natalia: *I know this is a difficult question to answer, and perhaps, an unreasonable question to ask, Mr. Jameson, but I am going to ask it anyway. Do you see any way that this "madness", as you call it, can be stopped?*

(Pause)

Nat: *First, there has to be the political will to stop it, on all sides. Then, with that in place, the political leaders will need to sit down and not leave the negotiating table until it is agreed, by all sides, that the solution cannot be found or enhanced by any side resorting to, or sponsoring, violence, in any form. From that point on, political leaders must ensure that aggression against another state or group of people does not occur, which means reining in militant groups, in their own countries, and keeping lines of communication open so that the road to a lasting and equitable peace is kept open. A political solution must be hammered out, which secures Israel's existence and a viable, independent Palestinian state. As things now stand, boundaries will have to be redrawn so that Palestine is not split apart into unmanageable pieces, and Israel, difficult as it may be, goes back to its 1967 boundaries in return for guarantees from its Arab neighbours that they will honour Israel's right to exist within those boundaries. A sovereign and secure Israel next to a sovereign and secure Palestine, working together, and working, also, with their neighbouring Arab countries, would transform the Middle East from a place of human and economic tragedy to an economic powerhouse, where Arabs and Jews can live peacefully together.*

Natalia: *Thank you, Mr. Jameson. It is clear that these are matters which are close to your heart, and understandably so. What you and your family went through is an experience that no one should have to suffer. We are running out of time, but are there any final words you would like to add?*

Nat: *Yes. I would implore everyone—men, women, young, and old—to write to their political representatives and demand an end to the violence. We have elected these leaders to run the world for us; our safety and our future are entrusted to their care. We must all insist that they live up to that trust.*

Natalia: *Thank you, Mr. Jameson. We appreciate you taking the time out to talk to us, and we wish you and your family the very best in the months and years ahead. We also thank you for your incisive suggestions regarding the way to make progress in the Middle East. Again, thank you!*

The cameras stopped rolling, and the floodlights went out. Natalia leaned forward and shook Nat's hand. "Thank you, Mr. Jameson. That was wonderful. Your wise words will be heard by millions of people. This will be part of BBC News, both here and internationally. It will run every hour, starting at four this afternoon."

Nat looked at his watch. It was a quarter past three. He unhooked his microphone. "Thank you, Miss Tolaram; it was my pleasure to be here with you."

She took his microphone and removed her own. Miss Tolaram stood up and gave him the brightest of smiles. "Would you care for a cup of coffee or a glass of champagne? The latter is an old tradition with BBC, although it is not consumed in anywhere near the quantity that it, apparently, used to be."

Nat smiled back. *My god, she is attractive!* He declined, anxious to get back to the embassy, and five minutes later, he was in a taxi on his way back to the office.

Chapter 34

Nat's secretary looked up as he passed her desk. "Hello, Mr. Jameson. Mr. Preston said he would like you to join him in his office when you return."

Nat changed direction. "Thank you, Angela."

He knocked on Preston's door and entered without waiting for a reply. Preston got up from his desk and walked over to his coffee machine. "You look bushed. Fancy a cup of coffee?" Nat accepted. Preston got busy making the coffee. He nodded towards the seating area at the back of which stood a large plasma screen. "We'll have our coffees over there and watch the four o'clock news. How did you make out?"

Nat came up next to him by the coffee machine. "OK, I think. Except I probably said too much."

They sat down, and Nat recapped the interview as best he could remember it. When he finished, Preston rubbed his chin and gave Nat a thoughtful look. "Sounds like you did pretty good except for the comment about Israel pulling back behind their pre-sixty-seven borders. That is not our official position, at least not yet." Preston drained his cup and set it down on the table.

"I know," said Nat. "But she asked me what I thought needed to happen for this madness to end, and I told her. I firmly believe that what I said needs to happen before we can begin to dismantle international terrorism in a lasting and meaningful way." There was a defiant tone in Nat's voice.

Preston grinned and slapped Nat's shoulder. "There, there... Keep your shirt on! I know you feel strongly about this. It's a good thing that our current president agrees with you."

The buzzer went off on Preston's desk. He got up and walked over. "Yes, Clara; what is it? ... In five minutes?" Preston consulted his watch. "Yes, thank you. We'll switch it on now." He looked over at Nat. "Please turn the TV on. The four o'clock news is about to start."

Nat found the remote on the coffee table and switched the TV on. The station was already tuned to BBC, and they sat through a number of program previews which went on for so long that Preston commented that, for a station which prides itself on having no commercial advertising, they sure spent enough time advertising themselves. Finally, the news was announced. The news anchorman started by giving a brief overview of the evening news.

Flash floods had caused serious damage to a hill town in Italy. The Spanish prime minister promised to bring the "new" Basque separatists, who claimed responsibility for the recent bombings in Madrid, to justice.

The flash floods, in the south of Italy, had claimed twenty lives and caused serious damage to the little hill town, where houses, bridges, and cars had been swept away in a torrent of mud and water.

And closer to home:

The investigation of the London Zoo bombings has resulted in two arrests, ". . . and," said the anchorman, "we have an interview with the deputy US ambassador, who experienced the attack first hand with his family."

A film clip showed a rescue team desperately trying to reach a woman who was trapped in her car sitting in the middle of a road that had been turned into a river. They had stretched a cable from the upper floors of houses on either side, and a rescue worker, in a harness attached to the cable, was pulled out until he was right above the car. He lowered himself down and, after a considerable struggle to convince the woman to let go of the car door she was holding on to, managed to strap her to himself, and she was pulled to safety.

The zoo episode was the last segment of the news, and they watched it in silence. When it was over, Preston reached over, got the remote, and turned the TV off. "Well done, Nat. I think you struck the right balance. You condemned the violence and focused the blame on the politicians and their lack of political will to find the solutions. You are angry and frustrated that, as you see it, the people in power are allowing the mayhem to continue. Rather harsh criticism, if you ask me, because the violence is largely out of their control, but equally, there is no way wars, or acts of terrorism, are going to solve these issues. You did very well." Preston rose and headed back to his desk.

Nat stood also. "Thank you, Jim. Are you saying I came over as a person who is mad enough to kill his own colleagues and betray his president?"

Preston smiled. "Only if you were Imam Badawi or anyone he might by now have shared your offer with. In that context, I would say you came over as a person who places blame for the state of affairs squarely on the decision-makers, the most powerful of them being the president of the United States of America."

"Well then." Nat headed for the door. "I guess we just go back to our waiting game?"

"That's right, Nat. That's what we do."

Chapter 35

It was three days later when Nat entered the kitchen and found Sonja reading the newspaper while eating her cereal and yogurt breakfast. She looked up. "Good morning, darling. I let you sleep. You tossed and turned all night."

Nat kissed her and looked at his watch. "Were you going to just let me miss work? It was Darwin who woke me up whimpering. Maybe he thought I was dead or something."

"I was only going to give you another ten minutes. It is only twenty past seven. By the way, you and Jim must have done a good job on Imam Badawi. He has taken out an ad in the paper. Look. . ." She turned the paper towards him, and there was a full-page ad with large letters in bold print:

STOP THE SENSELESS KILLING OF INNOCENT PEOPLE!
LET US WORK TOGETHER FOR A BETTER WORLD!
Imam Badawi
Central Mosque

Nat could feel his heart doing somersaults. There it was, at last, and big enough that he could not possibly have missed it! He grabbed the paper.

"Just a minute!" Sonja gave him a perturbed look. "We don't grab in this family, remember?"

Nat stared at the ad and then at Sonja. "I'm sorry, darling. I didn't mean to. It's just that—"

"It's just that what?"

Nat dropped the paper on the table and pulled Sonja out of the chair and into a tight embrace. "Come with me." Nat guided her through the dining room and into the garden.

"What are you doing?" Sonja twisted out of his grip.

"This is the start of Operation Endgame. Al-Qaeda has taken the bait, and we have to be careful what we say, in case our house is bugged."

Sonja looked puzzled. "What do you mean? Taken the bait?"

Nat stumbled in his words. He felt lightheaded. "This ad is—the. . . the signal that al-Qaeda has accepted my offer to kill the ambassador!" He could feel Sonja shivering in his arms. Fear was written on her face, but he could see that she was struggling for control.

"So soon?" Her voice was just a whisper.

He hugged her tightly and stroked her hair. "Now, now; don't start worrying. There is no risk in this until I get an audience with them, and that may or may not happen."

He knew that this was not necessarily true. If anything went wrong with "murder one" or with "murder two"—if they somehow found out that nobody had really been killed but they played along—he could be in deep trouble long before he got anywhere near al-Qaeda's headquarters. He did not really think that Sonja would believe his reassurances, and it took just a couple of seconds for that to be confirmed.

She leaned back and gave him a searching look. "Come now, Nathaniel Jameson; don't play me for a fool. If at any time they find out that your 'murder', or 'murders', are fake, you are in deep trouble. You'd be the last to know that *they* knew, and I hate to think what they would do to you." She shuddered at the thought, and Nat held her more firmly.

"That will not happen, darling. I have every confidence in the professionals who are going to make this happen. Furthermore. . . " He paused and gave her a reassuring smile. "I have every reason to think that I can hold up my end of the bargain."

She lifted a hand and stroked his cheek. "I know, darling. I know. I'm scared; that's all."

He bent down and kissed her softly. "It will be all right, honey. Don't—"

The phone rang. Sonja released herself from Nat's embrace and ran inside to the phone sitting on the counter below the cookbooks. "Good morning; Jameson residence. Hi Jim. . . . and a very good morning to you." She sounded bright and cheerful—like her normal self—no trace of the emotional trauma Nat knew she was in the midst of. "Yes, Jim; he's right here standing next to me already. Here. . . " She handed the phone to Nat.

"Good morning, Jim; how are—. . . . Yes, I've just seen it. Sonja showed it to me. Yes, Badawi is as good as his word. We have a lot to talk about when I get into the office." Nat hoped that Preston would get the message that the phone might be tapped. "The president will be pleased to see that things are moving in the right direction."

There was an edge of excitement in Preston's voice. He had clearly got the message. Nat looked at his watch. It had just gone 7:30.

"I should be in around quarter past eight if there are no traffic snarls."

"Okay, Nat. I'll see you soon. Drive carefully." Preston chuckled and hung up.

Chapter 36

Nat was at his desk at twenty after eight and grabbed the secure phone and dialled the number. The automatic answering system cut in at the third ring. "Code name, please."

"Endgame."

"Start report now."

Nat looked at his watch. It was quarter to three (in the morning) over there—too early for his contact, "Tom", to be at his desk.

Nat filed his report, trying to keep his voice as calm and neutral as possible. "They have taken the bait. There is a full-page ad in today's *Telegraph*, which is the cue for me to kill the ambassador. Please let me know when you want this to take place. I have memorised the details from our last conversation. End of report." He hung up and looked at his watch. Not *his* watch. He kept forgetting that this little baby was the wonder machine that might lead to the al-Qaeda leaders' death or capture; he hoped—capture and trial in an international court.

It was just before 8:30. Angela did not normally arrive until nine. She was the most exacting and punctual secretary he had ever had. He was about to walk out to the kitchen to get himself a cup of coffee when there was a knock on the door, and she appeared, gingerly balancing a tray in her right hand. "Good morning, Mr. Jameson. I heard you in here and figured you must have had a very early start. Thought you might like some coffee by now?"

"Thank you, Angela. You read my mind. You're in early yourself. Don't like it at home anymore?"

Angela smiled. "My chauffeur's car is in the garage. I took the Underground. It is much faster."

"So, you could get rid of the chauffeur and save yourself some trouble." Nat gave her a teasing wink. The "chauffeur" was Angela's fiancé. They were due to be married in the spring.

"Nah, I'd get union trouble instead." She gave him a wicked grin. "He loves taking me to work in the mornings. Besides, it's the best time to talk. No television, no computers, and no cell phone use in the car. He's all mine for an hour."

"I see your point." Nat returned to his desk, and Angela placed the tray with coffee and two Marie biscuits in front of him and left quietly without saying another word.

Nat took a swig of coffee and was about to send a biscuit after it, when his phone rang. It was Preston. "Please join me in my office, and bring your coffee and cookies with you. I saw Angela with the tray as I arrived. We need to talk." Preston left no room for excuses.

Nat grabbed his coffee and went across to Preston's office. The ambassador was all smiles. "So, *Agent* Jameson, your show must go on?" It was something between a question and an accusation. "And I must die." Preston heaved a theatrical sigh, and they burst out laughing.

When the laughter had subsided and Preston had joined Nat in the other side chair in front of his desk, Preston was all business. "I assume you have been in touch with Washington?"

"I have, but I don't expect to hear back from them until midday at the earliest."

"Good. Well, I broke the news to Janet, and she seems rather excited about the whole thing. ... Told me that she was looking forward to having an affair with my 'old friend'. ... Said maybe he'll be better in bed and spend a lot more time with her on things she likes to do. Women! They can be so cruel, can't they? Anyway, the important thing is I think she'll play her part, and play it well. That leaves me to do my part; well, I mean, having a convincing heart attack. ... Should be an easier role than Janet's, wouldn't you say?"

Nat nodded. "Yes; dialogue, just action, then inaction. Your most important role will be to remain 'dead'. My life will depend on it." The levity left the room like the air out of a balloon.

"I know," said Preston. "I've been thinking a lot about that in my waking hours." He pulled himself up in the chair, drained his coffee, and placed the empty cup on the desk. "I may not have your acting background or talent," he said, "but once I am physically unrecognisable, which is easy to do, I think I will *be* different just because I *look* different. I have to confess I am quite looking forward to this. I guess there's an actor of sorts in all of us."

"Yes," said Nat. "You'd better be. I depend on it."

Nat's secure phone rang at 12:30. "Hello, Nat. Tom here. Congratulations; you got them hooked. Now, let's see if we can play this thing until we land the big fish. I can tell you the president is very pleased with your news. He looks forward to seeing you when you come over for Ambassador Preston's 'funeral'. He has consulted with the NSC and tasked the CIA to move forward with this operation. The coast is clear." Nat was going to respond, but Tom moved on before he had a chance to get a word in.

"OK. So, this is the drill: The emergency response team will be in place next Wednesday morning. Your 999 call should take place at 10:00 a.m., give or take five minutes on either side. We don't want to leave the emergency tap on longer than absolutely necessary. With the number of people working in your building, someone could have a real emergency. You have a ten-minute window to make the call. Clear so far?" Tom paused momentarily.

"Yes, but I should like to make sure that next Wednesday works for Jim."

"Do that, and get back to me right away if there is a problem. Just to recap: We want you to be in the ambassador's office when he has his 'heart attack', and we want you to make the 999 call, then rush out of your office, and yell for assistance from your and Mr. Preston's secretary. The ambulance will arrive within ten minutes of the call. As I said last time we spoke, there will be a fully qualified doctor and nurse on board, and the doctor will pronounce Preston 'dead on arrival' at St. Mary's, and after the death has been recorded, the ambulance will continue directly to a 'morgue', our morgue, where Preston will be 'prepped' for his 'final journey' across the Atlantic. Any questions?"

Nat thought hard. "Last time we spoke, you said that you wanted me to accompany Preston in the ambulance. Why is that important?"

"For two reasons, Nat. First, if something goes wrong, there will be a need to improvise, and you need to know what happens at every stage of this operation. Second, by being there, you will be able to return to the embassy and report the ambassador's 'death' to the staff and to the media long before you could if you were not there yourself."

"Got it," said Nat.

"Your next step will be to brief the ambassador and run through the plan with him so that he knows what to expect at every stage. I assume he is comfortable with faking the heart attack?"

"He has done a lot of practicing," said Nat. "I am confident he will do his part well."

"OK, Nat. Speak to the ambassador; unless I hear from you to the contrary, it's all systems go next Wednesday. Please get back to me today if we need to change the date."

They said goodbye and hung up. Nat looked at his watch—12:45. Chances were, Preston had gone for lunch. Nat dialled his number, and to his surprise, Preston picked up on the second ring. "Yes, Nat. What's up?"

Nat recounted his conversation with Tom, and Preston did not interrupt once. "So, the question is: does next Wednesday work for you, or do you need more time?"

Preston hesitated. "Well, now. You're asking me if it's convenient for me to die next Wednesday, and I can tell you that it isn't, at least not from Janet's point of view. We are supposed to go for dinner, and then the opera, next Saturday. But next week is also full of events, so there is no convenient time to die in the foreseeable future, according to my calendar." Nat could hear the jest in Preston's voice. "However, since massive, deadly heart attacks rarely fit into anyone's schedule, I think next Wednesday is as good a day as any. The abruptness of it will make it feel more real, somehow."

"OK, Jim. Next Wednesday it is. I'll report back to Langley that we'll be ready." Nat hung up and dialled Langley.

This time Tom answered the phone. "Code name?"

"Endgame."

"Hi, Nat. What's the word? Next Wednesday not good?"

"No. . . I mean, yes; next Wednesday is fine." Nat cleared his throat. His words had sounded feeble and unconvincing. "Preston has a dinner and opera date with his wife for the following Saturday, but, as he put it, heart attacks don't happen when it is most convenient. We are both anxious to get on with it."

"Good," said Tom. "I'll put the wheels in motion. You know what to do. Once the ambassador is 'dead', you just do what you would normally do under those circumstances. Call his widow, notify the secretary of state, who, in turn, will notify the president, who will be pleased to appoint you to the job of chief of mission, no doubt. Your acting talents are about to be put to the test. There is no room for mistakes. One little slip of the tongue could give the game away. That's all for now. Any questions?"

Nat had many questions, but they had to do with future events—like Jim's 'funeral', Jim's and Janet's future together, his own future as the new ambassador, and on and on it went. He was trying to come to grips with the whole operation in his mind, but he knew it would be pointless to try and draw Tom into looking ahead too far. As he had said: "We'll take it one step at a time, Nat."

"No questions, Tom. I assume you'll brief me on next steps as things develop."

"That's right, Nat. That's how we'll do it. One more thing: your home phone is being tapped, so be careful. Good luck." Tom hung up, leaving Nat holding the dead phone in his hand.

He had a sudden feeling of dread. What was he getting himself into? What was he getting a lot of people into? Sonja and the children, Jim and his family, the vice president, the president, all were at risk in some way or another, and Nat was responsible for it. He replaced the phone on its base. His hands were shaking. He took a deep breath and spoke to himself.

"Calm down; calm down. OK. So, it was your idea, but it was endorsed by all the people involved. This is only happening because everybody agreed it was a *good* idea."

The killing of bin Laden had not had the desired effect. It had led to a steady growth in terrorism around the world. Loosely organised, regional terrorist groups had been harnessed into extensions of al-Qaeda, whose own ascendancy had been made possible by the larger-than-life image of its martyred, charismatic leader. Bin Laden had attained mythical status over the years of avoiding capture. It was important to get inside al-Qaeda's headquarters—very important.

Nat was beginning to feel better. What they were embarking on was the right thing to do. It was worth the risk. The image of a terrorist standing in Times Square, with a nuclear device strapped to his chest, came to him from nowhere. It was inconceivable to sit back and wait until that nightmare became reality.

CHAPTER 37

Nat spent the rest of the day dealing with normal embassy business and left the office early. He was anxious to get home to Sonja and the children, and he was anxious to tell Sonja what was happening. It was 5:30 when he arrived home.

He let himself in and was welcomed by Darwin, who rolled over on his back, wagging his tail furiously. Nat bent down and rubbed his chest.

"Hi, Darwin. How's my boy?" Darwin's tail sped up, slapping the tiled floor. "Careful, boy. You'll break that tail of yours." Darwin grinned from ear to ear. Nat stood up and looked around. There was no sign of other life in the house. *Where is everybody?*

"Hello, I'm home!" Nat made an amplifier with his hands. "Anybody home?" No response. He placed his umbrella in the stand next to the door, hung his overcoat in the closet, and headed for the kitchen, closely followed by Darwin—nobody. He ran upstairs to their bedroom—nobody, then up to the children's room—empty. Nat looked at Darwin, who sat patiently at his heels. "So, where is everybody, old boy?" Darwin looked bewildered, stood up, and wagged his tail. Nat was on his way downstairs again when he heard car doors close. He was halfway down the stairs when the front door opened and Tanya and Gregory tumbled in, followed by Sonja. They were carrying white cartons and grocery bags.

"Surprise, surprise, Dad. Guess what we're having for dinner?" Tanya reached him first, and when she reached up to give him a hug, it became obvious what was for dinner.

"Aha." Nat lifted her up and spun around. "Could it be a curry?"

Gregory joined in. "Not curry, Dad. Curries! We've got lamb, chicken, beef, and a mild shrimp for Tanya."

Sonja was taking in the happy scene from the doorway. "We thought it was time you had your favourite food. You deserve it." She came up and gave him a kiss.

"Guess what I think?" said Nat. "I think we *all* deserve it."

The packages were set down on the kitchen table, and Sonja took charge.

"You go and wash the day off, and the children and I will set the table and get the food ready. They have done their homework."

Nat did not need to be asked twice. "Good idea, honey. I've had quite a day." He gave her the look that said: "I'll tell you about it later" and disappeared up the steps.

When he returned, the big oak kitchen table had been transformed. Colourful dishes with steaming curries, one dish with white rice and one with brown rice, poppadoms, nan bread, chopped bananas, and condiments of all kinds sat on top of a bright red tablecloth with a border of black elephants. The napkins were royal blue and the plates black with a simple gold edge. Two brass candlesticks with white candles cast a lively light on the table and on the white lilies in a crystal vase in the centre.

"Wow! That is spectacular!" Nat was impressed. The aroma of all the different dishes and spices filled the room. It was good to be home.

Sonja handed him a scotch and Perrier, and holding her own drink in the other hand, she made a toast. "To our hard-working dad. We love you."

"Yeees, we do!" Tanya squealed.

"Thank you, thank you. I love you too. TGIF. We'll have a whole weekend together." Nat felt their closeness keener than ever.

"Dad, what's TGIF?" Gregory looked up from his lemonade.

Tanya jumped in. "It means 'Thank God it's Friday!' stupid."

"Huh," said Gregory. "There is no 'S' in TGIF." And they all laughed.

The conversation over dinner was lively. Tanya and Greg recounted stories from school. Gregory complained that his math teacher, Mrs. Baxter, was a "terrorist". When asked to explain himself, it turned out that she had made the whole class laugh when he got stuck on a long multiplication at the whiteboard.

"Well, Greg." Sonja put her napkin down. "That was not a very nice thing to do, but it does not make her a terrorist, now does it?" Greg conceded that maybe "terrorist" was not the right description and altered it to Mrs. Baxter being a "math bully."

"I had a run-in with a math bully at college," said Nat. "My teacher was a skinny little man with a hawk nose and thin lips. His eyes were two black slots. You could never quite tell if he was looking at you or not. He liked to make us squirm in front of the blackboard. I had some difficulty with algebra—linear equations to be exact—and he hung me out to dry in front of the class many times, until. . . "

"Until *what*, Dad?" Greg stopped the fork halfway to his mouth.

"Until I got mad and decided to work extra hard at home until I got good at it. And when I did get good at it, do you know what my teacher did? He winked at me! I didn't understand it then, but later I realised that he knew all along that I could do better if I worked harder at it. Why don't you try it and see what happens?"

Gregory looked skeptical "I guess I could try."

"Good," Sonja joined in. "It's an old saying that 'practice makes perfect', and it is as true today as it was then. Try fifteen minutes of extra math every day, and you'll be amazed what will happen."

Greg conceded defeat and nodded before concentrating on the plate of half-eaten curry in front of him.

When they came to the end of the meal, Nat looked at his watch. It was 7:15. "Look; turn on the TV. Dad's on BBC News tonight. We might catch the end of it."

Gregory jumped up and ran over to the TV/family nook in the large bay window off the kitchen. The others followed and sank down in two soft easy chairs and a three-seater couch.

Sonja gave Nat the elbow. "You didn't tell me you were being interviewed."

"Sorry, darling. I forgot."

The screen came to life, and the program had not got to the interview with Nat yet.

"Would anybody like a little ice cream for dessert?" Everybody declined. They were stuffed; besides, watching Dad on TV was more important than cramming down ice cream on top of a full stomach.

Finally, Ms. Tolaram's beautiful face filled the screen as she introduced her segment on the zoo bombing and the eyewitness account of Mr. Nathaniel Jameson, who had been there on the day with his family.

"There he is!" Gregory was half out of his chair.

"You look like a movie star, Dad," said Tanya.

"Hush," said Sonja. "Let's listen."

Nobody said a word until the interview was over. Tanya spoke first. "Wow, Dad. You were great! And you remembered my essay. Mrs. Jennings made me read it out loud in class. I got an A star for it."

"And so you should," said Nat. "You wrote from the heart and sent a very powerful message."

"Well done, darling." Sonja reached for the remote and turned the television off. "You sent a powerful message yourself. You're right; it *is* up to our world leaders to get together and work towards a safer, saner world. But how much control do they really have when it comes to terrorism?"

"More than you think," said Nat. "What is lacking is the *will* to deal with it. In some countries—like Iraq, Afghanistan, and Somalia—violence has become an acceptable part of the political game. The same is true for Palestine. Hamas wants to be seen as a legitimate government because they won in so-called free and fair elections, but they sponsor terrorism as a tool which they think will eventually rid the Middle East of the State of Israel. There is no real will to negotiate. The mindset is wrong. They see no other way to reach their goal. And yet, what they are really doing is playing into the hands of the Israelis, who use terrorist acts as a reason to tighten the stranglehold they have on the Palestinians."

"OK. Enough of that!" Sonja got up from the couch. "Let's clear the table and play crazy eights, shall we?"

Tanya and Gregory jumped out of their chairs, and Gregory ran straight for the cabinet, below the TV, where the cards were kept. They all helped clear the table and stack the dishwasher, and Sonja started the coffeemaker. They sat down at the kitchen table, and Sonja looked at her watch. It was quarter to eight. "We've got forty-five minutes before bedtime. Let's go!" Gregory shuffled and dealt first.

It was almost nine o'clock before Sonja realised what time it was. "Goodness, look at the time! You little monsters." The children laughed, then they all laughed. Gregory put the cards away, while Sonja made two cups of hot chocolate for them to take with them upstairs. "Up you go! . . . Face, hands, then the chocolate, and then the teeth. Dad and I will be up in ten minutes to say good night."

They heard the children's bedroom door close, and Sonja turned to Nat. "So, you've had 'quite a day'. Are you going to tell me about it?" She poured them both another cup of coffee and sat down opposite him at the kitchen table.

Nat lowered his voice to a whisper. "Have we had any gas men, or anybody else, come and check anything in the house?" Nat rolled his eyes and bobbed his head from side to side.

Sonja got the message. "No, we've not had anybody here."

Nat smiled and nodded. "Good; that means we can talk, at least for now, but Tom told me today that our phone is being tapped, so we have to be careful. I spoke to Langley today." Nat hesitated.

"And. . . what? What did they say?" Sonja leaned forward.

Nat took a sip of coffee, searching for the right words. "The day for Jim's heart attack is next Wednesday. Jim has practiced it to perfection." He told Sonja every element of the event, from Preston's performance to his body being flown out for "burial" at the family plot in Colorado.

Sonja listened quietly until he finished. "Poor Janet! It seems to me she's got the toughest acting job of all of you. Standing over your husband's coffin, knowing he's not in it, and grieving with family and friends, who are *really* grieving, is not going to be easy, is it?"

"No, but you know Janet; she's not your average, staid wife of a diplomat. She'll come through with flying colours."

"I would like to talk to her," said Sonja. "Can I give her a call?"

"No, you can't. Remember? Go and see her, or invite her over for lunch or something. Al-Qaeda's intelligence service will keep a close watch on us while this thing unfolds."

Sonja looked around the room. "So, for all we know, somebody could be listening to our conversation right now?"

"I don't think there is any risk of that until they see what happens as a result of the ad. And since we have not had any visits from gas men checking for leaks or any strangers coming into our house for any reason, we are OK for now."

Sonja shook her head. "No, nothing like that, and when I leave the house, I always set the alarm, so nobody could get in while we're away without it going off."

"You've made an important point, though," said Nat. "I'll discuss it with Langley. I'm sure they'll tell us that we must play along and give access to anybody who comes to plant listening devices. After all, we must remember—we've got nothing to hide."

"Are you coming to say good night or not?" A thin voice drifted down from the top floor. Sonja looked at her watch and jumped up. It was almost 9:30.

"We're on our way!"

They tucked the children in and kissed them good night. Gregory was already asleep by the time they closed the door.

When they came down to the landing in front of their own bedroom, and Nat made the turn to continue downstairs, Sonja held him back. "*They've* had a late night." She nodded up the stairs. "Why don't *we* have an early one?" She leaned into him, and he could feel the heat of her breath as she bit his ear. Her eyes seemed a deeper blue, and her mischievous smile got his heart pumping faster. "After all, we've all had quite a day," she added.

He put his arms around her waist, pulled her close, and kissed her. "You're right." His voice was tight as his body responded to the feel and smell of her.

She pushed gently away from him. "But, first, we have to take Darwin out, fill his water bowl, and turn out the lights."

"I'll do it. Darwin! Where are you?" Nat took the steps downstairs two at a time, with Darwin bounding after him. "Let's go, little feller; it's time for a pee."

CHAPTER 38

Preston called Saturday morning, apologising for interrupting Nat on the weekend. He said he would like to have a dress rehearsal for next Wednesday. Nat had received the call on his BlackBerry on the way to Stonehenge with Sonja and the children. Gregory was doing a special project at school on the old stone circle, and Sonja had determined it was a good excuse for them all to go down and take a look.

"Say no more. That's fine. How about tomorrow afternoon at 4 p.m.?" Nat had yesterday's conversation with Sonja about phone-tapping fresh in his mind.

It seemed that Preston understood. "That will be fine. We want to make sure we get everything right for the visit of the Chinese delegation."

"Understood. See you tomorrow afternoon."

Sonja raised her eyebrows. "What was all that about?"

"Pressing embassy business. I'll only be an hour or so tomorrow afternoon." Nat gave her a look that said it all. She knew, at once, it had to do with Operation Endgame.

They had a good time at Stonehenge. Gregory took a lot of pictures and did some sketching. He also got every brochure published on the subject. On the way back, they stopped in

Salisbury and had lunch in The Rose & Crown—a restored thirteenth-century coaching inn—where they had a lovely view of the cathedral across the river. Nat suggested a visit to the cathedral after lunch but was outvoted. The others were keen to get back to London before rush hour set in. Nat's argument—that most of the traffic would be coming *out* of London—fell on deaf ears. As it was, the return trip took two and a half hours. An accident on the M25 slowed the traffic down to a crawl for the best part of an hour.

"Aren't you glad we didn't go to see the cathedral, Dad?" Gregory poked his head between the front seats.

Preston was already in his office when Nat arrived promptly at 4:00 p.m. the next day.

He looked up when Nat entered. "Aha; here comes the vicious murderer." His voice was higher than normal.

"That's me, sir. I have come to relieve you of all worldly worries." Nat hunched over in the attitude of the Grim Reaper.

They decided that Preston's attack would come when he was standing holding a cup of coffee—the coffee that contained the substance which brought on the "heart attack" in the first place. They practiced the whole routine, from Nat entering Preston's office to Nat calling the secretaries for help. It all seemed quite straightforward. Once in the ambulance, he could relax until they got to St. Mary's Hospital, where it would be the responsibility of the doctor, in the ambulance, to ensure that they accepted his "dead on arrival" certification.

Preston had a question which Nat could not answer: When would he be able to see his wife again? Nat promised to bring this up with Tom in the morning.

It was 11:30 Monday morning when Nat's secure phone rang.

"Hello, Nat."

"Tom."

"Glad to hear you and the ambassador have had some trial runs for Wednesday. The answer to your question is that Mr. Preston will not be able to see his wife until he can be introduced as the old, long-lost friend. Remember the old friend did not show up at the funeral. The best place for that to happen will be outside the US, away from family and friends; therefore, we suggest that Mrs. Preston decides to get away from it and goes over to her house in France. The sooner she goes, the sooner Mr. Preston can see her again."

Nat was pleased to hear that Langley had accepted Preston's own ideas as to how to continue life after his "death". It would make it easier for everybody, and it was logical under the circumstances.

Nat asked if there were any further instructions, for himself, for Wednesday, but Tom told him that this was all for now. "You will be advised of the date of the funeral through the normal diplomatic channels, and you will obviously attend. Once you're in Washington, we'll go through the next steps. Call me when you get back to the embassy on Wednesday. We will receive a report from one of our other field agents on the emergency response team, but we also want to hear your version, and assessment, of the event. Have a good day."

Nat went back to Preston's office and gave him the answer to his question.

Preston was visibly relieved. "Great! I'll talk to Janet tonight. The house in France, and her painting, have always been Janet's refuge when she needed time to regroup. It will come as no surprise to anybody that she wants to have some time by herself when I'm gone. This is going to work just fine. Just fine." Nat could hear the excitement in his voice.

Monday and Tuesday were the longest days Nat could remember since he was in prep school waiting for the summer holidays, when one day had seemed like a week, and one week like a month. Preston had spoken to his wife, and Janet had said that she would be in France within two weeks of the funeral, ready to receive the surprise call from their old friend, who was living in Paris and had come across the death notice in the *Washington Post*, all by chance.

Nat had spent Tuesday evening, after the children had gone to bed, going through the overall plan for Operation Endgame again, with Sonja, who had listened intently.

CHAPTER 39

Nat got little sleep on Tuesday night. The events of the next day, and beyond, kept spinning around in his head. He went over hundreds of what-if scenarios:

What if the head of ER at St. Mary's didn't accept the ambulance doctor's dead-on-arrival determination? That would stop the whole plot dead in its tracks right there.

What if al-Qaeda got cold feet for some reason and pulled out after the first "murder"?

Assuming they got past the second murder, what if al-Qaeda's leaders still refused to meet with him? What if they offered him a ludicrous amount of money for him to kill the president; how should he respond?

What if? . . . What if? . . . What if?

He felt like he had just gone to sleep when the alarm went off at seven o'clock. He stopped it quickly, so as not to wake Sonja, only to discover, when he looked, that she was standing in the bedroom door.

"Good morning, handsome. Rise and shine! Today is the day that God made." She came over and kissed him lightly on the cheek. "I am making you bacon and eggs for breakfast; you need something solid in your stomach to get through this day. See you downstairs."

He showered, shaved, and put on his favourite herringbone navy blue and dark grey suit over a pale blue shirt, finishing up with a red and dark blue striped tie. He looked at the end result in the full-length mirror and thought *Dressed to kill*. He felt strangely calm. Perhaps it was the lack of sleep that had dulled his senses? He hoped not. This was the day when he needed to have his wits about him.

When he got down to the kitchen, the smell of fried bacon met him in the doorway. The table was set, and Sonja was preparing the eggs and the toast. He poured himself a cup of coffee and drank most of it in two long gulps. He needed to perk up. The *Daily Telegraph* was lying on the table next to his plate. A big fat headline announced that a car bomb had exploded in central Kabul, outside police headquarters. Reading on, it was reported that twenty passers-by and four policemen, who were in the entrance area when the bomb went off, had been killed. Another thirty people were seriously injured. It was thought that the attack was a joint effort of the Taliban and al-Qaeda. It was Nat's theory that the resurgence of the Taliban, in Afghanistan, was made possible by logistical and financial support from al-Qaeda, combined with income from the roaring drug trade, to which the Afghan government seemed to turn a blind eye.

Attempts to draw the Taliban into the political process had failed, for obvious reasons. Neither the Taliban, nor al-Qaeda, had any interest in being part of any democratic process; on the contrary, the Taliban's recapture of the country had created a safe haven for every terrorist faction in the world.

Sonja brought their breakfasts to the table. She had not allowed herself a treat of bacon and eggs but stuck with her alternate breakfast of half a grapefruit followed by Muesli and skim milk.

"I guess you don't have any idea when you'll be home tonight?" She looked up from cutting the grapefruit.

Nat put the paper down. "It shouldn't be very late. Preston's heart attack is scheduled for 10 a.m. If all goes well, I should be back in the office before noon. Obviously, there will be a lot of phone calls to make—local and overseas—but I don't see that going into the evening hours. Obviously, one of those calls will be to you, and you will have to tell the children when you pick them up from school."

"Yes, we're *all* becoming actors—*lying* actors. It is not a good feeling."

"I know," said Nat, "but the whole operation depends on it. We have to lie, and do it well."

They had to change the topic when the children appeared, ready for breakfast. Nat left early, while they were still eating, and arrived at the embassy shortly after eight fifteen.

The security guard gave him a friendly nod. "Good morning, Mr. Jameson. Have a nice day."

"Thank you, Walter; you too." *If you only knew what a day we'll have*, Nat thought. He looked at his reflection in the elevator mirror; his lack of sleep showed. Once in his office, he turned his computer on and scanned through his emails which were always filtered by Angela so that he only received the ones she could not deal with without his input. He trusted her judgment on this completely. One of the emails on his screen was from the Russian Embassy, directed to the US ambassador but copied to Nat by Preston himself. When he read it, Nat realised why Preston had copied it to him.

The ambassador of the Russian Federation, Mr. Yury Fedorov, invites the US ambassador to the Court of St. James to meet with him on Friday the 21st of October, at 12 noon, to discuss the matter of the nuclear warhead stolen from Russia and now, allegedly, in the hands of individuals in Iran, and other matters of mutual interest and concern. A light lunch will be served.

There was no signature, but it was clear that the email was sent by Mr. Fedorov's PA. Preston would not be able to keep his appointment with the Russian ambassador; although he had accepted the invitation, he knew that he would be "dead" and unable to attend, and Nat would be going in his place.

It suddenly struck Nat that he was taking on a huge task. Combining the job of ambassador with undercover agent attempting to infiltrate al-Qaeda was a daunting task. *But,* thought Nat, *I was the crazy guy who volunteered for it.* He would have to rely, heavily, on his successor, Tony Burville, but he was not at all sure that Tony was the kind of man that he could comfortably delegate ambassadorial duties to.

Nat had finished dealing with his emails when there was a knock on his door, and Preston entered, looking like he also could have done with more sleep the night before. He closed the door behind him.

"Morning, Nat. Just a quick word before the girls come." Preston stood in front of Nat's desk, and Nat gestured for him to have a seat, but Preston declined. "You look like I feel," he said. "Did you get any sleep last night?"

"Not much."

"Listen." Preston's voice sounded tense. "I am supposed to attend a luncheon hosted by the mayor of London today. I was wondering if, to set the scene, I should tell Clara, when she comes in, that I didn't sleep well last night and that I feel tired and would she please send my apologies."

Nat thought for a moment. "Yes, I think that is a very good idea. When the news comes out about your demise, the mayor's guests will nod, knowingly, and say, 'No wonder he didn't come, he obviously must have been feeling pretty awful'."

"Good," said Preston. "I thought you'd like it. I'll call Angela about quarter to ten and ask if she could let you know I'd appreciate seeing you on an urgent matter, immediately, and you'll come over; we'll get our coffees and get on with the show." Preston managed a strained smile.

"Very good, Jim. We may not get an Oscar for our performance today, but if it helps us to dismantle al-Qaeda, I'll be happy."

That broke the tension. They both had a good laugh.

Preston left, and Nat sat at his desk feeling nervous and excited. He took a few deep breaths, and his eyes wandered to the framed picture on his desk. Smiling back at him were Sonja, Tanya, and Gregory in Stetson hats, jeans, and riding boots. The picture had been taken last summer when they spent ten days at a dude ranch in Colorado. It had been a great vacation. Sonja was a very capable rider, and Tanya was not far behind, and what Nat and Gregory lacked in technical skills, they made up for in sheer bravado and guts.

The picture was taken at a cookout in the woods after a three-hour ride through spectacular scenery. Gregory's horse had been spooked by a rattlesnake on the way and had reared up. Miraculously, he had managed to stay in the saddle, and one of the wranglers had grabbed the reins and stopped the horse from taking off. Nat remembered how proud he had been at his son's calm and brave reaction to the incident. Gregory had basked in the praise from everybody, and it showed in the picture that he was feeling pretty good about himself. *I am a lucky man*, Nat thought, as he continued to study the photograph.

He was awakened from his reverie by Angela's call, wishing him good morning and asking if she could bring him a cup of coffee. He declined the coffee but asked if she could bring him a tall glass of ice water. His throat felt tight and parched. She appeared in less than a minute with his water and with two letters for him to sign. Nat looked at his watch. It was 9:15. Nat wondered if Preston had called his secretary to cancel the luncheon appointment at City Hall.

To his surprise it was Angela who provided the answer. "Oh, by the way," she said, "Mr. Preston asked me to send his apologies to the mayor. He is not feeling so well this morning—Mr. Preston, that is. . . . Didn't get much sleep last night, he said. Clara called in sick this morning too. Maybe there's a bug going around?"

"Let's hope not," said Nat. "We don't have time to get sick, do we?" He signed the letters and handed them back to her.

"No, sir. Certainly not." She smiled and headed for the door.

"Angela." She stopped in the doorway and turned around. "I was just joking. I don't want you to come to work if you're sick, ever. Understood?"

She nodded. "Yes, of course, sir." She closed the door softly behind her, and he could hear her footsteps as she walked back to her desk.

He had been less than three months at the embassy when he realised that Angela Pemberton was the best secretary he had ever had. She was fast and accurate when it came to typing a letter. She was good at shorthand, although he hardly ever asked her to do any, but, most important of all, she understood embassy business and could think for herself. Nat knew he would miss her when he took over as ambassador, and Clara would be his new assistant. Not that Clara wasn't good at her job; she was, but she just didn't have Angela's energy and can-do approach. Maybe the twenty-year age difference had something to do with it. Maybe that age difference, and Angela's good looks, had something to do with Nat knowing he would miss her. Nat preferred to think not. After all, he was a happily married man, and nobody could beat Sonja in the good-looks department.

Nat opened a file which he assumed Preston had left on his desk. It was a CIA report on the nuclear warhead stolen from Russia, and now, supposedly, in Iranian hands. He would need to know all he could about it before he met with the Russian ambassador. Nat did his best to focus on the material in front of him, but his mind kept drifting to what was going to happen in Preston's office. He kept looking at his watch every five minutes. At twenty minutes to ten, Nat put the file away and sat at his desk looking at the telephone, waiting for it to ring. Preston had said he would call Angela at quarter to ten, asking for Nat to join him in his office.

The minutes crawled along. Nat glanced out his window. The sky was a leaden grey, and there was a light drizzle of rain. The scene was like something out of a black-and-white movie.

The first ring on his phone gave him a jolt, and he picked up on the second. "Yes, Angela?"

"Mr. Preston would like to see you in his office. He says it is urgent."

"I'm on my way." Nat rose slowly from his desk. He looked at the picture of his family again. Their eyes seemed to follow him as he moved. *They must have looked straight into the lens when the picture was taken,* Nat thought.

He waved to Angela on his way across to Preston's office. He knocked on the door and heard Preston invite him to enter. Preston was sitting behind his desk looking very pale. *Looking just like a man who is about to have a heart attack?* Nat wondered. He closed the door and headed towards Preston's desk, but Preston stood up and pointed to his lounge area.

"Let's sit over there. Would you like a cup of coffee, Nathaniel Jameson?" Preston was grinning from ear to ear.

"You bet, Mr. Ambassador; I'd love a cup." Nat smiled back.

The play had commenced. Preston went over to his coffee machine and started to make their coffees. "I have an urgent matter to discuss with you," he said over his shoulder.

"So," Nat said. "Sir, what is it?"

Preston turned around with two cups of coffee in his hands. He lowered his voice to a conspiratorial level. "It is the matter of my untimely death."

Nat could tell by the mischief in his eyes that Preston was enjoying himself. "Untimely, sir? I thought we had agreed on ten o'clock?"

Preston had to control himself not to burst out laughing. "So we did; so we did." He looked at his watch and then at Nat. He handed Nat his coffee and gestured him to take a seat.

Preston remained standing and took a sip of coffee. "I must tell you," he said, "I am not feeling so good this morning. I have excused myself from the mayor's luncheon this afternoon." He looked at his watch again.

Nat looked at his. It was five minutes to ten. They looked at each other.

"Are you ready?" Preston's light-hearted tone was gone. All of a sudden, he was all business.

Nat looked at him, stood up, and extended his hand. "OK, Jim. I'm ready. Break a leg! . . . as they say in the theatre world." They shook hands. "Be careful when you fall so you don't break anything," Nat added, as he sat down again.

Preston took a few steps back towards his desk, but before he could reach it, he stopped dead and let out a loud groan. He dropped his coffee, and one hand went to his chest and the other to his throat. He gasped for air as he spun around towards Nat, one hand outstretched, the other clawing at his chest, as if he was trying to extract the pain.

"Aaah, aaah. Oh my God. Nat, help me!" His legs buckled, and he fell forward, face down on the carpet.

If Nat had not known better, he would have been certain that he was witnessing a man having a massive heart attack. Nat jumped up and ran over to Preston, who was moving slowly and groaning in pain. He bent down and started to turn Preston over when Preston wheezed under his breath, "Leave that for when you have called 999 and shouted for help!" He went back to groaning as Nat headed for Preston's desk. He dialled and was through on the second ring.

Nat did not have to pretend to sound agitated. "This is Nathaniel Jameson at the US Embassy in London. I am here in a meeting with the ambassador, and it seems to me that he is having a heart attack."

There was a moment's pause, then, "An ambulance is on its way. Loosen any restrictive clothing, but do not move him. Help will be there within ten minutes."

Nat hung up and ran to the door and tore it open. "Angela. Angela, come quickly; Jim's having a heart attack!" Angela came running in immediately. Nat was bent down over Preston. "Help me loosen his tie and open his shirt."

"Have you called 999?" Angela stared at Nat, wide-eyed.

"Yes. Yes, I have. Help me turn him over."

They got Preston over on his back. His eyes were closed, and his breathing was shallow and strained. A deep moan would halt the shallow breathing momentarily. Angela undid his tie and unbuttoned his shirt, which was brown with coffee stain. The cup and saucer were lying on the floor next to Preston's head. Nat removed his shoes.

Angela looked up at Nat, shaking her head. There were tears in her eyes. "Poor Mr. Preston! Why him? He looks like such a healthy and fit man. It doesn't seem possible that he should be having a heart attack."

Nat shook his head also. "No, you're right, but looks can be deceiving." They were both looking down at the man on the floor. He was still now but breathing in short, shallow gasps.

"Where *are* they?" Angela looked at Nat; tears were streaming down her face.

"They'll be here soon, Angela." Nat pulled her up. "Go to your desk, and call down to security and explain what has happened. I'll stay with Preston."

She disappeared, and Nat used the opportunity to bend down and whisper in Preston's ear. "My God, Jim, you had *me* going there for a while. Are you OK?"

Preston opened one eye. "Yeah, I'm OK, except for the coffee burning my chest. The chest pain is real enough." Suddenly they could hear a siren in the distance.

Nat looked at Preston's chest. It was deep red where the coffee had scalded his skin. "My God, Jim; I'm sorry. The coffee was my idea."

"Never mind," Preston whispered the words. "It sure makes the whole thing seem more real."

"Hush, Angela's coming back."

Preston closed his eyes and resumed the strained breathing and groaning. Nat stood up as she entered the room.

"The ambulance crew is on its way up." She was wide-eyed and out of breath herself, as if she had been running the stairs. She left the door open and ran back out to the reception area towards the elevators as the elevator doors opened, discharging the emergency crew of four people—two orderlies, one carrying a stretcher and a collapsible trolley, and the other what looked like a suitcase, and a dark-haired, Japanese-looking nurse, also carrying a smaller case. Last came the doctor, who carried nothing except the stethoscope hanging around his neck. Embassy staff were congregating outside the door, but the doctor turned and asked them to go back to their desks.

He moved quickly to the front and knelt down next to Preston, felt his pulse, and placed the stethoscope to his chest. He listened, just for a couple of seconds, before turning around to the nurse who had opened the case she was carrying and brought out a syringe and needle which she was getting ready. The doctor nodded in approval, and she handed it to him.

He rolled up Preston's left sleeve, felt for a blood vessel, and gave Preston an injection. Preston let out a moan which was no different from the others he had been producing, but Nat thought this might have been more real than the others. The orderly with the large case had produced a machine with an array of dials and proceeded to apply patches to Preston's chest.

The other orderly was putting an oxygen mask over Preston's face and placed the cylinder on the floor next to his shoulder. The first orderly finished placing the patches on Preston's chest and brought wires back to the machine with all the dials. The connections were made, and the doctor turned the machine on, which Nat assumed must be a heart monitor, and looked at the display for a few seconds. He stood up. "OK, let's move him onto the trolley." He then turned to Nat. "This man has suffered a massive heart attack. There is considerable damage to the heart muscle. Who is he?"

"The US ambassador, James Preston." Nat looked down at Preston. "How bad is it, doctor?"

"He is in critical condition. We will be taking him to St. Mary's, where he will receive the best care available."

Angela let out a pained cry and quickly covered her mouth to stifle a repeat. The orderlies had placed Preston on the stretcher, which they now lifted up on the trolley. The oxygen canister was placed between Preston's legs, and the nurse carried the heart monitor.

"Let's go!"

"Doctor!" Nat followed them out. "Could I come with you? I'm Nat Jameson, the deputy ambassador and a close friend of the ambassador."

The doctor pretended to hesitate. "Certainly. Carry this." He handed the medical case to Nat, and they carried on towards the elevators, where Angela was already standing, holding the doors open.

Once the doors closed behind them, the doctor patted Preston on the arm. "Sorry about the needle, Mr. Ambassador. It was just a little blood serum. You did a great job."

Preston lifted his head and opened his eyes. “Thanks. I’ve had a lot of practice.”

“My name is Dr. Bradley—Greg Bradley.” He shook hands with Preston and Nat. “And this is Nurse Chieko, Patrick, and Bill. I’ll fill you in on what happens next once we’re in the ambulance.”

The elevator came to a halt, and Preston laid his head back on the gurney and closed his eyes. The doors opened and they moved out into the entrance lobby. People stopped and stared at them. The security guard shook his head, his sad eyes following them as they moved through the exit doors to the ambulance waiting outside. *Angela must have told him who the ambulance was for*, Nat thought. Bill and Patrick placed the stretcher onto its track and slid it into place, followed by Chieko and Dr. Bradley, who beckoned Nat to join them in the back. Once he was in, Patrick closed the doors behind them and climbed in next to the driver and Bill in the front. They took off, siren wailing.

“OK, that went well.” Dr. Bradley gave them a reassuring smile. “But we don’t have time to rest on our laurels.” He looked at Preston, who had removed the oxygen mask and was propped up on one elbow on the stretcher. “Your last bit of acting today, Mr. Ambassador, will be for you to play dead. You will be ably assisted by the heart monitor which will show no blips when we arrive at St. Mary’s. You will have suffered cardiac arrest on the way. We have tried to revive you with the defibrillator but without success. When we arrive at St. Mary’s, I will certify that you were dead on arrival, and Nat, you, as the deputy ambassador, will insist that the body be taken, without delay, to a mortuary where the deceased will be prepared for immediate transport back to the US for the autopsy to be carried out in Washington. You will need to be very forceful about that." He looked at Nat. "In fact, you cannot take no for an answer. The ambassador must remain in the ambulance, or the game is up."

The ambulance wound its way through the congested roads of London. Progress, at times, was slow, when vehicles in front had no way to move aside and let them pass. This, as Dr. Bradley pointed out, was very much to their advantage, as the longer it took to get to the hospital the more real the "dead on arrival" scenario would seem.

"Please, Chieko; get the defibrillator out, and attach it to Mr. Preston's chest. I'll adjust the heart monitor." He leaned forward and pressed something on the back of the monitor. "Now it will look as if your heart is not beating even though it is," he said. "This little baby has been fixed to do that." He patted the monitor lightly and gave Preston a reassuring smile.

Nat could see the road ahead, looking through a small window behind the driver's seat. They had Hyde Park on the left, and traffic was flowing smoothly but slowly. Nat realised that they were traveling on Park Lane, heading towards Marble Arch, where, presumably, they would head left up Edgeware Road and left again on Praed Street, to St. Mary's. Nat figured at this speed, they would arrive in about ten minutes, which meant the whole trip would take no more than twenty minutes. Was that enough time to give up on a stopped heart? As they approached Marble Arch, traffic slowed to a crawl and then to a standstill. They were trapped by cars on all sides, siren blaring, but nobody had space to move out of the way.

Dr. Bradley gave them all a big smile. "Just what the doctor ordered," he said, looking at his watch.

After five minutes, the traffic started to inch forward, space opened to their left, and the driver swung the ambulance across and onto the sidewalk, where they were met by pedestrians, a few cyclists, and one young man on roller skates. They all looked stunned by the sight of the ambulance coming towards them but managed to get out of the way. The driver was moving cautiously but still passing the cars in the street. When they got to Marble Arch, the cause of the traffic cork became clear—a van had collided with a double-decker bus on the circle. Three policemen were directing traffic, and, when they saw the ambulance approaching on the sidewalk, they stopped the other traffic so that a clear route was created around the circle. They rejoined the street at the junction and continued around and up Edgware Road.

"All right," said Dr. Bradley, "let's get ready for arrival at St. Mary's. Chieko, make sure the monitor is in full view when the doors open. I'll be by the defibrillator, which will be off. We tried our best, but we could not restart his heart." He looked at Nat. "You and I will get out. I'll cover the medical side, and you'll insist that, as the ambassador is dead, you want him to be taken directly to the undertakers to be prepared for transport across the ocean so that the postmortem can be carried out in the US. Patrick and Bill will remain where they are, with the driver. With any luck, we'll be out of there in ten minutes, once the paperwork is in order. Are we all clear?"

They all nodded.

When they reached St. Mary's there was pandemonium at the emergency entrance. Patients were being removed from two ambulances, which must have arrived just minutes earlier. A doctor was supervising the efforts of half a dozen orderlies and nurses, who were pushing four trolleys through the emergency entrance doors. The doctor looked up as they pulled in and stopped. His face showed the strain of the morning's activities at the ER. *Not another one!* Bill jumped out and opened the back doors.

The doctor came running. "Another collision victim?"

Dr. Bradley jumped out. "No, no. Massive heart attack—cardiac arrest—resuscitation unsuccessful."

"Oh." The ER doctor seemed almost relieved. "We're snowed under with victims from the crash down the road."

Dr. Bradley nodded. "I can imagine. We got caught up in it on the way here. . . . Cost us at least twenty minutes; not that it would have made any difference. Our patient went into cardiac arrest as we left the embassy. We have been trying to revive him for the past twenty minutes."

"Embassy?" The ER doctor raised his eyebrows.

"Our patient is—was—the US ambassador here in London." Dr. Bradley turned around to Nat, who had stepped out and stood next to them. "This is the deputy ambassador, Mr. Nathaniel Jameson, and I am Dr. Bradley, in-house physician at the embassy."

"I'm Dr. Roberts, head of ER." He cast a look over his shoulder. "I must get in there. Bring your patient inside, and we'll deal with the formalities when I get a chance."

Dr. Bradley shot Nat a quick glance that said: *Nat, you're on.*

Nat cleared his throat. "Dr. Roberts, I would prefer that we take Mr. Preston directly to be prepared for sending back to Washington. We want the postmortem to be carried out there. I understand, from Dr. Bradley, that there is no chance that my boss and friend can be revived and that Dr. Bradley is prepared to certify that Ambassador Preston was dead on arrival. I trust this will be in order?"

Dr. Roberts hesitated, looked at Nat, then at Dr. Bradley and then back over his shoulder, towards the ER, where his presence was urgently needed. "Yes," he said. "Come with me. I'll have a nurse escort you to the admin office, where you'll find the necessary forms. Thank you." He shook Dr. Bradley's hand and turned and fell into a half-jog back inside, with Nat and Dr. Bradley following closely behind.

Dr. Roberts flagged a nurse down, on his way, and asked her to take them to the admin office. "I'll call and tell them I've agreed to you doing this. It's not normal procedure, as you know." He waved and disappeared into the emergency room.

Nat and Dr. Bradley reappeared through the emergency entrance doors fifteen minutes later. Nat breathed a sigh of relief. Everything had gone smoothly with the paperwork. Preston was in St. Mary's records as *Dead on Arrival.*

They climbed back on board the ambulance and drove off. As soon as they had left the hospital precinct, Preston sat up with a big grin, and they all laughed and applauded themselves for a job well done. The tension, which had been with them all morning, had evaporated, and they felt like they should be celebrating. It was agreed that Preston had been the star performer.

"I hope I never have a real heart attack," he said. "A fake one was bad enough. Anything in this truck for burned skin?"

Chieko opened a container full of bandages, bottles, and tubes, all neatly arranged in compartments. She brought out a bottle and asked Preston to remove his shirt. She studied the burn. "It is a superficial burn—nothing serious—but quite painful because of all the nerve endings in the surface layer of your skin." She asked him to lie down and applied a layer of white cream over the burn, then placed a large gauze bandage over the cream and fastened it all with medical tape around the edges.

"Ahh," said Preston, who sank back on the gurney. "That feels much better."

"Good," said Nat. "A dead man should not have to be in pain."

Everybody had a good laugh. Nat turned to Dr. Bradley. "Am I right in assuming that you are in charge of getting Mr. Preston back to the US?"

"Not quite. We'll take him to a safe house, just outside London, where he will be transformed into a new person with a new passport. He will be flown to Andrews Air Force Base. My involvement ends at the safe house."

Nat looked at Preston, who was sitting up again. "What happens when I get to the States?"

"You will go to another safe house, where the plans for your, shall we say, afterlife, will be worked out. I believe your own suggestions for this are the basis for what will happen."

"Good," said Preston. "My wife is looking forward to it, and so am I. Retirement, here I come."

Dr. Bradley knocked on the window to get the driver's attention and signalled him to pull over and stop. He looked at Nat. "There's a taxi stand around the corner. You need to get back to the office with the sad news and to pick up the pieces, doing both yours and the ambassador's jobs and working for us at the same time. You've got your work cut out for you. Good luck!" Dr. Bradley shook Nat's hand.

Preston gave Nat a serious look. "He's right, Nat. I wouldn't like to have your job description right now." He held his hand out. “Anyway, my friend, I wish you all the best. Play it safe. I hope to see you in France some time. I’m going to miss you.”

Nat could feel a lump in his throat. “Thank you, Jim, and thank you for going along with this. Without your support this would not be happening.”

“Right,” said Preston. “I’ve got the easy part from here. Early retirement; who would have thought?” They shook hands as Bill opened the door to let Nat out.

CHAPTER 40

It was noon when Nat arrived back at the embassy. Walter, the security guard, stood up as Nat entered the lobby; he could tell by looking at Nat that the news was bad, but he asked anyway and became the first person to receive the sad news of the ambassador's death.

When Nat stepped off the elevator, Angela looked up apprehensively. Nat shook his head, and tears welled up in her eyes, and she started to cry softly. "Oh, no." She sobbed. "He was such a fine man—always took the time to say a kind word." She looked around the room. "This place won't be the same without him."

"I know, Angela." He touched her shoulder and offered her his handkerchief, which she gratefully accepted, and blew her nose. "Angela, I need to go and see Mrs. Preston. I need for you to send an email around the embassy with the sad news, and please call our press liaison officer and ask him to inform Washington, right away, and the local media two hours from now, after I have spoken to Janet."

Angela collected herself, wiped her eyes with the back of her hand, and reached for the telephone on her desk. There was work to be done.

It was 12:30 when Nat rang the doorbell at Winfield House. He rang three times before the massive door opened. "Good afternoon, Harold."

The old butler squinted over his glasses. "Oh… Mr. Jameson… Nice to see you."

"Is Mrs. Preston at home?"

"Yes, sir; she is." Harold's temple creased in a frown. An unannounced visit by the deputy ambassador, midday, was unprecedented, and Harold had been around long enough to feel that it boded no good. He stepped back, to let Nat enter. "She's upstairs in her study. I will call her." He walked over to an ornate side table and dialled. "Sorry to disturb you, Mrs. Preston, but I have Mr. Jameson here in the lobby. He would like to have a word with you." He paused. "Would you like me to show him to the library?" Harold cast Nat a worried look. "Very well, ma'am; I'll send him up." Nat removed his overcoat and handed it to Harold.

"Mrs. Preston's study is up the stairs and to the left—second door on the right." Nat climbed the grand stairs slowly, heavy with the burden of his message, knowing that Harold would be watching his ascent. He turned left at the top of the stair and saw Mrs. Preston standing in the doorway to her study, holding the door open.

"Good afternoon, Nat. Please come in." She closed the door behind them, took his arm, and led him to a Louis XVI settee, covered in an oriental silk fabric. She took a similar seat opposite. She gave him a wink and a faint smile. "I guess coming here at this hour you are not the bearer of good news?" She spoke with a raised voice and cast a glance back towards the door.

Nat took the hint and played along. "I am afraid not, Mrs. Preston." Nat raised his volume to match. "I am here on the saddest of errands. I am sorry to have to tell you that your husband died from a heart attack this morning. He was rushed to hospital but died in the ambulance on the way. It was cardiac arrest, and efforts to revive him were unsuccessful, I'm afraid. . . "

Mrs. Preston leaned forward and lowered her voice. "I know Harold does not listen at keyholes, but we have two maids who I'm not so sure about. So, it all went well?"

"Very well. Jim did an outstanding job. He was so good that when he was lying on the floor in a pool of coffee, I had to ask him if he was all right, which he confirmed, except for a scalding on the chest from the coffee."

Mrs. Preston smiled. "Good, old Jim. He never does anything by halves. I'm glad I didn't see it. I probably would have had a *real* heart attack. I would offer you a cup of tea and a sandwich, but I'm sure a woman receiving the news I've just received would not be in any shape to even think of making such an offer." She pulled out a handkerchief and wiped her eyes. Nat could see them moisten. "You see, I'm prepared." She showed him the handkerchief, inside of which she held a slice of onion. She wiped her eyes again, and tears started to form in her eyes.

Nat smiled. "Brilliant, Mrs. Preston. That is your part from now, to play the grieving widow and to do everything which you would do if Mr. Preston really *was* dead."

"I know," she said. "Some of that will be easy; some of it will not, like calling my sons, for example, which I will do as soon as you have left. Where is Jim now?"

"Jim is at a safe house here in London as we speak, where they will change his identity and give him a new passport. He will be flown back to the US, to another safe house there, where he will remain until he can join up with you in France."

"I intend to go to France soon after the funeral." Mrs. Preston's eyes were red, and a tear was working its way down her left cheek. "I should be making the funeral arrangements, but I imagine that your people may have other plans?"

Nat shook his head. "I don't know how that's going to be handled, but I'll try to find out before the day is out."

"If we had been home in Colorado, I would be calling our local undertaker, and he would take care of everything." Mrs. Preston looked so forlorn that Nat had to remind himself that Jim was alive and well.

"This is different," said Nat. "Your husband *was*—we have to get used to saying it—a US ambassador, and therefore, it is reasonable to expect that the postmortem would be carried out in Washington and that your husband would be prepared for the funeral by a mortician in Washington before being sent for burial to Colorado. That is to say, *somebody* will be prepared and sent to Colorado to be buried. I will find out what the plan is when I speak to Langley this afternoon, and I'll call you when I have the answers."

"OK, Nat; I will let you go." She stood up, and Nat followed. "I know you have a lot to get on with. I have to tell you: when Jim first told me about your idea, I really thought you had lost your mind, but the more we talked about it, the more I came around to thinking that it was worth a go. How on earth did you come up with this idea?"

"I really don't know where it came from, Mrs. Preston; I just woke up with it one morning. It came from nowhere."

Mrs. Preston gave him a searching look. "You may have received your inspiration from a higher authority. Have you considered that?"

"It had occurred to me, but I'm not the person of obvious choice, if that's where it came from." Mrs. Preston touched his arm as they walked towards the door.

She looked up at him and gave his arm a squeeze. "Well, Nat, I wouldn't be so sure. You know, He works in mysterious ways."

Nat called Sonja on the way back to the office and gave her the bad news. She responded appropriately by getting into her part right away, knowing that someone was probably listening in on the conversation.

"Oh, my God! Poor Jim, and poor Janet. She must be devastated."

"I just came from there. She is a brave soul. After the initial shock, her main concern was for her children and how to tell them."

"I will go over and see her tomorrow," said Sonja. "She must feel very alone in that big house."

"I'm sure she'd appreciate that," said Nat and hung up after promising to come home as early as possible.

Nat could see George's sad eyes watching him in the rear-view mirror, while he maneuvered the Bentley through the heavy London traffic. Preston's driver had reacted very badly to the news of the ambassador's death, and Nat had spent the time, on the way to Winfield House, trying to console him.

It struck Nat that Preston would have the advantage of learning what people thought about him after he was "dead". And in his case, it would be mostly good news because Jim was a sincere, caring, fun-loving man. What was there not to like?

Back at the embassy, as the news of Preston's death had spread, a sombre mood had descended over the place. This was to be expected, but it was clear from people's reactions that Preston was held in higher esteem than Nat would have thought any boss in any large company would normally be held. It was not going to be easy to fill his shoes.

Angela had ordered him a light salad lunch, and he thanked her for her thoughtfulness but told her he was not hungry. She gave him some papers to sign, all, thankfully, routine. And when she left, he immediately dialled Langley.

Tom picked up after the second ring. "Hi Nat. Congratulations! I understand everything went well this morning. We've had a report from Dr. Bradley. Tell me how it looks from your end."

Nat gave Tom his account of the day's events, including his visit to Mrs. Preston.

"I hope to meet her one day," said Tom. "She must be quite a lady."

"She sure is. I don't think they come any better."

"Except for your *own* wife, perhaps?"

Nat mulled it over. "Yes, except for Sonja."

"I hope to meet you all one day," said Tom. "We'll all have a hell of a party if this operation succeeds."

"Tom, Mrs. Preston is anxious to know what the arrangements will be for the funeral. Can you tell me how that is going to be worked out?"

"OK, Nat. Let's take it from where things are right now. Preston is at a safe house in London, where his appearance will be changed by relatively simple means. His hair and eyes will change colour, and he will receive an artificial beard until he can grow a real one. He will fly back to Washington on the same plane that will bring his 'body' in a casket. The body is real and made up to look, as closely as possible, like Mr. Preston. We will be flying him out the day after tomorrow. Mr. Preston's new documents will show that he is a UK embassy functionary, tasked with bringing the ambassador's body home. Mr. Preston's looks and identity are temporary only and will change again before he leaves to eventually join his wife in France. Once Mr. Preston's 'body' is back on US soil, we want Mrs. Preston to call this number." Tom reeled off a Washington phone number. "And ask for Mr. Swainson, and we'll take it from there. It is our understanding that the Prestons have a family plot at their estate in Fort Collins. We would appreciate it if you would communicate this to Mrs. Preston." Tom did not wait for an answer. "Meanwhile, *Mr.* Preston will be taken to a safe house near Washington, where his final transformation will take place. I am not sure of the details, but he will not be recognizable, even by his own wife... at least not with his clothes on."

Tom's uncharacteristic moment of levity took Nat by surprise.

"We will arrange for Mrs. Preston to meet with her husband at the safe house after the funeral," he continued, "so that they can plan their future together."

"I think you will find they've already done that," said Nat.

"Very well; I think that is all for now, except, when the news of Mr. Preston's death hits the media, you will hear from your friend Badawi. Let him do most of the talking, and if he tries to draw you out on how you did it, say you are not prepared to divulge that information; just assure him that your method is not traceable, and leave it at that. We obviously want you to press for a meeting with al-Qaeda as soon as possible, and if we're really lucky, you'll succeed, but it is more likely that they will want further display of your sincerity. Offering up the vice president as the next victim should convince them that you are deadly serious about your commitment to the Muslim cause. However, we want you to insist that you will only kill the vice president if al-Qaeda is prepared to take the final step and prepared to admit you to their inner circle so that the 'execution' of the US president can be worked out in detail. Any questions?"

"Yes. What do I do if I *don't* hear from Badawi or somebody else?"

"Give it a few days, then contact Badawi yourself and keep the ball rolling. We are pretty certain you will hear from Badawi very quickly. We think the full-page ad was a message to you that al-Qaeda has taken your offer seriously. We are absolutely certain that the ad did not appear without the al-Qaeda's leader's knowledge and approval. So, it is fair to say that you have put us on the right track. We—and that includes the president—are very pleased with the way this is shaping up. Any further questions?"

Nat could not think of any.

"Good. If something comes to mind, you know how to get a hold of me. We'll see you when you come over for the funeral."

They said goodbye and hung up.

Nat picked up his other phone, rang Mrs. Preston, and passed on the information from Tom. Nat told her that Sonja would like to pay her a visit, and Mrs. Preston said she would love to see Sonja any time she could make it. Next, Nat called Angela to get an update on her progress with spreading the word of the ambassador's death. She confirmed that the State Department had been notified, and so had all the local media.

All embassy officers and staff had been informed via email. Angela did not let her grief get in the way of carrying out her duties. She told Nat that she had called Clara, Preston's PA, who was home sick with flu and that Clara had been devastated by the sad news. Nat was beginning to realise the extent of the misery Operation Endgame was creating for a lot of people, and he could not suppress a sense of guilt. Staff and colleagues were one thing, most of whom would soon get over it and move on, with the exception of Clara and Angela, who had worked with Preston very closely on an everyday basis. It was different with family and close friends. They were the ones who would suffer the most. Was it fair?

Images from the day at the zoo came back to him: the panic and sheer terror on the faces of adults and children caught up in a meaningless battle waged by religious fanatics who placed no value on human life, people who killed innocent people—women and children—around the world, Christian and Muslim, Buddhist and Jew. It made no difference. It had been named "terrorism", which seemed to lend it some element of legitimacy, but what it really was was cold-blooded murder on a grand scale. The mythical leader, the "messiah" of the mayhem, had been Osama bin Laden. His death had turned al-Qaeda into an even deadlier organisation, determined to avenge their hero and as dangerous as a wounded tiger. Nat rubbed his temples. Endgame *was* worth it. Catching the whole al-Qaeda leadership, and putting them on trial, would be better than killing them, which could turn them into the martyrs they were quite prepared to become. On the other hand, capturing them alive could lead to efforts to secure American hostages worldwide to use as bargaining tools for their release. There were no easy answers. *One step at a time*, Nat reminded himself. *Find them first. Whether they are caught dead or alive will be up to others.*

Nat was jolted out of his reverie when the phone rang. It was Angela, asking him if there was anything else she could do before she left for the day. Nat looked at his watch. It was five o'clock. He said no and told her to try to get some rest. Tomorrow was likely to be an even busier day.

CHAPTER 41

Preston's sudden death made the late evening news. Nat and Sonja had settled down in front of the TV in anticipation of that being the case. Nat had gone through the day's events over coffee, after the children had been tucked into bed. They had been shocked at the news of Mr. Preston's death, but Gregory was the first to recover.

"Does this mean you'll become ambassador, Dad?"

"I don't know, Son. That depends on the president"

"You will make a good ambassador, Dad." Tanya had made the president's mind up for him.

The news segment covering Preston's demise was brief and to the point but included a statement from the White House regretting the untimely death of the ambassador and expressing sympathy to his family. There was speculation that the deputy chief of mission, Mr. Nathaniel Jameson, who had been with the ambassador at the time of his death, would become the next ambassador to the Court of St. James. He was described as a career diplomat with extensive experience, well qualified for the job.

Not bad, for a liar and a cheat, Nat thought.

Sonja snuggled up to him on the couch. She was shivering a little. “Is it cold in here, or is it just me?”

Nat put his arm around her shoulders and held her tight. “Not really, honey. You just don’t think I’ve got what it takes to be ambassador.” Nat gave her a teasing grin.

She gave him a light elbow in the ribs. “You know that’s not true. You’ll make a fine ambassador, but are you going to be as good in your role as CIA agent? You have fourteen years of experience in the former and none in the latter.”

“Well, I guess that explains your shivers.” Nat encircled her with both arms. “But you don’t have to worry, darling. Janet told me that she thought this whole idea of mine, which I told her had come from nowhere, might have originated from a higher authority. If she is right—and I’m inclined to go along with her theory in the absence of having a better one myself—then I’m going to be all right; we all are. He wouldn’t put me up to all this to fail.”

Sonja gave him a thoughtful look. She lifted a hand and gently stroked his cheek. “No, he wouldn’t.”

The morning paper had an article on page two, with the headline

US AMBASSADOR DEAD FROM MASSIVE HEART ATTACK

US ambassador to the Court of St. James, Mr. James Preston, died yesterday from a massive heart attack. Mr. Preston, who had no history of heart problems, was taken to St. Mary’s but was declared dead on arrival.

The article described Preston’s career from beginning to end, including two tours of duty in the Gulf War. Nat was shocked. Why had Preston never told him about this? Preston had served with distinction and ended his army career with the rank of captain. The prime minister was deeply moved and saddened at the ambassador's death, describing him as the greatest champion of US/UK relations.

The ambassador is survived by his wife and two sons. Mr. Preston will be buried at his home near Fort Collins, Colorado, on a date to be announced.

Nat finished his breakfast early and left the house before the children came down. Sonja had asked him to slow down, but he was anxious to get to the office and get on with the day. She had given him a concerned look when he kissed her goodbye.

He arrived at the embassy shortly before eight and noticed the flag at half-mast already flying in the breeze. Good old Martin, the caretaker, must have made sure the flag was up with the sun. When he stepped off the elevator, the lights were on in the reception area, and Angela was at her desk. There was a whining noise coming from Preston's office.

"Good morning, Angela. You're in early?"

"Good morning, Mr. Jameson. Yes, I booked the cleaners for seven thirty to remove the stain on...on..." She faltered. ". . . on the carpet in Mr. Preston's office. I thought it would be easier for you to work from there for the time being?"

The cleaners appeared in the doorway of Preston's office, rolling out a steam cleaner and a trolley with cleaning equipment and detergents. "We're done, Miss. Good morning, sir." The taller of the two spoke with a hoarse cockney accent. "Good as new. Sorry about the governor, sir."

He must have seen a morning paper or last night's TV news, Nat thought.

Angela thanked them and asked that they send the bill for her attention. She gave the tall one her card. He looked at it and played with it between his fingers. "Nah, Miss." He shook his head and looked at his partner. "This one's on us." He raised a hand to his white cap in a military salute, and they left.

Nat told Angela he would stay in his own office, at least until Mrs. Preston had gone through and removed any personal belongings. He asked Angela to give him all the files in Preston's in-tray and to forward all incoming and outgoing emails on his computer, including his appointment diary.

Nat looked at Preston's appointment calendar for the rest of the week. He had Angela reschedule two meetings for early next week and asked her to confirm a meeting with the foreign secretary the following afternoon. He was in the middle of going through Preston's emails when the phone rang.

"Mr. Jameson, I have Imam Badawi on the line for you."

Nat's heart did a somersault. "Thanks. I'll take it."

"I shall not call it a good morning, Mr. Jameson, as I know it is not." Nat could hear the excitement in Badawi's voice. "I have read the sad news of Ambassador Preston's sudden death, and I am calling to offer my sincere condolences. Mr. Preston was a fine man."

"That, he was." Nat could feel sweat running down the hand which held the receiver. "It is a shock to us all here at the embassy. Mr. Preston had no history of heart problems." There was a pause, and Nat decided to wait it out, to hear what Badawi would come up with next.

Badawi cleared his throat. "It is a good thing we know not what tomorrow shall bring. We do not know when God will call on us and take us home. Until he does, we must continue the work he has given us to do while we are here. I hope that the ambassador's untimely death will not get in the way of our joint effort to rally Muslim leaders, and people of all religions, to come together to fight for a better world."

Nat heard the message, loud and clear. "No, Mr. Badawi, you can rest assured that I will do everything in my power to continue the quest we have started."

There was another short pause before Badawi spoke again. "I am glad to hear you say that, Mr. Jameson. I am collecting responses and ideas from Muslim leaders in the UK and overseas, and I would like to meet with you again, once I have had a chance to review and analyse the feedback." Badawi needed time to communicate with his superiors and receive their instructions before this could go any further.

"I should like that very much," said Nat. "Call me when you are ready, and we'll get together. I shall be away for a few days next week attending Mr. Preston's funeral in Colorado, but you can arrange a time for us to meet through my secretary should you call while I'm away." There was another pause, and Nat could hear Badawi's laboured breathing. The man was obviously feeling the strain as much as Nat was. Nat decided, again, not to fill in the gap.

"Who will be the next ambassador?" Badawi's question did not come as a surprise, and Nat had the answer ready. "That, Mr. Badawi, is up to our president. I hope to find out who it is going to be before I return to London after the funeral."

"Maybe you will become the new ambassador, Mr. Jameson?"

You sly bastard, Nat thought. *I told you when we last met that I thought I might become the next ambassador*. "That is a possibility but by no means a certainty."

"You would make a good ambassador, Mr. Jameson. I think it would help our cause of working together for a better world."

"That will continue regardless, but I agree that it could enhance our ability to create meaningful change. I shall do everything in my power to assist in anything that has the potential to halt the killing of innocent people, and I shall look forward to meeting with you when you are ready."

"Likewise, Mr. Jameson. I wish you a safe journey to Colorado."

They hung up, and Nat sat back in his chair, drew a long breath, and let it out in a slow whistle. So far so good. He thought the conversation had gone well. Badawi had given every indication that, as far as he was concerned, he wanted to continue their relationship. He was clearly waiting for instructions from a higher authority—hopefully, from the leader himself.

Nat asked Angela to hold all calls, dialled Langley, and filed his report on the conversation with Badawi. He was about to sign off when Tom came on the line.

"Hi, Nat. Sorry, I was on another call. So, the next move is up to al-Qaeda. We want you to try your best to achieve a meeting with them as soon as possible. There is only a slim chance that they will agree to that at this point, but it is worth a try. We expect their intelligence team will be taking a closer look at you, starting now; meaning—they'll likely try to bug your house, as well as tap your phone. That needs to be allowed to take its course. You have nothing to hide, remember; just be careful, even speaking to your wife in your own home, or in your or her car, for that matter. One slip of the tongue and this operation is history. We'll give it a few days, and then we'll have your house and cars checked for devices. It will help you to know where they are, and it will tell us, if they are there, that al-Qaeda is looking seriously at offering you a membership. In the meantime, it will be best if you avoid talking about this with anybody, anywhere."

They agreed that Nat would report again as soon as he heard back from Badawi, and they hung up. He dialled Angela and asked if there were any messages. There was one from Mrs. Preston, who had asked when she could come in and collect her husband's personal belongings.

Angela's voice trembled. "I told her she could come in any time she wanted, and she said that she would come in tomorrow afternoon. She... she sounded very calm and together. She's a very brave lady."

You have no idea how brave a lady, Nat thought. Aloud he said, "She is remarkable."

Nat spent the rest of the day studying the files he had requested from Preston's office. Intelligence reports on the missing Russian nuclear warhead indicated that this piece of hardware, in the hands of Iran, represented a real threat to security in the region despite the fact that the trigger mechanism was missing. This, according to the report, could be manufactured by the Iranians in a matter of months rather than years.

There was no hard evidence to prove that Iran were the recipients of the weapon, other than Colonel Ivanovitch's statements under interrogation.

The CIA was working hard on the ground in Iran, with their own agents and Iranian informants trying to verify the presence of the warhead on Iranian soil. Mossad, Israel's secret service, was also involved. A nuclear weapon in the hands of a government which had publicly announced the desire to wipe them off the map gave them every incentive to do a thorough job.

Chapter 42

The funeral service in the small Presbyterian church in Fort Collins was well attended. The minister had done his best to console the grieving family, likening the parting of Jim to the parting of a ship leaving harbour and people on shore waving goodbye until it disappears over the horizon. "To us it is gone, but to somebody else, it is appearing on the horizon, heading for another port," he said.

The hardest part for Mrs. Preston, and for Nat, was the tribute delivered by Mr. Preston's eldest son. It was a heart-wrenching story, paying tribute to a man who had always, despite his professional commitments, put family first. Mrs. Preston did not need onion in her handkerchief to bring on the tears, and Nat fought hard to control his own. The sense of guilt he felt to cause this anguish was overwhelming, and he knew that Mrs. Preston was feeling the same way.

When the service was over, they walked out into the crisp afternoon sun and drove to the Preston homestead, located twenty miles northwest of town, with breathtaking views of the Rockies across Horsetooth Reservoir.

The family graveyard held three generations of Prestons and was situated on a grassy knoll from which the land sloped gradually towards the lake. The setting sun turned the lake into a golden cauldron as the minister, coming to the end of the committal service, intoned, “We now commit his body to the ground—earth to earth, ashes to ashes, dust to dust. . . .”

Mr. Tilbury, the undertaker, scattered soil over the flower-draped coffin, looking very sombre but also very businesslike. Janet had told Nat, who had been staying the night at her country estate, that the funeral arrangements had gone smoothly, except when her sons had asked to view their father’s body. She had panicked and advised them not to do it, that he had injured his face when he fell, and that they would not recognise him. Better to remember him the way he had been in life.

To her great relief, they had taken her advice, and there had been no viewing. The service came to an end, and Nat was the first to go up to Janet and give her a hug. She gave him a gentle squeeze on the arm and a knowing blink of her wet eyes, as if to say, *It’s OK; we are doing the right thing. Go on; find them!* Shaking hands and offering his condolences to Preston’s sons was more difficult. The grief and pain of their father’s death were etched in their taut faces.

“I am so very sorry,” said Nat, and he really meant it. He hoped, when the time came, that they would forgive him—forgive *them,* Nat and their parents—for the anguish they had caused them.

The reception which followed was a typical Colorado affair, with food and drink aplenty, and soon the atmosphere lightened up, helped, no doubt, by the alcohol but mainly by the many happy memories which the attendees shared about Jim—Jim the hunter; the fisherman; the pool player; the caring husband, father, and grandfather.

If Jim could have been a fly on the wall, Nat thought, *he would have been a very happy fly*. It turned out to be a true celebration of Jim's life, and everybody, except Janet and Nat, felt better when they left. They had exchanged glances across the crowded room, which showed the pain their shared secret was causing them both. *Let this be over soon!*

At least the day was over for Nat. Janet was not so lucky. Her two sons, with their wives and children, were spending the night. She followed him outside to the taxi, which was taking him to the airport, and stopped before they reached the cab and grabbed Nat's hand and looked up at him. "That was as bad as I thought it would be."

"I know, Janet. I'm very sorry. I should never have asked you and Jim to be part of this." He gave her hand a squeeze, and she squeezed back.

"Yes, you should! Go out there and make it worth it! I had a lovely chat with Sonja before I came over. She is taking the bigger risk, and you are taking the biggest. If you can lead us to al-Qaeda, it will all have been worth it. Be careful."

They carried on to the waiting taxi. The driver was holding the door open. Nat turned to Janet as he got in. "Thank you, Janet. Sonja and I will come and see you in France, if you'll have us?"

Janet smiled. "That will be lovely. Safe journey." She waved, and the taxi driver closed the door.

Nat sank into the back seat as they took off. *And she doesn't mean—just to the airport,* Nat thought. He wondered how safe his "journey" *would* be over the next few months. If he succeeded in getting a meeting with the al-Qaeda leaders, he would be in the lion's den, vulnerable from the threat within—and from the outside when they came to capture them. But what was the point of worrying about that at this stage?

No doubt a special plan would be put in place should he get to that point, a plan which would, hopefully, minimise the risk to his own life.

He decided to put it out of his mind. A book he had read a few years ago, *The Power of Now*, by Eckhardt Tolle, suddenly came to mind. He had read it and tried to live by it, but he had lost it somewhere along the line. The basic tenet of Tolle's book was that we should not dwell on the past or focus too much on the future but live in the present. The past is gone. We cannot change it, and we are not guaranteed a future. *This is a good time,* Nat thought, *to try to get back to living in the present.*

He looked out of the car window and saw only his own reflection in the dark of the October evening. Traffic on the highway to Denver was fairly light compared to the traffic coming out of the city. He looked at his watch. It was seven o'clock. His flight to Washington was leaving at eight thirty, but the taxi driver had assured him he would get them there in good time. He would get to Washington around eleven thirty and hoped to be in bed at the Hay Adams shortly after midnight. His meeting the next morning with the president and the vice president was scheduled for nine o'clock.

Here I go again, thinking ahead, Nat thought, realising there was a limit to how tightly one could stay in the present without being a yogi or a Tibetan monk. His thoughts wandered to Sonja and the children in London.

Sonja had decided that she could not leave the children with a babysitter and join him at Preston's "funeral". "I know Janet will forgive me," she had said with a wistful smile.

Sonja had visited with Janet the day before Nat had left to attend the funeral, and, over a cup of coffee and biscotti, they had shared their fears and their pride in what their husbands were doing. Janet had dreaded the "funeral" but was looking forward to starting a new life with her incognito husband in France. She and Jim had picked the world cruise they would like to take, and after a few months in France, she would book it, and her "old friend" would come along for companionship. Sonja had shared her fear of Nat ending up in the midst of al-Qaeda and the consequences if something went wrong. They had finished their get-together by agreeing that all the grief, pain, and risk was worth it if it meant rolling up the terrorist network.

The flight from Denver to Washington was uneventful, but Nat was pleased to see that they arrived ten minutes ahead of schedule. He checked in at the hotel, and the receptionist handed him an envelope with only his name typed on the front—no identifying logo or address to suggest where it had come from. Nat put it in his briefcase, got his key, and wheeled his carry-on case to the elevators. He was in his room on the stroke of midnight.

He showered and brushed his teeth, set his travel alarm for 7:30 and placed it on the bedside table, climbed into bed, and was about to turn out the light when he remembered the envelope in his briefcase. He cursed himself for his oversight, got out of bed and retrieved the letter. "You're going to have to be sharper than this, if you're going to survive the game you're playing now," he told himself. He opened the envelope and pulled out a single sheet of paper. It was White House stationery on which was typed simply:

Dear Mr. Jameson,

A car will be outside at 8:45 tomorrow morning to take you to
your 9:00 a.m. appointment.
Yours sincerely,
Melinda Jackson

Nat remembered the perky curly-haired redhead with the bright smile who had met them when he and Jim had come for the first meeting with the president and the vice president. She was the president's deputy assistant for appointments and scheduling and, as Nat remembered, very good at her job. He returned the letter to his briefcase and climbed back into bed.

He was about to turn out the bedside light when it occurred to him that it would be a good idea to order a wake-up call, just in case his little travel alarm clock let him down. It never had, but it was better to be safe than sorry. It certainly would not do to be late for a meeting with the president. He booked the wake-up call, turned out the light, and sank back on the soft linen pillows. He felt tired but also excited. Operation Endgame was on track. Could they keep it that way and achieve their goal? A lot now depended on the al-Qaeda leadership. Would they take the bait?

Nat realised that how he dealt with Badawi next would be crucial to the success of the operation. Earning Badawi's unreserved trust would be key to gaining entry into the executive branch of bin Laden's "International Terrorism, Inc.", which was what al-Qaeda had become—a global corporation selling death and destruction—well organised and well funded.

Because al-Qaeda and other terrorist groups were immune to global financial troubles, as the 2007 mortgage meltdown had demonstrated, the attempts to choke off funding to them had been met with limited success. In fact, the terrorists were stronger financially than ever before, largely as a result of the booming drug trade which had taken on epidemic proportions. Nat thought the greatest contributor to the growth of terrorism worldwide was the West's pathological restraint in facing a ruthless enemy. Western news media had reported al-Qaeda kidnappers beheading their victims without passing judgment but had been up in arms about waterboarding, condemning the procedure as inhumane. Bin Laden had exposed the soft underbelly of Western society, and al-Qaeda continued to go for it with gusto. Did it make any sense to fight by the rules of the Geneva Convention against an enemy which placed no such constraint on its own actions? Did we need any more proof than we already had that it wasn't working? Iraq had been in turmoil since the allied pullout in 2010. The resurgence of the Taliban in Afghanistan had turned the country into a haven for terrorist groups. Extremist Islam was on the March in Africa and the Middle East, causing bloodshed and starvation on a scale which had been unimaginable ten years ago and denying that continent the economic stability and growth it could have achieved. The "Arab Spring", the popular uprising against long ruling dictators in most Middle Eastern countries, had turned into an "Arab Winter", with efforts to introduce functional democracies frozen out by sectarian violence sponsored by al-Qaeda, who wanted the whole Arab Peninsula to be run by Sunni fundamentalist clerics.

Worst of all—a cold shiver went through Nat at the thought—bin Laden had made it very clear, shortly after 9/11, that he would stop at nothing to achieve his goals, including the use of nuclear weapons if he could lay his hands on them.

Had al-Qaeda finally achieved this goal? Was the warhead missing from the Russian arsenal in *their* hands rather than in

Iran's? Nat started to play out a number of different scenarios in his mind. Certainly, Iran and al-Qaeda had one clearly articulated goal in common, and that was the destruction of Israel. Iran might be satisfied to use their nuclear capability as a lever and deterrent, but al-Qaeda would show no such restraint.

They had made no secret of their desire to acquire and use nuclear weapons, or other weapons of mass destruction, if they could acquire them.

CHAPTER 43

Nat woke with a start when the alarm clock went off in his ear. He rummaged around for it and killed it just as the telephone rang. He lifted the receiver and replaced it without listening to his wake-up call, remembering last time, when he had talked back to it. He had no idea when he had finally drifted off to sleep last night, only that his last thoughts had been about Sonja and the kids and the need to stop al-Qaeda before they got their hands on weapons of mass destruction.

He got up, showered and shaved, and put on a fresh but slightly wrinkled shirt. The dark blue suit and grey and silver striped tie were the same he had worn to the funeral. *Funeral?* Nat wondered what Preston was doing right now. Was he going through agonising plastic surgery, cursing the day he had agreed to be part of this outrageous scheme? Nat hoped not and thought it unlikely.

He looked at his watch—five minutes before eight, time to call Sonja, who picked up on the third ring.

"Good morning, darling. How are you doing?" There was a slight edge in her voice. She had been waiting for his call.

"Good morning, baby. I'm fine. The funeral was a moving experience, and Janet is holding up very well." He would have liked to speak openly to Sonja about it all, but Langley had made it very clear that this was not possible.

Sonja chose her words accordingly. "Poor Janet. She is a brave soul. She told me she wanted to go to France as soon as possible after the funeral."

"I know," said Nat. "I promised her we would come and visit her there, if she would have us, and she said that would be lovely. How are the children?"

"They're fine. Tanya is very pleased with herself. Mrs. Buxton told her that her essay was excellent. She made Tanya read it out loud to the rest of the class and told her that she would like to enter it in this year's national school essay contest. Greg is teasing her about it—says he wants the movie rights. Ten years old! Where does he get it from?"

"The internet," said Nat. "For all we try to limit their time on their computers, they learn a lot from them when they're not just playing computer games."

Sonja changed the subject. "Do you know when you'll be coming back?"

"Yes, I'm booked to fly back on American tomorrow—should arrive at Heathrow about 9:30 tomorrow evening. I'll take a taxi home. Should be there about eleven or so. Keep the light burning."

"You know I will, darling." Her husky voice had its usual effect on him as she brought the conversation to an end. "Good luck with the president this morning. Tell him you'll make one hell of an ambassador, and if he wants a character reference, tell him to call me. Bye, darling."

She hung up before he could say goodbye. Sonja was always very brief on the telephone; long distance or local call, it made no difference. She was not the kind of woman who would spend an hour on the telephone with a friend, talking about what she had bought at Harrods that day.

The president and vice president were seated in front of the fireplace in the Oval Office and rose when Hal Masters, the president's personal secretary, opened the door and announced Nat's arrival. "Mr. Nathaniel Jameson, to see you, gentlemen." He retreated and closed the door behind Nat.

The president approached, his hand outstretched. "Good morning, son. Welcome back. You've been busy since we met last." He gave Nat a robust handshake and turned to his vice president. "Jack and I have been following your progress closely."

The vice president nodded and shook Nat's hand. "So, we have, Nat, and it seems you are making good progress from what we hear."

"Coffee anybody?" The president gestured towards the silver tray on the coffee table behind them.

"No, thank you, Mr. President. I had plenty of that with breakfast," said Nat.

The president shook his head. "Mr. President here, Mr. President there. I thought I made it very clear last time we met that I want you to call me Ted."

Nat could feel the heat rising on his neck. "Yes, sir; that you did. I'm sorry, sir."

The president smiled. "And you're not in the army. Come and sit down, and give us your version of Operation Endgame thus far."

Nat gave them a detailed account of what had happened since they'd last met, leaving nothing out. Ted and Jack did not interrupt once.

When Nat finished, the president rose and went over to the coffee table. "Well, I don't know about you two, but I'm gonna have a cup." He poured himself some coffee and turned to Nat. "Your mission is even more urgent now than we thought. We have intelligence that suggests the missing warhead could be destined for al-Qaeda via Iran, not necessarily through any effort of the Iranian government but by a connection between Colonel Ivanovitch and a colonel in Iran's Revolutionary Guard, who our people believe may have links to al-Qaeda, near or at the top. Efforts to locate the warhead have, so far, not produced any results. As I'm sure you know, we have nobody on the ground in Iran close to the Revolutionary Guard or anybody with connections to al-Qaeda."

The president looked at his second in command.

"We have two priorities: find and secure the missing warhead and find and capture, or kill, the al-Qaeda leadership and cripple their terrorist organisation before they get their hands on a weapon of mass destruction."

The vice president nodded and turned to Nat. "... which is why it becomes urgent to get you on the inside of al-Qaeda headquarters as soon as possible. We are running out of time, which means we must try to move Operation Endgame forward as fast as possible."

President Adams drained his coffee and returned to the chair opposite Nat and the vice president. "To that end..." His pale blue eyes fixed on Nat, "... your nomination for the ambassadorial post has been vetted and approved by the Senate Foreign Relations Committee, and I expect to have Senate confirmation in two weeks. You're a slam dunk, Nat. No hearings. In the meantime, you are the acting US ambassador to the Court of St. James. Congratulations!" He leaned forward and shook

Nat's hand. "And, you'll be doing a lot more 'acting' as ambassador," he added, with a mischievous grin.

President Adams stood up and walked towards his desk, and the vice president and Nat rose with him. He turned to face them. "I know you will try to get an audience with al-Qaeda, based on having disposed of Jim, but I doubt that is going to work." He paused and looked at his vice president. "So, Jack, are you prepared to die sooner rather than later?"

"Whatever it takes, Ted. I signed on for this job to serve my country in the best way I possibly could. I must admit, when I took the job, it never occurred to me that I could serve my country best by playing dead. I'll be ready to go in a couple of weeks. Langley is working on my new "me", ready for introduction to Italian life in Venice. I have to admit, I'm really excited about the whole affair."

"Well, then." President Adams slapped his hands together. "Let's get on with it! Clear it with Langley first, Nat, but if you have not heard back from your imam friend one week from now, I'd get in touch with him and see if you can move this thing forward." He pressed a button on the desk, and his secretary appeared within seconds. "Hal, please escort Mr. Jameson to his car. And, turning to Nat, he said, "It was nice to see you again, Nat. I am very sorry about Jim, but we know that we have a good man in you to take on the mantle of ambassador. The UK Foreign Office will be advised before you get back to London. Good luck, and safe journey." They shook hands, and Nat followed Hal back to the waiting car.

CHAPTER 44

It was 11:15 when Nat turned the key in his front door. Darwin was sitting just inside the door, tail wagging, as Nat opened it, and rushed towards him before Nat could put his carry-on down. He rolled over on his back and squealed at the excitement of seeing his master. "Hush, hush, Darwin; you'll wake the whole house." Nat rubbed Darwin's stomach as he set his case on the floor. The lights were on low in the hallway and in the kitchen, and Nat was hanging up his overcoat when a voice came down the staircase.

"Welcome home, 'James'." Sonja was leaning on the banister of the first-floor landing. Nat spun around and looked up. She looked like a Greek goddess. The chandelier, above, turned her blond hair into a golden cascade running down to her honey brown skin, covered only partly by a pearly white silk nightgown. He was about to run up the steps when she pointed to the kitchen. "There's a mug of hot chocolate on the counter for you. Pop it in the microwave for thirty seconds. See you." She turned away and disappeared into their bedroom.

Nat could feel his heart thumping. Sonja had always had this effect on him. Ever since he had first set eyes on her in the Harvard library, she'd had the ability to send his heart racing.

It wasn't just physical, although he had to admit that was an important part of it. It was a deeper feeling of love that involved the whole person. Sonja was his soulmate, his best friend. They had their disagreements, and they argued from time to time. They were both strong-willed people, but nothing could break the strong bond that bound them together. Life without Sonja was unthinkable. They never talked about it, but Nat knew that she felt the same way.

He went to the kitchen where the mug of chocolate was sitting on the counter just below the microwave. He put it in and pressed the thirty-second button. As the seconds were counting down, the thought struck him: *I'm putting her life at risk, and my children's, with this crazy scheme of mine. I'm risking everything that makes my life worth living. I must be insane!* The microwave went *ding*, and he opened the door and retrieved the steaming hot chocolate. He was about to head upstairs when he realised that Darwin was at his feet, tail wagging. "Oh, what the hell, Darwin. Don't tell Mommy." He got a dog biscuit out of a jar on the counter and made Darwin sit up to receive it. The biscuit was gone in seconds. Nat turned the lights out in the kitchen, grabbed his case, and turned out the lights in the entrance hall.

Darwin ran ahead up the stairs and turned on the landing, tail wagging, as Nat followed, two steps at a time. "OK, boy. Remember, not a word to Mommy." Darwin turned and led the way into the bedroom, where the lights were off except for Nat's bedside lamp. Sonja appeared to be asleep, lying on her side without any covers. Her long legs and soft curves looked like an Impressionistic painting.

Nat dropped his bag and set the mug of chocolate down on his bedside table. He undressed hurriedly and lifted the cover to slip into bed next to her.

"No, you don't. In the shower! Get all that travel dirt off you, MR. AMBASSADOR!" She hadn't moved. She was driving him crazy.

He got out of bed, got his toilet bag out of his travel case, and headed for the bathroom. Darwin was in his basket, head resting on the sheepskin edge. His soft brown eyes seem to know it all. "It's all right for you," Nat whispered as he passed his basket. "But I still have my balls."

When Nat returned from the bathroom, his bedside light had been turned off, and the one and only nightlight on Sonja's side was casting a soft glow over the room. He could barely make out the naked form of the creature lying on his side of the bed.

CHAPTER 45

When he woke the next morning, the first thing he saw when he lifted his head off the pillow was a full cup of cold chocolate sitting on the bedside table. He turned to look at Sonja only to find that she was not there. He looked at his watch. *Seven thirty!* He had overslept. A faint smell of English bacon was drifting through the cool morning air. He was about to get out of bed when Tanya and Gregory burst through the door opening.

"Hi, Dad! Hi, Dad!" They jumped up on the bed and into his arms.

He gave them both a good squeeze and a hug. Tanya sat back and gave him a serious look. "Poor Mr. Preston. Were there lots of people at his funeral?"

Nat's brain ceased to function for a second. *I have to get used to this,* he thought, then said aloud, "Yes, sweetheart, the church was absolutely packed. It was a beautiful funeral. Jim was buried at the family plot on his own property, in the sunset, with the lake behind us."

"Poor Mrs. Preston," Gregory chimed in. "Was she crying?"

Nat thought he could at least give this question a truthful answer. "No, she didn't. She was probably all cried out before the funeral."

Tanya looked perplexed. "I'll cry at your funeral, Daddy."

"Oh, thank you, sweetheart, but I don't plan to die for a long time yet."

"Did Mr. Preston plan to die?" Gregory's question took Nat by surprise.

"Well, of course... no, son; nobody plans to die. It just happens, sometimes quickly, like in Mr. Preston's case, and sometimes not so quickly, like your great uncle Dave." It was time to change the subject. "Congratulations on the success with your essay, Tanya. I bet you'll do well in the national essay competition."

Tanya looked doubtful. "Do you really think so?"

"I know so."

"I've done a drawing." Gregory poked Nat's arm to get his attention. "... a drawing of what happened at the zoo. Maybe I can bring it home today."

"Please do, Greg." Nat ruffled his hair. "We'd all love to see it."

"It's a BBC van with flames and black smoke com—"

"BREAKFAST IS READY!" Sonja's voice rose up the staircase.

"OK, Greg. Later. We'd rather see it than have it described to us. Quick, get dressed!" He shooed them out of bed and headed for the bathroom.

When Nat arrived early at the embassy, Angela was already at her desk. "Thought you could do with some extra help," she said when Nat expressed surprise to see her there.

"That is very good of you, Angela, and I would really appreciate it for the next few days, but beyond that, there is no reason for you not to go back to your normal hours."

She smiled, nodded, and handed him a piece of paper. "Today is your luncheon with the Russian ambassador. It's on your computer calendar but with everything going on, I was going to stick this on your desk."

Nat looked at the piece of paper.

Reminder: Noon luncheon with the Russian ambassador, Mr. Yuri Federov, at the Russian Embassy.

Topics of discussion: Missing warhead and other matters of mutual interest.

"Thank you, Angela."

As Nat turned towards his office, Clara, Preston's PA, emerged from her office carrying a folder. "Good morning, Mr. Ambassador." She paused briefly to emphasise the greeting. "These are the latest CIA reports on the missing nuclear warhead." She handed him the folder. "I am sure you want to read them before you meet with the Russian ambassador this afternoon."

"Thank you, Clara; I most certainly do." He started for his office but paused in the doorway and turned around. "By the way, the Senate has not approved my appointment yet, so Clara, I would feel better if you continued to call me Nat, as you always have. And Angela, I would like it, also, if you would start to call me Nat. Mr. Jameson makes me sound like an old Irish priest."

Angela blinked. "Yes, sir." *That sounds familiar,* Nat thought. "And," he continued, "it would appear that I now have two secretaries, at least for the time being."

Clara cleared her throat. "Yes, Nat, for the time being. I have handed in my notice, not because of what has happened but for personal reasons. You know, I couldn't come over for

Mr. Preston's funeral because I had pneumonia?" She hesitated. "As it turns out, I also have emphysema—early stages. All that smoking years ago, maybe? Who knows? In any event, Charles and I have talked and decided that there are many parts of the world we would like to see before I have to drag oxygen around. I'll be leaving end of November."

"I am very sorry to hear that you are unwell," said Nat. "Your departure will be the embassy's loss."

Angela got up from her desk, went over to Clara, and took her hand. "I shall miss you terribly."

"Now, now." Clara patted Angela's hand. "I'm around for a while yet."

In his office, Nat opened the CIA file on the missing nuclear warhead. Doubt was cast on the validity of Colonel Ivanovitch's confession that he had stolen the device. The report suggested the possibility that the warhead was in Iranian hands as part of a two-stage transaction, sanctioned by the Russian authorities. Attempts to locate the device had failed. The Iranian colonel in the Revolutionary Guard, who was thought to have received the nuclear warhead from his counterpart in the Russian army, had claimed to be innocent of the charge but had nevertheless been found hanging in his cell. Suicide was the official version, but the report speculated that it could have been murder to prevent the man from talking to the UN inspection team, which would now be allowed in to search.

Nat thought this meant that if the device ever had been in Iran, it was no longer there, like Iraq and the weapons of mass destruction which had been spirited away before the inspection teams were allowed to enter that country. The report drew the unsatisfactory conclusion that the death of the Iranian colonel had made the task of finding the missing warhead a lot more difficult.

Nat closed the file, placed it in the safe, and looked at his watch as the phone rang. It was Clara telling him that George was waiting for him downstairs.

Chapter 46

George, Preston's driver—*No, my driver,* Nat thought—was waiting outside the Bentley with the door open. Nat slipped inside and sank back on the polished leather seat. It felt strange to be here alone. George was looking at him in the rear-view mirror.

"Will that be the Russian embassy or the embassy residence, sir?"

"The embassy, please, George."

"So, that will be 6 Kensington Palace Gardens then, sir."

"If you say so, George."

George knew London better than the back of his hand. He took them down Piccadilly, past Hyde Park, and along Kensington Road. The lunchtime traffic was heavy, but Nat figured they would be there on time.

It struck him as ironic that the Russian embassy was located on the most exclusive street in London. It had been nicknamed "Billionaires' Row" and had had residents such as the Rothchilds, in the past, and the Saudi royal family. A Russian American investment giant and an Indian steel tycoon were also located here. Today, most of the Victorian mansions housed embassies from around the world, including the Israeli Embassy.

Both ends of the street had armed police checkpoints, manned by the Diplomatic Protection Group (DPC)—a Special Operations branch of the London Metropolitan Police Force—because of the high-profile terrorist targets of the Russian and Israeli embassies.

George turned right onto Kensington Palace Gardens and stopped in front of the checkpoint. Nat rolled his window down and showed his diplomatic pass. The guard nodded and waved them on. They proceeded down the tree-lined avenue and stopped in front of the wrought-iron gates of the Russian Embassy, where Nat presented his credentials again. The guard consulted a paper in his hands, nodded, and returned to his station.

The gates swung open, and George proceeded slowly to the main entrance. A man emerged from the front door as George held the car door open. The man introduced himself as Piotr Ustinov, the ambassador's secretary, and welcomed Nat to the embassy. He spoke with a heavy accent, and Nat found it hard to understand what he was saying. Something about being sorry for the death of Mr. Preston, and "Congratulations on your appointment, Mr. Ambassador." Mr. Ustinov led Nat through the entrance lobby and up the grand stair to the ambassador's office.

Ambassador Federov rose from his desk and came towards Nat, hands outstretched, with a wide grin. He was a large man in every direction, his double-breasted suit straining to contain his bulk. Nat hoped that his plain red tie was not a political statement.

"Welcome. Welcome and congratulations, Mr. Ambassador!"

Nat's hand disappeared in a double bear grip as Federov pumped his hand vigorously—no words of condolence over Preston's demise.

Nat retrieved his hand. "It is a pleasure to be here with you, Ambassador Federov. I wish the circumstances which have brought us together would have been more pleasant."

Federov bowed and invited Nat to take a chair next to the fireplace, and placed himself in a matching chair opposite. "So do I, Nat. May I call you Nat?"

"Please do, Mr. Ambassador."

"Call me Yuri. How is the family, Nat?"

"Very well, thank you. And yours?"

"Very well also, thank you." Federov's eyes turned into narrow, black slits as his smile fought for space in his fleshy face. "Well, well." He slapped his knees. The pleasantries were over.

Federov adjusted himself on the chair, which seemed to have disappeared beneath him. He cleared his throat. "Uh-hum, I know foremost of our concerns is the disappearance of the nuclear warhead, yes?"

"Indeed." *Let him do most of the talking*, Nat thought.

"Colonel Ivanovitch will be prosecuted to the fullest extent of the law. He has confessed that he arranged for the device to be shipped to his counterpart, Colonel Razar, in Iran, hidden in a massive piece of earthmoving equipment sold to the Revolutionary Guard for one of their many civilian infrastructure projects. A search of the machine turned up nothing." Federov paused, reached for a folder on the table between them, and pulled out a photograph of a transfer dump truck and trailer. "This is the vehicle." He turned the picture around so Nat could see it. "The Colonel—I mean Ivanovitch; he is stripped of his rank—told the investigators that the warhead was hidden under a fake steel floor in the trailer. However, when the vehicle was located in Iran, the fake floor had been removed, and so had the warhead. Fortunately, as you know, all the trigger mechanisms for this type of device are accounted for. Nevertheless, the Iranian authorities are assisting us in our search to find the weapon, and we are confident that we will recover it." Federov leaned back in his chair to indicate that he had come to the end of his account of the missing warhead.

Nat noted the omission of any mention of Colonel Razar's "suicide". "It is a great shame that Colonel Razar is no longer alive." Nat deliberately did not use the phrase "committed suicide", letting Federov know that he suspected foul play on the part of the Iranian authorities without saying so.

Federov took his meaning. "Yes, quite so. Had he lived, we would likely have located the warhead by now. The Iranian authorities tell us that they believe he committed suicide to avoid what he knew would be death by firing squad, for treason, after a painful stay in the notorious Evin prison."

Nat decided to let it go. He looked at the picture of the dump truck and trailer again. It was a monstrous size. Judging by the two men in hard hats standing next to it, the wheels were over six feet in diameter, and the top of the wheelhouse looked to be about twenty feet high. The length of the trailer alone was over forty feet, plus the truck itself—about the same length—big enough to easily hide the SS-23 Oka warhead which was missing from one of the many Russian stockpiles of mothballed tactical nuclear weapons.

The phone rang on Ambassador Federov's desk, and he stood up and walked over to it. "*Da, Magda, spa-see-ba.*" He hung up and turned to Nat. "Lunch is served." He gestured to a side door and led Nat to a dining room adjacent to his office. The table was set with white linen, silver, and crystal.

Nat observed the schnapps glasses and thought, *No vodka for me, Mr. Federov; I need to keep a clear head.*

A crystal vase with red tulips sat in the middle of the round table, which Nat estimated could accommodate at least ten people. It was set so that Federov would sit at twelve o'clock and Nat at 12:15. They were seated, and the first course arrived immediately—Beluga caviar blinis. Nat had eaten the light pancakes with smoked salmon or caviar before but never with Beluga caviar. A young waitress dressed in a traditional black silk dress with a white apron, low-cut white lace blouse, and a white lace headdress, appeared with a bottle of water and a bottle of white wine. Nat accepted the water but declined the white wine.

"My friend," said Federov, as he stuffed the corner of his napkin under his shirt collar, "you must try our exquisite Russian wines. They are one of our best kept secrets. The ones I have selected today come from Chateau Le Grand Vostock, one of our very finest vineries in the South near the resort of Anapa. The five hundred hectares of vineyards at Chateau Le Grand Vostock go back to the nineteenth century when the land was given to General Karsov in reward for his victory over the Turks at the siege of Kars. The general saw the potential of the land for wine production. You may not realise it, but the land is in the same latitude as Bordeaux, and the terrain and the soils are very similar. A new winery was built there in 2003, and they are producing wines of a very good quality."

That explains your red nose and translucent skin, Nat thought. Aloud he said, "I had no idea. Thank you; I will try some."

The waitress filled their glasses and withdrew.

Federov raised his glass to Nat. "*Vashee zda-ró-vye*! [Your health!]"

Nat responded, "*Na zda-ró-vye*! [Thank You!]"

Federov raised his eyebrows in surprise, then a rumble started from somewhere deep inside his ample frame. The rumble erupted in a deep, staccato laugh. "Very good! Very good!" He put his glass down and slapped his fleshy hands together in a short applause. "So, we continue our discussions in Russian?"

"I'm afraid not," said Nat. "That is the extent of my Russian vocabulary, with the exception of *da* and *nyet*."

Silence fell over the room as they sampled the blinis. They were delicious and were complemented by the dry, crisp white wine.

Federov made short work of the blinis and the glass of wine. Nat was still on his first blini when Federov had finished his two. There was no doubt the man liked food. Federov put his utensils down and wiped his mouth on the napkin without removing it from his collar. He leaned back and looked over at Nat with a serious expression on his face.

"I am so sorry about what you and your family went through at the zoo. It must have been very frightening for you all, especially your children?"

"It was, but everybody is coping very well. Thank you for asking."

"And, on top of that, my good friend, Ambassador Preston dies, and you have to step in and fill his shoes. It is a good thing that you are a young man with plenty of energy. I was shocked at the news of his death. There is 'slim and trim Jim', as I used to call him, dead from a heart attack at sixty-five, and I am still here, with my 240 pounds and high blood pressure, eating, drinking, and smoking my Havana cigars. It's not right."

Nat shook his head. "It came as a shock to all of us. Jim appeared to be in excellent health." Nat took the last mouthful of caviar and placed the knife and fork on his plate.

The waitress reappeared instantly and removed the empty plates. Federov gave her a stern look and switched his gaze to his empty wine glass. She got the message and returned quickly with the white wine. Nat declined; he still had half a glass left.

Nat thought it was time to get the conversation back to the issue of the missing warhead. "Our experts tell us that it would not be impossible for somebody with the right technical knowhow to create a trigger mechanism that would make the warhead fully functional."

"That is true." Federov downed half the wine in his glass. "But they would need to have both the skill and the necessary equipment to succeed. Neither of these, fortunately, are available to al-Qaeda or any other terrorist group, as far as we are aware."

"So we are told also," said Nat, "but we do know that Iran has scientists who are beginning to be knowledgeable in this field. As far as my government is concerned, Iran is a rogue state, in violation of a number of UN resolutions, hell-bent on the eradication of Israel, who destroyed their uranium enrichment plants in self-defence. Is it not possible that Iran is behind the theft of the warhead—that the Iranian colonel was acting not only with the full knowledge of the Revolutionary Guard but with the full knowledge of the Iranian government?"

Federov drained his glass and gave Nat an alarmed look. "Obviously. . ." He coughed and cleared his throat. ". . . it cannot be ruled out entirely, but we believe this to be a highly unlikely scenario. As you know, Iran has now agreed to give access to UN inspection teams to help in the search for the warhead. It is not likely that they would have agreed to this if they have something to hide."

Nat had to concede that this made sense. The door opened, and two waitresses appeared, one carrying a tray with two steaming deep dishes and the other a tray with a bottle of vodka and a bottle of red wine.

One of the steaming dishes was put in front of Nat and the other in front of Federov, who leaned forward and inhaled the steam with a big grin on his face. "One of my favourite meals."

To Nat it looked like a beef stew, which, he had to admit, was one of his favourites also.

"Let me explain." Federov adjusted his napkin. "What we have in front of us is reindeer stew, which is smoked reindeer meat stewed in the broth from the bone with potatoes, carrots, onions, and fresh cranberry salad on the side. I hope you will like it."

"Thank you; the aroma is wonderful. I know I will like it."

Nat accepted the offer of a glass of red wine but declined the vodka. Federov took both. He raised his wine glass. "To our success in finding the missing warhead... soon." They drank, and Nat was surprised at the smoothness of the wine—every bit as good as his favourite Margaux. He nodded in agreement with Federov's toast and in appreciation of the wine. "Surprised?" Federov's eyes were twinkling. "This is another wine from the same chateau. It is called Cuve Karsow."

"It is a wonderful wine," said Nat. "I had no idea you produced such excellent wines in Russia."

"Ah, my friend, we Russians are full of surprises. The West will find out as you get to know us better."

Will we, now? Nat thought. *Perhaps more than wine secrets.*

They concentrated for a while on the reindeer stew, and Nat had to admit that, again, he was impressed. It was a simple meal but delicious. They covered topics ranging from the chaos in the Middle East to Chechnya, where ethnic unrest had resurfaced. The need for closer cooperation in the fight against terrorism and the US president's upcoming European tour in February next year to further the cause of that cooperation were also discussed. Federov was full of praise for President Adams, for his openness and directness in dealing with matters of international concern.

"You will see more and more support coming from us in the fight against terrorism," he pledged. "It is a battle we must win."

Dessert was an apple and blueberry tart with cream. Nat went easy on the cream and said no thank you to an after-dinner drink. Federov polished off half a bottle of vodka, plus the wine, but it seemed to have no effect, except his face had gone a deeper red, and his narrow black eyes were shinier.

Chapter 47

Nat was in the back seat of the Bentley at three o'clock, heading back to the office, when his cell phone rang. He fumbled to retrieve it from his overcoat, which was lying on the seat next to him.

"Jameson here." Silence. "Hello, this is Nathaniel Jameson. Who is this?"

Nat could hear faint, heavy breathing, then, "Good afternoon, Mr. Jameson, Imam Badawi. I trust I find you well?"

Nat's heart started to pump faster. "Never better, Mr. Badawi. How are you?"

"Very well also, thank you." There was a pause as Badawi drew a deep breath. "I was hoping we could get together soon." Badawi sounded like he was short of breath. "So I can share with you the progress I have been making with our drive to discourage terrorism around the world. I think I have made good progress."

Nat swallowed. "That is good news, Mr. Badawi. I am on my way back to the embassy right now. How about I stop off at your office on my way? I could be there in about fifteen minutes."

"Excellent, excellent! I shall be waiting for you."

Nat slid the privacy window open so that George could hear him. "Change of plans, George. Please take me to the Central Mosque. Imam Badawi has some good news for us regarding his efforts to bring leaders of all faiths together to condemn and combat terrorism."

George looked at Nat in his mirror. "Very good, sir, good timing." They were just coming up to Hyde Park Corner, and George turned left up Park Lane.

Nat got a glimpse of a man standing on the soapbox dressed in a worn-out overcoat and a Chelsea Football Club scarf wrapped around his neck. At his feet stood a placard, with words written in poor script with a red marker: "The end of the world is near! Are you ready?" *The end of the world is near! Are you ready?*

There was a dozen or so people gathered around him on the chilly October afternoon.

"Lunatic!" George shook his head in disgust. "If I'd had a shilling for every time the end of the world has been announced from that soapbox, I'd be a rich man." George gave the steering wheel a thump to reinforce his point.

"Thank God they were all wrong, George. Sorry about the money, though." Nat leaned forward so that George could hear him better.

George chuckled. "Of course with all of these Muslim fanatics running around trying to get atomic weapons, and with a Russian warhead gone missing, maybe this guy's got it right, at last. God help us all."

Maybe he is right, Nat thought. He felt a chill go down his back. The conversation with the Russian ambassador had disturbed him. It was quite obvious that neither Colonel Ivanovitch nor Colonel Razar could have acted alone. You didn't stroll out of a nuclear warehouse with a fifteen-hundred-kilogram warhead hidden in your overcoat, nor did you lift it into a ten-ton trailer and weld a quarter-inch-thick false floor over it by yourself, in your back garden, at night. The same applied to Colonel Razar at the other end. Laser cutting the false steel floor, lifting the warhead out of the truck and taking it somewhere. Where? That was the question which sat like a cold lump in Nat's stomach. Were the Iranians working on the trigger mechanism and getting ready for a shot at Israel? They had the delivery capability, for sure, but hopefully, they would realise that a swift retaliation from European and US nuclear weapons would be the result.

If, on the other hand, the weapon was in the hands of al-Qaeda, they would not have the same concern. Presumably, they could not develop a trigger mechanism, nor did they, as far as Nat knew, have the ability to deliver the warhead on the end of a missile. The importance of getting into al-Qaeda had never felt more urgent. Maybe this meeting with Badawi would get him there? Maybe not. Nat could feel his pulse racing. He sat back in his seat and took some deep breaths. *You better calm down, Mr. Ambassador, or you'll have a real heart attack and blow this whole operation*, thought Nat.

"Here you are, sir." George pulled up outside the office entrance to the Central Mosque.

Nat looked out. "Thanks, George." Nat let himself out. "Wait for me here, please."

"Yes, sir. Good luck, sir." George switched the engine off and reached for his *Daily Mirror*.

A young man was waiting outside the front door. He introduced himself to Nat and escorted him to Badawi's receptionist, who was dressed in the traditional burqa without the face cover. She spoke perfect English.

"Good afternoon, Mr. Ambassador. Go right in; Imam Badawi is expecting you."

Nat knocked on the door and entered. Badawi rose from his desk and met Nat halfway. He was dressed in a traditional white robe over pale green trousers and a white turban with a double-twisted gold braid. He looked every bit the Muslim leader that he was. His tinted horn-rimmed glasses made it impossible to see his eyes.

"Welcome. Welcome, Mr. Jameson. It is so nice to see you. Will you take some tea?"

Nat really did not feel like tea, but he knew that it would be rude to say no. "Yes, thank you. That would be very nice." *This is my day for being showered with welcomes*, Nat thought.

Badawi opened the door to the front office. "Aisha. . . " The rest was in Arabic, which Nat took to mean something like *Aisha, bring us some tea, please.* The tea must have been prepared already because they had only just sat down when Aisha appeared carrying a brass samovar and two shallow gold-rimmed blue cups on a brass tray. She placed it on the table between them and withdrew quietly.

"It is very good to see you again, Mr. Jameson." He poured the tea out and handed Nat a cup. "Much has happened since we last met. You kept your promise and succeeded in your mission, and I have spoken to my people about where we go from here."

My people, Nat thought. *You must have been promoted since we last met*. "I told you what I would do if you placed the ad. I told you I meant what I said and that I could make good on my promise. I did, and now I have a request for you."

"And what is that, Mr. Jameson?"

I wish I could see your eyes, Nat thought. *You look like Ray Charles in a turban.* "I want you to arrange for me to meet with the whole of al-Qaeda's leadership."

Nat's request hung in the air while Badawi sipped his tea. He placed his cup gently down on the table. "That, Mr. Jameson, is what we have to talk about. I have had word back from Omar, and this is what he said: 'Your commitment to the Muslim cause, and your killing of the ambassador, is much welcomed at the very highest level.' These words come from the leader himself and from his Shura Council. However, as you will appreciate—and these are Omar's words based on the response he received at the highest level of al-Qaeda. The security of our beloved leaders is paramount. Very few know of their whereabouts, and it is important that we keep it that way. The council has recommended that we do not breach the wall of security which now surrounds them, based on this one demonstration of sincerity and commitment to our cause. Our supreme leader, in turn, has this proposal for you—he welcomes the opportunity for al-Qaeda to execute the president of the United States of America. To demonstrate that you are in a position to deliver this opportunity, he asks if you would be willing to dispose of his vice president. This will demonstrate your unquestionable commitment to the cause and your ability to gain access to the very top, for al-Qaeda to deliver the final blow. Upon learning that the vice president is no longer, you will be taken to meet our leader and his top advisers and operatives, where, together, you will plan the ultimate strike against the arch-enemy of the Muslim world."

Badawi leaned forward and poured himself some more tea. Nat debated whether to continue to push for a meeting now but decided against it.

The leader's request was like a gift from heaven. Nat stared down at the table, appearing to be struggling to find an answer. He took a sip of his tea, raised his head, and looked straight into Badawi's dark glasses. "Mr. Badawi, as much as I am disappointed not to be able to meet your leader soon, I appreciate his—and his advisers'—reluctance to move ahead so quickly. It so happens that I will be returning to Washington in November upon Senate confirmation of my appointment to succeed Mr. Preston. I will be meeting with the vice president then, and this may present me with the opportunity to carry out your request. My commitment to the Muslim cause, and my desire to save the lives of innocent people, has not diminished since we last met. In fact, it has grown stronger. I will endeavour to eliminate the vice president if al-Qaeda and its affiliates hold off on any further attacks on civilians or any target where collateral damage to civilian life and limb is possible. The campaign you are spearheading with your fellow clerics and other religious leaders worldwide to end terrorism will be seen to have a positive effect as incidents of random acts of violence subside. I must have your leader's word that he agrees with this before I take this step."

It was Badawi's turn to hesitate. He stroked his beard and licked his lower lip. "A personal call or email is not possible, as I am sure you will understand, these can be traced."

"Understood." Nat decided to go for broke. "All I need is a piece of paper that says 'I agree', signed by your Supreme Leader. I believe him to be a man of principle, and that he would not go back on his word."

Badawi removed his glasses and proceeded to clean them with a handkerchief he had pulled from his pocket. “I will see what can be done,” he said. “A piece of paper cannot be traced unless it is mailed. It could work.” He replaced his glasses.

“Very well.” Nat placed his empty cup on the table and stood up. “Our work has just started, Mr. Badawi, but if we succeed, we will have helped to change the world. I must stress again that, for me, the reason for doing what I am doing is to stop the senseless killing of innocent people. I got no satisfaction from killing the US ambassador, and the same will apply in the case of the vice president. That is a means to an end, the end to random killing. I shall await the note from your leader.”

They shook hands, and Nat took his leave.

It was four thirty by the time Nat got back to his office. There were a number of papers on his desk needing his attention, but he ignored them all and dialled Langley on the secure phone. Tom answered on the third ring.

“Hello, Nat; how are you doing?”

“Very well, I think.” Nat related the conversation he had just had with Badawi.

“Excellent! It’s prophetic that they suggested the vice president as your next victim. It is beginning to feel like this was meant to be.” Tom paused for a moment. “OK, Nat; here are the next steps. The president wants this to move forward with all possible speed. The Senate will confirm your appointment at the start of their next session, which is the twelfth of November. You will be invited to a meeting with the president and the vice president on the sixteenth of November, which gives you the opportunity to carry out your treasonous deed. All the arrangements have been made in preparation for the vice president’s fatal ‘heart attack’. We were just waiting to hear back from you as to whether it would become necessary or not. Now that we know it will, everything will be ready for your visit in two weeks' time. We have had to enlist the services of the president's physician, Brigadier General Dr. John Stubbs, who will happen to be in the White House when the vice president takes ill. He, and a special emergency response team, will take care of everything, after the VP 'takes ill'. You just need to be there. You will be meeting with the VP in his office. The president will not be with you. The purpose of your meeting is for the vice president to make your appointment as ambassador official after the Senate's confirmation of your appointment. The two of you will be alone, which gives you the opportunity to do what you have promised Imam Badawi you will endeavour to do. You will remain in Washington until after the vice president's 'funeral', which will be four days later. His will, which is real enough, requires that he be cremated. You will spend the four days at Langley going through the plans, which have been prepared on the assumption that you will now get an audience with al-Qaeda. Any questions?"

"Yes, Tom. Who is going to take care of embassy business while I am away?"

There was a moment's silence at the other end. "Your replacement, Tony Burville, will be heading to London next week. He will report to you for duty next Wednesday."

Nat bit his lip. Just as well Tom could not see his face. Nat was not looking forward to having Tony Burville join his team. The man was an insincere show-off, more concerned with image than with substance. They had been stationed together in Lisbon as foreign service officers at the start of their careers. That was twenty years ago, and Nat had to concede that a man can change a lot in twenty years. Aloud he said, "OK, good. He will need to get up to speed quickly. All going well, I'll not be able to focus as much on the embassy business as I should."

Tom chuckled. "Listen, my friend. If you get inside al-Qaeda HQ for us, I think you'll be forgiven."

CHAPTER 48

Anthony Burville arrived as planned the following Wednesday. Nat barely recognised him. He had put on a lot of weight, and his red hair had withdrawn from his scalp and was clinging, precariously, by his ears and on his neck. His pale green eyes had not changed, except the white was tinged with red. He wore a crumpled grey suit and a loud red tie.

He had greeted Nat as his long-lost friend and had been effusive in congratulating Nat on his promotion to ambassador. Nat received him in his new office, and they had coffee and reminisced about their early years together. Burville's seemingly fond memories gave Nat a tinge of guilt about his own feelings for the man. *I must give him the benefit of the doubt*, he admonished himself.

Sonja had. When she heard of his appointment and impending arrival, she had insisted that Nat invite him home for dinner when she learned that he was divorced and coming to London on his own. "We must make the poor fellow feel welcome," she had said, knowing Nat's sentiments about the man. She had insisted that Nat invite him over after his first day on the job, and that is how Nat found himself fighting the rush-hour traffic on a rainy October evening with Anthony Burville sitting next to him, talking incessantly about his experiences in the diplomatic core since they had worked together. He had moved around quite a bit—Stockholm, Warsaw, Cairo, and Islamabad—the last two postings as deputy chief of mission.

Nat thought he might be annoyed that he was making yet another sideways move, but Burville spoke with enthusiasm about his London posting and the chance to work with Nat again. Nat had briefed him on the state of affairs at the embassy, including his recent meeting with the Russian ambassador and the groundwork which was being done for the president's European tour next February. To his surprise, Burville responded with intelligent and constructive comments. Maybe twenty years and life's experiences had changed the man for the better?

It was six thirty when they pulled up in front of the townhouse in Cadogan Gardens.

"I thought you would have moved in to Winfield House by now." Burville opened the door and stepped out.

Nat came around the car and locked it with the remote. "That is not going to happen for a few months yet. There are some issues with the heating system which need to be sorted out. They tell us we will not move until mid-January."

Burville looked up at the redbrick townhouse "Too bad; I like this place already."

Ah, thought Nat, *that sounds more like the Tony Burville I remember*.

They were walking up the front steps when the door opened and Sonja stood in the doorway dressed in dark slacks and an Irish cardigan. She was all charm, greeting Burville enthusiastically. She took his coat and hung it on the coat stand in the entrance hall.

Burville looked around and back at Sonja. "Very lovely; very lovely."

Nat wasn't sure if he meant the house or Sonja, and he thought Sonja had caught the same vibe, judging from the momentary frown which crossed her face.

I warned you, Nat thought and gave her a knowing look.

"The children have had their supper," she announced to no one in particular. "They'll be down to say hello when they have finished their homework."

She led the way into the living room where the fireplace was lit and Nat's butler's tray was set with three glasses and an ice bucket. Beyond it on the coffee table by the fire were a vegetable dip, celery sticks, and a bowl of green olives.

"Make yourselves comfortable. I'll be back in a minute." Sonja disappeared into the kitchen.

"What can I offer you to drink?" Nat picked up a glass.

Burville hesitated. "What are you having?"

"Scotch and Perrier water."

"I'll have the same, thank you."

Nat mixed the drinks and handed a glass to Burville and held his glass up to him. "Here's to you, Tony. I'm glad you're here. I'm going to need all the help you can give me."

"Cheers, Nat; I'm very pleased to be here. I look forward to working with you again."

They sat down opposite each other in the two soft leather sofas which were arranged in front of the fireplace. Golden reflections of the flames danced on the glass coffee table between them.

They both placed their glasses down on the table, and Nat offered Burville the vegetable dip and celery sticks. Burville leaned forward and helped himself. He put two sticks together and buried them in the dip up to his fingertips.

I bet you do that with cream dips too, Nat thought. *No wonder you have grown to such formidable proportions.*

"A real shame about Preston." Burville spoke through the mouthful of dip. "Who would have thought it? He always seemed like a guy who took good care of himself—always slim and trim. What happened exactly?"

"Died from a massive heart attack... gone before we could get him to hospital." Nat took a swig of his drink, surprised at how easy it was to lie about this.

Burville shook his head. "Well, you never know when your time is up, do you? That's why we have to live life to the fullest while we're here." He drained his glass and took another handful of dip, followed by a pinch of green olives.

Is that how you lost your wife? Nat thought. He took Burville's empty glass and stood up. "Can I get you another?"

"Yes, thanks...with less water, please."

That explains the red eyes; you like your drinks strong, and plenty of them, Nat thought.

Sonja walked in with the children as Nat poured Burville his second scotch. She introduced them to him, and they shook his hand. An awkward moment of silence ensued. Talking to children was obviously not one of his strong suits.

It was Gregory who broke the silence. "Mom says you have come to take over Dad's job."

Burville stared down at him. "That's right. Your dad's the big cheese now, and I'm the little cheese." He turned and gave Nat a wink. Nat tried to smile, but Gregory burst out laughing.

"You're pretty big for a little cheese, aren't you?"

"GREG!" Sonja gave her son a stern look.

Nat's smile became real, and, to Sonja's relief, Burville threw his head back and shook with laughter, spilling some of his drink in the process. "I need to be big to fill your father's shoes." His cheeks trembled as he laughed again.

Nat handed Sonja a gin and tonic, and she sat down on the sofa where Nat had been sitting. "OK children; run along. I'll be up in half an hour to tuck you in."

"Good night! Good night!" They waved and disappeared.

Nat realised that those were the only two words his daughter had said to Burville. *She's a good judge of character*, he thought.

They had dinner around the oak table in the kitchen. Roast beef and Yorkshire pudding. The most English of meals, accompanied by a fine Margaux. Sonja had opened two bottles for the three of them, thinking that would be more than enough, but Burville was knocking it back at an alarming rate, so Nat opened a third bottle. They were on the cheese and biscuits when Sonja got onto the topic of Burville's most recent posting in Islamabad. He spoke with great enthusiasm about his four years in Pakistan, saying he thought that more than any other country, Pakistan was the country where the battle against Muslim extremism would be won or lost. When Sonja asked him why he thought this was so, he laid the blame squarely at successive Pakistani governments' failure to provide adequately funded public schools.

"You may have heard about the flow of funds from the Saudi Wahhabi sect to build thousands of Wahhabi madrassas in Pakistan, particularly in the border regions with Afghanistan. This is Saudi oil wealth pouring into Pakistan to fund the building of mosques and schools, many of which become the incubators of Islamic extremism. The money is smuggled in suitcases or through the hawala money transfer system, which is impossible to trace. We are talking about thousands of schools and mosques, most of them built since 9/11. The poor people are easy targets for exploitation." Burville paused and arranged some cheese on a biscuit and downed it in one mouthful, followed by a gulp of red wine.

"Surely, all Wahhabi schools can't be bad?"

Sonja's question hung in the air, unanswered, while Burville chewed another piece of cheese. The man had an amazing appetite and a great capacity for alcohol. Nat was impressed that after three scotches and eight glasses of red wine, Burville was not slurring his words. The only telltale signs of overindulgence were his watery red eyes and the complementary red of his fleshy cheeks.

He focused his watery eyes on Sonja. "No, not every madrassa is teaching jihad, but a Lahore-based journalist who is considered to be the world's leading authority on the subject estimates that more than eighty thousand young madrassa students have become Taliban recruits over the past ten years."

Nat nodded in agreement. "The World Bank estimates that 15 to 20 percent of madrassa students are receiving military training as their main focus of education, to the detriment of subjects such as science, math, history, and geography. As long as this continues, we are not likely to win the war in Afghanistan or the war against extremism worldwide. I agree with you; we need a major push by Muslim leaders, not only in Pakistan but in all Muslim countries, to focus their attention on affordable public education. All the fire power, and shock and awe we can muster, will get us nowhere unless the education issue is addressed."

Sonja, who had gone to the kitchen to get the coffee, returned just in time to catch the end of Nat's sentence. She placed the tray down on the table. "Yes," she said, "education is the key, and I know of somebody who is doing something about it. Have you heard the name Greg Mortenson?" They both looked at her. "Does the Central Asia Institute ring a bell? You should know, Anthony. Of all the people in this room, you should know."

Burville looked like he was struggling to focus his mind. Then a light seemed to go on somewhere in his addled brain, and a smile of relief and recognition spread across his face. "He came to the embassy once in my first year in Islamabad. He has been building schools in rural Pakistan and Afghanistan since 1996. An amazing fellow—started singlehandedly and built the first school with his own money, for children, in a small village in northern Pakistan. They had no schoolhouse and no teachers. The man has gained a near godlike stature in rural Pakistan."

It was eleven thirty, and many yawns later from Sonja, before Burville took the hint and asked Nat to call him a cab.

They were clearing the table and stacking the dishwasher when Sonja made the observation that Burville was hardly the best person they could have picked to fill the vacancy at the embassy. "He certainly drinks too much." She stated the obvious. "And, not remembering Mortenson, having met him in person, shows that he must have pickled his brain completely."

Nat could only agree but expressed that, to his surprise, Burville seemed very alert when it came to embassy business.

"Just as well." Sonja poured the washing-up liquid in the machine and closed the door. "You are going to be preoccupied with other matters in the next few months."

CHAPTER 49

It was four days later when Nat had a plain white envelope on his desk marked "Private & Confidential". There was no stamp. The letter had been hand-delivered. Inside was a single sheet of paper on which was written, in a shaky hand:

Dear Mr. Jameson,

Your commitment to the Muslim cause is appreciated very much.

I agree with your terms.

Allah be with you!

Shura Council Director

Nat felt the hairs rise on the back of his neck. This was it! Or was it? Anybody could have signed it. Nat had no idea what the Leader's signature looked like. There again, who would dare fake his signature? *I have no choice but to take this at face value,* he thought.

The flight to Washington—first class—was perfectly fine, but Nat had to admit that it didn't come close to the comfort of flying private. They landed in the dark, at 6:30 p.m., and Nat was installed in a suite at the Hay Adams half an hour later. He showered, put on the dressing gown hanging on the bathroom door, stretched out on the king-size bed, and pulled the telephone on the bedside table with him. He called Sonja's parents first. Sonja's father confirmed that they would join them for Christmas in Switzerland, and they chatted for a while about family matters and Nat's impending appointment as ambassador to the Court of St. James.

"We are very proud of you," he said. "We know you will do an outstanding job."

My God, thought Nat, *I hope you're right*. "Thank you, Raoul; I shall do my best."

They talked on for a while. Raoul apologised for his wife, Fatima. "This is her night out with the 'girls'—dreadful habit. I have to make do with a TV dinner."

They hung up. Nat called his mother and got the answering machine. "I'm in New York for a couple of days... will be back on the sixteenth of November. Please leave a message."

Nat realised that he had neglected to tell his mother and Sonja's parents that he was coming over. So had Sonja. *We are not acting as we would normally*, he thought. *Something to be more careful about*. He left a message and hung up. He debated whether to call Sonja but decided it was too late. It was 11:30 over there. He ordered some soup and a sandwich from the room service menu and did a mental run-through of tomorrow's event in the vice president's office. The meeting was scheduled for 10 o'clock the next morning. The VP would fake his heart attack at 10:15. Nat would alert Hal Masters, the president's PA, across the hall, who would know that Brigadier Dr. John Stubbs was waiting outside to meet with the president and would, naturally, appeal for his assistance.

Dr. Stubbs would take it from there. He would call the emergency team, consisting of CIA special ops people, who would, with Dr. Stubbs attending, take the vice president by air ambulance to Washington Hospital Center, where he would be pronounced dead on arrival. Nat had had many questions about how this would be accomplished, but Tom had told him not to worry. It was "all taken care of"; the "funeral" would take place four days later, at Arlington Cemetery, where the vice president would be buried with full military honours. Nat would spend three days at Langley working through the plans for his meeting with the al-Qaeda leaders. He would return to London, confirmed as the US ambassador to the Court of St. James, following the funeral.

It was Hal Masters, the president's PA, who met Nat in the reception hall at the White House the following morning.

"The president would like to have a quick word with you before you meet with the vice president." Hal led the way down the corridor to the Oval Office and opened the door. "I have Mr. Jameson for you, Mr. President." He closed the door behind Nat, leaving them alone.

"Well, hi there, son! Nice to see you." President Adams rose from his desk and approached Nat with a big smile, his hand outstretched. "You're doing well, really well." He pumped Nat's hand while holding his elbow with the other. "I just wanted a quick word before I hand you over to Jack." Adams gestured Nat to sit down in front of his desk and retook his chair behind it. "I have been following your progress closely, through regular briefings from Langley, and I wanted to tell you that I'm very impressed with what I hear. I don't know how on earth you came up with this plan, but you did, and now you're doing a bloody fine job implementing it. If you lead us to the heart of al-Qaeda, you will have done us, and the rest of the world, a great service. You and I both realise that even if we dispose of the whole of al-Qaeda's leadership, it is not going to be the end of international terrorism, but it is going to be a significant step towards that end."

Nat thought of the conversation over dinner with Burville, and Sonja and her mention of Greg Mortenson and his amazing work, through the Central Asia Institute. "It would seem, Sir, that, unless countries like Pakistan and other Muslim countries get on top of their inadequate public education systems, we are not going to see an end to terrorism. Thousands of extremist madrassas are turning out suicide bombers and Muslim 'freedom fighters'. . . " Nat mimicked the inverted commas with his index fingers. ". . . faster than we can kill them off."

Nat gave the president a brief recap of his conversation with Sonja and Burville. The president listened intently, and when Nat had finished, he rose from his chair.

"That's very interesting, son. We have provided millions of dollars to the Pakistani government towards improving their education system through USAID. Regrettably, we have no control over how the money is being spent. Maybe we could do better by funding CAI and Mortenson. We'll talk about that some more once we have dismantled al-Qaeda. First things first, as they say." He pushed a button on his desk, and Hal Masters appeared within seconds. "Hi Hal; *Ambassador* Jameson is ready to see the vice president now." He placed emphasis on the word *ambassador*.

Nat stood, shook the president's hand, and followed Hal across the corridor to the vice president's office. Hal knocked on the door and opened it. "I have Ambassador Jameson for you, sir." He stood back and gestured for Nat to enter.

The vice president smiled as he stood up behind his desk and invited Nat to take a seat in front of it. "Hello, again, Nat.

You've been a busy man since we met last." They both sat down. "You will have a cup of coffee with me, won't you?" He gave Nat a wink.

"I would love one, sir." Nat smiled back. They went over to the lounge area, where the table was set for coffee, including a tray of assorted biscuits. They sat down and the vice president poured the coffee.

Just like his boss, Nat thought.

The vice-president lowered his voice. "Ted and I are very pleased with the way things are going. I didn't think it would be my turn so soon, but. . . " he hesitated and looked down at an envelope in front of him. ". . . but I'm ready as soon as I have dispensed with the important business of confirming your appointment as ambassador to the Court of St. James." He handed Nat the envelope. "And here it is."

"Thank you, sir." Nat did not open the envelope but placed it in his inside jacket pocket.

"I should add that this is not a temporary appointment. Mr. Preston made it quite clear before his 'death'. . . " The vice president gave Nat a conspiratorial look. ". . . that he had no desire to return to diplomatic service, having, as he said, '. . . made the ultimate sacrifice.' " They both laughed.

Vintage Preston humour, Nat thought. Aloud he said, "Sir, I—"

The vice-president cut him short. "How about granting a 'dying man' his last wish?" There was a twinkle in his eyes and a wicked grin on his face.

"Certainly, sir. . . ?"

"Call me Jack!"

"Yes, sir... Jack... I was going to say that I think that decision was made for him by his wife, Janet. She's been after him for the past few years to hand in his notice. I suspect that was the 'deal' she struck with Jim when she agreed to go along with this."

"I don't blame her," said Jack. "This crazy scheme of yours, brilliant as it is, will be a life-altering—pardon the pun—*experience* for all of us." Jack looked at his watch. "Anyway, Dr. Stubbs is out there waiting for us. It's time we got on with it. If you don't mind, I'll have my heart attack over there and slump over my desk. Don't like the idea of falling down and maybe hurting something." The vice president looked at his watch again. It said 10:16. "We're a minute late. Are you ready?"

Nat nodded. They walked back to the vice president's desk and sat down. Jack winked. "OK, here it goes!" He gasped and grabbed at his chest, pulling buttons out of his white shirt. "Ahhh, my God! Jesus!" He was holding his breath; his face was going a deep red.

Nat jumped up and ran into the hallway yelling for help. A door flew open down the corridor, and Hal Masters came running out.

"The vice president is in trouble! I think he's having a heart attack!" Nat sounded out of breath and had a look of shock on his face. Another man—a security guard—appeared out of nowhere, and Masters waved his hands as the guard ran towards him.

"Craig, Dr. Stubbs is in the waiting room. Get him, quickly!" Craig disappeared and returned, at a full gallop, seconds later, followed by the president's physician, who wasted no time in lifting the vice president's limp body from the desk and gently placing him down on the floor. He felt for a pulse on the side of the neck and turned to Masters.

"Call 911!"

Masters disappeared back into his office, leaving Nat and the security guard with Dr. Stubbs leaning over the still body of the vice president, pumping his chest with both hands. Jack groaned and gasped for air—a reaction which was real enough—as the pumping action forced the air out of his lungs.

Dr. Stubbs turned to Nat. "See what I'm doing? In a moment I want you to take over doing this so I can get to my case up there." He nodded towards his medical bag sitting on the counter. "Ready?" He moved away, and Nat took over. Dr. Stubbs got a syringe and needle out of his bag and extracted a small glass bottle, sucked the fluid out, and gave the vice president an injection in his left arm. He turned to the security guard. "Go outside, and make sure the coast is clear for the emergency team. Clear the way for them. Tell people to get back in their offices." He knelt back on the floor and felt for Jack's pulse, which was faster and stronger than ever.

He whispered so that only the three of them could hear, "Well done, sir. Try to calm down. We don't want you to have a real one. The emergency team will be here shortly, and we'll get you out of here."

He had barely finished his sentence when three men appeared in the doorway.

Dr. Stubbs took charge of the proceedings. "I've done all the primary treatment procedures. Hook him up to the monitor, and let's get him on the stretcher and out of here."

The eyes of people standing in their office doorways followed the stretcher as they wheeled the vice president out to the waiting ambulance. Nat was left alone in the vice president's office and was still sitting on the floor, holding his hands to his temples, when Hal Masters returned. “Mr. Jameson, are you all right?”

Nat pretended not to hear.

“Mr. Jameson, are you OK?”

Nat rose slowly and turned around. “I can’t believe it! I can’t believe it! First Jim, and now this!” He shook his head and slumped down on the visitor’s chair in front of the vice president’s desk.

“Now, now, Mr. Jameson. It’s not your fault.” Masters went to the telephone on the vice president’s desk and dialled. “Briefing room. I know he’s busy. This is an emergency!” There was a short pause. “Mr. President, I am sorry to interrupt, but I must tell you that the vice president has taken ill. Luckily, Dr. Stubbs was on the scene immediately and took charge. The ambulance is on its way to the hospital as we speak. . . . Yes, sir. Mr. Jameson is right here. . . . Yes, Mr. President; here he is.” Masters held the phone out to Nat.

The president’s voice boomed into the earpiece. “What happened, son? You were there with him, right?”

“Yes, sir. I think it must have been a heart attack.”

“Christ, poor Jack! That’s bloody awful.” There was a short pause. “Look, son, I’ll abort this briefing now and see you in my office in two minutes.” The president hung up, and Nat handed the receiver back to Masters, who replaced it on the cradle.

“He wants to see me in his office in two minutes.”

Masters nodded and led Nat back to the Oval Office. “Can I offer you something to drink while you wait?”

A stiff scotch would go down well right now, Nat thought, but he asked for a glass of water. Masters pressed a button on the president’s desk and ordered the water, which arrived in less than a minute.

“Take a seat over there.” Masters pointed to the lounge seating by the fireplace. “The president will be with you shortly.” Masters withdrew to his own office.

Nat was wondering what was happening with the vice president. Would Dr. Stubbs pronounce him dead, or would this happen, somehow, at the hospital?

When he had asked Tom, his CIA contact man, these questions, he had just laughed and told him not to worry about parts of the operation he was not directly involved with. “You have enough on your plate. Just rest assured that the vice president’s ‘death’ will seem every bit as real as that of the ambassador’s. This is easier,” he added. “We’re on home turf.”

“Are you OK, son?” The president came in and went straight to his desk and reached for something underneath the desktop. “We’ll keep this conversation off the record,” he said as he turned and came towards Nat with a big smile. “How did it go in there? Did Jack do a good job?”

Nat stood up and they shook hands. “An outstanding job, Mr. President.”

“Sit down, Nat, and tell me where we are with this operation from where you sit.”

Nat pulled the envelope with the Leader’s note out of his pocket and handed it to the president. “If this is real, sir, and I have no reason to believe that it is not, I will get to meet him and his executive, hopefully soon after the news of the vice president’s death is made public.”

The president smoothed the note out on the coffee table as he studied it. “Poor handwriting. How do we know that it’s the real thing?”

“We don’t, sir, but I think it’s highly unlikely that anybody would dare fake his signature.”

“Yeah, you’re right. In any case, we have to take it at face value. If you had questioned it, it would have slowed us down, and time is not on our side.” The president handed the note back. “Langley tells me that they are extremely concerned over the missing nuclear warhead. We know that it went to Iran, and with the Iranians now agreeing to give access to a UN inspection team to help look for it, we can be almost certain that it is no longer there; so, where is it? Our boys at Langley believe that the warhead may be in terrorist hands as we speak. Whose and where? We don’t know, but it is reasonable to assume that al-Qaeda would be involved. They have the motivation and the resources, and they and Iran are aligned in their desire to wipe Israel off the map. The need to get inside al-Qaeda has never been so urgent.” The president paused. “So, Nat—Ambassador Jameson—” He fixed Nat with a firm gaze. “Go get them, son! And God be with you.” He pressed a button on his desk, and Masters appeared, it seemed, immediately, looking very sad and dejected. “Any news, Hal?” The president placed a hand on Nat’s arm, as if to help steady himself to receive the news.

“Just in, Mr. President. Not good.” Masters was struggling to get the words out. “Dead on arrival, sir.”

“Oh, no!” President Adams shook his head. “Poor Jack, poor Jack.” He let go of Nat’s arm and went around his desk and sat down, staring at his hands, which he folded in front of him. Then he straightened up and looked at Nat and Masters standing in front of him. “Well, Jack got his wish.”

“His wish, sir?” Masters’ facial expression reinforced his question.

“Yes Hal; Jack always said that, when his time was up, he would like to make a quick exit, and he sure did.” The president sighed heavily and went back to studying his hands.

Nat thought he was playing his part like a pro. The thought that we are all actors on the stage of life flashed through his mind—*some of us more than others*.

"Well, that's that. God rest his soul. He was a good man. A good vice president and a good friend. I shall miss him." The president's words seemed to hang in the air until he slammed his fists on his desktop and stood up. "Right, let's get on with it! Hal, see to it that the ambassador gets back to his hotel." Then to Nat: "I'd like you to remain in Washington for a few days so that you can attend Jack's funeral. Does that work for you?"

"Certainly, Mr. President. I would like that very much."

"Very well. I'll see you in a few days' time." They shook hands, and Masters escorted Nat out of the Oval Office.

CHAPTER 50

Nat arrived back at the Hay Adams Hotel just before midday. A stunningly beautiful receptionist, of Japanese origin handed him a plain white envelope with just "Ambassador Jameson" typed on the front. He opened it immediately once he got to his suite:

A car will pick you up tomorrow morning at 9:00 a.m.

Black Lincoln Town Car flying two American flags and the Diplomatic Service Emblem.

P.S. Please destroy this note.

The paper was unheaded, and there was no signature. Nat tore the note into pieces and flushed it down the toilet. He suddenly realised that the rest of the day and evening were his own and decided that the first thing to do was to call Sonja. It was 5:15 p.m. over there. He went for the phone on the writing desk, then changed his mind and switched on the TV and found CNN News just as a reporter said: *A report has just come in that Vice President Burton died suddenly this morning, apparently of a heart attack. We will bring you further information on this as it becomes available.*

The reporter continued with the other news items on his agenda—no expression of feeling or regret.

What are we coming to? Nat thought. *The death of our vice president becomes just a byline? Are we about to lose our humanity?* He turned the volume down on the TV and dialled Sonja.

She picked up on the third ring. "…Jameson. … Hello, darling. … How awful. We've just seen it on the news." Nat realised she was there with the children.

"Yes, I've just come back from the White House. He had just handed me the envelope with the confirmation of my appointment when he toppled over. The president wants me to stay for the funeral, so I'll be here for another four or five days. How are you doing?"

"We're fine, Nat. How awful for you! Poor Mr. Burton. We miss you, and we are all very proud of you. Tanya and Gregory are right here. We are making baskets for the Christmas tree we'll have in Switzerland this year. They're doing a great job. Here's Gregory; he's been making signs at me ever since he realised it was you on the phone." There was a short pause.

"Dad?"

"Yes, Greg. How are you?"

"Good, Dad. I was wondering…" He hesitated. "Ambassador Preston died, and they made you the ambassador. Now, the vice president has died. Will they make you vice president?"

"No, son; that's not going to happen. Besides, I'll have enough on my plate being ambassador."

"I guess so, Dad. I was just thinking that if you became vice president, we could go everywhere with you in a private jet."

"Tough luck, Greg, but you never know; maybe one day we'll all fly in one together. Hey, you could become vice president, or even president, yourself, one day and then you could take us along in *your* jet."

"Yeah, I could." Gregory clearly liked the idea.

"Listen, son; the harder you work at school the better the chances are that you could one day have your own plane. Have you done your homework yet?"

"No, Dad; we don't have any," Gregory added, hurriedly. "When are you coming home?"

Nat could hear in his son's voice that he missed his dad, and he felt a pang of guilt. *I certainly haven't enhanced my ability to spend more time with my family*, he thought. "I'll be staying for the vice president's funeral, so I'll be gone for another five days or so."

There was silence at the other end, then "Bye, Dad. Here's Tanya."

Tanya was full of excitement. Mrs. Buxton, her English teacher, had said that the results of the national essay competition would be announced before the Christmas break. "And, Daddy, Mrs. Buxton said she thought I had a good chance of getting one of the three prizes!"

"I bet she's right, sweetheart." Nat remembered clearly the simple and profound words of his daughter and her plea for a sane, peaceful world.

She described the complexities of paper basket weaving, and said, "Tomorrow we are going to start on the gingerbread house. The roof will be covered in M&Ms."

"Yum, yum, that sounds lovely, baby. How are we going to get it to Switzerland?"

"In a box, of course, Daddy." There was a hint of exasperation in Tanya's voice. Adults could be so stupid sometimes.

"Oh, good. Why didn't I think of that? Have you got planning permission for it?"

"Daaaad." Tanya giggled. "You're being very silly."

"So, I am. Could you hand me back to Mommy, please? Bye, baby." There was no reply as Tanya was handing the phone back to her mother.

"I spoke to your dad. Your mom was having a night out with the girls. Raoul said they will join us in Zermatt for Christmas." Nat realised, as he spoke, that he did not know, himself, when they were supposed to leave for Switzerland. "When are we going?"

Sonja laughed. "Oh, Nat, I guess you've been a bit distracted lately. We're booked on BA for the morning of the seventeenth of December. I think the flight leaves at eleven thirty. I will speak to my parents. I was hoping that we could all go together. What about your mother?"

"According to her voicemail, she is returning from a trip to New York today. I'll try her again this afternoon."

"OK, darling. Take good care of yourself. Stay in touch." Sonja hung up.

Nat was left holding a dead phone in his hand. He shook his head, chuckled, and replaced the receiver. How was it that he had found the only woman in the world who did not like talking on the telephone?

Nat called room service and ordered pea soup and a turkey sandwich, a bottle of Perrier water, and some coffee, and while he was waiting for it to arrive, he tried his mother's number again—still no answer. It was so frustrating. She would be flying from New York to Washington and then driving herself home to Harrisonburg. If only she had not thrown away her cell phone when she retired from the *Post*.

Then a thought struck him. He would call his friend Peter Morris at the State Department. Peter was a seasoned communications security expert. He would know how to find out which flight Nat's mother was on, if anybody could. They had stayed in touch over the years. Nat found the direct number on his iPhone and dialled.

"Hello, Nat, I mean Ambassador Jameson. Congratulations! Long time, no hear." Peter Morris's cheerful voice sounded as optimistic and upbeat as ever.

"Hi, Peter, how are you?"

"Well, Mr. Ambassador, old chap. If life got any better, I'd think I'd died and gone to heaven. Talking about dying, it seems to be following you around? First Jim, and now the vice president. What have you been up to, my friend?"

"Good God, Peter; don't joke about it. My son just asked me if this meant I would now become vice president, and now you sound like you think I'm going around killing people for personal advancement. Give me a break. The last few weeks have been pretty trying to say the least."

"I know." Peter was suddenly very serious. "I'm sorry, Nat. I know what you've been through. I saw you on television after the zoo bombing. You said all the right things. How are Sonja and the kids?"

"They're holding up very well, thank you." Nat gave Peter a condensed version of their ordeal at the London Zoo and got Peter to update him on his life since they had last spoken almost a year ago.

Peter was still a bachelor at forty-eight, and it looked like a situation which was not going to change anytime soon. Despite a number of affairs along the way, he had never popped "the question" to any of them. The reason given for this, by

Peter himself, was that he had not yet—and he stressed the *yet*—found a woman who was "worthy" enough.

Having caught up on each other's lives, Nat came to the main reason for his call. "Peter, I wonder if you could do me a favour?"

"Absolutely; as long as there is no money involved." They laughed.

"No money, unless you are going to charge me for your services."

"Try me."

"My mother is returning from New York today, and she'll be flying into Washington, I imagine, sometime this afternoon. She does not have a cell phone, so I can't communicate with her, but I'd like to intercept her before she gets in her car and drives home to Harrisonburg. I thought maybe with your resources and clout you might be able to find her for me?"

"Piece of cake. What's her name?"

"Amy."

"I'll call you back in a little while." Peter's unbridled confidence gave Nat hope that maybe he would end up having dinner with his mother that evening.

His lunch arrived, and he ate it watching CNN News. Floods in China, massive forest fires in New Zealand, landslides in California. Extreme weather was on the rise worldwide, but that did not stop man from adding to the world's woes. Two suicide bombers had blown up a Shiite mosque full of worshippers in Baghdad, killing 180 people and wounding 200. A plot to blow up the German Reichstag had been foiled, and a group, linked to al-Qaeda, with some sixty members, was behind bars awaiting trial.

Then appeared a short segment on the life and work of the deceased vice president. Jack had excelled in college football, graduated from Harvard top of his class, and entered politics at twenty-seven as aid to a Virginia senator. His contribution to the nation was second to none. The service was to be held in Washington Cathedral, with interment to follow at Arlington National Cemetery, with full military honours, on the nineteenth of November—three days away. You had to hand it to CNN; they were first with the news most of the time.

He was only halfway through the sandwich when his cell phone rang.

"American Flight 2508, arriving at Reagan National at 2:50 p.m. Anything else I can do for you, Mr. Ambassador?"

Nat laughed. "That's brilliant, Peter. Thanks. That'll be all for now. I'm here for a few days; maybe we could go out and have some dinner together one night?"

"My calendar is free; give me a call."

"Thanks again, Peter. You've made my day. I'll call you."

CHAPTER 51

Nat arrived at Reagan International at two thirty and took up position close to the doors in the arrivals area. He looked forward to seeing his mother and to giving her a big surprise. She would wonder how on earth it could be that her son, who, as far as she knew, was in London, was there at the airport to greet her.

The airport was busy, even though it was too early for the rush hour of commuters. Nat saw the heavily armed guards patrolling in pairs. He observed four different teams in the short wait before his mother arrived.

Mrs. Amy Jameson cut a fine figure for a sixty-five-year-old. She was tall for a woman, five feet nine inches, so with high heels, which she was wearing as she came through the arrival doors, she stood out from the crowd. Nat spotted her immediately. Her grey, almost white, hair was well shaped, falling in waves just short of her shoulders.

The camel-hair overcoat had a simple Coco Chanel look, but it did not look at all old-fashioned on her. She was pulling a brown leather carry-on case which complimented her coat. She did not notice Nat until she was almost next to him and he called her.

"Mother!"

She looked up and stopped dead in her tracks. First came the expression of shock and disbelief. "Nat?" Then the big, warm smile as she came towards him with her hands outstretched. "What on earth are you doing here?" They embraced, and Nat realised he was holding on a bit longer than usual. It was so good to feel his mother's arms around him. When they disengaged, she held on to his hands and took a step back so that she could see him better. "Are you OK?"

He laughed. "Yes, Mom, I'm OK, and, to answer your first question, I'm here to ask you out for dinner."

"Sure." She gave him that 'mother knows better' look. "You came to Washington to ask me out for dinner. That's as commendable as it is unbelievable." Her blue eyes sparkled with joy and mischief. "Try again: What are you doing in Washington?"

Nat cleared his throat. "Well, hum, you see, I should have called you a week ago to tell you what was going on, but I didn't get around to it somehow." He was groping around to find the right words for his gross oversight but could not find any. "The truth is, Mom, I came to Washington to be appointed ambassador to the Court of St. James." He looked at her apologetically.

"London ambassador, you mean." She mulled it over. "Well, that's a good reason to come to Washington. When did this happen?"

"This morning. It was Vice President Burton's last official act before he died. I was with him when it happened."

"The vice president... dead?" Her eyes widened. "I had no idea. What happened?"

"He died from a massive heart attack, Mom." It was more difficult to lie to your own mother. It made him feel like a real crook. He tried to shake the feeling.

"Wow! Poor fellow. He seemed like a decent man. Spoke with heart. Not a common trait in politicians." Nat's mother handed him her carry-on and stroked his cheek. "You know what? I'd love to have dinner with you if you can find me a place to stay."

"No problem, Mom. If worse comes to worst, we can share my suite at the Hay Adams." Nat grabbed the handle of her carry-on and headed for the exit.

"Suite at the Hay Adams, huh? You ambassadors are all the same." She gave him a gentle nudge in the ribs.

They found her 1996 model Volvo station wagon in the long-stay car park after a few attempts, and Nat took the wheel and drove his mother back to the hotel. On the way, he told her how he had tracked her down to meet her at the airport, answered all her questions about Sonja and the children, and reassured her that their lives were back to normal.

"Well," she said, "you'll discover soon enough that a 'normal' life for an ambassador and his family is somewhat different from what you have been used to."

You have no idea how far away from "normal" my life is right now, Nat thought. Aloud he said, "You're right. The biggest change will be for Sonja, who'll have to accept that we'll have servants once we move to Winfield House. She's not going to like that, I know."

"Oh, she'll get used to it. Most women would be envious."

Nat shook his head. "Sonja has refused to even have a part-time maid up to now; she's going to find it hard to adjust to a house with staff."

The hotel was full, but it was no problem because the couch in Nat's suite was a well disguised sofa bed. Nat would take the sofa bed; he insisted. It was agreed that the sofa bed would be made up when they were having dinner, which Nat booked for seven o'clock.

Nat's mother took a bath while he watched TV. She emerged twenty minutes later in a bathrobe and a towel wrapped over her wet hair. She sat down next to Nat on the sofa, put an arm around his shoulders, and pulled him towards her. "This is such a lovely surprise—to be here with my boy." She gave him a kiss on the cheek. "My boy, the ambassador! I feel like celebrating. Any champagne in the minibar?"

Nat switched off the TV and went to check. He opened the door of the minibar and pulled out a bottle. "Will this do?" He held a bottle of Veuve Clicquot aloft, swinging it lazily backwards and forwards.

"That's just the ticket." He found two champagne flutes sitting on a tray on top of the minibar, together with two tumblers and two wine glasses. He opened the champagne, taking great care not to create an eruption of bubbles, explaining the fine art of uncorking a bottle of champagne as he proceeded.

"You hold the cork and the neck of the bottle in your left hand, tilt the bottle gently to the left, then you grab the bottom of the bottle with your right hand, twist while you retrain the cork with your left, and..."

Pouffe. A small puff of air emitted from the bottle. "...and you don't lose any of the bubbles or any of the champagne." He filled the glasses and handed one to his mother.

She raised her glass to him. "Congratulations, son. I know you will do your best in your new job. The very best of luck to you!" They drank.

"Thank you, Mother. I need it—the luck, I mean. Representing the US internationally is getting more and more complicated. Our world is getting more and more complicated, politically and economically. Foreign relations has become a minefield. The emergence of China and India as major global players is changing how we do business. So is the ever-present fact of international terrorism, which affects our lives on a daily basis."

"Have they caught the people who were responsible for the zoo bombing?" Nat's mother sat back down on the couch.

"Two individuals are in custody, but it is believed that there were more people involved."

Nat's mother shook her head. "Unfortunately, our Western legal processes are, I believe, interpreted as weakness. It takes years, sometimes, before people are brought before a court, and then many walk free because of lack of compelling evidence. To those who live by the justice of the sword, we must seem incredibly weak and vulnerable."

Nat decided to change the subject. "What were you doing in New York?"

"Oh, just visiting some old friends." She paused and looked at Nat over the edge of her champagne glass. There was something in her eyes that made Nat feel uneasy. She kept looking at him. She took a sip of champagne and looked down as she put the glass on the coffee table. "That's not entirely true, Nat. I have been a bit stingy with the truth lately."

You and I both, Nat thought. He raised his eyebrows. "What's up, Mom?"

She sat back in the couch, folded her hands in her lap, and looked straight at him. "I've been going to Sloan Kettering for treatment for the past six weeks, radiation first—three sessions—then two weeks from now will be the first dose of chemo... colon cancer." The words hung in the air like two black clouds in a clear sky.

Nat drew a sharp breath. "Oh, Mother!" He leaned forward and held her hands. "Why didn't you tell us?"

"I was going to, but then you had your zoo episode, and I felt you had enough on your plate." Tears welled up in her eyes as she attempted a feeble smile.

Nat pulled her to him and held her tight. "You poor thing. You poor thing. You don't have to do this alone."

The tears flowed as she let herself go. They just sat there and held onto each other until the tears subsided.

"Silly me!" She sniffled and straightened up and smiled up at him. "Could you get me a Kleenex, darling?"

He left her, reluctantly, and returned moments later with a handful of paper tissues from the bathroom.

She blew her nose and placed the tissue in the pocket of the towel robe. Then she slapped her knees and gave Nat a bright smile. "Anyway, darling, I'm giving you the wrong impression. The doctors say the tumour has responded well to the radiation treatment, the last of which I had today. There will be three doses of chemo at four-week intervals. That's when my hair will fall out. I told them to tell me the truth, that I could handle the facts, and they told me I have a 70 percent chance of a full recovery. If I were a betting woman, I'd say those are odds worth betting on." She smiled and took a sip of champagne. "Of course, I'm not supposed to touch this stuff."

"Then don't, Mom." Nat took her glass. "There will be plenty of time for champagne when you get the all-clear."

She nodded and looked at her watch. It was getting on for 5:00 p.m. "Do you know what? I think I'd like to take a little nap before dinner."

"Good idea, Mom; you do that. I'll catch up on the international news, then I might take a short snooze, myself. This has turned into quite a day for us both."

Nat's mother retired to the bedroom, and Nat turned on the CNN Headline News channel but could not concentrate on what was on the screen. It was just after ten o'clock in England. He decided to call Sonja.

She answered on the fourth ring. "Jameson residence." Nat told her how he had been able to intercept his mother at the airport and that she was having a rest before dinner. "Sonja, Mom just told me that she is undergoing treatment for colon cancer. . . . Decided not to tell us because of the zoo episode."

"Oh, my god, Nat; that's dreadful. Poor Amy!"

"She was at Sloan Kettering for the last radiation session today." "No wonder she is tired," said Sonja. "What do the doctors say?"

"That's the good news. They say the tumour has responded well to the radiation, and now they are following up with chemotherapy. They give her a 70 percent chance of a full recovery."

"That's very positive, Nat, and your mother has the right spirit to conquer this. Do you think we should change our plans for Christmas? It'll probably be difficult for Amy to travel while she's still having treatment."

"I don't know. I'll ask her tonight. Knowing Mom, she's going to want to carry on as normal a life as possible."

"Yes, you're right." There was a short pause. "Nat, do we tell the children?"

Nat thought for a moment. "Not yet. I'll talk to her about that too. At some point they should be told, but I think we should let her decide when and how."

"I agree, darling. Are you OK?" The concern in Sonja's voice warmed Nat's heart. "You've had quite a day, yourself." Nat assured her that he was fine. "I'll have to take your word for it, darling. Give my love and best wishes to Amy. Tell her I'll call her when she gets home. I love you."

"I love you too, honey." They hung up.

The Lafayette Restaurant was full of business people relaxing after a hectic day in the office. The sound of voices and laughter mingled with the sound of crystal touching crystal. A pianist provided a soothing musical background.

Nat and his mother were seated at a quiet corner table with views over Lafayette Park towards a floodlit White House. Nat's mother ordered a simple salad for her starter and the halibut for her main course. Nat ordered tuna carpaccio for his starter and went for the filet mignon for his main course. He ordered a large bottle of Perrier water and decided to forgo the red wine to keep his mother company. A waiter arrived with a basket of bread and another with the bottle of Perrier and poured a glass for them both.

"Well, this is such a treat." Nat's mother lifted her glass, and they had an alcohol-free toast to each other and to a long and happy future.

Nat's mother gave her son a teasing look. "You must forgive me," she said. "Maybe it is the journalist in me, but you have witnessed two tragic, sudden deaths just weeks apart. First Ambassador Preston and now the vice president. If I were still an investigative reporter, and you were not my son, I would have wanted to ask you some searching questions."

Nat's heart started to beat faster. He knew she was having him on, but she made him feel uncomfortable. He had to play along.

"Fire away, Mrs. Jameson."

She took a sip of Perrier water. "Well, Mr. Ambassador." Her eyes twinkled with mischief. "Two prominent men have died suddenly, and you were at the scene in both instances. What would you say the odds were of that happening?"

Nat studied the tablecloth. "I'm not a gambling man, but I would say the chances of that happening would be one in a few hundred million?"

"If that." She studied him intently.

Nat started to feel a knot tighten in his stomach. Was she joking, or was she serious? Then, all of a sudden, she reached across the table and touched his hand.

"Forgive me, Nat. Two tragic deaths is not a laughing matter. I don't know what came over me." Thankfully, at that very moment, two waiters appeared with the starters and created a natural break for a change of subject.

"I called Sonja while you were resting and told her about your situation. She sends her love and best wishes and said to tell you that she will call you when you get home."

"Bless her. You are lucky to have a wife like Sonja to support you with all you are heading into."

"Yes, I am very lucky." *If only you knew how blessed I am*, he thought. He had a sudden urge to tell his mother about Endgame, but he knew that was not possible; instead, he switched the conversation to Christmas. "Sonja thought we should forget about Switzerland and have Christmas together here. What do you think?"

"Absolutely not! I don't want any change of plans on my account."

"But do you think you'll feel up to it? The air travel and all?"

"You bet I will! I've already got my ticket. I'm leaving here on the evening of the twenty-third of December, and I'll be with you in Zermatt midafternoon on the twenty-fourth."

Nat could tell there was no point in putting up an argument. "OK, but if you change your mind, let us know, and we'll all come over here."

She nodded, then focused on finishing her salad. They were in the middle of the main course when Nat's cell phone rang.

"Sorry, Mom. I thought I'd turned it off." He looked at the caller ID, but the number was not recognised.

"No, no, that's OK; take it. It could be important." Nat's mother busied herself with the food in front of her, while Nat accepted the call.

"Hello, Jameson here."

"Good evening, Mr. Jameson; I just wanted to say that our thoughts are with you. Can you tell me when you will be returning to London?" Imam Badawi had not introduced himself, but the voice and accent were unmistakable. Nat had no doubt who was at the other end of the line.

"I shall be back in London on the twentieth, the day after the vice president's funeral."

"Yes, very sad, very sad. Bad news for America." Badawi's gravelly voice sounded cheerful, despite the words. "Please call me when you get back; we have much work to do together."

Nat could feel his heart pick up the pace. "I will call you as soon as I can upon my return."

"Thank you. I look forward to hearing from you."

"Good night." Nat turned his phone off and returned it to his jacket pocket. "That's enough of that. The Russian ambassador seems anxious to meet me. Sorry for the interruption."

"Don't be. A call from the Russian ambassador after midnight his time must be pretty important, don't you think?" Nat's mother put her knife and fork down, showing that she had finished her meal. She had hardly eaten anything.

"He wants to talk about the missing warhead, I would imagine. It is a big embarrassment for the Russians and a big worry for the rest of the world. There is a real concern that it could end up in the hands of terrorists. We must find it and find it fast." Nat was only halfway through his steak and felt that he could really do with a drink, after all. "Would you mind, terribly, if I had a glass of wine to help me finish this steak?"

"Not at all. Go right ahead."

Nat got the attention of a waiter and ordered a glass of 2003 Pomerol.

"I've been reading about the missing warhead," said Nat's mother, "and, if I were an Israeli, I would be very worried right now."

"Why just if you were an Israeli?"

The waiter returned with Nat's glass of wine.

"Because, the Iranians have made no secret of their desire to see Israel wiped off the map, and we know that the warhead went from Russia to Iran."

"True," said Nat, "but we also know that Iran has agreed to allow a UN team in to help search for it, and they wouldn't do that if it was still there and they planned to use it against Israel, would they?"

Nat's mother hesitated. "No, unless they've hidden it so well that they are sure it can't be found."

“Or it has been passed on to someone outside Iran, someone like al-Qaeda, for example,” added Nat.

“You mean a team effort by like-minded people?”

“Precisely.”

“Good God, Nat! Are you saying that the nuclear warhead could be in terrorist hands as we speak?”

“I am saying it is a possibility which we cannot afford to ignore.”

“So that means we are at a stage where we must get to al-Qaeda?”

“Yes, that is true. We must find them.”

“But we can’t, can we? We haven’t caught a major al Qaeda operative since al Zawahiri.”

“True, but I have been told by the highest authority—”

“You mean, the president?”

“Yes—the president—that a major, international operation is being staged to infiltrate al-Qaeda.”

“A race against time.” There was a note of resignation in Nat’s mother’s voice.

“Well, don’t forget the trigger mechanism is still intact in Russia, and the delivery system, the rocket and fuel, is also not readily available. It will take time and substantial resources to get a fully functional weapon system assembled.”

“And, whoever they are, if they got it all together, who knows who they would aim it at? I said Israel, but it could be Washington or New York, right?”

“It could be anywhere,” said Nat, “but Israel would be an easier target, unless they can get their hands on an intercontinental ballistic missile.”

“Iran has those types of missiles, so if they are the culprits, they just need to work on the trigger mechanism.”

Nat's mother paused as the waiters cleared their plates. One of them returned to take their dessert order. They declined dessert but ordered a decaf cappuccino each. The coffee returned moments later with a small silver plate of biscotti.

"Ah, my favourite." Nat took a biscuit and dipped it carefully in his coffee.

"I don't think ambassadors should dunk in public." Nat's mother waved an admonishing finger at her son.

"Sorry, you're right. Bad habit."

They lingered over the coffee. Nat told his mother about Tanya's essay and reassured her that Sonja and the children were coping well with the aftermath of the zoo bombing. He also shared his reservations about Anthony Burville, his new deputy chief of mission.

"So, I imagine that means you are anxious to return to London as soon as possible."

"Yes, there is a lot to be done, and a lot of it can't be delegated, even to a good assistant, never mind to a fellow like Tony."

She patted his hand gently. "You have to learn to delegate and to pace yourself so you don't end up where Ambassador Preston went."

Nat produced what he hoped was a reassuring smile. "Don't worry, Mom; I'm not going there any time soon."

"Good," she said. "That makes two of us. Neither am I." Nat's mother looked at her watch as she yawned discreetly behind her raised wrist. "Oh, my... nine thirty. Time for bed for an old lady. What are your plans for tomorrow?"

Nat told her that he was being picked up at 9:00 a.m. and that he would be tied up in meetings most of the day. He suggested that she stay on so they could have another evening together, but she said she needed to get back to her animals. She had one dog and one cat being boarded at a local kennel while she was away.

"I'll leave shortly after you tomorrow morning."

CHAPTER 52

Nat and his mother had finished their breakfast fifteen minutes before he was due to be picked up. When Nat asked her if she would find her way back home from the centre of Washington, she assured him that it would not be a problem.

"My Garmin has never let me down," she said, referring to her GPS navigation system.

They said goodbye, and Nat got her to promise that she would keep them posted on her progress and let them know if she changed her mind about Switzerland. She scoffed at the suggestion but agreed that, of course, she would.

His car arrived just as he headed for the front door. The driver remained behind the wheel, while a man got out of the back seat, as Nat came through the front door. He was tall with dark brown hair and a hawk-like nose, supporting a pair of dark horn-rimmed glasses. Nat estimated that he was in his mid-forties. He held the door open and extended his hand when Nat approached.

"Good morning, Mr. Ambassador. Very nice to meet you in person. My name is Tom." He smiled as he closed the door, went around to the other side, and got in next to Nat. "Hi Nat.

I gather you had a very successful meeting with the vice president yesterday." Seeing Nat's worried glance at the back of the driver, he added, "He can't hear us unless we want him to and press this button." He pointed to a red button on the bulkhead in front of them. "If I press it, the button goes green." The glass, which separated the driver from the back, was so clear that Nat had not noticed it.

"Wow! Hi, Tom. I thought, for a horrible second, you'd blown it. I didn't notice the glass." A smile of relief spread across Nat's face.

"I guess I should be offended that you thought me capable of making a mistake like that, but I'm not." He gave Nat a big grin. "You're our greatest asset right now. The director calls you 'our star performer'."

"That's not right," said Nat. "I haven't 'performed' much yet. So far, it's been Ambassador Preston and Vice President Burton who've done most of the performing."

"Don't sell yourself short, Nat. You came up with the idea, you sold it to Imam Badawi, and you have played an active role in executing the plan, successfully, to this point. Of the few people who know about this operation, there is great excitement and anticipation from the president on down. I am here so that we get you through security at Langley, no questions asked."

They soon turned onto the George Washington Memorial Parkway, and Tom pressed the button in front of him. "Dan, stop when you can, and remove the flags, please."

"Yes, sir. Will do." Dan's voice came through loud and clear.

"Thanks." Tom pressed the button again and leaned back in his seat. He looked at his watch. "We'll be there in ten minutes. I'll take you to Benson's office, and then you'll meet some people who'll run through the next steps and prepare you for your meeting with al-Qaeda." Nat felt a chill run down his spine. Tom's certainty that it was going to happen turned it from dream to reality.

It was really going to happen, and it would happen soon. Nat looked out at the shimmering glimpses of the Potomac River, caught between the trees which lined the parkway. It was a beautiful sight in the bright morning sun.

"I have gone through hundreds of scenarios in my mind of how and where that might happen," said Nat. "My preferred version is that we meet at the Ritz, in Paris, where they live, disguised as Middle Eastern businessmen. Your people should be able to get to us easily in a location like that."

"Yeah, that would be great, but I doubt we'll be that lucky. We are pretty sure they are still holed up somewhere in Pakistan."

Nat gave Tom a sideways glance. "That will take longer, right?"

"Not necessarily. We have about three hundred special ops forces in Pakistan right now, all very low-key, but embedded in that group are sixty or so marines and Navy Seals who are, in fact, a special task force, ready to act on intelligence on the whereabouts of wanted persons in Pakistan. Wanted by us, that is. No doubt they will be placed on high alert once you tell us you have your invitation to meet with al-Qaeda leaders."

"Glad to hear that," said Nat, "but what makes you so sure I'll get that invitation?"

Their driver pulled in at a rest area, stopped, and got out, leaving the car running, and removed the flags.

Tom pressed the button as they took off again. "Thanks, Dan." He pressed the button again and returned his attention to Nat. "You'll get that invitation because al-Qaeda will not be able to pass up an opportunity like this. Killing the president of the United States of America will fulfil their dream of avenging the killing of bin Laden. Right now, they are probably thanking the prophet for having sent you to help their cause."

"But will they believe that it's for real, or will they smell the trap and let me walk into theirs?" Nat put into words his own worst fear and felt better immediately after he had said it.

Tom shook his head. "Highly unlikely, unless something goes wrong and it gets out that you didn't kill anybody. But that's not going to happen; I can assure you. And, don't forget, once you are sure that you are in the midst of al-Qaeda's headquarters and you press the button on your watch, our special ops people will be all over you in a matter of hours. Your greatest risk will come from friendly fire, but we'll go over with you a whole bunch of what-if scenarios to help prepare you for all that. Right... here we are."

They pulled up outside the Old Headquarters Building. The driver jumped out and held the door for Nat, while Tom helped himself out on the other side.

CHAPTER 53

CIA Director Charles Benson was all smiles when Nat and Tom entered his office.

Tom closed the door behind them as Benson rose from his desk and stretched his hand out to shake Nat's. "Good morning, Nat. It's good to see you again. Are you well?"

"Very well, thank you."

Benson had a firm handshake. He gestured for them both to be seated and sat down himself. A frown spread across his face. "We don't go by last names around here, and we don't call each other 'sir' either. You've been in England for too long, maybe?" The smile returned. "Please call me Charlie." He continued before Nat could respond. "First, let me say that we are extremely pleased at the way Operation Endgame is unfolding. The 'deaths' of Ambassador Preston and the vice president have been successfully executed, and we have good reason to believe that this will achieve the desired result of you getting an audience with al Qaeda and his top people. That being the case, we now need to prepare you for that event."

Benson paused, and looked at Tom. "As Tom may have told you, the disappearance of the Russian warhead has created a new urgency to get inside al-Qaeda. We are very fortunate that you came to us with a plan that greatly enhances that possibility. The president is following this operation every step of the way. He says that dismantling the al-Qaeda network will greatly enhance his ability to broker a Middle East peace settlement, which is at the top of his agenda for next year. He also believes—and we agree with him—that there is a good possibility that al-Qaeda may be involved in the disappearance of the Russian warhead. If that is the case, then it is only a matter of time until they find a way to make a trigger mechanism, and that time would be greatly reduced if the Iranians are involved. Erasing Israel from the map is a goal Iran and al-Qaeda have in common. The notion that they could be working together to achieve that objective is not so far-fetched. The fact that the Iranians have agreed to allow UN inspection teams in to help search for the warhead means that it is no longer there. So where is it? We are throwing a lot of resources at finding the warhead, but infiltrating al-Qaeda is equally important, particularly if it turns out that, finding one, we find both." Benson let the words sink in before he continued. "So, Tom is going to take you to a briefing room where you will meet two of our special ops experts. They will show you some videos—some of real training exercises and some animated footage—demonstrating how our commandos will mount the attack on al-Qaeda's headquarters. Obviously, this will differ depending on the location and physical nature of their hideout. The object of the exercise is to catch them all—dead or alive—with as many of his group as possible and making sure that you come to no harm in the process." Benson hesitated and fixed his eyes on Nat. "And this is the time when I have to tell you that we cannot guarantee your safety; there is a risk that you could be injured or even killed in the attack. I would be lying to you if I told you otherwise."

Nat swallowed hard. This had been on his mind since the beginning, but hearing the words still sent a shiver through him. It crossed his mind that perhaps, in the scheme of things, he might be expendable, but he decided not to ask the question. *Maybe I don't want to know the answer?* he thought.

"Any questions?" Benson's words took Nat by surprise. Could the man read his mind?

"None that come to mind right now." Nat smiled. "But I will probably have many as the day progresses."

"Very well, then." Benson rose from his desk. "Tom will take you to the briefing room, and I'll join you for some lunch later."

The briefing room was a small auditorium with raked seating. When they entered, two men, casually dressed, rose from seats in the back row and came towards them. Tom made the introductions by way of first names only.

Leslie, the older of the two, was introduced as a clinical psychologist who specialised in the workings of the minds of fanatics, and Travis was a special operations strategist with ten years' experience in the field.

"I shall leave you in their capable hands," said Tom, when he had finished the introductions. He looked at his watch. "Benson and I will join you for lunch in the cafeteria at twelve thirty."

Tom took his leave, and Leslie invited Nat to take a seat midpoint of the raked seating. They placed themselves either side of him. Travis had a remote control in his hand. "We'll start, first, by taking a closer look at some of the men you are going to meet, including one you are not going to meet because we killed him back in 2011. It's all yours, Leslie."

The lights dimmed, and the projection screen came alive with an image of a younger bin Laden, taken during the 1980s Afghan war.

Leslie started his narrative. "So here is the man who started it all. The heroic jihadist who threw the Russians out of Afghanistan, or so he was seen by many Muslims around the world. Had Russia not attacked Afghanistan, it is very unlikely that al-Qaeda would exist as we know it today. Bin Laden took a just war against Russia in Afghanistan and hijacked it into a jihad against all 'infidels', i.e., non-Muslims and Muslims who don't practice the most extreme forms of the faith. His actual contribution to the war effort was minimal, but the kudos and the following he was able to extract from it were phenomenal." The next slide showed bin Laden in a camouflage jacket, holding a Russian AK-47 assault rifle. Leslie continued. "Urban legend has it that Osama killed a Russian soldier with his bare hands and took his rifle and jacket. Stories of his bravery in battle abound and contribute greatly to his stature in the world of Islamic extremists. At the end of the Soviet/Afghan war in 1989, bin Laden returned to Saudi Arabia a hero of jihad. Al-Qaeda had been formed in August of 1988 at a meeting between senior leaders of Egyptian Islamic Jihad including the deceased second leader of al-Qaeda, Ayman Al-Zawahiri." Leslie flicked to a picture of a bespectacled man with a long grey beard and a black turban. "Bin Laden was preparing for the next 'battle', which he predicted would be against America. There were two reasons for this prediction, one being that Osama had always considered the presence of US troops in the 'holy land' to be a profanity, and two being that the US support for Israel had made it possible for the Jews to continue their oppression of the

Palestinians. Bin Laden and Zawahiri, therefore, turned their attention to the West. Various terrorist plots, including a plot to blow up a New York skyscraper, were discovered in 1990. That same year saw another event which was to have a profound effect on Osama and his terrorist network—the Iraqi attack on Kuwait in August of that year. Bin Laden tried to convince King Fahd and the minister of defence of Saudi Arabia not to turn to America for support, which would perpetuate the presence of foreign troops on Arabian soil. He offered to supply his own mujahideen fighters in the defence of Saudi Arabia and its oil fields. His offer was turned down, and this turned bin Laden into a fierce critic of King Fahd and the Saudi regime. Bin Laden kept up his criticism of King Fahd, was expelled from Saudi Arabia in 1992, and went to live in exile in Sudan. This did not seem to have a negative impact on his 'war on the West', as can be seen from the string of attacks which followed: The 1992 hotel bombings in Yemen, the 1993 World Trade Center, and the 1992 attacks on US troops in Mogadishu."

Leslie was pressing the remote as he spoke, showing a picture of each event. "Then followed the 1998 US embassy bombings in Kenya and Tanzania and the bombing of the USS *Cole*, in Yemen, in 2000." More pictures. "And then, Osama's crowning achievement: 2001, 9/11, the World Trade Center and the Pentagon. The most spectacular and deadly terrorist attack on American soil—the attack that changed everything." Leslie was flicking through a number of images in quick succession. "These are images imprinted in every American's soul, and these are the same images that elevated bin Laden to godlike status in the minds of many Muslims. It is also, we believe, the event that, after years of avoiding capture, made bin Laden think that he himself was a prophet, second only to Mohammed and the man Allah had chosen to establish Islam as the dominant world religion." The screen went blank, and the lights came back on. Leslie turned to Nat. "This is to give you some sense of why we believe that bin Laden was a man who not only believed in his own ability to outwit the mighty US of A and her allies but believed that his powers to do what he did came from God—the only true God—Allah. He believed he was chosen to fight this fight." Leslie paused, looked at his watch, and then at Nat and Travis. "Shall we take a little break and have a cup of coffee?"

A table at the back of the auditorium was set with a coffee urn, cups, plates, and a selection of cookies, and Travis led the way. They helped themselves to coffee, and Leslie and Travis each took a doughnut. Nat stayed with just the coffee. Sonja would not be impressed if she saw him eating junk food. They remained standing by the table, and it was Travis who spoke first, between mouthfuls of doughnut.

"We don't know the details, but we've been told that you're involved in a mission, the aim of which is for you to infiltrate al-Qaeda."

"That's right." Nat smiled. "I have some contacts that may make that possible." He realised that he could not explain it any further.

"Better you than me." Leslie shook his head. "That sounds like a very dangerous assignment, to me."

Nat chuckled. "Is that a question or a statement?"

They all laughed.

Back in their seats, Leslie explained that he would show a video, first broadcast by Al Jazeera in 2004, in which bin Laden accepted responsibility for the 9/11 attacks. "In it, you'll hear Osama explain the justifications for the assault on the twin towers and what inspired him to do it." Leslie pressed the remote, and an amateur-quality film started to roll, showing bin Laden, in a white turban and robes, under a gold mantle, standing at a lectern with a manuscript in his hands. The background was a featureless brown. He started speaking in Arabic, and English subtitles appeared at the bottom of the screen. He spoke in a low, monotone voice.

There was no sign of agitation or anger. It was as if he was lecturing a group of students on current affairs. He warned the Americans that, "... the best way to avoid another Manhattan is not to threaten the security of Muslim nations, such as Palestine and Lebanon." The inspiration for the attack on the twin towers came from looking at "... the destroyed towers in Lebanon; it sparked my mind that the tyrant should be punished with the same and that we should destroy towers in America."

He went on to say that the conditions which provoked 9/11 had not changed and declared, "We are free people who do not accept injustice, and we want to regain the freedom of our nation."

He compared America to corrupt Arab governments and mocked the Bush administration: "It is easy for us to provoke and bait this administration. All we have to do is to send two mujahideen to the farthest point east to raise a piece of cloth on which is written 'al-Qaeda', in order to make generals race there and cause America to suffer human, economic, and political losses... This is in addition to our having experience in using guerrilla warfare and the war of attrition to fight tyrannical superpowers, as we, alongside the mujahideen, bled Russia for ten years, until it went bankrupt and was forced to withdraw in defeat."

Leslie paused the film and turned to Nat. "Take note of the reference to the Soviet/Afghan war. He gives all the credit for the outcome of that war, first, to himself and his own fighters and, second, to the Afghan mujahideen. No mention of the three billion dollars' worth of support from the United States. It did not suit his purpose to acknowledge the vital role that American weapons and logistical support played in the defeat of the Soviets. This was a man who altered reality to suit his own purpose. He used his own interpretation of the Quran to justify his actions, and he did not do it to deceive you; he firmly believed that his actions and those of his followers were not only justified but required, by Allah, of any true believer."

Leslie restarted the video. Osama dismissed Bush's statement that Islamic extremists hate freedom: "It is known that freedom-haters don't have defiant spirits like those of the nineteen; may God have mercy on them."

"We'll carry on to the end, but remember that statement. It is central to what made bin Laden tick, and it is central to the belief of his successor and the whole al-Qaeda leadership." Leslie spoke without taking his eyes off the screen.

The video finished with bin Laden criticising President Bush's actions on the day of the 9/11 attacks, saying Bush had left fifty thousand citizens in the two towers to face their ordeal alone, while he was busy reading a children's story, referring to Bush's visit to an elementary school where he was listening to the children reading *The Pet Goat* when the twin towers were attacked.

Travis, who had remained quiet for the duration of the video, coughed and cleared his throat. He turned to Nat as he dropped his feet off the chair back in front of him. "So, you see, the man we killed was not 'all there', to quote the Cheshire Cat in *Alice in Wonderland*. And that's where he was—in Wonderland. Unfortunately for us, since his death, al-Qaeda has been recruiting candidates for self-sacrifice like never before. The would-be martyrs are lining up to get to their wonderland, lining up to meet scores of virgins who they couldn't even look at in this life."

Leslie gave Travis an exasperated look. "OK, Travis, we all live in our own wonderlands. The difference is some are more real than others." He turned to Nat. "Let's go back to the statement about the 'nineteen'—the nineteen terrorists who hijacked three planes on the eleventh of September back in 2001. In Osama's mind, the nineteen hijackers loved freedom. Their fight was for the freedom of oppressed Muslims, the fight goes on under the current leadership. Killing Zawahiri, impressive as it was, did nothing except making the organization more secretive. We believe they are now spread out all over the place, which makes communications more difficult and weakens their ability to plan and coordinate terrorist actions, but judging by the frequency of attacks, the organisation still functions well enough."

"Ayman al-Zawahiri. . . " The screen filled with images of the man. ". . . was, as I'm sure you know, an educated man. Came from an upper-middle-class Egyptian family, most of whom were doctors, as he was. He excelled in school and has been described by many as an intellectual. He came out in favour of the revolutionaries in the Middle East uprising but not because he believed in democracy. Palestinians under the Israeli heel is his main gripe, but his enemies are also Arab rulers who do not follow his own strict interpretation of the Muslim faith. He talked about freedom from oppression, and yet he wanted the world to be ruled by fundamentalist Muslim, totalitarian regimes. He did not see the contradiction. The words 'democracy' and 'self-determination' did not exist in Zawahiri's vocabulary." Leslie looked at his watch. "We've got fifteen minutes until lunch. Any questions on what you have seen and heard so far?" He turned to Nat.

"Yes, a few. Did Zawahiri speak English at all? All his messages seemed to have been in Arabic."

"He could speak English and French. Bin Laden, too, could speak some English, but don't forget what we are looking at are propaganda tools aimed at the Muslim world. They know that we will translate them for our purposes. Zawahiri was quite capable of carrying on a conversation in English should he choose to do so."

"What about his personal life? Do we know much about that?"

"We know a reasonable amount." Leslie picked up a file from the chair next to him. "Ayman al-Zawahiri was born in 1951 in Maadi, a suburb of Cairo. His father came from a large family of doctors, and as you know, Zawahiri was a doctor himself. He excelled in school and loved poetry. Joined the Muslim Brotherhood when he was fourteen years old. Married in 1978 and had four daughters and one son and, ten years later, another son who had Down Syndrome. His wife and one of his daughters were killed when the Americans bombed a Taliban headquarters building in Afghanistan shortly after 9/11, in November 2001. He had another daughter in 2005. Zawahiri rose to become one of Egyptian Islamic Jihad's foremost recruiters and organisers, and it was his goal to one day overthrow Egypt's secular leaders. A failed coup against Anwar Sadat in February 1981, just prior to his assassination, resulted in the rounding up of some fifteen hundred people thought to be terrorists, and Zawahiri was one of them. He spent three years in jail, where he claimed that he was tortured. He was exiled from Egypt and went to Saudi Arabia for one year, practicing medicine. It was here that he first met bin Laden in 1986. He then travelled to Peshawar, where he worked in a hospital, treating wounded refugees. In Peshawar, he met up with bin Laden again, and it was here that he started to rebuild the EIJ, the Egyptian Islamic Jihad. The two realised that they had a lot in common and joined forces in 1988 under the al-Qaeda banner. Zawahiri has travelled extensively through Western Europe, shaved off his beard, worn Western clothing, and travelled with false passports. He came to the US in 1993, addressing several California mosques, again traveling under a false identity."

Leslie flicked through another series of photographs of the al-Qaeda leader as he continued talking.

"Zawahiri was the brain of al-Qaeda since its inception. Bin Laden was the inspirational leader and the man with the money to make things happen. You'll remember that Zawahiri came out in strong support of the Arab Uprising. For al-Qaeda, this was a golden opportunity to rid Middle Eastern countries of their secular leaders, doing what al-Qaeda has been unable to do in thirty years of trying, and an opportunity, as they saw it, to turn these countries into true Muslim republics. Not democracies, as we, and the majority of the protesters, were hoping for but fundamental Muslim states under Sharia law. The enemies of Islam, according to al-Qaeda, are many. The West, of course, but also Muslim countries whose leaders do not subscribe to their strict Wahhabi religious movement within Sunni Islam. The four principal enemies of Islam, according to al-Qaeda, are America, Israel, Shia Muslims, and 'Heretics'. In fact, bin Laden claimed that the only truly Islamic country in the Muslim world was Afghanistan when it was under Taliban rule."

"So, when he claimed to speak and act for Muslims," Nat interjected, "he was not being very truthful."

"Not at all, and this is a state of delusion that is typical in most fanatics. What made Zawahiri more dangerous than his predecessor was that, while he shared bin Laden's radical Islamist views, he was a cold, calculating technician of terror and destruction."

"Tell me, isn't Wahhabism the dominant form of Islam in Saudi Arabia?"

"It is; and here is another contradiction—bin Laden hated the Saudi regime even though they adhere to the version of the Muslim faith that he subscribed to, himself, and even though a lot of Saudi oil money has financed al-Qaeda operations over the years and built a lot of mosques and madrassas around the world." Leslie looked at his watch again. "OK, we better break for lunch. Can't keep the boss waiting."

CHAPTER 54

They met up with the CIA director at the entrance to the cafeteria. Benson smiled. “Good timing. Tom sends his apologies. Something came up. He’s glued to his screen. How are you fellows doing?” The question was aimed at nobody in particular, but Nat thought it was for him to answer.

“Good. I’m finding out things about al—”

“Shh. . . ” Benson placed his index finger over his mouth. “No names, please.”

“. . . about the people I hope to meet soon,” Nat corrected himself. “. . . things that begin to make me understand what makes them tick.”

“Excellent, that’s the idea. Forewarned is forearmed. Let’s eat; I’m starved.”

They helped themselves to lunch at the counter and settled down at a quiet corner table where they could talk without being overheard.

Benson dug into his lasagna, Leslie—a meat pie, Travis—a cheeseburger and fries, and Nat—a chicken salad. Nobody said a word for a couple of minutes, until Benson looked up from his lasagna.

"I had a call from the president this morning; he is following this operation like a hawk. He told me that he wants all our special ops personnel around the world to be placed on high alert from the moment you get back to London so that our response time is the shortest possible, wherever al Qaeda's top brass are hiding."

There was a moment's pause, and Nat decided to ask the question he had wanted to ask when they broke for lunch.

"Leslie mentioned that a lot of Saudi oil money has gone into financing al-Qaeda operations around the world. On top of that, we know that sixteen of the nineteen hijackers who attacked us on 9/11 were Saudi citizens, and yet, we consider the Saudis our closest ally in the Middle East. Why is that?"

Benson looked at Nat, raised his eyebrows, and produced a deep sigh. "Now, that's a hell of a question, and one that should be answered by the politicians rather than by someone like myself. Anyway, since you've asked, I'll try to give you my take on the situation. I'll have to be careful not to give away any state secrets." He smiled as he put his fork down and nudged the plate of half-eaten lasagna away. "As you know, our military presence in Saudi Arabia started with Operation Desert Shield in 1990, when Saddam attacked Kuwait. US-led coalition forces, including Saudi Arabia, Britain, and Egypt, fought the UN-sanctioned war, which brought Iraqi troops to heel very quickly. Our troops remained after the war had been won, under Operation Southern Watch, to enforce the no-fly zone over Iraq and to ensure that Saddam didn't try it again." Benson took another forkful of lasagna before he continued.

"We had some sixty thousand troops in Saudi Arabia at the height of the fighting. The majority of our troops were withdrawn from Prince Sultan Air Base in 2003, leaving about five hundred in Saudi Arabia, with forty-five hundred troops redeployed to Al Udeid Air Base in Qatar."

"Wasn't that move at the request of the Saudis, who were coming under a lot of criticism from bin Laden for allowing the continued presence of infidel troops in the holy land?"

Benson looked like Nat's question had taken him by surprise. He pinched his nose as he searched his mind for an appropriate answer. "That is one theory, yes."

The tone of his voice suggested he was not about to reveal any other theories on the subject. "So, you can see," he continued, "the Gulf War forged a strong relationship between us and our coalition partners. Our relationship with Britain, which has always been strong, grew stronger, and our relationships with Saudi Arabia and Egypt took on a new dimension of cooperation." Benson stopped, apparently at the end of his explanation.

Nat was not satisfied with the answer. "You didn't answer my question. I am well aware of the history you describe, but it hardly explains why our most ardent enemies come from just those countries."

"I think it does." Benson left the statement without further explanation.

"How?" Nat persisted.

Benson chewed his lip and hesitated, debating with himself whether he should continue. He sighed and folded his hands in front of him. "I think it does because we, the US, spent years supporting repressive regimes in those countries on the basis that they were our allies in the Middle East. We criticise the Chinese for their poor record on human rights, but we ignored the same from Hosni Mubarak because he was anti the Muslim Brotherhood and, supposedly, a 'friend' of Israel. Muslim militancy grew strongest in the countries where oppression of the local population went hand in hand with support from the US. That is why, in my opinion, the majority of those who were prepared to lay down their own lives to punish America came from Saudi Arabia and Egypt."

Benson looked at his lasagna, picked up his fork, changed his mind, and put the fork down again and added the knife to it. His appetite for lunch was clearly over. He looked at his watch. "Time to get back to work. I'm expecting a call from my Russian counterpart this afternoon on the subject of the missing nuclear warhead. Apparently, Colonel Ivanovitch has suffered a stroke and cannot be interrogated about his involvement in the disappearance of the device." Benson got up from the table. "We don't like this turn of events. When you combine this news with the Iranian revolutionary guard's suicide in jail, who could therefore also not be interrogated about the part he played in receiving the warhead in Iran and what he did with it, it starts to have a very bad smell." He paused and looked at each of them, in turn, before he continued. "It is beginning to look like the Russian and Iranian authorities could be involved. If that is the case, could they have created an unholy alliance with al-Qaeda to further the objective of obliterating Israel?" Benson lowered his voice. "We must find al Qaeda's headquarters, and find it soon. Have a productive afternoon. Prepare him well." Benson's parting words to Leslie and Travis underscored the importance of Nat's mission.

Back in the auditorium, Leslie spent another half hour showing videos of interviews with Zawahiri before he handed over to Travis.

Nat estimated that Travis was in his late-forties. He looked very fit. The short-cropped greying blond hair and pale blue eyes behind steel-rimmed glasses gave him a distinctly military look. That looks do not always deceive became clear when Travis gave a quick summary of his own background.

Travis was a retired Delta Force commander with extensive field experience, including Yemen, Somalia, and Afghanistan. He had been involved in the hunt for bin Laden at Tora Bora, where they destroyed al-Qaeda's base but failed to capture or kill the man himself, which had been the main objective of the operation. The maze of caves and bunkers, which had served as bin Laden's headquarters for ten years, were demolished by arial bombardments and ground artillery. Travis explained that had the Delta snipers been allowed to get directly involved in chasing after the al-Qaeda fighters who fled across the mountains into Pakistan, chances are they would have found their man. The decision-makers, meaning the politicians, had insisted that the Afghan mujahedeen had to be in the forefront, and Travis said, the "muhj" fighters, who always left the battlefield at night, let hundreds of al-Qaeda fighters disappear across the border, and, obviously, bin Laden and Zawahiri had been among them.

He recalled that Lieutenant Colonel Ashley's request to close the mountain passes and trails with mines had been rejected. The mines would, no doubt, have killed a lot more al-Qaeda fighters and might have got bin Laden in the process. There was no doubt in Travis's mind that the decision to allow the ground forces to be headed by Afghan mujahedeen commanders had led to the failure of the Tora Bora mission.

"So," he said, "this time, if you lead us to al-Qaeda's headquarters, the president has assured us that catching them will be a Delta Force operation. The scale and nature of the operation will depend on where you find them, but wherever that may be, we shall be knocking on their door within eight hours. Since we don't expect them to open it and invite us in, we will bring a group of highly trained and well-equipped individuals who don't take no for an answer. Whether they live in a cave in Pakistan or Afghanistan, or wherever they might be hiding out, they are likely to be surrounded by security people who will sacrifice their lives to guard them. This means you'll hear us coming, and this will be the most dangerous time for you, for two reasons. One: when all hell breaks loose, they'll realise that their hideout has been discovered, and he is likely to connect the dots and realise that it has something to do with your presence. They may try to kill you there and then, and for obvious reasons, you will not carry weapons of any kind to defend yourself."

Nat felt his heart picking up the pace. The image of having his throat slit while the fighting was going on outside flashed through his mind. If he noticed Nat's discomfort, Travis did not let on.

He continued: "It is therefore best if you can put some distance between yourself and the terrorists. Escape may be impossible and too risky, but if we attack at night, which is what we plan to do, you may be in a bedroom by yourself, and you may be able to lock the door and buy some time. We are tasked with getting the al-Qaeda people dead or alive, so being away from them when we attack is going to be the safest scenario for you. We will do everything we can to get to you as fast as possible, but remember getting al Qaeda's top brass is our first objective. Your safety is second."

Travis paused and gave Nat a long hard look that said, *Just so you know what you're up against.*

Nat could feel that the tightness in his gut was winding a bit tighter, but he nodded. "I am under no illusion as to what your priorities are. I just hope you'll do your best to keep me intact."

Travis smiled. "I like that word, 'intact'. We will do our utmost to keep you intact, but you could be hurt in the process. The team that goes in is well versed in dealing with the freeing of hostages, and you are in the same boat, except you volunteered to be there."

Travis turned the screen on, showing a picture of bin Laden flanked by al-Zawahiri and Mohammed Atef at a press conference pre-9/11. "As you can see, one thing which will help us is the clothing. Al-Qaeda comrades are always wearing the same clothes and full beards. I note you don't have a beard. Don't grow one, and don't let anybody talk you into wearing a white turban and flowing robes; stick with your Western clothing. Blue jeans and your favourite football team jersey and cap would be great, but I guess we'll have to settle for a business suit. Just make sure you wear a bright tie. Red would be good." Travis put the remote down and reached for a laptop on the seat next to him. "Let's run through some attack scenarios."

The screen came alive with a cartoon image of a compound of buildings seen from the air.

"OK, here we have a make-believe al-Qaeda compound similar to one we destroyed at Tora Bora. Once your locator has given us their presence, our intelligence boys will bring up a satellite image of the location, which will enable us to study the physical characteristics of the area in great detail. We will have real-time, detailed video showing anything or anybody moving around between buildings. We will be able to estimate the approximate number of enemy combatants and size our task force accordingly. In this situation, we'll approach the site in attack helicopters with plenty of firepower, including grenade and rocket launchers. One group will secure the perimeter. Nobody will be allowed to escape. This time they either get captured, or they get killed. The other group will go in with AK-47s, grenades, and machine guns, pistols, knives, and clubs. We'll look like a band of Ninja Turtles, dressed in night camouflage fatigues, black Kevlar helmets with flip-up night-vision goggles, and black vests with ceramic plates capable of stopping a round from an AK-47 rifle. We'll be wearing web gear containing grenades—some of them stun grenades—ammunition, special knives, explosive charges, fuse igniter systems, quick-tie tourniquets, and a special medical kit to stop bleeding. Silenced scoped sniper rifles and scoped machine guns will cover the perimeter—three hundred and sixty degrees. Nobody is going to slip away, not even by air. Ground-to-air missiles are part of the arsenal we're arriving with. You'll hear us coming. We expect them to put up a good fight, but they don't have the tools or the training to match us. If you are not in a separate room already, try to get to someplace on your own. In the panic and confusion, you may be able to find a place to hide. Do not—I repeat, do not run outside and away from the building you're in, whatever happens, or you'll be shot by one of our people. When you hear us getting close, start shouting your name repeatedly and the word 'here'. This will help us locate you and make sure we don't throw a grenade in the wrong direction. Close combat is tricky business, but we expect to have the element of surprise in our favour as well as all the other advantages I have mentioned already. Any questions so far?" Travis opened a bottle of water and took a long swig.

"Yes," said Nat. "As you pointed out, I will not have a weapon of any kind to defend myself with. Should the time—from when you start your attack until you reach me—become quite a long time, and they have added two and two together and realised that I am responsible for them being attacked, I imagine they might want to do something about it before you have a chance to stop it. It would be nice to know some self-defence routines to improve my odds of survival should that situation arise."

Travis replaced the screw cap on his water bottle and returned it to the seat next to him. "You're a mind reader. I was coming to that next. Tomorrow and the next day will be devoted to teaching you ways not only to defend yourself but how to turn your hands and feet into lethal weapons. I can assure you, you'll feel a lot better after this crash course. In the meantime, let's run through this video of a Delta Force attack on a compound with two hundred al-Qaeda fighters."

Travis pressed the remote, and the film started to roll showing eight AH-6 attack helicopters and three MH-6 transport helicopters approaching the compound. Four of the attack helicopters landed a distance away from the compound, landing at 1:30, 4:30, 7:30, and 8:30, and the other four attack helicopters continued in close to the edge of the buildings, landing at twelve, three, six, and nine o'clock. The three transport helicopters landed behind the outer ring of helicopters, dividing the circle precisely in three.

Men, dressed in combat gear, much as Travis had described, with the exception of the night-vision goggles, as this was a daytime operation, jumped out of the choppers—six from each. The men on the perimeter spread out evenly, to form an almost equally spaced ring consisting of snipers and machine gunners, and they were already in place when the four attack helicopters, close to the buildings, landed and started to discharge their men—six each—who stayed together as a group and headed for the nearest buildings. Enemy fighters appeared on some of the rooftops and were picked off by the snipers. Enemy fighters came running out of some of the buildings firing at the approaching Delta Force operatives who fanned out in pairs as they returned fire. The enemies withdrew to the shelter of the buildings, and the soldiers put on a zigzag-dash straight for the buildings where enemy fire was now coming from the windows and other openings in the perimeter buildings. Some enemy fighters appeared again on roofs but were quickly taken out by the snipers.

The first Delta fighters reached the relative safety of the walls of the outer buildings and tossed grenades through the windows. A grenade was fired at a door from a grenade launcher and blew the door off its hinges. Two Delta soldiers took up positions either side of the opening and tossed in a grenade each. Black smoke and a cloud of dust erupted through the opening, and the Delta group of six men entered the building under the cover of the smoke.

Travis pressed the pause button. "This gives you some idea of what will be happening outside. At this point, if you are not already alone, try to separate yourself and find a place to hide if you can. Our men will be coming through the buildings room by room using grenades, rifles, and pistols. Here we go."

Travis restarted the film. The roof of the building was peeled off to reveal a maze of corridors and rooms, giving a bird's-eye view of the whole compound, showing Delta teams penetrating the compound from four sides. Nat noted that all the Delta operatives had mics attached to their helmets.

"The team leaders are in contact with each other, describing what they are encountering, and reporting progress. This is important to minimise the risk of friendly fire incidents." Travis had answered the question Nat was about to ask before he had asked it. He paused the film again and pointed to a room in the middle of the compound where one person was lying on a mattress on the floor.

"This is a hostage, and the object of this exercise is to free the hostage, obtain any intel that may be available on computers and on paper, and destroy the compound. The grenades being used, as they move room to room, are stun-grenades only, designed to disable rather than kill."

Travis restarted the film, and the scenes of close combat reminded Nat of some of the games he had seen his son play on the computer. The enemy fighters were putting up fierce resistance but were outgunned and outmaneuvered. Their response was erratic and uncoordinated. Nat noticed that the two guards outside the room where the hostage was held had not moved from their posts, despite the chaos around them. The Delta groups were advancing slowly from all sides towards the middle. The group which had entered the building first reached the hallway where the two guards stood. The guards fired at them, and the Delta team withdrew around a corner, where the group leader communicated to his counterparts that he believed they had located what looked like it could be the room where the hostage was held.

He took a grenade from his belt, pulled the pin, and held it for what seemed, to Nat, an eternity, then he swung his hand around the corner and rolled the grenade down the corridor in the direction of the guards.

As it exploded, the whole group of men rushed down the corridor through the cloud of dust and found the guards lying on the floor, presumably dead. One of the men attached a small explosive device to the door, blew it open, and two men entered the room while the other four remained on guard outside. The hostage was lying half under the mattress when they found him. The team leader spoke to him very briefly and brought him to his feet. He was stunned and disoriented. As they led him out, the team leader communicated that the target had been found. The men formed an enclosure around the freed hostage as they retraced their steps through the maze of corridors.

Travis explained, “The task now for this group is to get the hostage to safety as quickly as possible. The other three groups inside will continue the fighting until there is no further resistance, then they’ll collect any info they can find before they lay charges to reduce the whole compound to dust.”

The group with the hostage met sporadic resistance on their way back outside but returned effective fire. Once outside, they headed for the helicopter, which was sitting about a hundred yards away, with the rotor spinning, ready to take off. Nat counted five dead enemy fighters lying on the ground outside. Presumably, they had tried to escape and were picked off by the snipers or the machine-gunners.

They reached the helicopter and hoisted the man inside, and the helicopter rose into the sky and headed away from the scene. A barrage of fire burst from the perimeter to create cover for the departing helicopter. An enemy fighter who appeared on the roof with a stinger missile was cut down as he raised the launcher to his shoulder. The helicopter disappeared in the distance.

"Mission accomplished." Travis stopped the film. "There is more, but I think we don't have to bore you with the rest. The six men who brought the hostage out return to continue the fight. The enemy is overwhelmed, the majority are killed, and just a handful give themselves up. Information is found on future al-Qaeda operations, including a list of sleeper cells in various Western countries, including our own. No senior al-Qaeda are found—to that extent, the cartoon you just saw mimics reality," Travis added ruefully.

The screen went blank, and the lights came back on.

"Any further questions arising from what you have just seen?" Travis reached for his bottle of water.

Nat realised that his mouth felt parched and found his own bottle of water next to him. He opened it and finished half of it before he spoke, a little out of breath. "Wow, that was quite a show! I have one question: Am I crazy to put myself in harm's way like this?"

Leslie, who had been sitting quietly all afternoon, suddenly came to life. "The short answer is yes. Do you want the long answer?"

Nat nodded.

"The long answer goes something like this: Somebody, or some situation, has created an opportunity that you believe could enable you to infiltrate al-Qaeda at the very highest level. How or why that is so, I have no idea. It sounds pretty far-fetched. Now, we combine this belief with the narrow escape you and your family had at the London Zoo, which I am aware of, and we have a man who has a personal incentive, and a personal desire, to fight back. Any person who voluntarily puts himself in harm's way, just like the soldiers we saw in the video, must be a little out of the ordinary to risk their lives for what they believe in. The difference is that we don't call those kinds of people crazy; we call them heroes. So, I think you have to accept that to do what you propose to do, you are a bit crazy, but 'heroic' would apply equally. Hopefully, you won't be a dead hero if Travis and his Delta Force boys do their job; which, also being a bit crazy, they are likely to do." Leslie gave Nat a searching look. "What I don't understand is why a man with your background—an ambassador and family man with no experience or training as a spy or a fighter—would think that he could possibly succeed in pulling off an operation like this."

Nat knew he could not explain why he thought he could succeed, but he felt he had to give some sort of answer. "What if I were to tell you that it is precisely my background and position that have created the possibility that I might succeed?"

Leslie thought for a moment before he replied. "I would have to accept that possibility and wish you the very best of luck." He smiled and looked at his watch and then at Travis. "It would appear that we have a very unique opportunity, here, Travis. There is something different about Nat here. He seems to be a man with great focus and purpose. I would say we are very fortunate that his purpose right now is to find Zawahiri for us. He might just do it." He rose from his seat, smiled, and reached his right hand towards Nat. "It has been a real pleasure meeting you. I wish you the very best of luck. I'll leave you in Travis's capable hands." He picked up his empty water bottle and walked out of the auditorium.

Travis spent another hour showing Nat films of real training raids and finished with a video showing a training session in hand-to-hand combat.

"Just to give you a little taste of what you'll be doing over the next two days," he explained.

It had just gone five o'clock when Travis turned the lights off in the auditorium and escorted Nat back to the main entrance, where a limousine sat outside waiting for him.

CHAPTER 55

It was five thirty when Nat entered his suite at the Hay Adams. He went straight for the telephone on the writing desk and dialled Sonja.

"Jameson residence; good evening."

Nat could feel himself reacting to the sound of her voice. "Hi, darling, it's me."

"Hey you. How are you? I miss you terribly."

"I miss you too, baby." Nat knew that Sonja knew that they had to be careful what they said on the phone. He asked after the children, and Sonja filed a full report on their well-being. The Christmas baskets had been completed, and tomorrow was gingerbread baking time, to create all the little creatures which would fill the baskets on the Christmas tree.

As usual, Sonja was the one to bring their conversation to a close. "Please call my parents while you're there. Mom called, very concerned about you when they heard the news of the vice president's sudden death and the fact that you were right there when it happened."

Good girl, Nat thought. *If they're listening to our conversation, this is what they need to hear again and again.*

Sonja continued. "She called me on the hour after it happened, worried that this was going to be too much for you so soon after Jim's death. I told her you were doing fine, but I know she'd like to hear it from you. Must go darling. Love you." *CLICK*.

Nat shook his head and smiled to himself as he hung up. Good old—old? ... no—gorgeous, sexy, clever Sonja. *What would I do without her?*

Thankfully, that was not a condition he needed to worry about in the bigger scheme of things, but he realised *I'm doing without her right now, and it hurts like hell.*

He was reaching for the phone to call Sonja's parents when it rang. It was Peter Morris, his friend from the State Department who had traced Nat's mother's flight yesterday. Peter sounded as bouncy and cheerful as ever.

"Hi Nat. Peter. Decided not to wait for your invitation. How about coming out and having some dinner with me tonight?" Nat hesitated for a moment, and Peter broke in: "Not to worry, pal; I'll let you pay. After all, you owe me for finding your mother."

Nat laughed. "All right then. When and where?"

"How about Sequoia at seven thirty?"

"Sounds great." Nat remembered the chic Georgetown restaurant, with its magnificent views of the Potomac and the Kennedy Center, from visits there with Sonja in the early years of their marriage.

"Good. I'll pick you up at seven fifteen." Peter hung up, and Nat pressed the hook button, got a dial tone, and dialled Sonja's parents' number.

It rang and rang until eventually voicemail picked up. Sonja's father's voice responded. "I am sorry, but we are out of town for the next few days. In the meantime, you can reach us on Fatima's mobile." He gave his wife's mobile number, and finished with "We look forward to hearing from you."

Nat dialled his mother-in-law's number. It rang four times before she picked up.

"Hello?"

"Hello, Mother." Nat called his own mother "Mom" and Sonja's mother "Mother". How it had ended up that way he could not remember. It was just the way it was.

"Oh, hi, Nat. My poor boy. How are you doing?"

"I'm doing just fine."

"Just fine? You and your family almost get blown up, your own boss dies in front of you in London, and the vice president dies in front of you in Washington, and you are doing 'just fine'? Give me a break. I know you are not Superman. Tell me the truth."

Nat laughed and gave her a distilled and censored version of life since the day at the zoo. She listened quietly without saying a word until he came to the end of his story. "So, I'm here until after the vice president's funeral on Saturday. How are you doing?"

"We're doing fine." She paused. "Well, actually, we're in Boston right now. I'm going to have a cataract operation tomorrow—both eyes at once. I said to Raoul that I'm not going to have Christmas with you all in Switzerland this year without seeing you clearly. I've been putting it off for a couple of years. Can't drive at night anymore. It's a real nuisance."

"When will you be back in Washington?" Nat was hoping he might see them before he returned to London on Saturday evening.

"We're here until next Wednesday. They won't let me travel until they are sure that everything is OK."

"I go back on Saturday evening after the funeral, so I'll miss you yet again." Nat was referring to the fact that this was his third trip to Washington in so many months and that he had not caught up with his in-laws once.

"Never mind. I told Sonja we'll get to London on the fifteenth of December so that we will be on the flight with you all on the seventeenth. Sonja said she'll book us a room at No. 11 Cadogan Gardens, just five minutes' walk from your place. When we get there, I'll be able to see, with my own new eyes, how well you are really doing." She chortled before she continued. "I'd put Raoul on, except he is downstairs having a haircut. Said he has to look his best before I can see clearly again. Huh! Men, honestly." She made Nat promise that he would call again before he left for London and said a bright and cheerful goodbye.

Nat knew where Sonja got her bright and cheerful disposition from. He looked at his watch. It was quarter to seven—just time for a shower and a shave before Peter arrived.

Nat was down in the lobby at ten after seven. The place was teeming with people—businessmen and women, mostly—winding down, some with a drink, some without, after a busy day at work. Nat took a chair, which gave him a clear view of the entrance doors, and picked up a copy of the *Washington Post* lying on the table in front of him.

PRESIDENT ADAMS CALLS FOR AN INTERNATIONAL TASK FORCE TO BE FORMED TO COMBAT TERRORISM.

The headline was accompanied by a picture showing the president giving a speech to the general assembly at the United

Nations building in New York. Nat started to read the article, which reported the president's idea of what, in effect, amounted to an international army assembled from forces in individual countries around the world. He had got to the part where the president stressed that piecemeal and sporadic fights against international terrorism had failed and that an organised, and well-funded, international response was needed, when Peter Morris came through the front door. He had not changed much in the past five years. He was tall and slim with curly sandy-coloured hair almost to his shoulders, and blue-grey eyes separated by an aquiline nose. The only change, which threw Nat at first, was that he was clean shaven. When Nat had last seen him, he had sported a full beard. "It makes me look more intelligent," he had said when Nat had asked him which woman he was hiding from this time.

His limp, caused by a skydiving accident, and his corduroy jacket and faded blue jeans had not changed. Nat wondered briefly if they would allow him into the restaurant dressed so casually.

Peter headed for the reception as Nat stood up and waved. "Over here, Peter."

Peter turned, and a smile spread across his face as he came towards Nat, hands outstretched. "Hey, there you are. Great to see you." He grabbed Nat's hand in both of his and shook it vigorously. "Man, you look great! Sonja must be doing a good job looking after you."

"You don't look so bad yourself...for a bachelor," Nat added, and they both laughed.

"Let's go! My horse and carriage are waiting outside."

The "horse and carriage" was a sleek BMW 5 Series Sedan, six-cylinder, Twinpower Turbo Valvetronic, fuel-injected engine,

306 hp, as Peter managed to describe his car before Nat was settled in the black leather-upholstered passenger seat next to him.

"Wow! You missed your calling. You should have become a car salesman," Nat observed.

Peter patted the dashboard. "This is my first love now. Never gives me any hassles. Goes where I want her to go, always ready and willing, not to mention. . . able."

He pressed the electronic start, and they drove off past the doorman, who nodded his approval and gave them a thumbs-up. Peter was a good driver, moving his car deftly through the evening traffic. Nat could tell he was enjoying himself.

"So, what do you mean, this is your 'first love' now? What happened to Peter the 'Lady Killer'?" Nat sat back in the comfortable seat.

Peter allowed himself a quick sideways glance. "He almost got killed last year."

"Oh, yeah? How did that happen?"

"I came *this* close to proposing." Peter showed a gap of half an inch between his thumb and index finger. He shook his head, and his eyes had taken on a wistful look as he focused on the traffic in front of him.

"What happened? Was she ugly, with buck teeth and a wooden leg?"

"Ugly? You must be kidding. Since when did you see me out with an ugly girl? She was drop-dead gorgeous. Six feet tall, long black hair, full lips, brown eyes you could drown in. The body...the body..." Peter was lost for words.

Nat helped him out. "I take it her body was OK."

"It was bloody incredible, stupendous."

"So, what was the problem?"

"She's a medical doctor, an internist at the Washington Hospital Center; she's from Bogota, where all her family lives." Peter stopped.

"OK, so, she's a doctor, she's from Colombia, she's drop-dead gorgeous; I can't see, for the life of me, that any of these facts are reasons not to marry the girl."

Peter turned the wheel hard onto K Street, burning some rubber as he accelerated out of the turn. Nat had no doubt they would reach their destination in record time.

"She wasn't the problem. It was her family."

"Her family? Not wealthy enough for you?" Nat applied an imaginary brake as Peter came up fast on the car in front of them.

"No; they were wealthy enough, only I got the sense that the business they were in—her two brothers, that is—had something to do with a Colombian drug cartel."

"You mean, they talked openly about it?"

"Not in so many words, but they told me they were in the import/export business, and that, together with their expensive gold watches and jewellery, gave me the sense that I was talking to members of the Colombian mafia."

"Did you confront your girlfriend with your suspicions?"

"I didn't have to. She told me that she didn't like some of the company her brothers kept but that there was nothing she could do about it."

"What about her parents? What did they think?"

"That was just it. They were beyond thinking. Juliana's father was a well-known plastic surgeon in Bogota until he had a stroke four years ago. His wife cares for him at home, poor woman. He's a vegetable—can't talk, can't walk, can't feed himself—just sits there like a statue with eyes that can move, probably the reason her brothers ended up doing what they're doing."

Peter turned the wheel and exited K Street down a ramp which led to the parking lot below the restaurant. It was obvious that he knew the place well. He parked close to the elevator, which brought them up directly into the restaurant.

The hostess who greeted them was all smiles. "Hello, Peter, nice to see you back with us again."

Peter turned to Nat and winked.

"I had to bring my friend here for the views." The way he said it was clearly intended to suggest that the hostess was one of the views Peter admired.

There was an extra sway in her hips as she showed them to a table by the window.

When she left them, Peter leaned forward and whispered conspiratorially. "This is one place I'm guaranteed to get a table no matter how busy they are." He looked around the room and added, "Unfortunately, it does not mean that the service is any better. They tend to be a bit slow around here."

To prove his point, a waiter did not appear for over four minutes to take their drink order. "See what I mean?" Peter said, as he saw the waiter approaching. Nat ordered a scotch and Perrier, and Peter a vodka martini.

They waited another five minutes before the drinks were placed in front of them, but they were already so deep in conversation that neither of them noticed the delay.

"Here's to the new ambassador." Peter raised his glass to Nat. They clinked and took a sip.

"Thank you, Peter. I wish the circumstances under which I got here had been better, but...here I am, ambassador to the Court of St. James; who would have thought?"

"I did," said Peter. "I knew you would get there someday. You just got there a bit faster than I thought you would; that's all."

The waiter returned with two menus and a wine list. When he hesitated as to who to give the wine list to, Nat stretched his hand out.

"That's for me; thank you."

"Very good, sir." He smiled and withdrew.

They studied their menus, and Peter picked the leek and potato soup to start and the rack of lamb for his main course. Nat went for the tuna tartare to start, followed by the filet mignon. Nat turned his attention to the wine list.

He looked over at Peter. "I assume you will drink some red wine with your lamb?"

"Absolutely! Is the Pope Catholic?"

Nat smiled. "Good. I am one of those strange people who drinks red wine with everything, including fish and seafood. Drives Sonja crazy." Nat's finger ran down the list of reds and settled on a Chateau Margaux 2008. He read it out to Peter. "Sound all right to you?"

"Hey, you're the wine connoisseur. Margaux sounds great."

They chatted and sipped their drinks while they waited for the waiter to return with their starters. Peter told Nat what he had been up to since they last met a year ago, and it was clear that his taste for adventure had not diminished after his skydiving accident. While he had given up skydiving, he had added swimming with sharks at the Barrier Reef and motocross racing on super bikes in the desert.

The waiter arrived with their starters, placed them on the table, and asked Nat if he had chosen the wine. Nat gave him his choice.

"Excellent choice, sir."

Nat handed him the wine list and watched him head back towards the kitchen. The man had a peculiar gait. He seemed to crab sideways across the floor, like a boat without a rudder.

"How did your mother take your surprise presence at the airport?" Peter paused the spoon on its way to his mouth to get the question in.

"Very well, considering she had no idea I was even in the country. We had a lovely time together. She's quite a lady. Still got the sharp edge of the reporter in her." Nat debated whether he should mention her illness but decided against it. Peter had never met his mother. To her, he was a stranger, and illness is something you share with family and friends and your doctor.

The waiter returned with their wine and poured a small amount into Nat's glass for him to taste. Nat swilled the wine around in the glass and brought it to his nose before he took a sip. Both Peter and the waiter gave Nat their full attention as he performed the wine-tasting ritual with a deftness that could only come from years of experience.

"Thank, you. That is very nice." Nat nodded his approval, and the waiter bowed in acknowledgment.

"Shall I pour now, sir?"

Nat looked at their drinks and shook his head. "No, thank you. We'll finish our drinks first and let it breath for a while."

"Very well, sir." He placed the bottle on the table, bowed, and withdrew.

"Very impressive. I'm pretty much a box-wine man myself," said Peter. He finished his soup and sat back in the chair. Then he leaned forward again, and looked intently at Nat before he spoke. "There is something I have to ask you, Nat. It seems to me you have had a hell of a few weeks lately. First the zoo bombing involving your whole family and then the death of your predecessor followed by that of the vice president, both of which occurred right there in front of you. You seem to be all right, but how are you bearing up?"

"I think I'm doing OK, but I have to confess that I've had moments when I have wondered whether bad luck is following me around but affecting only people around me." Nat paused. "So far."

"I hope not." Peter downed the rest of his martini. "I shouldn't be sitting here having dinner with you if that were the case." He gave Nat a mock wide-eyed shocked look.

Knowing the truth, Nat felt he could play this along a bit.

"I'm glad we are. If you survive the evening, I'll know the other two were just a coincidence."

"Thanks a lot. I guess that's what friends are for." Peter stared at his empty martini glass.

"Would you like another martini?"

"I could do with one, but I better not. I wouldn't want to miss out on some good red wine for once."

Nat took the hint and poured them each a glass.

"Tell me," he said, "I've got a question for you. I had a meeting recently, with the Russian ambassador, where the main topic of conversation was the missing warhead. I left that meeting feeling uneasy, feeling that I was being fed a story. What are your thoughts on this situation?"

"Well..." Peter straightened up in his chair, took a sip of wine, and cleared his throat. "I have a theory, which many of my colleagues and friends think is way out of the ballpark, and you'll probably agree with them."

"Try me."

“OK. Mine is a conspiracy theory—a plot on a grand scale—which, if it succeeded, would change the balance of power in the world.”

Peter finished his introduction with another sip of wine, then cleared his throat again.

“It starts with Ayman al-Zawahiri. Unlike his predecessor in al-Qaeda, he travelled extensively on behalf of his organisation. Not since we got bin Laden, of course, but in the nineties and beyond. Among the countries he visited were Russia and Iran, and it is thought that in the latter, he worked with the Islamic Republic of Iran on behalf of al-Qaeda. And, why not? Al-Qaeda and Iran want the same for the Middle East, namely that every country in the region should be run as fundamentalist Islamic republics and that Israel should be erased from the map. Russia has tried to do a balancing act between support for Israel and support for the Palestinians, but they have been selling weapons to the Arab nations surrounding Israel. So, even though Stalin adopted a pro-Zionist approach to Israel back in 1948, thinking that Israel would become a socialist state, the support for Arab states fighting against Israel has been a fact of life since the Suez Crisis in 1956. In a way, I think you could say that the Soviets supported the Palestinians and the surrounding Arab states because we supported Israel, and this has continued after the dissolution of the Soviet Union. So, Russia and America continue their struggle for power with the Arabs and the Israelis as the pawns.”

Peter paused and drew a deep breath.

“So, this is my theory: I think Russia and Iran have agreed to supply al-Qaeda with a nuclear weapon for the specific purpose of using that weapon against Israel. It’s a classic win-win situation, or should I say win-win-win situation. Al-Qaeda and

Iran achieve their objectives of wiping Israel off the map, and Russia, who supplied the vital hardware to make it happen, and therefore, supposedly, a strong ally of the Muslim world—the fundamentalist part, that is—will have created an unholy alliance capable of controlling the world's oil supply. This would be a real game-changer and a nice payback to America for busting Communism and the Soviet Republic and for giving them a bloody nose in Afghanistan, which started the destruction of the USSR." Peter grabbed his glass of wine and took a long swig.

"Wow, Peter! That's some theory! Has it reached to the top?"

"I don't know how far it has gotten, but I know that the boys at Langley have been running a lot of 'what-if' scenarios, both before and after the so-called theft of the Russian warhead. I am pretty sure this is one of them. It is just not possible for two men in isolation to steal a weapon of this size and conceal it the way they did. A lot of people would have had to be involved."

"I agree with you there, the..." Nat stopped as the waiter returned to clear away the starter plates. Nat had finished his tuna tartare, but Peter had let half his soup go cold as he delivered his conspiracy theory.

The waiter turned to leave but stopped and turned back towards Nat. "Would you like me to bring some water for the table, sir?"

Nat looked at Peter. "Still or sparkling?"

"Either is fine with me."

"Sparkling, please."

"Very good, sir."

The waiter left, and Nat picked up where they had left when he was interrupted. "I agree—there had to be a lot of people involved in the stealing of the warhead—but I think it is a stretch to say that it is state-sponsored. What about the Russian mafia? I imagine they would have the resources to pull something like this off."

"Possibly, but who did they sell it to—the Iranian National Guard or just a group of renegade officers who have decided to take the politicians seriously and make their wish come true?"

"Something like that." Nat refilled their wine glasses just as the waiter returned with their main course. He was followed by a young man, bringing Perrier water and glasses.

Conversation halted until the waiters had disappeared and Nat and Peter had tasted their food.

Nat broke the silence. "If your theory is right, and Russia and Iran have entered into an unholy alliance with al-Qaeda to wipe Israel off the map, we will have World War III, unless we can stop it."

Peter looked up from his plate. "For sure. Which means we have got to find that warhead, sooner rather than later." He stabbed a lamb chop with his fork and worked the knife to get the meat off the bone.

They ate for a while in silence.

"Am I right in thinking that Iran has now allowed an international inspection team into the country to conduct a search?" Nat broke the silence.

"Yes, they started their work two days ago."

"I don't think they'll find anything in Iran." Nat took a sip of wine before he continued. "Particularly if this is a state-sponsored event, as you suggest it could be. And if it isn't in Iran any longer, does that mean it is in al-Qaeda's hands?"

Peter put his knife down and picked the remains of a lamb chop up with his fingers. "Shame to waste it," he said as he put a clean bone down on his plate.

"The president has told the CIA to make finding al-Qaeda's headquarters their top priority. It was one of the last words the vice president spoke to me before he had his heart attack. The president agrees with you that the warhead may be destined for an al-Qaeda-sponsored terrorist group." Nat felt he could at least share this fact with Peter.

They finished their main courses, and the waiter came and took their plates and cutlery away.

"Would you care to see our dessert menu?" They both declined, but Peter asked for an espresso, and Nat ordered a decaf cappuccino.

Peter was stirring a second spoonful of sugar into his espresso when he looked up and placed the spoon carefully down on the saucer.

"I would say it's beginning to feel like we are living in a very dangerous world; wouldn't you agree?"

Nat nodded in agreement. "Yes, it does feel like we're getting to the point where it's a 'them-or-us' scenario. We either get them or they'll get us."

"It's got me thinking." Peter took a sip of coffee, and stared, distractedly, at a spot over Nat's shoulder.

"Thinking what?"

A smile spread slowly across Peter's face as he continued his thought: "Thinking that maybe I should propose to Juliana after all."

"Good idea, Peter. Sounds to me like you could do a lot worse."

"That's for sure."

By the time they left the restaurant, it had been established that Peter would be making a call over to Washington Hospital Center in the morning to invite Juliana out for dinner.

“I still have the ring I never gave her. I hope she’ll still have me,” he added.

CHAPTER 56

Nat entered the gym at Langley at eight thirty the following morning. He had been picked up by the same driver, minus Tom, and the driver had got Nat through security by passing a note, together with Nat's passport, to the guard at the gate.

Tom had met him at the entrance to the Old Headquarters Building and had escorted him across a courtyard to the gym, where Nat had been introduced to his close combat instructor, Gavin Wilson. Gavin looked to be in his mid-thirties—with close-cropped blond hair and steel blue eyes. He looked fit and muscular under a camouflage training suit. He went straight to business as soon as Tom had made the introductions.

"Have you had any previous experience with hand-to-hand combat?"

Nat had to confess that with the exception of a short stint with jiujitsu in high school, he had no real knowledge or experience in this field of human endeavour.

"No problem. What I'll teach you over the next two days is quite different. Have you heard of Krav Maga?"

Nat shook his head.

"Krav Maga is a contact combat technique, derived from street-fighting skills, developed by Imi Lichtenfeld in the 1930s to help protect the Jewish community in Bratislava, Hungary, from Nazi militia—self-defence without weapons. The Israeli Special Forces were the first to embrace this method of close combat fighting and developed the techniques to what we today call Commando Krav Maga. The principles are simple." Gavin counted them off on his fingers as he continued. "Counterattack asap, or attack preemptively, targeting the body's most vulnerable areas—eyes, jaw, throat, groin, knees—neutralising the opponent as quickly as possible by responding with an unbroken stream of counterattacks, and, if necessary, a takedown and/or a joint break, maintaining awareness of surroundings while dealing with attacker to look for escape routes, further attackers, objects that could be used to defend or attack, and so on." Gavin paused and took a swig from his water bottle, put it down, and stepped out onto the gym floor before he continued. "We will teach you a series of punches: straight punch, palm-heel strike, low punch. . . " Gavin demonstrated each punch as he spoke. ". . . hammer-fist, hook uppercut, chop, moving across the floor, side kick, back kick, heel kick, slap kicks, axe kicks, knee strikes, and sweeping."

Nat could not help feeling he was watching a macabre form of ballet. *How am I going to remember all this?* Gavin must have seen Nat's concerned look.

"Don't worry. We will focus on just a few in each category, and we will also introduce you to some nerve points. Nerve points are pressure points on steroids, and attacking an opponent's nervous system is a very effective way to stop him dead in his tracks."

Gavin headed back to the chair where he had put his water bottle and drained it. He nodded towards a door at the far end of the gym. "Go to the changing room over there. You'll find a training suit. Put it on, and we'll get cracking."

When Nat returned, Gavin stepped out onto the floor, handed him a boxer's head guard, and donned one himself. "Here; put this on. We'll start with some punches."

They spent the next two hours on punches, and Nat felt, at the end of it, that he had gained a good grasp of a number of punches, including the palm-heel strike and some of the elbow strikes. He was amazed how effective it was to use his "attacker's" own momentum to increase the force of his own strike.

He was breathing heavily as they went over to a row of bleachers where Gavin pulled two bottles of water out of a carton. He spun around and tossed one to Nat, who caught it one handed. Gavin laughed. "Good reflexes. That always comes in handy in this business. You're doing well. I think you'll come out of here quite capable of taking care of yourself."

Nat took a long pull on the water, looked at his instructor, and spoke between deep breaths of air. "I thought I was fitter than this. Obviously, thirty minutes a day of aerobic exercise is not enough."

Gavin smiled. "Actually," he said, "you're doing fine. I turned the tempo up a bit to see how you would respond." He nodded in the affirmative. "You're doing OK."

They returned to the floor ten minutes later and spent another two hours on kicks. Nat was amazed to learn how easy it was to break somebody's leg or knee with a well-aimed and well-timed kick. In fact, he thought he preferred kicks to punches, especially the kick to the groin. Gavin had explained that "...a well-placed hard kick in the balls will drop a man faster than anything else, and he won't be able to get up again for quite a while."

Nat knew the truth of this statement from when he had played soccer in high school. He had stopped what was intended to be a cross to the other side of the pitch, in a distance of less than ten feet, when the ball hit his groin. He remembered the excruciating pain that rose from his balls into his lower abdomen and upwards, until he puked on the grass, and his legs buckled beneath him, and he was lying in agony on the field. Yes, sir; a kick in the balls would do the trick.

Gavin looked at his watch. "OK, let's break for lunch. The director asked me to take you back to his office. I don't know what you are up to, but I get the sense that it is something very important. It is not every day that the boss takes such a personal interest in somebody." He raised a hand defensively. "You don't have to say anything. I know you can't."

Director Benson's secretary smiled when Gavin and Nat stopped in front of her desk. She pressed a button and spoke into a small microphone which was attached to her head. "Gavin is here with your guest, Mr. Benson." She listened for a moment and then nodded and pointed to the door. Go right in, sir."

"I'll see you later. Enjoy your lunch." Gavin turned around and headed for the elevator.

Charles Benson stood up, came around his desk, and met Nat halfway across the floor. "Hi Nat. Good to see you." They shook hands. "How was your morning?"

Nat smiled. "Interesting and physically demanding."

"Yeah, well, you look like you can handle it." Benson steered Nat in the direction of his lounge seating, where the table was set for lunch.

Benson gestured for Nat to take a seat. "I decided we'll eat here today." He looked at his watch. "We are getting a call from the president within the next thirty minutes. His secretary called earlier this morning saying his boss wanted to have a word with us."

There was a knock on the door, and two young girls appeared, one carrying a tray of sandwiches and the other carrying a tray with an assortment of sodas. They placed the trays on the table and left as quietly as they had arrived. Benson thanked them and returned his attention to Nat. "The president is anxious for Operation Endgame to proceed with all possible speed, so I think he wants to talk to us about how to accelerate the process of getting you inside al-Qaeda. Help yourself." He gestured to the table. "You must be hungry after the workout you've had this morning."

"Thank you." Nat leaned forward and picked what appeared to be a BLT sandwich on whole wheat. He had not noticed it before, but he realised that, in fact, he was hungry—very hungry. Thankfully, the plate of sandwiches would easily have been enough to feed four people.

Nat selected sparkling water rather than the sodas. Sonja would have been proud of him. Benson went for the Coke and a turkey sandwich. Silence reigned as they sampled the food and drink.

It was Benson who spoke first. "As you can imagine, the combination of a missing nuclear warhead and the chatter we are picking up—indicating that al-Qaeda is coming up with something big—is making everybody very nervous. Every day that goes by without us finding it increases the danger that it can be rendered functional and used against us. When I say: 'us', I don't necessarily mean: 'against Americans'. Depending on where it is, and who's got it, it may explode just about anywhere. Once the trigger mechanism has been made, they—whoever *they* are—would not necessarily need a sophisticated delivery system to detonate the device. It could be smuggled over land to where they want to wreak havoc rather than be delivered on the end of a rocket." Benson took a bite of his sandwich and reached for his Coke.

Nat took the opportunity to respond. "I have a meeting lined up with Imam Badawi next Monday morning. I will appear to have kept my word. The ambassador and the vice president are 'dead'." Nat fingered the inverted commas. "And now it is al Qaeda's turn to add me to their team, if he wants to eliminate our president. I have to confess that I am concerned that, in the event they are in possession of the nuclear device, they might not want anyone, including a seemingly trustworthy traitor like myself, to be in the picture." Nat took a swig of water and was about to continue when a buzzer went off on Benson's desk.

Benson looked at his watch, stood up, and gestured for Nat to join him. "That will be the president now, right on schedule." He sat down behind his desk and pressed a button. Nat remained standing.

"Good afternoon, Mr. President. Yes, he is here. I'll transfer to the speaker."

He waved at Nat to take a seat. The president's gravelly voice filled the room. "Hi Nat. How's it going?"

"Very well, sir. So far, so good."

"I should say, assuming all goes well at Jack's funeral on Saturday, we're halfway there." Nat could hear the urgency in the president's voice. "The next trick will be to get you inside al-Qaeda as soon as possible. You'll have to use your best efforts to convince your imam friend that there is no time to waste if they want my head on a platter." He chuckled, and added, wistfully, "And tell them, if they detonate a nuclear device, the deal is off. Your proposal is all about stopping the senseless killing of innocent people and making the power brokers pay."

Benson nodded his head and gave Nat a thumbs-up. "Brilliant idea, Mr. President. Nat and I were just talking about how, if they have the device, it might affect Nat's ability to get inside al-Q. If they have to choose between detonating the warhead or killing the US president, I would think they would go for the latter. They could always do the other later. How could Nat stop them? they would think." Benson looked up at Nat. "What do you think, Nat?"

"I like it. I think it could have the effect of getting me in there sooner rather than later."

"Precisely, son," the president broke in. "And time is what we don't have any longer. We either get to the head of the snake and cut it off, or we die of the consequences of not getting there. This is crunch time. Charlie tells me he's picking up stuff on the net, and in the air, which suggests something big is being planned. We have to stop it." He paused briefly. "Of course, I'd like to think I was the 'big thing', but my gut tells me they've got that warhead stashed somewhere, and they're working on getting it ready for action."

Benson looked at Nat, as he spoke. "Three days of unfettered search for the warhead has turned up nothing in Iran. We have twelve international UN inspection teams spread out over the whole country. It is a big country, but if we have not found anything in ten days, I am inclined to believe it is no longer there."

"I agree," said the president. "I very much doubt the Iranians would have been so accommodating to allow us in to search if there was any chance we would find anything, unless, of course, the government is not involved, and they're as scared of what might happen as we are."

"If it is there, we'll find it, Mr. President." Benson's reassurance did not do much for Nat. A country who could build a massive subterranean plant, capable of uranium enrichment, without the West knowing about its existence, could do anything. It would seem the president felt the same way.

"I hear you, Charlie. And I sure as hell hope we find it, but if we don't, I hope Nat is knocking on al-Qaeda's door. Good luck. Keep me posted."

The president rang off, and Benson hung up, looked at his watch, and then at Nat. "Let's finish our lunch. Gavin will be back to collect you in ten minutes."

Gavin spent the afternoon polishing Nat's kicks and punches. The tempo was high, and Nat was dissolved in sweat long before Gavin called it a day. They showered and changed, and Gavin escorted Nat back to the main entrance, where a limousine was waiting to take him back to his hotel.

Gavin stretched his hand out to say goodbye. "You did well today. I would say you are a natural. Tomorrow we'll focus on nerve points. See you tomorrow morning."

They shook hands, and Nat climbed into the back of the car.

"Where to, sir?" Nat saw the driver looking at him in the rear-view mirror.

"The Hay Adams hotel, please." Nat sank back into the seat. He felt tired, but it was a good tired. He felt relaxed and energised at the same time, and best of all, he was beginning to feel that he could defend himself should the need arise.

It was just after six o'clock when he arrived back in his suite, the lamp on and the telephone blinking. He pressed the message button, and Peter's cheerful voice greeted him.

"Hi Nat. Good news! Juliana has agreed to have dinner with me tonight. I'm going to ask her to marry me. Wish me luck!" Nat could hear the excitement in his friend's voice. He made a mental note to call Peter in the morning to see how he made out.

Having decided it was too late to call Sonja, Nat spent the next half hour calling his mother and Sonja's parents. He found his mother in good spirits. She thanked him for the previous evening and told him that she was on her way out to play bridge.

"I'm paired with Leslie tonight. We're going to win. She has a memory for cards that is outstanding. She can recount who played what—when—the whole evening. Regrettably, her culinary skills are not up to the same standard, and we're at her place tonight."

Fatima, Sonja's mother, had had her cataract operation, and it was Raoul who answered the phone.

"It all went fine. She can't see anything at the moment because she's got patches over both eyes, but they can come off tomorrow evening. Here she is." Raoul handed the phone over to his wife.

"Hello, Nat. How are you?"

"I'm fine, thank you. More to the point: how are *you*?"

There was a brief pause before she answered. "Well, now I know what it is like to be blind. It is a very strange feeling. I feel... I *am* totally helpless, but do you know what? ... I can *hear* much better. The doctor said the operation went very well, and I shall be seeing like a hawk in a couple of weeks."

Nat went down for dinner at seven and was back in his suite at nine thirty. He turned on the TV and found CNN. He followed the news for ten minutes in anticipation of getting some news on the search for the missing warhead but gave up when none was forthcoming. He felt very sleepy and decided it would be a good idea to have an early night. No doubt tomorrow would be another strenuous day at the gym. He set a wake-up call on the TV for 7:00 a.m. and went to sleep as his head hit the pillow.

Nat called Peter on the way to Langley to find out how the evening with Juliana had gone. He got the voicemail, saying, "Sorry I missed your call; please leave a message." Nat chuckled and said, "Guess you're still in bed, so Juliana must have said yes. Give me a call when you get a chance."

Gavin was already there when Nat entered the gym at 8:15 a.m., even though the agreed start time was eight thirty.

"Good morning, Nat. How are you this morning? Feel stiff and battered?"

Nat realised, to his own amazement, that he felt no ill effects from yesterday's session. "No, strangely enough, I feel fine."

"Good. That will make today easier." Gavin pointed a remote control at a spot in the ceiling, and a projection screen came whirring down. "We'll start, this morning, by focusing on just a few nerve points. There are many more, but for our purpose—in close combat fighting—these are the most useful ones. Before we look at the specific nerve points and how we attack them, let me give you a brief rundown on what they are. I am sure you have heard of pressure points and how they are used in acupuncture and massage therapy. Nerve points are pressure points on steroids—the most sensitive points on the body. Striking or gripping these points, we can produce immediate results by interrupting the nerves that stimulate muscle movement." Gavin pressed a button, and the screen came alive with a computer-generated image of a male body spinning slowly around. Gavin clicked the remote and froze the image in sideways position, then zoomed in on the head. "The head, obviously, is a treasure trove of good nerve points. The temples—a pulsing circle identified the area—are extremely sensitive, and a well-placed blow here will knock a person out cold or even kill a person. . . . The hollow under our cheekbones, the ears—a slap on the ears with a cupped hand upsets the balance and can even render someone unconscious. . . . Eyes—very sensitive—poking or hitting the eye will stop an attacker very quickly, giving you a chance to get away or to strike a debilitating blow or kick. . . . The front, back, and sides of the neck." Gavin spun the model around, and the exact nerve points were identified by the pulsing circles. He turned the model face on.

"Then, moving down the body, we come to a very important area for self-defence—the hollow where the neck and the chest meets, between your collarbones. A dig down with three fingers here will bring your opponent to the floor like a rag doll. . . . The inside crease of your arm at the elbow—a strike here will render the arm useless for quite a while." Gavin kept moving down the body. "As I am sure you are well aware, the groin is a very sensitive area. A knee or a kick, properly placed in this area, will bring your opponent to the floor and leave him there. . . . The back of your thigh towards the top, the side of your thigh, roughly in the middle. . . . Straight in with the knee—not an upwards movement—in these spots will bring your attacker down. And finally. . ." Gavin zoomed in on the inside of the model's ankle. ". . . just below the bony protrusion on the inside of the ankle is a spot very sensitive to pain and damage. A well-aimed kick to this area will put your attacker out of business." The screen went blank, and Gavin reached for his bottle of water. "Any questions so far?"

"Yes, knowing where they are is all very well, but how do you get to them in a fight? Your opponent is not likely to be standing still so you can just pick your spots and go for it."

"No, and we'll get to that next. First, I'll run some instruction videos of a move and combinations of moves, and then we'll try it out ourselves."

They spent the next two hours studying videos and trying out moves. Gavin was the aggressor, and Nat had to defend himself. At first, Nat found it very difficult, but as the morning wore on, he started to feel the pace and the rhythm of the moves and started to enjoy the process.

They broke for lunch at twelve thirty, and a tray of sandwiches and soft drinks had been set up on a table at the back of the gym.

"I hope you don't mind," said Gavin. "I thought we'd run through some more combat videos while we eat."

They watched a dozen short instruction videos while they ate, and when they had finished their sandwiches, Gavin jumped to his feet, went over to a box, and pulled out a motorcycle helmet, which he put on himself.

"OK. We're going to spend the afternoon practicing a combination of moves at speed and strength. It is very important that you get to know what it feels like to land a good slap, punch, or kick at full strength." As he spoke, he bent down into the box again and pulled out a set of American football protection pads and put them on and finally handed Nat a pair of elbow guards. "You will need these; a motorcycle helmet is a lot harder than the side of my head."

Nat donned the elbow guards.

"Remember the ear slap, elbow jab—side of face—and head butt? We'll do it in slow motion a couple of times first, then I'll want you to do them as fast as you can. In the end, it's all about speed, rhythm, and accuracy. I'm well protected, so don't hold back. Give it everything you've got." They moved out to the middle of the floor.

"Remember, the slap to the ear is fingers closed with a cupped hand... slack wrist. It's the whipping action of the wrist that creates the

power of the blow."

They went through the sequence in slow motion twice. "OK, now, go for it!"

Nat went for it with all he had to muster. *SLAP! TWANG! BANG!* Gavin staggered backwards.

"Not bad as far as placement is concerned but much too slow. Do it again!"

And so, they did, again and again, until Nat thought his hand was going to drop off.

It was a half hour later when Gavin finally said, "That will do. That's good. Now you've got it. Now we add straight leg up into the groin. You only get three tries." He grinned. "I've got a hockey cup but even so."

The addition of the groin kick went surprisingly well.

"OK. Good! Then we add the knee to the inside of my thigh. This is a good variation to help destabilise your opponent."

Off they went again until Gavin was satisfied. They spent the rest of the afternoon practicing combination moves, and Nat's excitement grew as Gavin, one by one, expressed satisfaction that Nat had mastered the techniques they had been practicing. It was five thirty when Gavin declared that Nat had, as he put it, "... passed Self-Defence 101. You've done very well. What you've learned over the last two days will serve you well should you find yourself in a tight spot. We're done here."

They showered and changed, and Gavin escorted Nat out to the waiting limousine. Nat thanked him and stepped into the back seat past the driver, who was holding the door for him. A final wave, and the car headed back towards the city. Nat sank back, exhausted, in the soft leader seat, when his phone rang.

"She said yes!" Peter's voice trembled with excitement. "And we are getting married in Bermuda in May! You're invited!"

CHAPTER 57

Washington National Cathedral was filled to capacity for Vice President John Burton's "funeral" the following afternoon. From the president on down, the pews were filled with members of cabinet, senators, House representatives (from both sides), high-ranking members of the armed forces, and White House staff, who had all braved a chilly November afternoon to pay their last respects to "VP Jack", as he was affectionately known to many. On entering the cathedral, they had been greeted by the National Symphony playing the mournful yet warm "Adagio for Strings" by Albinoni: a moment to reflect on the fragility of life and to thank God that you were sitting in a pew and not lying in the flag-draped coffin on the raised podium in front of the altar.

After wishing everybody welcome, with simply "Mr. President and distinguished guests" and ". . . we are gathered here today to celebrate the life of Jack Burton...hmm. . . Vice President Burton," he corrected himself, Bishop Francis Waddington led the congregation in "Onward Christian Soldiers", ably assisted by the cathedral organist.

Nat sat in the middle of the twentieth right-hand row in the main aisle and had a clear view of the altar and the coffin.

The latter was framed by four cascading flower arrangements on pedestals at each corner of the casket. The colours were red, green, white, and blue.

Nat noticed that TV cameras were positioned discreetly at strategic points in the space, and he wondered if the vice president would be watching his own "funeral" from some safe house in the countryside. It struck him what a weird and uncomfortable experience it would have to be, and he felt a pang of guilt again that this was all his own doing. The grandness of the space, and the grandness of the occasion, somehow magnified the atrocity of the deception. On the other hand, Nat realised that this event would be shown on news programs around the world and would be seen by millions of people, including, he hoped, The Supreme Leader and his top advisers. He felt certain it would have the desired impact and pave his way to al-Qaeda's door.

Bishop Waddington remained at the microphone on the temporary rostrum, which had been set up behind the flag-draped coffin.

He started the proceedings by reading from the New Testament, John 11:17-27: "I am the Resurrection and the Life; whoever believes in me, even if he dies, will live..."

Who had picked that reading? Nat wondered. It was certainly appropriate for the occasion.

The bishop came to the end of the reading and paused for a moment, bowing his head before he straightened up again and announced, simply, "The president will deliver the eulogy." He yielded the microphone to the president, who rose from his seat in the front row. He walked slowly up to the rostrum, which he grabbed with both hands, and leaned forwards towards the microphone.

"Jack was a fine man, a good vice president, and a good friend. I first met Jack at Harvard and got to know him in our last year when we tripped the light fantastic in the Hasty Pudding comedy show."

The president told the story of how he and Jack had stayed in touch from university days into their political careers, which they both started as assistants to senators in the late seventies.

He touched briefly on their two tours of duty, together, in Gulf wars. "This was the experience which soldered our relationship. We watched each other's back, and we learned to rely on each other. Jack was awarded the Purple Heart for bravery in action, an action that saved my life. I was shot in the thigh when we came under heavy fire from a group of enemy soldiers, and Jack carried me on his back to an evacuation point and saved my life."

President Adams narrated his friend's illustrious political career which led him to become vice president. He explained his choice for vice president like this: "It wasn't that I owed him one, which I did. I wanted the best man for the job, and I got him. The best advice he ever gave me was this: 'Remember, we are all made of the same stuff—Christian, Jew, Muslim, black, white, rich, poor. We dwell on our differences, but the truth is—we're all made of the same stuff—flesh, bone, and blood. We are one kind, humankind, and we all journey together on this ball we call Earth.' I shall miss his wise counsel. I shall miss him for the good friend that he was, and we shall all miss him for the dedication and commitment he brought to his job as vice president. Jack, I thank you. We all thank you. Rest in peace."

The president stood for a moment, hands still, clasped to the sides of the rostrum, and stared out at the congregation, then he let go and returned slowly to his seat. Nat wondered what was going on in the president's mind. Giving an emotional and personal eulogy to a man you knew still to be alive could not have been easy, but the president had pulled it off and sent the world a powerful message in the process. WE ARE ALL MADE OF THE SAME STUFF. *You certainly played your part well,* Nat thought. *Now it's up to me to get to the heart and brain of terrorism.*

Jack's secretary read from Romans 6:3-9: "Let us walk in the Newness of Life..." Then they all sang a last hymn, "Abide with Me", and the National Symphony Orchestra played John Rutter's "The Lord Bless You and Keep You" as the congregation rose to join the cortege to Arlington National Cemetery for the interment.

The flag-draped casket was carried to the waiting hearse by six Marines in dress uniform who placed the coffin carefully in the all-glass enclosure of the hearse. A line of black limousines, with the president's special car in front, were parked behind the hearse. Nat had received a formal invitation to the vice president's funeral in which he had been asked to take the sixth limo for the cortege to Arlington, and when he got to it, there were already two men seated in the car, one in the front passenger seat and one in the back seat. Nat did not know the man in the front seat, but he recognised the man seated in the rear immediately when the driver held the door open.

"Hello Nat. Long time, no see." The grey-haired, heavy-set man stretched his hand out and smiled through a finely trimmed full beard.

Apart from his beard having turned grey, Sam Watson had not changed much in ten years, when Nat had met him at a reception for European trade delegates in Washington. Sam had just been appointed ambassador to Spain a few weeks before, and Nat had taken an instant liking to the man.

"Mr. Watson. How are you?" They shook hands as Nat climbed in.

"Sam! Please! Don't 'Mr. Watson' me! I might be twenty years older than you, but I don't feel it." Sam turned to the man in the front passenger seat. "Harry, meet the new ambassador to the Court of St. James. . . . Harry Reed, our colleague in Paris."

They shook hands, and Nat settled back in the seat next to Sam who continued the conversation. "Terrible shame about Jim and the vice president. Good thing we don't know what tomorrow might bring. One moment we are here in the thick of it and next we are gone—actors on the stage of life."

Actors, indeed, Nat thought. *If you only knew.*

The vice president knew what his "tomorrow" would bring, on this occasion.

"You must be feeling your blows these days." Sam gave Nat a concerned look. "First the London Zoo bombing, then Jim's sudden death, and now the vice president's death, both in your presence. You must be feeling that bad luck is following you around?"

"Yes, you could say that, but I guess you could also say I'm the lucky one. I'm still alive, and so is my family." Nat felt the familiar unease when somebody brought up his presence at two sudden deaths. It seemed so obvious that somehow he was connected with them.

The car moved forward.

Four civilian police escort bikes flanked the hearse, and the same number surrounded the president's car, which followed fifty yards behind. The motorcade to Arlington moved slowly through the falling autumn leaves, which danced down, lit by a pale afternoon sun, giving the funeral procession the feeling of a festive ticker-tape parade.

The motorcade came to a halt under a long line of bare oaks. The honour guard retrieved the flag-draped coffin from the hearse, and the procession continued on foot, led by the bishop, the president, and his bodyguards. They reached the gravesite, and the coffin was placed on a cradle over the open grave. As people gathered around, the nineteen-gun salute commenced, shattering the stillness of the crisp November afternoon. A grey cloud of smoke drifted through the air, and Nat could feel the sharp smell of cordite fill his nostrils. He looked at the crowd gathered around the grave. There must have been at least five hundred people there, saying farewell to their vice president, who was probably watching the ceremony on TV.

Nat realised that he was looking forward to having this all behind him. The falseness and deception of it all left a bitter taste in his mouth. He swallowed hard and closed his eyes to block out the scene which unfolded in front of him.

"This must be difficult for you, being the last person to see him alive."

Sam Watson touched Nat's arm as he leaned and whispered in Nat's ear. Nat just nodded. What could he say? Every word he could say would be a lie. He was tired of lying, yet he knew that he had a lot more lying to do ahead of him.

The nineteen-gun salute was followed by "Taps." The lone bugler stood on a slight hill nearby. When the last mournful sound of the bugle died away, the honour guard stepped forward around the casket, picked up the flag, stretched it out in the air over the casket, and proceeded the folding of the flag, twelve times, in honour of the fallen soldier. Nat looked away.

He could not stand to watch this most solemn of burial rituals knowing that the vice president was both safe and sound. *On the other hand,* he thought, *he did make a big sacrifice. He gave up the vice-presidency.*

When Nat looked up again, the flag was in a neat triangle with only the stars showing. One of the guards held it to his chest, then held it out in front of himself and marched over to the president. The president saluted as the guard handed him the flag and, relieved of the flag, returned the chief's salute and marched crisply back to his position at the casket.

The casket was lowered into the grave until the top of it was level with the ground, and the minister committed Jack's "body" to the ground—"earth to earth, ashes to ashes"—and the casket continued down to its final resting place.

The congregation stood still. The only sound to be heard was the rustle of dead leaves swirling around on the road behind them.

The bishop moved first. He walked over to the president and shook his hand. It struck Nat that Jack must have had no next of kin to hand the flag to or to extend condolences to. The president had stepped in as the person closest to the vice president.

A line was forming, of people who wanted to shake the president's hand, and Nat decided he ought to join the line.

It was twenty minutes later when Nat found himself in front of a very sombre-looking president. Nat extended his hand and offered his condolences. The president held Nat's hand as he responded.

"Jack told me, before you arrived to receive your appointment as ambassador, that he felt you had a lot to offer in your new role. So do I. What a shame Jack will not be here to see it."

Nat thought he saw a faint wink of the president's left eye, but he could not be sure. It could have been a bit of autumn dust carried by the wind. The firm squeeze of the president's hand, however, was unmistakable in its message: *Right. Now it's over to you, son. Show us the way to al-Qaeda before it's too late.*

Nat nodded and produced what he hoped was a reassuring smile and yielded to the next person in line.

CHAPTER 58

They could have been mistaken for a group of friends gathered around the television set to watch the Super Bowl, except for their flowing robes, turbans, and the absence of Buds and junk food.

The men, huddled around a small television screen, were not watching a game of football; they were watching the funeral of the American vice president. Nobody said a word. They were sitting on the floor, backs against a whitewashed stone wall, with the television raised on a small box in front of them. It was not until the coffin disappeared into the ground that any reaction was displayed at all and then spontaneous applause and shouts of "Allah Akbar!" (God is great!) filled the room. A large carafe of tea appeared, mysteriously, and the death of the vice president of the "evil" United States of America was celebrated with great joy and laughter.

After a while, the man who seemed to be the one the other four deferred to raised his right hand, and the room fell silent. He spoke Arabic with a low, raspy voice. In the monologue that followed, the words "Jameson" and "Adams" could be heard repeatedly, as could the words "Imam Badawi".

A mumbled discussion followed. Then the conversation seemed to die, and the man with the large steel-rimmed glasses and big ears, who seemed to be their leader, lifted both arms in the air. He looked at each man in turn, moving to the next person after he received a nod from the previous one. Clearly a vote was being taken. It was a unanimous vote in favour of . . . something.

Imam Badawi was in the middle of a lesson when there was a knock on his classroom door. He invited the person to enter, but the door opened just enough for him to see the face of his secretary, who beckoned him to come to the door. He asked one of the students to continue the reading from the Quran and went over to the door. "I am sorry to disturb you, but there is a call for you . . . a man. He said, 'Tell him it's from his barber in Manchester.' "

Badawi's heart did a somersault. He walked out into the hallway, closed the door behind himself, and headed down the corridor at a pace which his secretary found hard to maintain. He sat down at his desk, breathing heavily, and waited for Aisha to put the call through.

"Hello, Iqbal, how are you?" Badawi struggled to sound calm.

"Hello, my friend. I have never been better." Badawi thought he could sense a strain in Mahoud's voice as he continued. "I had a visit from our friend Omar this morning, and we would like to come and see you later today if that works for you."

"Yes, of course; you are welcome here at any time." Badawi's heart was pounding in his chest.

Was this it? Had Mr. Jameson's plan been accepted?

"Very, well. We should be there around six o'clock this evening. We would be pleased to take dinner with you if that suits you."

"Excellent! I look forward to it."

Mahoud hung up, and Badawi was left holding the phone and staring at it as if it was about explode. Mr. Jameson had kept his promise. The ambassador was dead and the vice president was dead. It was time to start the final act—the killing of the president of the United States of America.

Badawi asked Aisha to arrange for a catered dinner in the room next to his office, which was really a meeting room but used as a private dining room for special occasions. Badawi had no doubt that this would be a special occasion. He gave her a list of the food he wished to serve, and she wrote it down and withdrew to go to place the order with the caterers down the road.

Badawi returned to his class, but he was unable to concentrate on what was going on there. Jameson had picked him to offer his assistance to al-Qaeda and the Muslim cause. Badawi had used his connections to get the proposal to the al-Qaeda leadership, and here he was, in the middle of an operation the likes of which al-Qaeda had never even thought possible. He felt a surge of pride. He raised his eyes to the ceiling and thought of his parents, who had died in an American drone attack in Pakistan many years ago. *Your blood is being avenged,* he thought. *When the president of the United States breaths no longer, I shall have peace in my soul.*

CHAPTER 59

The table was laid out with lamb, chicken, and lentils in steaming serving dishes on a black and gold damask tablecloth. The lamb, taba hajah, was marinated and cooked in oil and topped with chopped greens. The chicken was Andalusian, baked until golden brown and served with rice, and the lentils were cooked with onions and spices and served with cooked eggs around the perimeter of the dish. The dessert, khush kanana, was a pastry made from flour and sesame oil with a filling of almonds, sugar, and rosewater. A small enamelled bowl of hais, little balls made of dates, ground nuts, breadcrumbs, and butter, were placed next to each table setting.

The caterers had just finished setting out separate jugs of mint and lemon drink, made from watered and flavoured sugar syrup, when Badawi's guests arrived and were shown in to his office next door. Omar came first, dressed in a grey pinstriped suit, looking like a Lincoln's Inn lawyer, followed closely by Mahoud, the Manchester barber, in his baggy trousers and worn tweed jacket. Neither man looked like he could possibly have any link to a terrorist organisation.

Badawi rose quickly from his desk and met his guests halfway. Omar smiled and stretched his hand out.

"My dear Imam Badawi, I must congratulate you. Your friend, Ambassador Jameson, is coming through ... flying colours." They shook hands as Mahoud appeared next to Omar.

Badawi shook Mahoud's hand. "Yes, Mr. Jameson is as good as his word." Badawi attempted a smile, but he was too tense to make it more than a grimace. Badawi did not return to his desk but invited his guests to join him in the room next door. "I have arranged for us to have our dinner next door, where we can eat and talk in private." He gestured to the door on his right.

"Excellent. Privacy is what we need for what we have to tell you, my friend."

Mahoud smiled and gave Badawi a reassuring look as he spoke.

Badawi seated his guests, and the caterers, turned into waiters, poured the flavoured waters and removed the lids from the steaming dishes of food.

Omar looked at Badawi with raised eyebrows and then at the waiters. Badawi got the message and addressed them. "Thank you. That will be all. We will help ourselves." They bowed and withdrew immediately.

Omar sat back, surveyed the table, and smiled. "This is a feast that you have prepared for us, Imam Badawi. Are we celebrating something?" He winked at Mahoud as he helped himself to some lamb and then some chicken and rice and lentils.

Badawi cleared his throat. "Yes, we are. We are celebrating the beginning of the end of American tyranny in the world. Allah brought to me the man who has proven that he can help our Muslim cause and rid the world of our worst enemy. He has done what he said he would do. He has killed the US ambassador and the vice president. He has shown that he is worthy of our trust. I would say we have every reason to celebrate."

Mahoud looked at Badawi over a plate full of food. "I agree." He raised his glass of lemon drink. "Let us drink to the impending demise of the president of America." Omar and Mahoud responded, and they toasted the end of President Adams.

"That," said Omar, as he replaced his glass on the table, "is what we are here to talk about. I have received word, from the very highest authority, that Mr. Jameson shall be welcome to attend a meeting at, to me, an undisclosed location at the beginning of the first week of December." Omar fixed a stern gaze on Badawi and paused while he took a piece of lamb on his fork and brought it to his mouth slowly. He chewed, pensively, put the fork down, brought the napkin up, and dabbed his mouth before he continued. "I have been told that you must ask your friend to allow three days for the visit, starting from the third of December or as close to that date as possible. Mr. Jameson will obviously have to come up with a reason for being away from the embassy for a few days, but for a man of his resourcefulness, that should not be a problem." Omar allowed himself a hint of a smile. "He will be picked up, by car, from a location of his own choosing, and you, Imam Badawi, will get him to confirm to you the date and place when this is to occur."

Badawi raised a hand, as if he was a student in class requesting to speak. "What if he says he cannot get away anywhere near that time because of work commitments?"

Omar leaned forward and placed his elbows on the table, either side of his plate. "Then you must tell him that it was a real shame that an ambassador and a vice president died for nothing. A day or two before or after the third—OK—but you must make him understand that the timing is very important from our point of view."

Omar paused and it was Mahoud who picked up the conversation. "You will have noticed that there have been no, as they call it, 'acts of terror' sponsored or carried out by al-Qaeda since your friend made his offer. However, other plans are afoot, and the elimination of the president must come first. I cannot say why that is so except to say that the other plan, or plans, are of great, or even greater, magnitude."

They ate in silence for a while. Badawi was not hungry and was just picking at the food on his plate. His guests, on the other hand, were digging into their food with great enthusiasm. It was Badawi who broke the silence.

"Since the third of December is only a week away, I imagine you would want me to get in touch with Mr. Jameson soon?"

Omar stopped chewing and put his knife and fork down. "The sooner the better." He picked his utensils up and continued eating.

"I suggest you call him this evening and ask for a meeting with him tomorrow." It was Mahoud who had spoken.

Badawi could not figure out which of the two men were in charge. Omar was the man who appeared to be the leader, but Mahoud also spoke with authority. "In fact, by calling him tonight, we'll know that the wheels have been set in motion, and we can report back."

Omar looked up from his food and nodded in agreement. "Yes," he said. "Why don't you call him now? You don't seem to be very hungry tonight."

Badawi looked at his watch; it was seven fifteen. More than likely, Mr. Jameson was also in the middle of dinner with his family.

The Jamesons were seated around the kitchen table eating apple crumble for dessert when the phone rang. Sonja gave

Nat a look that said, *Let it ring; we're having dinner*, but Nat got up, lifted the phone from its base on the kitchen counter, and walked out into the hallway before he pressed the reply button.

"Jameson residence; good evening."

"Good evening, Mr. Jameson; Badawi here. Sorry to call you at this hour; you are probably in the middle of dinner."

Nat assured him it was no problem.

"I have some important news, which I would like to share with you as soon as possible... in person," Badawi added.

Nat could feel a tightening in his throat. Was this it? Would he receive his invitation to al-Qaeda headquarters? "How about you come to my office tomorrow morning at ten. Would that suit you?" Nat tried to sound calm, while his heart was beating in his chest.

"Your office? Are you sure...?" asked Badawi.

"Yes, my office at ten."

"Very well. I'll see you tomorrow."

Chapter 60

Nat had not had much sleep the night before, but he arrived at the embassy shortly before eight. To his surprise, he found that Anthony Burville, his successor as deputy chief of mission, was there ahead of him. He appeared in the doorway of Nat's old office.

"Good morning, boss. Having an early start too?"

Nat cringed. *How did a man with such poor people skills survive in the diplomatic corps? By always being kept in the background*, he thought, as he gave Burville a quick "Good morning" aloud and headed for his own office.

"How was the funeral?"

Nat stopped dead in his tracks, then turned around to face his deputy. "It was a very fine and dignified event. The president delivered an excellent eulogy. Did you not watch it on TV?"

"I did," Burville conceded.

Which should have made your question unnecessary, Nat thought. He was not prepared for what came next.

"You sure have been to a lot of funerals lately."

Nat thought there was a strange undertone, of something, in Burville's voice, or was it just his own imagination?

"More than I would have liked, for sure."

"Not only that, but you were present when they died. Doesn't that unnerve you?"

"It does." Nat was going to keep his answers as short and simple as possible. He could not let go of the feeling that he was being interrogated.

"I'm surprised you haven't had a visit from the police asking some searching questions about these deaths."

Nat could see, from the supercilious grin on Burville's face, that the man was trying to be funny. Instead, he was just trying.

"I guess they would have, had the deaths been from strangling, stabbing, or a gunshot wound. Massive heart attacks are as natural and common a cause of death as you can find—too common—as it turns out." *Time to change the subject.* "Have you had any communications from the Russian Embassy on the subject of the missing warhead while I was away?"

"We did, but only to say that the search for it has turned up nothing."

"Did you speak to the Russian ambassador himself?"

"Yes. He called yesterday afternoon. He didn't seem very concerned. When I suggested it could have ended up in terrorist hands, he just said that they had no proof of that and that he thought it was unlikely. . . . Didn't make much sense to me."

"I agree," said Nat. "This whole affair stinks to high heaven. The president has put every intelligence resource, and our defence systems, on high alert. He believes the warhead is in terrorist hands as we speak, and I'm inclined to agree with him. Anything else happen while I was away?"

Nat continued into his own office, followed by Burville, who spent the next twenty minutes running through mainly mundane embassy business.

The Chinese ambassador wanted to meet Nat, in his new capacity, to discuss the details for a bilateral meeting on trade between his country and Nat's. The currency issues between the two countries had not been resolved and were far from mundane. The president had worked hard with the Congress and Senate to reduce America's dependence on Chinese financing, and deficit spending had been greatly reduced, but a balanced budget was still an elusive goal. The aftermath of the Covid-19 pandemic was still a sore point between the two nations and had hampered further trade negotiations, which were considered, by world leaders, to be critical for the world economy.

Nat asked Burville to deal with a number of matters, knowing that depending on what Badawi had to say, he might be out of the office for a while. *For a while?* Nat shuddered at the thought that his absence from the office might be forever. No. This was not the time for negative thinking.

His thoughts went to Badawi, and it struck him that maybe Nat had made a mistake inviting him to his office. Burville was the type who would just assume that his presence was required and burst in uninvited. Nat realised that it would be difficult to explain why his presence was not wanted. He looked at his watch. It was almost nine o'clock. Angela would be at her desk any moment. He buzzed her, and she picked up immediately. "Good morning, Angela. How are you today?"

"Very well, thank you. Couldn't be better."

"Excellent. Listen, could you please try and get Imam Badawi on the phone for me? We are getting together this morning, but I would like to have a word with him first." If Burville asked, there was a simple answer.

Nat waited less than a minute before Angela called back. "I have Imam Badawi on the line for you."

"Thank you. ... Good morning, Imam Badawi, how are you?"

Badawi's gravelly voice sounded lower than usual. "Good morning, Mr. Jameson. Thank you; I am well. Can you not make our meeting this morning?" Nat could hear the strain in his voice.

"Yes, yes I can. I would just like to change the venue. How about I pick you up outside your place, and we take a drive?"

"Yes, I would like that. I shall be waiting for you." Nat could hear the relief in Badawi's voice.

When they hung up, Nat immediately reached for the secure phone and called Langley. Tom picked up on the second ring, and Nat told him about his impending meeting with Imam Badawi. Tom stressed the importance of agreeing to any procedure or process which was presented as a pre-condition for achieving the meeting with al-Qaeda.

"Also, I can tell you we are proposing to do another sweep of your house today to see if there are listening devices of any kind. Please tell your wife to expect two men from the gas company to come and check the house for gas leaks."

When Nat pulled up in front of the Central Mosque at five minutes before ten, Badawi was already standing on the sidewalk waiting. He wore a shiny green suit, which sparkled in the pale autumn sunlight as he raised his arm to open the passenger-side door. Nat leaned over and opened the door for him.

"Please, step in. Hope you didn't mind the change of venue. My new second in command, Mr. Burville, is a nuisance. ... Might just have poked his nose in on our meeting, and it wouldn't have looked good if I'd thrown him out."

Badawi made himself comfortable. He was all smiles behind his dark glasses. "No, Mr. Jameson. I like this better."

Nat pulled out from the curb and headed down Park Road. He had no route in mind—no destination—he would just drive around with the flow of the traffic, going nowhere in particular.

It was Badawi who spoke first. "I want to congratulate you, and thank you, on behalf of all Muslims. What you are doing for our cause is a miracle, and we give thanks to Allah for bringing you to us."

If you only knew, you wouldn't be thanking me, Nat thought, but aloud he said, "Now you know that I am sincere. I said what I was prepared to do, and I have done it. Now we have to develop the strategy for the final stage." Nat stepped on the brake and reached out his left hand to hold Badawi back as a courier on a motorbike cut across in front of them. "Crazy driving. Sorry, Mr. Badawi; are you OK?"

"Yes, thank you; I am fine." Badawi brought his handkerchief out and dabbed his forehead.

Nat turned right onto Baker Street. Maybe this wasn't the best place to have the talk they were about to have. "Let's drive over to Hyde Park and drive through the gardens. It will be less busy there and easier for us to talk."

Badawi nodded. "Good, good. I like that idea."

Badawi adjusted himself in his seat, removed his glasses, and polished the lenses before he returned the handkerchief to his pocket. He held the glasses in his hands as if he were not sure whether to put them on again. Then he cleared his throat and turned towards Nat, his black eyes sparkling in the low autumn sun. "I have been asked to invite you to a meeting, and I'm afraid it is short notice."

Nat could feel his heart picking up pace. He allowed himself a quick glance at Badawi. "When and where?"

"Third of December."

Wow, you weren't kidding about the short notice, Nat thought. "Where?"

"I don't know. I was told that you will be picked up by car from a place of your own choosing. There is some flexibility—a day or two either way—but no more. they told me you should make allowance for three days."

To Nat's surprise, a deep sense of calm flooded over him. Finally, what they had all been working on for the past months was paying dividends. The deception had worked, and he would be trusted to enter the inner sanctum of al-Qaeda. *And I am ready?* he thought. *I am ready*.

"December third is fine. I want to move this ahead as fast as we can. There have been no al-Qaeda-sponsored attacks on civilians since the zoo bombing, and now that we have brought the struggle to a new level, I trust that attacks on civilians will be a thing of the past."

Badawi mumbled something in reply. Nat couldn't quite make it out, but it sounded like an agreement. He turned right on Oxford Street, heading towards Marble Arch, where he could take off into the park on the Ring Road and then across the Serpentine Lake into Kensington Gardens.

What pretext would he come up with for being out of the office for three days? It would have to be something where his story could be corroborated should someone make enquiries as to his whereabouts.

Nat turned onto the Ring Road. The thought struck him that the simplest scenario would be to call in sick. Sonja would cover for him, and he would ask to be picked up from his house while the children were at school.

He stopped the car in the middle of the bridge over the Serpentine, leaving the motor running. Badawi did not look at the scenery. His dark eyes were staring at a point on the dashboard immediately in front of him. The tranquil scenery around them was lost on both men.

It was Nat who broke the silence. "This is how we will do it, Mr. Badawi. I will call in sick on the morning of the third; that way, I can be picked up from home midmorning, say ten thirty?" Nat pulled out a business card and wrote his home address on the back. "Here, this is where I'll be, standing on the sidewalk outside my front door."

Badawi took the card and studied it. "So, you are not at Winfield House?"

"No, not yet. The place is undergoing renovations. We won't be moving in until early next year." *Which, at this rate, probably means we won't be moving there at all,* Nat thought. "Will I need to bring anything with me, like an overnight bag with toiletries and so on?"

"No, Mr. Jameson. I was told that you are to bring nothing with you unless you are on medication which you cannot be without. Everything you need for your stay will be provided to you."

Nat shook his head. "I don't take any medications... except a little whiskey now and then," he added, with a smile.

It was Badawi's turn to shake his head. "No alcohol, I am afraid."

"I know. Just kidding. Anything else I need to know?"

Badawi thought back to his meeting with Mahoud and Omar. He could not think of anything else that he had been asked to convey to Mr. Jameson—their gratitude, a time and place to pick him up, and the fact that he needed to come empty-handed. That was it. And Mr. Jameson had made it so much easier—by agreeing to the third of December—mission accomplished. Badawi allowed himself a broad smile.

"No, Mr. Jameson; that is all. Of course, if there is any change to what we have agreed here today, then I will be in touch with you."

"Very well." Nat pulled away from the curb and looked at his watch—*the watch*. It was ten forty-five. "Shall I drop you back at the mosque?"

"Yes please; I have a class at eleven thirty."

Nat fought the London traffic and arrived at the mosque twenty minutes later. When he pulled up at the curb and stopped, Badawi did not jump out immediately, as he had done the last time they had taken a drive together. Instead, he turned to Nat, both hands outstretched. There was a solemn expression in his eyes.

"Thank you, my friend. Thank you for all that you have done and all that you will do to right the wrongs that have been perpetrated against my people. I am proud to be part of this mission. You have changed my life, and, with your help, we will change the lives of millions of Muslims. Allah Akbar! God be with you."

He opened the car door, to step out, when Nat held him back. "There is one very important thing you must make clear to your leader. As I'm sure you know, a nuclear bomb has gone missing, and our president believes it is in al-Qaeda's hands as we speak. If it is detonated, many innocent lives will be lost, and our deal is off. We are doing this to stop the killing of innocent people."

Badawi turned and nodded. "That we are, Mr. Jameson; I'll make sure that message gets delivered." He opened the door, climbed out, shut the door gently, turned around, and gave a farewell wave as Nat pulled out from the curb.

I wonder what will happen to you, if I succeed, Nat thought. Then, as an afterthought, *I wonder what will happen to me, if I don't succeed? Better not to think about it.*

For the rest of the journey back to the embassy, he also pondered what would happen if he succeeded. Would he and his family have to live with special protection for the rest of their lives? Would they be given new identities? Where would they live? Surely, not in London. He had not come up with any answers by the time he got back to his office and decided the only thing to do was to focus entirely on each day, one day at a time. The next thing to do was to report to Langley and bring Sonja up to speed with what was happening.

Chapter 61

"That is excellent news, Nat. Speed is of the essence. We are beginning to think that the nuclear warhead is in al-Qaeda's hands as we speak and that the Russians, and the Iranians, are helping them to construct the trigger mechanism. We can't prove it, but for all we know, they could be ready to launch at any time if our suspicions are correct. Six days is short notice, but we'll be ready. The sooner you lead us to al-Qaeda the better."

There was an unmistakable sense of urgency in Tom's voice. "Langley is abuzz with activity, with lots of disturbing chatter being intercepted. Something big is going down soon, but where and when? We just can't tell. Good you got the message in there about the deal being dead if a bomb goes off."

There was a short pause, which Nat did not fill. He was waiting anxiously for Tom's instructions. "OK, so you are getting picked up next Thursday. Since they have told you to allow three days, it is very likely that you will be flown somewhere. Not that we ever thought al-Qaeda's headquarters were in England," he added. "Even though you have proven yourself, to the extent that you have been invited to a meeting, they will likely want to keep the location a secret, even from the person who, they think, has murdered two very prominent Americans. This means it is likely that you will be drugged so that you will not know where you are when you wake up or how you got there. But not to worry; none of that is important." Tom coughed. "Excuse me. I've got a bit of a cold." Nat heard him blow his nose. "Anyway, as I was saying, for you to know where you are and how you got there is not important; what is important is that you are able to establish that you are indeed in the company of al-Qaeda's top brass. Only when you are certain that this is the case do you press the watch. After that is done, all you can do is wait. If you can, keep them busy—keep them distracted. The less they are alert to the outside world the better for us when we arrive."

"We arrive? Are you going to be on the assault team?" Nat had a fleeting vision of Tom in combat uniform.

"No, no." Tom chuckled. "This is the royal 'we'. When I say 'we', I mean our boys who are coming to capture the enemy, if they can, or kill them, and get you out of there." Tom coughed, again, before he continued. "You know what to do when you hear us coming, and you know how to defend yourself. I wish you all the best of luck. Any questions?"

"Yes. Assuming all goes well and we are successful, I imagine al-Qaeda will wish to take revenge, going after myself, my family, and others who were involved, such as Mr. Preston and the vice president, perhaps even the president himself. Any plans afoot to tackle this?"

"Yes, of course. For the operation to be labelled a success, we will have captured, or killed, most, if not all, of al-Qaeda's leaders, and we will have gathered a mother lode of intelligence, which will enable us to roll up a large number of al-Qaeda-linked cells here at home and abroad. This will greatly reduce their capacity for retaliation in the first place. Secondly, after discussions with Ambassador Preston and Vice President Burton, it has been agreed that they will not be resurrected from the dead but will live out their lives in their new identities. You and your family will receive high-security protection, and you will be moved back to an undisclosed location in the US so that we can carry out risk assessment studies and decide on a long-term solution. Security will be beefed up around the president and his family as a matter of course. If this action becomes the success it has the potential to become, then it will result in a world where threats from terrorist groups will cease to exist over the next few years. Does that answer your question?"

Nat hesitated. He had lots of questions swirling around in his mind, such as the children's education. Was it possible to get children to change their identities, if that should become necessary, without them blowing their cover? But he replied, "I guess it will do for now."

"Very well, then; before we hang up, I want you to press the crown in on your watch."

"Right now?"

"Yes, please."

Nat pressed the crown and heard a faint click and felt a vibration in his wrist. *Silence*.

"Very good, Nat. You're all set. Pull the crown back out."

Nat readjusted the crown.

"One more thing." Tom cleared his throat. "We have swept your house again for listening devices and found none. Still, use extreme caution when you speak with your wife. Good luck."

Across town, Imam Badawi lifted the telephone off its cradle and dialled Mahoud, his barber friend in Manchester. He had rehearsed what to say, in case his phone was being tapped—something which was highly likely following the zoo bombing incident.

"Good afternoon, Mahoud. I trust you are well?"

"Very well, thank you."

"Good, good. I have good news, further to our recent meeting: the package can be collected on the third of December at 10:30 a.m. Location details will follow."

Badawi would send Nat's address by personal courier that afternoon. There was a moment's silence at the other end as Mahoud was processing the encrypted message.

"Excellent, my friend. I shall arrange for it to be picked up. And thank you again for dinner. It was lovely."

"You are very welcome. We must do that more often."

"I agree."

They said goodbye and hung up. Badawi copied Nat's address on a piece of paper and placed it in an envelope. He called his secretary to come in, gave her the envelope, and asked her to find a student with a driver's license, to have it delivered to Manchester.

When Nat arrived home at six that evening, he found Sonja and the children bent over something on the kitchen table. They were concentrating so hard that they had not heard him open the front door.

"OK, so, what are you up to?" He stepped into the kitchen and opened his arms to catch the children.

"Dad!" They spun around and ran towards him. "We're putting the roof tiles on the gingerbread house. Look!"

Gregory wriggled free of Nat's embrace and pointed to the kitchen table. Sonja straightened up, wiped her sugar-coated hands on her apron, and gave him a big smile. The children dragged him over to the kitchen table, in the middle of which sat the gingerbread house with a zigzag pattern of M&M's stuck down with icing sugar. One slope was done, and the other side was half-finished.

"We're allowed to eat one M&M when we have finished a row," Gregory announced.

"But he's eaten more. Look at him." Tanya pointed to her brother's chocolate-stained lips, which seemed to substantiate her allegation.

"No, I have not." Gregory was not going to allow circumstantial evidence to interfere with his plea of innocence.

"Now, now, children. Back to work, while I get your dad a drink." Sonja gave Nat a quick kiss on the lips and walked over to the liquor cupboard.

Nat followed behind her. "Thanks, honey; I could do with one."

She gave him a look as she poured whiskey into his favourite tumbler. And Nat gave her a look and nod that left her in no doubt that something special had happened today.

She handed him the scotch. "Tell me about it?"

"Later." His eyes squinted towards the children behind him, who were again absorbed in the roofing of the gingerbread house.

He could tell Sonja understood the nature of what he was going to tell her by the way she looked up at him as she poured herself a gin and tonic. There was love, worry, and pride shining out of those blue eyes, and Nat had to swallow hard to get rid of the lump that had all of a sudden formed in his throat.

Sonja put her left hand on his and raised her glass to him. "To you, my darling." They both took a long swig. Then she put her glass down and shifted gear. "OK, Dad. Come and help us finish this roof." She grabbed his hand and led him back to the kitchen table.

One hour later, the gingerbread house had been completed, amid laughter and light conversation about the upcoming Christmas holiday in Switzerland. The table had been cleared, and everybody had helped make a chicken, cheese, and macaroni dinner, which had been eaten amidst lively banter until it was time for the children to go to bed.

Gregory had tried, as usual, to delay the inevitable, and Sonja had, as usual, dismissed his many pleas to stay up longer. Once they were tucked up in bed and kissed goodnight, they had fallen asleep very quickly, as could be expected from tired little elves.

Nat and Sonja had just made it back downstairs to do the dishes when Sonja closed the kitchen door behind them and turned to him. "Right. So, tell me what's happening. The gas company came yesterday, as you said, and found everything to be in order."

Nat put an index finger to his mouth. "Yes, I know, and all appears clear, but Tom says extreme caution is advisable." Nat led her to the kitchen table, and continued in a low voice. "You better sit down, darling." She did as she was told. He sat down opposite her, took her hands in his, and continued in a low voice. "I met with Imam Badawi this morning." He felt Sonja's hands tighten around his own. He squeezed back. "Yes, baby, it has happened. I have been invited to a meeting, I hope, at al-Qaeda's headquarters."

Sonja's eyes widened. "When?"

"Next Thursday."

Sonja closed her eyes, and when she opened them again, Nat could tell she was struggling to conquer her fear. "So soon?" She looked down at their hands and locked her fingers into his.

"Yes, darling; they'll be picking me up from here at ten thirty in the morning, and I've been asked to allow three days for the visit."

"Three days? Where could they be taking you?"

Nat smiled. "If we knew that, honey, I wouldn't have to go."

"Silly me." Sonja smiled apologetically as tears welled up in her eyes.

Nat got up from his chair, still holding her hands, and pulled her to him in a tight embrace. He could feel Sonja shivering as she started to cry softly against his shoulder.

"Now, now, darling. Everything is going to be OK." He stroked her hair gently.

"I know, I know. I'll be fine in a minute." She looked up at him, bravely smiling through the tears. "I just need to let it sink in."

He bent down and kissed her wet, salty lips. They stayed locked in a silent embrace for another while, until Sonja extracted herself slowly and went over to the kitchen counter to a box of Kleenex. She blew her nose, discarded the tissue, took another, and wiped her eyes.

"I never dreamed that being married to you would get quite this exciting."

Sonja was back in control of her emotions.

"It's time I paid you back, then, isn't it? I have always found living with you to be very exciting." The way he said it could not be mistaken.

"Oh, you're just saying that to cheer me up." She gave him one of those teasing smiles, which always drove him crazy.

“Yes, just to cheer you up.” He came up to her, pulled her close, and kissed her with an urgency that took him by surprise.

She pulled away, breathlessly. “What about the dishes, darling?”

“They have to wait.”

He lifted her up and carried her upstairs.

CHAPTER 62

Nat had spent the next four days making sure that there were no loose ends at the embassy. Anthony Burville had been briefed on everything that was going on and seemed to relish the fact that Nat was delegating a number of matters of importance, including another meeting with the Russian ambassador for an update on the search for the missing nuclear warhead.

Tom had called from Langley the day before Nat was due to be picked up, to tell him every special ops team around the world was ready to go into action. "We will get there quickly, wherever they take you. Good hunting!" were his parting remarks.

"Thanks." Nat replaced the secure phone in its cradle and sat staring at it while images of possible scenarios played out in his mind. What if al-Qaeda's headquarters were miles from nowhere, in a desert or a jungle? It might take quite a while before the special ops team got there. Tom had said, "... in a matter of hours," but what if it became days?

The possibility that al-Qaeda's leaders were hiding in an urban centre in Pakistan or out in the mountains near the Afghan border appealed to him. The US had substantial resources in that part of the world, and he was sure they would find him quickly, if this turned out to be where he was taken. The buzzer on his desk jolted him out of his thoughts.

"Mr. Jameson, I have Andrew Jefferson on the line for you; shall I take a message?"

Nat had told Angela, his secretary, earlier in the afternoon, that he thought he was coming down with something, paving the way for Sonja to call in the morning to say that he was down with a dreadful cold and would not be coming to the office. "No, Angela, I'll take the call."

"Hello, stranger. Long time no see."

Andrew's Scottish lilt felt reassuring. "Hi, Andrew. Yes, I'm sorry. Sonja and I have been talking about having you over, but with one thing and another, we just haven't got there yet."

"No worries, my friend. We can see from the news that you have had your hands full." There was a clear tone of concern in Andrew's voice.

"Thanks, Andrew. Things have been a bit hectic lately."

"A bit hectic? You're some lad, my friend." Andrew chuckled. "First the zoo, then your boss dies, and then the vice president, and you're in the middle of it all. You can take the 'bit' out of hectic, I'd say. I called for three reasons: first, to find out how you are doing; second, to congratulate you with your appointment; and third, to find out if you and Sonja would like to have dinner with us Sunday evening?"

"Thank you, Andrew—One, I'm doing fine; two, filling Jim's shoes is not going to be easy; and three, I'm coming down with something. . . haven't felt right all day. Can we take a rain check on dinner?"

Tomorrow was Thursday, and he was being picked up at ten thirty in the morning. Badawi had been told that Nat should allow three days for the visit. That was the visit as they envisaged it, not as it would turn out. Nat had no idea when he would get back. Come to think of it, he didn't even know if he would come back. He shuddered at the thought.

"You're worn down, Nat. Your resistance is low. If you take some time off and let Sonja look after you, you'll probably be good as new come Sunday. Why don't we leave it open? Call us on Saturday."

Nat could not think of any excuse to say no, so he said, "Thanks, Andrew. You know we'd love to see you."

"Great! You take it easy, and we hope to see you Sunday."

"Likewise." *And I mean that in the sincerest way*, Nat thought. "Thanks for your call, Andrew. Goodbye."

"Goodbye, my friend."

They hung up.

Nat looked at his watch. It took him only a fraction of a second to realise again that it was not his and how a firm push on the crown would unleash an operation which had the potential to change the world. The time was five fifteen. Angela called to say that she was leaving and asked if there was anything else she could do for him before she left. He said no; she said, "Get better. Take some time off." He said that he might just do that.

Nat was tidying up his desk when Burville stuck his head in the door. "My God, you look dreadful! You're as white as a ghost. What's the matter?"

Nat managed a feeble smile. "Nothing. I'm coming down with a cold, that's all."

"Go home, put your feet up, and get Sonja to make you a hot toddy—whiskey, honey, and lemon. That'll fix you up." Burville was generous with the medical advice.

"Thanks, Tony. I'll give it a try." Nat switched his light off and headed for the door.

Burville was walking back to his own office. "I'm just going to finish some background reading on the missing warhead situation," he said as he turned around in the doorway. "Hope you feel better in the morning."

"Thanks, Tony; so do I. Have a nice evening." Nat went out to the elevator lobby thinking he probably wouldn't feel better in the morning at all.

He arrived home just after six. Darwin gave him his usual enthusiastic welcome, always first at the door when he opened it, followed closely by Gregory and Tanya, who leapt into his arms as soon as he had put his briefcase down. Sonja appeared in the kitchen doorway smiling, wiping a glass on a kitchen towel. Nat took it all in and knew, that very moment, that he was doing the right thing. They deserved a saner, safer world to live in, as did millions of other families around the world.

The children were anxious to tell him about their day, and he tried to follow two simultaneous accounts, while he was putting his overcoat in the hall closet.

"OK, children, save the rest until Daddy has had a shower; you can tell him the rest over dinner. Help me set the table." Sonja gave him a kiss and shooed him up the stairs. "Go on; wash the day off."

The hot water felt soothing. The tension of the day eased, and he started to feel... *What was that feeling?* He felt a sense of deep happiness. The years of frustration from living in a turbulent and dangerous world, and from watching and listening to news of terrorist attacks claiming innocent lives across the globe, were washing down the drain with the hot water. He was no longer going to be a passive bystander, watching the world fall apart. He was going to do something about it. The fear was gone.

When he came back down to the kitchen, the table was set for dinner, and a lovely smell drifted from the stove, despite the exhaust hood's best efforts. Nat took a long sniff of the air. "That smells good!"

"Guess what it is, Daddy." Tanya was placing a thick red candle in the middle of the table and held off lighting it, waiting for her father's answer.

"Judging from the copper casserole, I would say it must be a casserole of some sort."

"Ha ha! Very clever, Dad. Right on." Gregory gave his father full marks as he looked up briefly from a game he was playing on his mother's iPad.

Tanya was not impressed. "What kind of casserole, Daddy?" She lit the candle.

"Irish stew?"

"Bingo!" Gregory clapped.

"Your dad's got a very reliable nose. Let's eat." Sonja picked up the casserole dish and placed it in the middle of the table. "Help yourselves. Dad first; he has to go on another trip tomorrow." She gave Nat a quick glance.

"Again? You're always going away." Gregory gave his father an accusing look, but then he brightened up. "Are you going on the Gulfstream?"

Nat fumbled the answer. "I don't think so… I mean… No, I'm not. British Airways this time."

"Where to, Dad?" It was Tanya's turn.

Nat had to think fast. "Singapore. Short trip… I'll just be gone for a few days." *I sure hope so*, he thought as he helped himself to some stew. When everybody had served themselves, Sonja did something which was not the norm in the Jameson household.

"Let's all hold hands and thank God for this meal and for bringing Dad safely back to us."

Greg looked perplexed and was reluctant to extend a hand to his sister.

"Come on, Greg." Sonja gave him a look that made argument a nonstarter. When their hands were joined, Sonja looked down, closed her eyes, and said simply, "Thank you, God."

"So, now you can tell me what kind of day you have had. Tanya first." Nat was anxious to move the conversation away from his travel plans.

"I had a great day," said Tanya. "Mrs. Buxton told me that she would like to enter my zoo story in an international essay competition. She said it sends a very important message, and she thinks the whole world should hear it."

"The whole world? That's impossible," Greg observed. "Some people can't read, and some people who live in the jungle don't have television or radio or a computer." He took a big mouthful of stew to underline the challenge in his statement.

"That is true, Greg, but I think what Mrs. Buxton is saying is that the more people who hear or read the story the better." Sonja gave her son a gentle smile.

"What was your day like, Gregory?" Nat knew that his son was miffed about the attention Tanya had received from the essay and that he had been teasing her about it.

Greg looked up from his plate, chewing on a generous mouthful of his mother's delicious stew. Sonja stretched a hand out and touched his arm.

"Swallow that first. We don't talk with our mouths full in this house."

Greg swallowed, opened his mouth to speak, and then swallowed again. Finally.

"We played terrorists in the big break, blew up the gym building, and set fire to the headmaster's house."

"You what?" Tanya's voice came out in a high-pitched squeal. "For real?"

"Of course, dummy. Of course, for real." Greg gave his sister a disgusted look. "And you're supposed to be so clever?"

"Now, now, Greg; your sister is very clever, and so are you, but I don't think it was very clever to play terrorists." Sonja shifted her gaze from her son to Nat, saying with her eyes: *You take it from here, Dad.*

"Mom, is right, Greg. I know it was only make-believe, a game, like you might have played cowboys and Indians, but that was way back when; it's history. Terrorism is a miserable fact of life today in our own world, and many people have experienced it firsthand, like we did."

Greg looked down at his plate, chasing a piece of meat around with his fork. Then he looked up. "We have played cowboys and Indians, too, but Ernest said we had it all wrong, because the cowboys were always the good guys and the Indians the bad guys. He said, 'You Americans, who came and stole the Indians' land and hunting grounds, were the villains.'" Greg tried to mimic Ernest's posh English accent.

Ernest was one of Gregory's English classmates, who lived on a large country estate in West-Sussex. Greg had once been invited over to play and spend the night and had come home in awe over the retractable roof over the swimming pool.

Nat gave his son a thoughtful look. "It is true. Our treatment of the Indians is not part of our proudest history, but you must tell Ernest that the Americans he is talking about were English, Irish, Italian, German, Dutch, and more, who emigrated to the New World to find a better life."

"It didn't become a better life for the Indians," Tanya observed.

"No. Sadly, it became a matter of survival of the fittest, and the Indians were forced off their land and onto reservations, some of which are still in existence today." Nat thought, as he was saying it, that terrorism went back further than he cared to think.

"But we are the good guys now. We don't blow up people; the terrorists do." Greg's words came out as an indisputable statement of fact, but Nat was thinking, as he heard them, that the Palestinians in Gaza and the West Bank would not necessarily agree with that statement.

But aloud he said, "No, we don't."

Sonja changed the subject. "Today it is only ten days until we get on the plane to Zurich, and since Dad will be away for a few days, I need the two of you to be really helpful in getting organised for the trip."

The children promised to clean their rooms, put their school books neatly on the shelves, and help pack their own suitcases. Greg counted up a list of the toys he wanted to bring, and Sonja laughed.

"Come now, Greg; you would need an extra suitcase for all that. You can bring just a few things, things that will fit in your one and only suitcase."

It was nine o'clock by the time the children were in bed. They had been tucked up and kissed goodnight, and Sonja had left to get on with tidying up the kitchen. Nat turned the lights out but lingered in the doorway. He turned around and tiptoed back to their beds. The moon was casting a blue glow over the two little heads, which lay peacefully on the pillows. He bent down and kissed his son on the forehead.

Greg was asleep already. Nat went over to Tanya's bed. She was lying on her back with her blond hair spread in a halo around her head. He bent down and kissed her on the forehead, but as he pulled back, her eyes opened wide, and she was looking straight into his.

"Bye, Daddy; I love you. Be safe," she whispered.

Nat stroked her cheek. "I love you too, baby. I'll see you soon."

She nodded and closed her eyes, then sighed deeply and turned on her side. Nat stood up. It was hard to leave the room tonight. He had to force himself to turn around and head for the door. Once he got there, he turned around for one last look at two small dark shapes in their beds, distorted by the moonlight. He closed the door, swallowed the lump in his throat, and started down the stairs.

Sonja had stacked the dishwasher and was handwashing the bone-handled knives when Nat returned to the kitchen. He came up behind her and put his arms around her. She leaned against him and tilted her head back as he kissed her neck. She had a special "Sonja" smell—not perfume but a slightly sweet natural smell, and he loved it. He had always loved it from the first time they had kissed.

She put the last knife in the drying rack and spun around in his arms.

"Do you know what, Mr. Jameson?" Her blue eyes were sparkling with mischief.

"No. What?" Nat pulled her closer.

"You are something else. You sweep a girl off her feet, drag her around the world, make her very happy, and then you say, 'Now I have to take some time off to fix the world.' You're not an easy man to keep up with."

"But you will agree, in that case, that life with me is not boring, will you?"

He bent down close until he could feel the sweetness of her breath, his lips almost touching hers. She closed her eyes; her lips parted and touched his for an instant. Then she whispered, "Agreed." Their lips found each other, and the world around them ceased to exist.

Chapter 63

They all had breakfast together the next morning, and Sonja drove the kids to school at eight. She was back just after nine and made the call to the embassy, telling Angela that Nat would not come to work, as he had developed a bad cold.

She was shocked when she saw that he had not even packed an overnight bag. “How can you manage without even a change of clothing? I don’t like it, Nat. I don’t like it at all. It’s as if they think you won’t be needing it.” Her voice trailed away as the full implications of her statement dawned on her.

“No, no, darling, not at all. They have to keep me alive if they want to get to the American president, and don’t forget, that’s what this is all about as far as they are concerned. Badawi told me everything I need will be provided, except my Scotch, which, I told him, was the only drug I took when he told me I could bring medication if I was on any.”

Sonja managed a strained smile. “You really are a piece of work. Do you know that?” She brushed an imaginary piece of lint off his suit jacket.

Remembering Tom’s advice to dress as loudly western as he could, to stick out visually from the enemy when the special ops team arrived, Nat was wearing a navy blue suit, a white button-down shirt, and a red tie.

Of course, if they insisted on giving him Arab clothing while he was there, he would not be able to refuse without arousing suspicion. He did not share that thought with Sonja, who kept looking at her watch while she busied herself tidying up after breakfast. Nat poured himself another cup of coffee and sat down at the kitchen table with the *Daily Telegraph*. The headline read:

POLICE FOIL PLOT TO BLOW UP NO. 10

Two men were held in custody, and links to al-Qaeda were suspected.

Sonja finished up at the sink and turned around. "You look like it's just going to be another day at the office. Either you are cracking up, or you're tougher than James Bond."

Nat put the paper down. "Neither, my darling. But I'll tell you one thing: I feel really good about what we're doing, about fighting back." He pointed to the newspaper on the table. "There will be more and more headlines like these unless we take drastic action, and I feel good about being part of it." He patted his knee. "Come and sit down."

She sat down and put her arms around his shoulders and looked into his eyes. "Part of it, you say? Don't sell yourself short. Without you, this wouldn't be happening. This is your operation, my darling." She leaned into him and hugged him. "And I'm so very, very proud of you, and so very, very scared."

"We're all in it together—you, Jim, Janet, the vice president, the president, and all the people who are part of making it happen."

He snuggled her and squeezed her tighter. "And without your support, my darling, this thing would never have moved off the runway."

"I know. . . I know." She whispered the words, and he could feel a warm wet tear trickle slowly down his neck.

He held her away so that he could look into her eyes, which were brimming with silent tears. "I will be fine," he said. "I don't know how I know, but I know I'll be fine." He leaned forward and kissed the saltiness of her lips. He looked at his watch. It was almost time to go. The car would be arriving in less than ten minutes. "Right, darling. It's time for me to get going."

She slid off his lap, and they stood up together. She kept holding on to him, raised a hand, and straightened his tie. "Promise me you'll be careful. I know they have taught you some tricks, but please, darling, don't take any chances."

"I promise." Nat started to move towards the entrance hall, still holding her close.

Once there, she freed herself and got his overcoat from the closet. "Umbrella?"

He smiled and shook his head. "They might think it was a secret weapon and take it away from me. And that. . . " He pointed to the umbrella with an exaggerated gesture. ". . . is my favourite umbrella."

They both burst out laughing. She helped him on with his coat, buttoned it, and gave him a quick kiss. "Off you go, then. Come back soon!"

He could tell she was fighting back the tears. He wanted to hold her and kiss her again but thought better of it. Sonja had said her goodbye; best not to prolong the agony. "I'll see you soon." He gave her a light kiss back.

As he walked towards the door, he felt something scrape his leg. He looked down and saw Darwin standing there with those shiny brown dachshund eyes looking up at him, his tail wagging. Nat bent down and held Darwin's head in his hands and wiggled it side to side.

"You be a good boy, Darwin, and look after them for me until I get back." Nat ruffled his ears and stood up. Darwin looked from Nat to Sonja and back at Nat again, his tail kept going slowly. It was as if the dog knew that this was no ordinary morning.

Nat gave Sonja a last look, opened the front door, and stepped out into the cool December morning.

CHAPTER 64

A black Mercedes was parked across the street. The tinted windows made it impossible to see if there was anyone in the car. Nat looked up and down the street. There were many cars parked on both sides.

He descended the three steps from his front door to the sidewalk and waited. The street seemed dead, then a dark blue Audi appeared around the corner and came slowly up the street. *This is it*, Nat thought. He could feel his heart pick up the pace. As the car approached, Nat stepped closer to the edge of the road, but the car did not stop. He took a deep breath, realising he had been holding it. He took a few more deep breaths, trying to slow down his heart, which was pounding in his chest, when the back door of the Mercedes opened, and a man stepped out, leaving the door open. He was tall and dark, olive-skinned, and dressed in a pinstriped dark grey suit. He was wearing a pair of dark, almost black, sunglasses. He crossed the street towards Nat and stretched his hand out.

"Mr. Jameson, very nice to meet you. My name is Omar, and I have been given the great honour to accompany you on your journey to meet with my superiors. Please," Omar gestured towards the car, "after you."

Another Omar, Nat thought. *Is that the standard, secret name for you all?*

They crossed the street, and Nat climbed in. Omar closed the door behind him and came around the other side. Nat noticed a small leather case lying on the console that separated the two back seats. It looked like the kit he had at home with his razor, scissors, comb, and nail file. *Why would they give that to me now?* he wondered as Omar took the seat opposite.

"Drive on!" Omar barked the order to the driver, who Nat could not see through the tinted glass screen which separated him from his passengers.

Omar reached for the leather case and turned to Nat. "For reasons, which I am sure you will appreciate, it is imperative that the location of al-Qaeda's headquarters remain secret. Not that we believe you would voluntarily divulge them; we don't, but it is much safer for all that you simply don't know."

Nat's heart did a somersault at the confirmation that his destination was indeed, al-Qaeda's headquarters.

Omar opened the leather case, revealing a syringe and needle held down by Velcro straps. "Do not be alarmed; I am a qualified surgeon—obstetrics, to be precise. A little prick in the top of your hand, and you will miss the journey and wake up at our headquarters. Pull over and stop, Amin!"

The driver responded instantly. Nat placed his right hand obligingly on the centre console, while Omar attached the needle to the syringe, held it up, and squeezed a few drops out.

"Lean back, please. Relax. Pleasant dreams."

Nat leaned back and closed his eyes. He felt a sting in the top of his hand, and seconds later, a warm sensation spread down from the top of his head, then nothing.

The ambulance drove straight out to the waiting Gulfstream medevac jet. A stretcher was brought out by two orderlies and hustled into the cargo door at the back of the plane, assisted by the steward who appeared in the doorway. The doctor, in a grey pinstriped suit, was handling the paperwork with an airport official.

The pilot had cleared the plane for take-off. The cargo door closed; the doctor sprinted up the short passenger steps, and as the door rose up behind him, the pilot revved the engines and started to taxi towards the runway. A flight plan had been filed for Johannesburg, where the patient was to undergo brain surgery. Time was of the essence.

Two minutes later the air traffic controllers in the tower at Luton Airport saw the gracious silver bird take off steeply, shimmering in the wintery morning sun. Five minutes later the plane reached its cruising altitude of forty-seven thousand feet, and the seatbelt signs were turned off.

Omar pressed the attendant's button and removed his seat belt. The purser, a slim dark-haired man in his mid-twenties, appeared from the galley at the rear. He wore black pants and a grey and white vest over a white shirt. His nose was too big for his face, and his dark brown eyes were small and piercing and too close together. The ensuing conversation was held in Arabic.

"I want to move our passenger into the cabin so I can keep an eye on him. It is very important that he arrives in good condition. I need to check his vital signs from time to time and put him back to sleep should he wake up on the journey."

The young man nodded. Omar stood up and followed him to the back of the plane, through the toilet room, and into the cargo compartment at the very back of the plane, where Nat was lying on the stretcher in the walkway running along the storage area. Omar indicated to the steward that he should move across to the foot end of the stretcher. The space was so narrow that the steward had to walk with one foot, either side of it, to get there. They picked the stretcher up, and Omar backed up slowly. The cramped space made it difficult to make the turn through the first bathroom door, but they managed it on the third attempt, then straight through the bathroom and into the main cabin, where they laid the stretcher down on a couch which was running along the fuselage at the rear of the main cabin.

"Secure him with the seat belts." Omar straightened up and rubbed his hands together, as if lifting the stretcher had hurt them. "We have precious cargo here. We do not want to lose him in an air pocket."

He returned to his seat and strapped himself in. He reached for his briefcase, which was stored in a leather pocket at the side of his seat, and pulled out a folder. He extracted a single piece of paper and studied it briefly, then pushed the call button. "Saif, give this to the captain; there is a change of flight plan."

"Very well, sir." The steward disappeared and returned moments later. "Can I bring you something to eat and drink?"

"Just some tea. I am not hungry yet."

Saif disappeared and returned with a tray, upon which he balanced a gold-rimmed black tea mug, a matching cup, and a matching bowl of fresh figs, together with a small glass of honey. He pulled the table from the armrest, rested the tray down, and poured the tea.

"Will that be all, sir?"

"Yes, thank you."

Omar added two spoons of honey and stirred them in absentmindedly. His thoughts were on what lay ahead. The supreme leader had been very clear in his instructions: "Bring Mr. Jameson to us, make sure he has no idea where you are taking him, and do not tell anybody why he is being brought here."

He took a sip of the hot liquid and sank back into his seat. His thoughts went to what was going to happen next. With Mr. Jameson's help, al-Qaeda would stage an operation which would shake the world and shift the balance of power in their favour. The assassination of the American president would restore al-Qaeda's influence in the Arab world and make Western leaders realise that the continued support of Israel, in their occupation and humiliation of the Palestinian people, and Arabs in general, was no longer sustainable. He wondered what al-Zawahiri had meant when he said that this would be a perfect prelude to the "shock and awe" operation, which was in the works for the West... an operation which would make the attack on—and defeat of—Iraq seem like child's play.

Omar looked over at Nat, asleep on the stretcher, opposite. Why would a man in Mr. Jameson's position do something like this? What was it that motivated the man to kill his own boss and the vice president of the United States of America, in order to he could prove he was worthy of al-Qaeda's trust? Why was he prepared to go so far out on a limb to help the Muslim cause? Omar shook his head and drew a deep breath. It was beyond comprehension. He finished his tea, leaned back in his seat, and closed his eyes. Moments later, he was asleep.

It was a very strange space—a tunnel made of soft green velvet. The floor, walls, and ceiling were uneven and continuous, like someone's intestine, and he found himself moving through it, slowly at first and then faster and faster, until all of a sudden, there was a blinding light coming towards him, and the green tunnel dissolved in an explosion of light.

Nat opened his eyes but closed them again quickly. Where was he? He opened his eyes again, just a fraction, enough to get a faint impression of his surroundings. It took him just seconds to recognise that he was in a private jet. Immediately to his left was Omar, who seemed to be fast asleep, and there was no one else in the cabin. He tried to move his hands and legs, but it was as if they did not exist. His mouth was dry, and he felt very thirsty. As his mind cleared, he realised that he was lying on a stretcher set on a couch and that he was strapped in, presumably with the standard safety belts across his chest and legs.

He risked turning his head towards the bulkhead to see if he could get a glimpse of the outside. A louvre, captured between the inner and outer layer of glass, was half shut, allowing a narrow view of pale blue sky. Nat sensed a movement to his left and quickly closed his eyes and lay stock still, breathing evenly. Moments later, he could feel someone grabbing his left wrist and turning it to face upwards.

Nat concentrated on keeping his wrist and arm totally limp. He realised that Omar was taking his pulse. *I hope it doesn't give me away*, Nat thought. Omar dropped the wrist, and moments later, Nat could feel what he instantly recognised to be a stethoscope in the area of his heart.

It was held there for no more than ten seconds. Nat sensed that Omar was moving away from him and opened his eyes a fraction, enough to get a blurred view of Omar returning to his seat and reaching for something in the pocket next to his seat. *The leather case. . . !* Nat shut his eyes quickly.

Obviously, Omar had determined that he needed to do a booster shot. Nat had hardly finished the thought when he felt a stinging sensation in the top of his left hand, and the world disappeared in black fog.

He had no idea how long he had been out when he came to again, but he sensed by the sound of the engines that they had started their descent. He could hear and feel some commotion in the cabin but did not dare open his eyes for fear that Omar would knock him out again. *This way, I might get an idea of what kind of place they're taking me to*, he thought.

The engine noise changed to a higher pitch, and the nose of the plane felt like it was angled upwards. They were landing. Nat opened his eyes slightly and saw greenery speed past the window, as if they were landing in the middle of a dense forest. The plane touched down, decelerated, made a sharp left turn, taxied briefly, and came to a full stop. Nat heard Omar release his seat belt and saw, through narrow slits of his eyes, the steward enter the cabin from the front of the plane. Omar spoke to him, and Nat felt the straps across his legs being released, followed by those across his chest. Two men, who Nat had not seen before, appeared in the cabin.

They were dressed in grey and pale green combat uniforms and black headbands. Omar spoke to them, and they nodded their heads. Nat wished he could understand what was being said.

They approached him, lifted the stretcher off the couch, and walked down the gangway towards the front exit. As they turned left at the exit, Nat got a glimpse of the pilot and co-pilot, who had turned around in their seats to get a look at their mystery passenger. They looked like a pair of British Airways pilots, which, clearly, they were not.

The air outside was hot and dry. Where was he? The stretcher tilted as they started to move down the steps, and Nat got a glimpse up into what appeared to be a massive camouflage net supported on very tall, triangular truss columns. The pattern of green looked like what he had seen when they were landing. My God; was it possible... a covered airstrip?

They reached the bottom of the steps, and Omar passed them and headed for a group of men standing a stone's throw away. They were all wearing variations of traditional Muslim dress. Nat decided this was probably as good a time as any to "wake up". He opened his eyes fully and raised both hands to his eyes and rubbed them. He raised his head, looked around, and was stunned. The intricate web of steel cables and fabric which soared overhead, supported on white, steel columns, was a feat of engineering virtuosity worthy of publication in the world's most prestigious architectural magazines. Nat had just enough time for a quick glance back in the direction they had landed and saw the light at the opening through which the pilot had squeezed the plane. Next, he was brought up in front of the welcoming committee. One of the five men stepped forward and spoke to Nat's porters. The man at the foot end lowered the stretcher to the ground as the man at the head raised his end, and Nat found himself standing.

He felt dizzy and swayed from side to side. The men who had carried him grabbed him and held on to him as the man in front stretched out his hand.

"Welcome, Mr. Jameson. I am sorry you are feeling groggy, but as I'm sure you will appreciate, we take our security very seriously."

Nat did a double take as he offered his hand. The man spoke fluent American! Nat struggled to see as he looked at the bearded man in front of him. As his eyes focused, he realised why the man sounded so American. He was none other than Adam Gadhan, the infamous American who had converted to Islam in his teens and moved to Pakistan in the late nineties.

What are you doing here? Nat thought. *According to our intelligence sources, you died in a drone strike.*

Gadhan's quarterback smile broadened. "I am glad to see I'm not the only American taking up the Muslim cause. My name is Adam."

They shook hands. Nat cringed at being classified as the soulmate of the only US citizen who had been charged with treason since World War II.

"Let me introduce you to some of my colleagues." Adam turned around to the men behind him. "This is Adnan el Adrani."

The man took Nat's hand in both of his. "*Ahlan wa sahlan*." And shook it vigorously. Then a boyish smile spread across his face, and he continued in American. "That means 'hello'. I am very pleased to meet you, and I know I speak for all of us when I say that we are grateful to you for your support of our cause. Your actions speak louder than words, and you have earned your place at our table." He bowed and made room for the next person.

Nat was impressed at the man's command of the English language and thought how much better he would have been off, himself, if he could have spoken some Arabic.

"And here is Khalid al-Habib, our military commander in chief."

Al-Habib smiled and bowed but did not offer his hand.

"And this is Saif al-Adel, our tactical expert and trainer of jihadi fighters."

Nat remembered that this was the man who had been bin Laden's security chief. But what was he doing here? It was said that Adel had spent time in Iran with other al-Qaeda top brass. What was going on?

Adam turned to the last of the group. "And this is Hamza al Jawi, our external operations chief." Hamza bowed and smiled but also did not extend his hand.

"And now I shall escort you to your quarters. It's not Ritz-Carlton quality, but you will be comfortable there." Adam took Nat's arm and turned him towards a long, low concrete building which ran down one side of the covered airstrip. The camouflage cover sailed over the building onto columns that jutted out from the roof.

Nat estimated that the building was more than two hundred feet in length. The walls were rough concrete, left natural, and judging by the pattern of deep-set, square windows, the walls were thick. The roof was flat, which gave the structure the appearance of a bunker.

Adam led the way through a pair of heavy metal doors which led into a simple reception space with a polished concrete floor on which stood a steel desk and an unoccupied chair. The space was about thirty by thirty feet square. The walls were the same bare concrete, devoid of any decoration. The space was lit by two square windows either side of the door they had just entered, supplemented by artificial lighting provided by bare bulbs strung under the concrete ceiling on metal hooks. The only concession to decoration were two carpets; their vivid colours and geometric design against the polished concrete floor reminded Nat of something he had seen in a five-star hotel in Marrakech.

Nat realised that Omar had vanished while Nat was being introduced to the welcoming committee, who all disappeared down a corridor in the opposite direction to which Adam took Nat.

"You will have the VIP guest room. It's not five-star, but it is comfortable. It's one of only two rooms with its own shower and toilet accommodation."

Nat was making up a mental picture of the layout of the place as they proceeded down the narrow hallway, which was lit by square roof lights every ten feet or so. There were no windows even though it would appear that the corridor ran along the perimeter opposite the side of the landing strip. Nat figured they had entered roughly in the middle of the length of the building, with the hallway running both ways along the perimeter, creating a solid barrier to a compound that looked inward towards the landing strip. A quick look backwards confirmed that he was right. The hallway went straight back at least a hundred feet.

Nat counted half a dozen rough wooden doors as they passed them on their right before Adam stopped at the seventh door. It was a heavy wood door like all the others. Adam opened it and invited Nat to go first. The room looked to be about ten feet wide by fourteen feet deep—same coarse concrete walls, same polished, concrete floor. A square window sat at the end of the room, about five by five, Nat judged, which gave a view out to the soaring camouflage structure over the airstrip. There was one bare lightbulb in the concrete ceiling.

A single bed was in the middle of the long wall to the left as they entered. It was covered with a plain grey wool blanket, through which could be seen the contours of a pillow. There was a crudely made wardrobe placed immediately to the left of the door and a table positioned below the window.

If this is the VIP suite, they sure don't spoil themselves, Nat thought.

The only decoration in the room was another vibrantly coloured rug on the floor next to the bed, not unlike the Berber rug Sonja had bought in Marrakech three years ago.

"Well, as you can see, it is not up to the standard we are used to from home, but here is the pièce de résistance." Adam opened a smaller wooden door to the left of the bed. "Voilà! Your very own bathroom, and if you don't think this is impressive, wait till you see my accommodation."

To Nat's surprise, the bathroom was better than he had come to expect. Not only were the floors polished concrete, but so were the walls, which had a bluish grey tint. The whole space was no more than four by eight, with a white wall-mounted hand basin, a glass shelf, and mirror above on which were laid out a plastic razor, a plastic cup with a toothbrush, and a small tube of toothpaste. The toilet was to the right of the basin, followed by the shower area, which filled the end of the space. There was no enclosure for the shower, and Nat could see a plastic soap dish in one corner. Hopefully it had soap in it. There was none at the hand basin. The space had no natural lighting, but there was what looked to be a narrow fluorescent fixture over the mirror and the obligatory naked light bulb in the ceiling for general lighting.

Adam was waiting for the verdict.

"If there's a bar of soap in the soap dish over there, I'll be fine."

Adam went over to investigate. "There is, and towels and clothing should be in the wardrobe." They returned to the bedroom, and Adam opened the double doors of the wardrobe to reveal two white towels on a shelf, and the two drawers below it had three pairs of socks and underwear. It was what was hanging on the rod which caused Nat's heart to sink. There, on two hangers, were one white and one dark brown cotton robe with matching pants...one gold and one black corded waistband, and a white turban. So much for dressing so he would stand out from the crowd when the SEALS came storming in.

"I hope they fit you." Adam closed the wardrobe. "We want you to be comfortable, and besides, you're one of us now. You have earned your uniform. How did you do it?"

"Do what?" The question took Nat by surprise. He needed time to construct the answer.

"Kill the ambassador and the vice president?" Adam gave Nat an admiring look. "They think I'm a bad person. Wait until they find out about you!"

"They will never find out, unless you folks give away my secret, which would not be in your best interest. Not, at least, if you want to eliminate the president, which I assume you do since I was invited here?"

Adam nodded. "Indeed, we do, and the consensus here is that Allah sent you to help us achieve the goals which we have been fighting for all these years." Adam seemed to have forgotten that Nat had not answered his question. "There is great excitement and anticipation among the al-Qaeda leaders here that your presence will do much to enhance our cause."

"I have delivered on my promises so far, and I intend to do so in the future."

"Good." Adam turned and headed towards the door and turned around as he reached it. "I should warn you that they are going to ask you to kill the president also. It would be easier for you than for anybody else."

"I am not prepared to do that. I made that very clear from the outset. Besides, if I were to be present at yet another death of a high-ranking American official, it would not take long before somebody started to get suspicious that these deaths might not have been natural, and my usefulness to al-Qaeda would be over."

Adam stood framed in the doorway. He raised a hand in a farewell gesture. "I hear you, but I know they'll be pressing you hard to change your mind." He looked at his watch. "It is eight o'clock. Dinner's at nine—last door on the right, down the hallway. Have a shower and change. You'll be surprised how much more comfortable our clothes are." He smiled. "Just one more reason I became a Muslim. See you in a bit."

Adam closed the door, and Nat sat down on the end of the bed. It felt strange to be in a "hotel room" without having any luggage to unpack. That, and the austere surroundings, created a surreal feeling. Where was the supreme leader of al-Qaeda? Where was Abd al-Rahaman, their explosives expert, or Mustafa Hamid... who Washington thought was al-Qaeda's link to the Iranian government?

Without these key members of al-Qaeda present, the operation would not be the success they had hoped for. Could he even "pull the trigger" with only a handful of al-Qaeda leaders in attendance?

Nat stood up. Time to have a shower, clear his mind, and focus on the task at hand. Maybe there were more leaders in the compound, and he just had not met them yet. Nat undressed and laid his clothes on the bed, went to the wardrobe, brought out the hanger with the white robe and pants, and picked a pair of underwear and socks from the drawers.

Ralph Lauren! Nat smiled. Did they just want to make him feel at home, or were they all wearing American fashion-label underwear?

He removed the clothes from the hanger, laid them on the bed, put his own clothes on the hanger, returned it to the wardrobe, and grabbed a towel. Maybe he could put them on again when he heard the SEALS coming? Nat shook his head. One step at a time, as Tom said.

He walked into the shower and turned on the tap. There was only one tap and one shower head, high on the wall. Nat jumped back. The water was cold. He let it run for a while. It did not warm up, and Nat realised that this was it. Cold showers! These people certainly did not believe in pampering themselves. He stepped under the cold stream of water, which took his breath away. He grabbed the soap and rubbed it on quickly, forcing himself to stay under the cold spray, and soon the shock of the cold water was replaced by a pleasant, tingling sensation. The water did not feel cold anymore. He finished with the soap and lifted his face towards the stream of water, which felt like fine needles pricking his skin. He rinsed off thoroughly, enjoying the invigorating sensation of the water.

CHAPTER 65

When he had dried himself and put on the light cotton clothing, he felt like a new man. He realised that the anaesthetic had made him feel groggy and that the cold shower had revived him. He was ready to face the challenges that lay ahead. He looked at his watch—the watch—and toyed with the crown. When would he be able to press it? It was almost nine o'clock. Time to go for dinner. As he started down the long corridor, Nat realised that the camouflage canopy not only covered the runway but sailed over the building also, which meant Langley would not be able to get any useful satellite images of the compound to assist the SEALS in planning their attack. *Well,* he thought, *there's nothing I can do about that other than trust them to still do an outstanding job.*

The last door on the right was open, and Nat could hear agitated voices seeping out into the corridor. As he entered the room, all heads turned his way, and conversation halted abruptly. The man who sat at the far end of the table, below a large painting of Osama bin Laden, was instantly recognisable. It was Zawahiri, who was supposed to have been killed in Kabul.

The room erupted in spontaneous applause. Adam, who sat close to the door at the other end of the table, got up and walked over to Nat.

"There you are. . . looking much better. Let me introduce you to your host." Adam led Nat down the length of the table, and the applause seized abruptly when they stopped in front of al-Zawahiri. Adam bowed. "It is my pleasure, and a great honour, to introduce to you my countryman, Nathaniel Jameson."

Zawahiri rose from his chair. His eyes were twinkling behind his steel-rimmed glasses. He offered his hand. "Welcome, my son. You are the miracle we have been praying for." His English was excellent. – *So you played a hoax on us before we played one on you*, Nat thought as he reached for the outstretched hand.

Nat took his hand. "I am pleased to be here, Dr. Zawahiri. Very pleased." More than you can imagine, he thought.

Zawahiri pointed to an empty chair to his right. "Please have a seat next to me. You must be surprised to see me, but we thought this was the best way to keep me safe. Nobody keeps looking for a dead man, and this has enabled me to travel freely around the world, which has been very useful in coordinating our efforts worldwide."

Seals are in for a big surprise! Nat thought.

Nat sat down, but Zawahiri remained standing. He looked out at the men seated around the table. Nat did a quick count and realised there were twelve men in the room, excluding himself, but no sign of Omar. This was looking much better. He debated whether he should press his watch there and then but decided to wait. Maybe he could learn more by spending some time with these people, maybe things that could not be discovered were they all to fight to the death in the attack which would follow.

Zawahiri started to speak, and Nat could, at first, not understand a word of what he said. Zawahiri raised his head to the ceiling and thanked Allah.

"Allah Akbhar!" A long monologue followed, in which Nat recognised "Jameson" and "Preston", "London" and "Burton", from which he deduced that Zawahiri was relating to his audience that Nat had killed the US ambassador and the US vice president. And when Zawahiri stretched both hands out towards him, Nat thought he might have said something like: "... and that is why he is sitting here at our table, right here, next to me."

Applause filled the room and continued until Zawahiri raised both arms in a gesture of "silence". He remained standing and turned towards Nat. "I told our brave fighters that we now have among us the bravest of them all. I told them what you have done and why you are here. Tonight, we will eat and relax, and tomorrow we will be joined by four other key members of our organisation, and then we will go to work. Tomorrow, a representative from fourteen of our twenty affiliates worldwide will be here." He sat down, and conversation resumed around the table in a low murmur.

"So, what do you think of our little hideaway, Mr. Jameson—a little on the primitive side for you?" Zawahiri's smile did not make it to his eyes.

"I haven't seen much of it, but that airstrip canopy is impressive, and my accommodations are quite satisfactory, thank you."

Zawahiri bowed in acknowledgment. "We believe in a simple life—a life of devotion and prayer. Our fight is for a world that makes this its priorities. The world is full of debauchery and evil. Many people have lost their way, lost their connection with God, the almighty Allah, who created the miracle that we are all part of. Our struggle is to return people to the right path so that we can all live our lives to His glory." Zawahiri smiled. "But I don't mean to lecture. I don't need to lecture a man who has made common cause with us to make the world a better place."

The words jolted Nat. He had heard them before and thought them before, and to hear them coming from the al-Qaeda leader hit a nerve. *They are just as sure as we are that their cause is right*. It was difficult to accept.

"You must be hungry. Let us eat." Zawahiri clapped his hands three times. The room fell silent, and moments later two women, Nat presumed, entered the room carrying a large covered silver tray each. They were totally covered in dark brown flowing gowns and niqabs (veils) with narrow slits for the eyes, and floated like ghosts across the floor.

One of the dishes was placed immediately in front of Nat and Zawahiri, and the other at the opposite end of the table. The dish, with its high dome cover, looked to be at least three feet in diameter. Each woman grasped her lid handle with both hands; they looked at each other and removed the lids in unison to reveal the golden-brown bodies of roasted lambs surrounded by an assortment of vegetables, dates, and figs. The steam, which rose from the dish, reached Nat's nostrils, and the delicious aroma made his mouth water.

"*Bismillah wa ala Barakatillah*." Zawahiri raised his eyes to the ceiling as he spoke. All eyes around the table were on him.

Zawahiri turned to Nat. "That means: '. . . in the name of Allah and with the blessings of Allah, and so we eat.' Please help yourself."

Nat looked around and saw that all eyes were now on him. There were no utensils next to his plate and none on the serving dish. Nat hesitated.

Zawahiri smiled. "We use our hands—both hands for serving ourselves and the right hand for eating. Dig in."

Nat reached out and pinched a piece of meat, which came off easily in his hand, and placed it on his plate.

"Please, please, help yourself. You have come a long way. You must be very hungry." Zawahiri urged him on.

Nat took a handful of couscous and some greens, which looked like it could be steamed spinach. Zawahiri followed suit, and only after he had helped himself did the others around the table help themselves. There was no conversation, and nobody started eating. Nat held back, despite feeling ravenously hungry, to see what they were all waiting for. He noticed that again all eyes were on Zawahiri, who very slowly picked up a piece of mutton and put it in his mouth, and before he had swallowed it, the room came alive with people eating and talking. Nat dug into the food in front of him. He could not remember ever having had a meal which tasted better.

Even allowing for the fact that he was starving, the moist, tender and flavourful meat, which seemed to melt on his tongue, complemented by the lightly scented couscous and the lemony greens, made for a very pleasant culinary experience. Nat had to restrain himself not to eat too quickly. He noticed that the people around him were picking very slowly at their food. It seemed that the conversation and the companionship around the table were more important than the food.

A delicate hand holding a white jug appeared over his right shoulder and poured water in the glass in front of him. Nat turned to see one of the veiled women standing behind him. He could only see her big dark brown eyes.

"Thank you." He smiled at her, and she did something with her eyes, which a Western woman would have needed to be in a bikini to achieve. It was a sexy, flirtatious gesture so powerful that, if Nat had not experienced it himself, he would have said it was impossible. She moved on to serve others.

As if he had read his mind, Zawahiri turned to Nat. "It is through a woman's eyes that we can learn of her true beauty. Contrary to common, Western belief, we cherish our women. They are God's gift to man. So, like any treasure, we must guard them with great care." He looked at Nat's plate, which was empty. "Please, help yourself to more food."

Nat did not have to be asked twice. He had just finished replenishing his plate when Zawahiri leaned towards him. "How did you do it? Being a doctor myself, I am intrigued at what you did. Inducing heart attacks is not easy, and inducing them with a poison which escapes the scrutiny of an autopsy is, I would have thought, almost impossible. How did you do it?"

Nat remembered Tom's advice not to let himself get drawn into how he had accomplished the assassinations, but sitting here, in the middle of an al-Qaeda "banquet" surrounded by his new "friends", that seemed to be a wholly inappropriate response. Nat could feel his pulse quicken. What to say? He had, to satisfy his own interest, looked up ways to induce heart attacks on the internet and, in his search, come across a substance, potassium chloride, which is a common substance in many prescription drugs and breaks down into potassium and chlorine in the body. Slightly elevated levels of PC would not be red-flagged in an autopsy report.

Nat took a drink of water, wiped his hands on his napkin, and turned to face the al-Qaeda leader. "I did a lot of research on the best way to go about this. As you will appreciate, when I first broached this subject with Imam Badawi, I had been thinking about all this for a long time. For over a year, in fact, and I had developed a plan." *And that's the God's honest truth*, Nat thought, *but not the plan we're talking about*. "I came across a substance called potassium chloride, found in a number of prescription drugs but also, as I discovered later, in some over-the-counter drugs; it breaks down into potassium and chlorine, both of which are found naturally in the body."

"Ah ha! Very clever." Zawahiri's eyes twinkled wickedly.

"Too much potassium in the body causes tachycardia, fast heart rate, which leads to ventricular fibrillation and cardiac arrest."

Zawahiri stroked his beard. "How did you administer it?"

"In cups of coffee. The ambassador was easy. We frequently had coffee together from the machine in his office. Last time we did, I made the coffee and slipped the PC in with the sugar. It was easy. The vice president was more difficult, but I was very lucky. We met in his office, where he presented me with my official appointment as ambassador to the Court of St. James, and he asked me if I would have a cup of coffee with him. He poured coffee for us both, and then he excused himself and went to the bathroom. 'Old man syndrome,' he said, when he returned a couple of minutes later. It gave me the opportunity to spike his coffee." Nat stopped and looked at Zawahiri. It sounded too good to be true, and he wondered if his host had heard the saying that if something sounds too good to be true, it normally is.

Zawahiri stared at Nat, blinked, and sat back in his chair. He looked around the room at the men, who were eating and talking quietly together. He started to laugh, softly at first, and then louder and louder, until all conversation ceased and all eyes were on their leader. Zawahiri raised his hands, subdued his laughter, and started to speak in Arabic.

Nat's heart beat faster. What was the man saying? Was he suspicious that there was something wrong with Nat's story? An image of being dragged off and having his throat slit flashed through his mind.

"*Alhamdulillah*!"

Zawahiri ended his monologue, and all eyes shifted to Nat. To his relief, he saw no expressions of hostility. Quite the opposite—there were smiles, nodding of heads, and grunts of approval. Nat turned to Zawahiri. "What did you say to them?"

Zawahiri smiled, leaned forward, and picked a fig from the serving dish and studied it intently before putting it in his mouth. He chewed it slowly, still smiling, and swallowed. "I told them what you told me and that we all now are living the miracle that could only have been bestowed on us by God. Alhamdulillah. All praises and thanks be to Allah." Zawahiri leaned towards Nat and touched his arm. "Yours was a long journey to get here, and I don't mean the flight from England. I mean your journey from being a trusted American diplomat to becoming a champion of the Muslim cause, a journey so difficult that only Allah could have shown the way. Alhamdulillah!"

Nat assumed a thoughtful expression. "Yes, it has been a long journey, and one that I chose reluctantly. I do not believe in killing. I want to stop the killing, but for it to stop, we have to stop those who are ultimately responsible for it."

Zawahiri picked another fig and leaned back in his chair as he put it in his mouth. Chewing it slowly, he fixed Nat with his black eyes. There was an intensity and coldness in the stare which made Nat feel uneasy. Killing innocent people was al-Qaeda's substitute for more difficult military targets.

Zawahiri finished his fig and wiped his hands on his napkin. "And we both know who is ultimately responsible; you have focused on him yourself. It is your president, who, along with his predecessors, has continued to support an illegitimate Israeli regime against the Palestinians, who were driven from their homes many, many years ago. The Israelis and the Americans have killed many women and children, many of our young boys fighting for freedom; they have died by the thousands. God bless them." Zawahiri leaned forward, his face close to Nat's. "So, we kill their women and children and their young men."

Nat could feel the hairs stand up on his neck. There was no visible emotion in the man's softly spoken words, just a quiet promise that this would continue, forever if necessary. Agreeing wholeheartedly with Zawahiri on the injustices committed against the Palestinians, Nat had to remind himself that al-Qaeda's goals went way beyond an equitable peace in the Middle East.

"It is all this senseless killing that I want to stop, Dr. Zawahiri." Nat stared back. "As you know, I was at the London Zoo with my family when it was attacked recently. We were lucky, but we could have been killed, and that experience made me more determined than ever to be part of a process that will stop this madness once and for all. I am very pleased that you have kept your word not to carry out any further attacks on civilian targets and that our—that is to say, your target now is the American president. As you know, I am willing, and able, to create the opportunity for that to happen but not to do it myself."

"I know." Zawahiri stroked his grey beard. "That is one thing I hope to change your mind about."

"No chance. We have a deal. I've carried out two major parts of my side of it, and I will deliver the last part of my side of that deal." Nat's appetite had vanished, and his body felt heavy. He felt a sudden urge to yawn and put a hand over his mouth to cover it. "I'm sorry." Nat emptied his glass of water. "I feel bushed, as we say back home."

"No, no, do not be sorry. Of course you must be tired. Adam will take you back to your room. Tomorrow we will get down to business."

Nat started to get up from his chair. His limbs felt like lead. The room was filled with the murmur of conversation and seemed to sway gently. He steadied himself on the table. Next thing he knew, Adam was standing next to him, pulling his chair back. Zawahiri rose to his feet, and the room fell silent. He spoke a few words in Arabic and turned to Nat. "Sleep well, my friend; tomorrow will come, God willing."

"Thank you." Nat forced his legs forward. He could feel all the eyes on him as Adam led him down the length of the table and out into the hallway.

CHAPTER 66

He woke from a knock on his door. It opened, and Adam entered, followed by a veiled woman carrying a tray. "Good morning, Nat. Breakfast in bed. A first in al-Qaeda history. Even bin Laden never had that." Adam stood aside and let the woman with the tray pass him. She placed the tray at the end of his bed, bowed, and backed out of the room.

Nat struggled to get his brain in gear. Yesterday seemed like a dream. He looked out of his window at the dappled sunlight filtering through the airstrip camouflage net. His eyes automatically went to his watch. It said 8:30 a.m. He sat up in bed. "Good morning. What's the time?"

Adam looked at his watch. "It's ten thirty. We let you sleep. The other participants have arrived, with the exception of Ali, who's joining us from Iran, but he should be here shortly. Our meeting is scheduled to start at eleven, but you can be fifteen minutes late to let Zawahiri have a few words with the new arrivals before we get started. We meet where you ate last night. See you soon."

Adam withdrew, and Nat looked at the tray at the end of his bed. On it was a glass of something, which looked like orange juice, only darker, a cup of very dark tea, two pieces of almost black bread, and a glass jar of some kind of marmalade. Nat sipped the tea. It was very sweet—honey, not sugar. He tasted the juice. It was not orange juice; mango maybe? He picked up a piece of bread, and, with an ornate silver knife which lay next to the jar of marmalade, spread some of it on the bread. Sonja would have approved. There was no butter. The marmalade was not marmalade but fig paste. It was delicious. Nat washed the mouthful down with tea. Just as he did, he heard the distant whine of a jet engine. The sound grew louder and louder until it seemed to fill the room.

Nat got off the bed and went to the window and saw a private jet pull up less than fifty yards away, coming to a stop next to six other private planes. Al-Qaeda's austerity measures obviously did not extend to air travel.

The scene outside reminded him of the scene at Bermuda's airport when he had taken his family there for a vacation two years ago. Opposite the commercial air terminal, he had counted twelve private jets, no doubt belonging to international insurance and reinsurance executives who had set up business there and made the island their home. The comparison sent chills down his back. What he saw outside the window confirmed that al-Qaeda was a well-organised, and well-financed, international organisation, but their business was not insurance or manufacturing. Their business was murder and mayhem.

He returned to his breakfast, and while he finished it, he wondered where he was in the world. Based on Adam's information, they were two hours ahead of London, which meant he was about thirty degrees east of London. Judging by the heat he had experienced when he arrived, and last night at dinner, it suggested that he was a lot farther south. The Middle East or Africa maybe?

He finished his breakfast, shaved and showered, and put on the brown cotton robe and pants, with the black braided waistband and the white turban from last night. He looked at himself in the mirror, where a blond blue-eyed "terrorist" stared back at him. He looked at his watch, which said ten past nine, which meant it was ten past eleven. He debated adjusting the watch to show the correct local time but thought better of it. The only time he would touch that crown was when he depressed it to bring in the SEALS. He took a deep breath and a last look in the mirror and headed for the door. He stopped halfway through it and returned to the wardrobe, where he extracted a photograph of Sonja and the children from his suit jacket, took a quick look, and stuffed it in a deep pocket on his baggy cotton pants. It made him feel better somehow.

He headed out again and down the monotonous hallway. The sun created hotspots under the skylights, and the corridor was hot. The door to the room they had met in last night was closed, but Nat could hear a murmur of voices inside. He knocked, opened the door, and stepped inside. A cool gust of air greeted him. Thank God! The room was air-conditioned. All conversation stopped. Adam jumped up from his chair and went to meet Nat, who waited by the door, which he closed behind himself.

"There you are. We are ready to start. Come this way." Adam held him lightly by the left elbow and guided him towards the head table, which was set at right angles to the long table at which they had eaten, making a short "T".

Ayman al-Zawahiri was seated in the middle of the head table, flanked by two men on his left and one man on his right. There was an empty chair immediately next to Zawahiri—the place of honour. As Nat and Adam approached, Zawahiri rose and started to clap. The three men next to him followed suit, and by the time Nat and Adam stopped in front of the head table, everyone was on their feet clapping but stopped the moment Zawahiri spoke.

"Welcome. Welcome, my friend." Zawahiri offered his hand to Nat, and they shook. "Did you sleep well?"

"Very well, thank you. I went out like a light."

"Good, good." Zawahiri was dressed in a grey silk tunic with a gold and white braided waistband. He wore the same white turban he had worn last night. He turned to the men on his left. "Let me introduce you to some of our new arrivals." He pointed to a suntanned, grey-haired, and grey-bearded man to his immediate left who wore dark horn-rimmed glasses and looked like he could have been a Harvard professor. He extended his hand. "This is Mustafa Hamid, a diplomat of great skill and our link to the Iranian government."

Nat's heart did a somersault as he shook Mustafa's hand. Al-Qaeda's link to the Iranian government! *I wonder if you know something about the missing Russian nuclear warhead?* Nat thought, as he nodded and smiled at the man.

"And, next to him," Zawahiri continued, "we have Abu Khalil al-Madani, a man of many talents, not the least of which are his excellent connections throughout the Arabian Peninsula." Zawahiri turned to the man sitting beyond the empty seat to his right. "And this is Bazam Abu Salih, who is the coordinator of our affiliates around the world, and with twenty of them in total, he is a very busy man."

And, pointing to a man standing behind his chair, in front of Nat, "And last but not least, this is Ibrahim Hassan al-Asiri, our bomb expert.

He has had some spectacular failures, such as what your people called the 'underwear bomb' and the intercepted shipment of printers destined for Detroit, but he is currently working on a bomb which will be a spectacular success."

Hassan extended his hand across the table. He did not smile, and there was an arrogant expression in his dark, cold eyes. His lips were shut tight between a thin moustache and a scraggly goatee. Nat estimated that he was in his early thirties. With the introductions over, Zawahiri gestured for Nat to take his seat, then he looked down the long table, called someone in Arabic, and waved for him to approach the head table.

Nat recognised the man who came towards them, carrying his chair, as the man who had spoken English with an American accent, Adnan el Adrani, who came behind the head table and placed his chair behind Nat's.

Zawahiri sat down next to Nat, and everybody sat down. "Adnan will be your translator. He spent fifteen years in your country, so he is almost as fluent in English as he is in his mother tongue."

Nat turned around, smiled, and nodded at his interpreter, who nodded and smiled back.

"So, let us start." Zawahiri clapped to get everybody's attention, then switched to Arabic, addressing the assembly. Adnan started to translate.

"You all know why you have been summoned to this meeting. To bring you all here goes against our policy of never having more than two or three of us together in one place, but this is a moment in our history as an organisation which demands that we all come together to make decisions which will have a fundamental impact on the future of our organisation and the future of the world." Zawahiri paused to let his words sink in. "As you all know, we have been working steadfastly to acquire the means to force the Jews out of Palestine and the Americans out of the Arabian Peninsula, and our sabotage and guerrilla activities are moving us, slowly, closer to achieving those objectives—too slowly, until recently. Thanks to our Iranian and Russian friends, we are close to having a weapon so powerful that, if used correctly, it will change the balance of power in the Middle East."

Nat could feel his pulse quicken. Was Zawahiri referring to a nuclear weapon? Nat had a vision of Tel Aviv in ashes with hundreds of thousands of lives lost. Another Hiroshima.

"But now we also have, thanks to a very brave man, an opportunity not only to change the balance of power in the Middle East but to change the world order, which, for too long, has been dominated by the United States of America." Zawahiri paused and gave Nat a sideways glance. "And that man is sitting here, right next to me, Mr. Nathaniel Jameson, the US Ambassador in London, who has joined us in our fight for justice."

Zawahiri turned to Nat, and the room burst into applause. He put a fatherly hand on Nat's shoulder as he continued. "By killing the US vice president and a US ambassador, he has earned the right to sit at this table, and we thank Allah for having brought him to us. Mr. Jameson is offering us the opportunity to kill the man who is the embodiment of all that is evil... the man who, more than anyone, stands in the way of us achieving our goals: the president of the United States of America. He will not do it himself; I have asked him, because it would be easier for him than for us, but I understand that not only would this ruin his life and that of his family, but it would also mean that we would lose a valuable partner in the fight for the Muslim cause, which, no doubt, will continue after the president's death." Zawahiri reached for his water glass and took a long drink. He placed it back on the table, folded his hands, and leaned forward.

"So, I have called you here today to ask you first: do we want to take this opportunity? And, secondly: to agree, with Mr. Jameson's help, how we do it. Let's start with the first question."

Zawahiri's sentence was drowned out by shouts, reinforced by raised fists. The noise subsided and was replaced by a hum of voices, as the men exchanged words across and along the table. Zawahiri let this continue for a while before he raised his hands, and the room fell silent.

"Good. That means we can get on to how we achieve it." He turned to Nat and switched to English. "So, Nat, I hand over to you. What are your thoughts on how we go about this?"

Nat cleared his throat. He sensed Adnan, his interpreter, move so that he sat to Nat's right side so that he could hear better what Nat was going to say.

Nat turned to Adnan. "Are you ready?" Adnan nodded, and Nat turned back to face his audience.

"It is not common knowledge, but an ideal opportunity to kill the American president will present itself in February when he comes to Europe for a visit with European heads of state." Adnan's monotone voice started up, and Nat paused until he had finished his sentence. "The purpose of this visit is to get European support for a multinational task force, or army, to fight terrorism, as we call it," Nat added, as Adnan started his translation.

It was strange to address an audience in a language he knew most of them did not understand and to see their eyes switch from himself to his translator as they alternated. It was like playing a verbal game of tennis.

"On his one-week trip, the president will visit six countries—England, Germany, France, Italy, Spain and Russia—and he will meet with heads of state, government officials, and people who, through their connections in the Arab world, are seen by the US to be in a position to help the cause."

Nat paused to let Adnan come in.

"A number of Arab business people will be identified, who will be invited to meet with the president at various points along the way, and it is my thought that one of those people who will receive such an invitation will be our assassin." Nat paused, again, and waited for the Arab words to stop. "This could be a bona-fide businessman with links to al-Qaeda or an al-Qaeda operative who is given a false identity and background to qualify him for such a meeting in the opinion of the decision-makers in Washington."

Adnan hesitated, as if he had difficulty finding the right words. Nat turned around and found his interpreter staring at him wide-eyed. "I would be the perfect person for that job," he whispered.

Zawahiri turned and spoke in English. "Not now! Translate! We will talk about who it should be later." Adnan resumed his translation.

"A bona-fide businessman would obviously be preferable, as the background checks on anybody meeting with the president will be thorough." Nat was starting to feel himself running out of steam. Time to throw the discussion open to the floor.

Adnan finished the sentence, and Nat scanned all the faces across the table, trying to make brief eye contact with as many as possible, and continued.

"I would like to hear your ideas and thoughts on how we can best achieve our objective, given these circumstances."

When Adnan finished, Zawahiri was the first to speak. He spoke in Arabic, and Nat had to wait for the translation. "As some of you who are directly involved already know, we are close to having a nuclear weapon ready for... for firing." Adnan was struggling to find the right word.

There it was, confirmed! *Our worst fears...confirmed!* Nat could feel a cold lump form in his stomach.

Zawahiri continued. "The firing mechanism was completed recently, and we are now looking at finding the best delivery method. Delivery to where? You may ask, and the answer to that question is: to our arch enemy, Israel!"

Nat could feel his heart starting to pound. Al-Qaeda were in possession of a fully functional nuclear weapon which they planned to use against Israel!

The room burst into applause, which Zawahiri cut short with a wave of his right arm. He carried on, clearly excited. He spoke faster and louder, but Adnan's translation came with the same subdued monotone, which made the words seem even more sinister.

"We have been exploring a rocket delivery but have dismissed it in favour of a less spectacular, but more reliable, method which involves shipping the bomb to Israel hidden in a combine harvester. Four of our people in Israel, who have been there for nearly twenty years, are established farmers in the Jezreel Valley, south of Haifa." Zawahiri paused, turned to Nat, and smiled. "Can you imagine? Deeply embedded al-Qaeda operatives in Israel—we have over one hundred of them altogether." He turned back to his audience and switched to Arabic. Adnan resumed his translation. "The bomb will be transferred from the harvester to a heavy freight truck which, at the right time, will be driven to Tel Aviv and parked near Independence Hall."

Nat could feel sweat running down his back despite the air-conditioned coolness of the room. It struck him how incredibly fortunate it was that he was sitting at this table right now, how very fortunate it was that the deception had worked and that this diabolical plot would be foiled. He felt a sudden chill, and goose bumps rose on his arms. What was he waiting for? He pulled his hands down from the table and rested them in his lap, then he bent forward and slid his hands under the table. His right thumb found the back of the bezel, and his index finger touched the crown. He applied pressure—nothing. He applied more pressure—still nothing. What was wrong? He felt the panic rise in his chest. He pressed harder and felt a slight vibration as the crown slipped down into place. It was all he could do to suppress a deep sigh of relief.

"Mr. Jameson! Are you all right?" Zawahiri's words jolted Nat out of his trance. The old man was staring at him with raised eyebrows, his eyes barely visible behind the reflection in his glasses.

"Yes, Dr. Zawahiri; I'm fine, really." Nat placed his hands back on the table. "But I am shocked at what I hear. My offer to kill the US ambassador and the vice president, and to create the opportunity for you to eliminate the president, was based on your agreement that there would be no more killing of innocent people. And you are describing a plan that will kill millions of innocent people."

Zawahiri shook his head and spoke in a fatherly tone. "No, my friend. That is where you are wrong. There are no innocent

Israelis! They killed our sisters and brothers and stole our land. There are no innocent Israelis."

Nat decided he had nothing to lose to debate the point. The clock was ticking. He wondered how long it would be before the SEALS arrived.

"I do not agree with you. I believe the vast majority of Israelis would like nothing better than to live in peace, side by side with the Palestinians. It is their leaders who are to blame, not the Israeli people."

Zawahiri frowned and rubbed the sides of his nose with his index fingers. It was as if he was weighing the merits of Nat's point. He folded his hands in front of him, as if in prayer. "I do understand what you are saying, and maybe we can achieve our objectives now, with your help, without having to detonate the bomb." Zawahiri paused. He looked out at the al-Qaeda leaders in front of him. Nat could see he was thinking hard. Then a smile spread across his face. "Yes, I have an idea. Let's see whether it can get the support of the council." He turned to face the audience, most of whom had not been able to follow what had just been said, and switched to Arabic.

"My friends," Adnan's monotone translation resumed, and Nat had to concentrate on the sound coming from behind him while his eyes followed Zawahiri and the men around the table. "Our new brother is pleading for the lives of the Israelis."

The room erupted in angry shouts and drumming of fists on the table.

Zawahiri raised his arms. "Quiet! Quiet! I have an idea which I want to share with you. With Mr. Jameson's help, we will kill the president, and then we present the world with an ultimatum: All Israelis must leave Israel by the first of May or a nuclear bomb will destroy Tel Aviv on the fourteenth of May, on the seventy-fifth anniversary of the establishment of the State of Israel." Zawahiri paused to let his words sink in. A dead silence filled the room. "What do you say?" Zawahiri looked at each man in turn.

Abu Salih raised his right arm.

"Yes, Bazam, you have the floor."

Salih rose from his seat and looked past Nat towards the al-Qaeda leader. He cleared his throat and spoke Arabic in a low but high-pitched voice—a boyish voice, Nat thought. "If Osama had been here today, he would have said we must not take the lives of thousands of our brothers, who would surely die along with the Jews, should we explode the bomb in Tel Aviv." Adnan's translation finished almost as Salih finished his sentence.

Salih continued. "I believe we must keep the nuclear threat as a means to achieve a peaceful end to the Israeli state. We have a big tactical advantage. We are not a country, like Iran, threatening to destroy the Jewish state, against which the Jews could launch a pre-emptive strike. We are everywhere and nowhere. Where would they strike?"

Salih paused, looked at Nat, and smiled. "Our new brother has done more to quietly further our cause in just a few months than we have been able to accomplish in years. If we can now, finally, with his help, succeed in killing the president of the United States of America, the world will realise that it can no longer be business as usual. In particular, politicians will understand that those who pursue unjust agendas, wherever they are and whoever they may be, will be punished. And it is by this realisation that we will achieve justice in Palestine and justice for Muslims worldwide."

A low murmur of voices filled the room as Salih took his seat. It was difficult to judge how his words had been received.

Zawahiri raised his hands and spoke quickly. Adnan did not translate, but Nat could understand what was happening. There was a showing of hands. First, what seemed like two-thirds of hands went up, and on the second showing, the remaining third. "Sorry, Mr. Jameson. I should have been translating that for you. The majority voted in agreement with Salih's sentiment."

CHAPTER 67

The remainder of the morning was taken up by every person present standing up and expressing an opinion or asking questions. Nat could feel himself losing concentration. The strain of listening to the translation over the words of the speaker was taking its toll.

Lunch was served at 1:00 p.m. and consisted of a delicious white fish, couscous, and lentils.

When the remnants of lunch were cleared away, Zawahiri called the assembly to order, and a discussion ensued on who was going to be the man to assassinate, or, as many put it—execute—the US president. It was going to be a suicide mission, and the room was full of volunteers. . . . *maybe*, Nat thought, *because none of them have a chance of being picked.*

In the end, it was Zawahiri, having listened patiently to them all, who came up with the solution, a solution which took Nat completely by surprise.

"I believe the man for this is Tariq Abu Habedi."

Nat had met this well-spoken, and utterly charming, Israeli Arab businessman and member of the Knesset when he visited London, heading up a delegation of Ta'ayush activists—a movement of Jews and Arabs working together to break down the barriers of racism and segregation between the two groups. Nat remembered Jim Preston had been impressed with the man as someone with a vision for how to achieve peace in the Middle East.

Habedi, a member of al-Qaeda? Prepared to become a martyr for the fundamentalist Muslim cause! It was hard to comprehend.

"He is a well-respected businessman," Zawahiri continued, "a member of Knesset and a member of the Arab Association of Human Rights. He was a man who believed that Arabs and Israelis could live in peace, shoulder to shoulder, but his idealism has been killed by repeated Israeli transgressions and humiliations. He came to us. We did not target him. His hatred for the Jews can be a powerful tool in our hands." Zawahiri paused to let Adnan catch up with his translation, and then turned to Nat.

"So, my friend, do you think you could get this man a meeting with your president?"

"I am amazed that you have a man of this calibre available. I met Mr. Habedi myself when he came to London two years ago as head of the coalition of Arabs and Jews working together to create a true Arab-Jewish partnership in the Middle East. My boss—my ex-boss," Nat corrected himself, "was very impressed, and so was I. And, yes, I think he is an excellent choice. As a power broker for peace, I am confident that I can arrange for him to meet with the president when he comes to Europe."

Zawahiri slapped his hands together, then stroked his beard, as Adnan finished his translation. Murmurs of approval and smiles filled the room. Zawahiri rose and clapped his hands again to get everyone's attention.

"Alhamdulillah!" "Thanks be to Allah!" The room erupted in praise for Allah.

Zawahiri remained standing and waited for the praises to come to an end. Then he turned to Nat, gestured for Nat to stand, and spoke in English. “I speak for all of us when I say that we thank you for your courage and for your commitment to the Muslim cause. Your vision and your bravery will change the world.” Zawahiri paused as Adnan translated. “Tell us, how will you arrange for Habedi to meet the president?”

“When I return to London, I shall be working on the plan for the president’s visit, and I will strongly recommend Habedi as a man the president ought to meet. His credentials speak for themselves, and he will, no doubt, pass all the background checks. I shall then arrange for Mr. Habedi to meet with the president during his stay in London. He will, in all likelihood, be staying at the Royal Palace, but meetings with private individuals will take place in a suite at the Savoy or the Ritz.”

“Excellent!” Zawahiri did not wait for Adnan to finish his translation, but when Adnan did, there were murmurs and nods of approval from al-Qaeda’s top leaders.

Nat looked at his watch. It was four hours since he had pressed the crown. Local time was 3:00 p.m. How long would it take the SEALS to arrive?

Nat started to worry that some of the attendees could be leaving the compound before they arrived, but those fears were allayed when Zawahiri continued. “So, as you Americans say: let’s look at next steps.” Adnan started to translate, but Zawahiri cut him off. “No need, we are just going to flesh out some details, then I shall take our friend for a tour of our facilities, and tonight we will have a celebration dinner and honour Allah, who is providing our way forward to victory.”

Nat could feel the knot in his stomach ease. If the SEALS were not here by nightfall, something would have gone very wrong.

"A messenger will be sent to Habedi, and he will learn about our plan. I know he will be excited and pleased," Zawahiri continued, "and you and I will communicate via Imam Badawi from now on. He is a fine man, and his role in all this will not be forgotten."

Nat nodded. "He is a sincere and dedicated man, and we have built a good relationship over the years. That's why I felt I could approach him with my idea."

"Allah works in mysterious ways. He brought you together for this purpose."

They spent another half hour going over how to ensure that their communications were safe. Zawahiri apologised for being so secretive about the location of al-Qaeda's headquarters but said that should something go wrong, God forbid, and Nat was subjected to US torture, the cruel methods of which were legendary in al-Qaeda circles, the location of their hideaway would be safe. Nat assured him that he understood completely. Zawahiri brought the meeting to a close, and the room emptied slowly as the men talked among themselves on the way out. There was a palpable buzz of excitement in the air.

"Not you, Hassan. You come with us." Zawahiri waved to Ibrahim Hassan al Asiri, al-Qaeda's foremost bomb expert. "I want to show our friend our most prized possession."

They left the room and headed down the long corridor, past Nat's room and past the entrance lobby, where a veiled woman was sitting typing away on an Apple laptop. They continued down the corridor in the opposite direction, almost to the end, before Hassan turned left at a pair of heavy steel doors. They were padlocked, but Hassan pulled a key out of his pocket, unlocked the doors, and swung one of them open. He walked in and found the light switch, and the room was bathed in fluorescent light by rows of fixtures suspended from the concrete ceiling. The room had the look and smell of a mechanic's workshop. A wooden workbench ran the length of the space on the far side of the room, in the middle of which stood a massive metal cradle on wheels holding a green tapered metal cylinder looking like a big tapered bullet, about from four feet to two feet in diameter and about twenty-five feet in length.

Zawahiri and Hassan headed straight for the cylinder, which sat up at eye level. Hassan patted the side of the cylinder. "This is our pride and joy—a Russian Oka SS-23 missile with an AA-60 nuclear warhead. It is really a museum piece, mothballed by the INF Treaty (Intermediate-Range Nuclear Forces Treaty) in the late 1980s."

He spoke in very broken English but with a big grin on his face. "It is a hundred-kiloton implosion nuclear bomb... enough power to level Tel Aviv. And over here..." He moved over to the workbench along the wall, "an exploding-bridgewire detonator which I have built myself from drawings provided by our Iranian friends."

Nat could feel the chills running down his spine. He did not know a lot about nuclear technology, and a thought had struck him: if the SEALS came barging in here with one of their stun grenades, would it set off an atomic explosion?

Nat turned to Zawahiri. "You promised me that this will now just be used as a deterrent. I need your solemn promise that this is a fact before I deliver up the president to Mr. Habedi."

Zawahiri shot Hassan a quick look before he answered. "You have my solemn promise."

The disappointment on the young man's face was palpable. All that hard work for nothing?

Zawahiri read his thoughts. "Do not look so dejected, Hassan; the bomb would not be a threat without your trigger mechanism. You have done an outstanding job."

That brought a glimmer of a smile to Hassan's face, but the disappointment at not being able to kill hundreds of thousands of Jews was evident in his eyes and body language.

Zawahiri turned to Nat and put a hand on his shoulder. "So, there you have it, my friend; you came to us just in the nick of time, as you Americans put it. Without you, this bomb would have gone off on the fourteenth of May next year, but now it looks as if we can achieve our objectives without that taking place. And I will tell you, I am pleased. Killing innocent people to force the hands of politicians is not as effective as killing the politicians themselves. I am sure history will show that you were right about that."

That is not what history will show, Nat thought, but aloud he said, "Thank you, Dr. Zawahiri; we cannot make the world better by punishing the innocent and letting the guilty go free. That is why I am here. I would not be doing what I am doing if I believed otherwise." Nat held Zawahiri in his gaze. Zawahiri looked away first, and Nat could see that he was emotional. His eyes were shiny, and he struggled to speak as he stretched his arms out and held Nat in both shoulders.

"Nat, my friend, we have—al-Qaeda has—struggled for many years fighting for justice. In that struggle we have made mistakes; one of those mistakes is that we have killed many Muslims. Our beloved leader, Osama, shortly before his death, admonished us for killing so many of our own, and he wanted us to focus on killing our real enemies." Zawahiri let go of Nat's shoulders before he continued. "As I am sure you are aware, Osama had set in motion a plan to kill President Obama and General Petraeus shortly before he died. Since then, we have looked at many ways to try and accomplish the death of your current president, and other high ranking US officials, but the security surrounding them is too tight, and we had nobody on the inside until you came along and started to do the job for us. I am very sorry that Osama is not here with us right now. He would have been very excited about seeing his dream turning into reality."

They left the workshop, and Zawahiri dismissed Hassan and took Nat outside under the impressive canopy of the runway camouflage net. He pointed to it. "This was designed by a very talented Yemeni engineer and architect and was built by our own construction company three years ago. This was all planned by Osama. What a shame he did not live to see it. The plan was to get him out of Abbottabad. The Americans were getting too distrustful of the Pakistani military leaders, some of whom had given him protection. This was designed to be his new hideaway and the permanent headquarters for al-Qaeda Inc. as well as for our Somali branch: Al Shabaab. The West does not seem to realise it, but al-Qaeda forms the organisational backbone of al-Shabaab with me as their leader."

It struck Nat that Zawahiri was speaking of al-Qaeda as a CEO of a multinational Fortune 500 company might have. And judging by the six private jets parked along the edge of the runway, they had more in common than anyone realised. The notion that al-Qaeda was on its "last legs" did not square with what Nat was both hearing and seeing. *God, I hope the SEALS get here soon!*

Zawahiri showed Nat the "control tower", which was not a tower at all but the end of the building they were in, where an all-glass corner gave views to the landing approach and the runway. "We have two fully qualified air traffic controllers working for us," Zawahiri announced proudly, "as well as two fully qualified mechanics. And, of course, so are the pilots and co-pilots. In fact, three of them are US trained and certified."

Zawahiri looked at his watch and then at Nat. "It is almost five o'clock. It will soon be time for evening prayers. Will you join us?"

Nat hesitated. Tom had said to try to separate himself from the others if he could, and this seemed like an ideal opportunity to do that even though there was no way of knowing when the SEALS would show up.

"I feel really tired," said Nat. "I would like to have a rest before dinner."

"I understand, my friend." Zawahiri looked at his watch again, "We will eat at seven tonight. You go and have a rest, and we will see you at seven. Can you find the way back to your room?"

Nat nodded. "Yes, thank you. Of course I can." *The simple layout of the building will make it easier, also, for the SEALS when they arrive,* he thought. The long, straight corridor, and all the rooms off to one side, facing in towards the landing strip, should be a lot simpler to attack than the maze of a floor plan he had seen in CIA's demo videos.

Back in his room, Nat lay down on the bed, fully dressed. He debated changing back into his suit and tie for dinner but decided against it. It would look very suspicious that he was dressed to stand out from the crowd when the attack came. Besides, if the nuclear bomb went off, it would not matter what he was wearing. His thoughts drifted to Sonja and the children. Would they all have Christmas together? He could just see Sonja putting up a brave front, "business as usual", in front of the children, while inside, she was in a state of turmoil, waiting anxiously for news that it was over and that her husband was safe. What a woman! Nat sighed deeply and closed his eyes. He realised that he felt every bit as tired as he had suggested to Zawahiri. The constant tension was taking its toll.

He thought he could hear Sonja's voice in the distance. She was saying something to him, but he could not make out what it was. Then he saw her. All of a sudden, she was much closer, standing almost next to him.

"Come home to us soon." She was smiling as she put her arms around Tanya and Gregory, who were standing next to her. He had not noticed them before. He tried to get the words out, "I will," but there was no sound. He tried to shout it. The whole world erupted in noise, and he found himself sitting bolt upright in a bed covered in diamonds. As his conscious mind kicked in, he realised that the diamonds were fragments of shattered glass.

He looked towards the window and saw that it was no longer there and that a bright orange light was pouring through it together with the roaring sound of flames. He jumped out of bed and was over by the window in two giant leaps. He peered out but withdrew quickly from the heat blasting through the opening, but what he had seen in that split second told him the SEALS had arrived. The jets parked outside were engulfed in flames which rose into the camouflage canopy above. Nat could feel his heart racing.

Calm down; control yourself! This is the moment you have been waiting for. He took three deep breaths, ran over to the door, and put his ear against it. First there was no sound, then suddenly he heard loud shouts and running feet. More explosions were coming from outside, then machine-gun fire which sounded like it was coming from above him.

He heard more excited voices from the corridor. Should he stay in his room or join the melee outside? The former would give him away as an accomplice of the attackers, and the latter would put him at a higher risk of getting hurt by friendly fire. The decision was made for him. The door flew open, almost knocked him over, and Adam appeared, followed by two al-Qaeda fighters who had not been present at the meeting or the dinner the night before.

"Come with us; we're under attack!" Adam's posture was hostile. He turned, and Nat followed, with the two fighters coming close behind. Adam broke into a run down the corridor. There was a loud explosion above them as they ran. The ground shook, and the air filled with concrete dust. They did not break stride until Adam stopped in front of a door. He knocked and put his ear to the door waiting for an answer. . . . Another loud explosion nearby and more concrete dust. Adam did not wait for an answer but swung the door open. Nat was pushed through and found himself standing face to face with Ayman al-Zawahiri, whose eyes were wide and black with rage.

"Was it you? Was it you? Have you betrayed us?" His shrill voice was just audible over the background noise of explosions and machine-gun fire.

Nat shook his head and did his best to look as shocked as he knew he would have been had he not been prepared for what was happening. "No, no! Not me! I killed two prominent

Americans to be here. Why would I do that and betray you? It makes no sense!"

The last words were drowned out by another loud explosion.

"Did you? Did you?" Zawahiri was shaking with rage, or was it fear? "I am not so sure. It may be somewhat academic now, but I intend to find out." He looked at Adam and shouted, "Make him talk!"

Nat saw Adam's right hand go across his body, and, moments later, Nat was staring at a Muslim sword—a scimitar—a curved, single-edged blade, just like the one in the Saudi Arabian flag. Adam held it sideways, twelve inches from Nat's nose. Spit was dribbling out from the corners of his mouth as he spoke with clenched teeth. "Do you recognise this?" He did not wait for an answer. "This is a slightly shortened version of a ceremonial sword, which we use for executions." He placed his left index finger on the sharp blade. "It is so sharp that it can cut a man's head clean off with one swift stroke. I would hate to have to do that to a fellow American." Adam's eyes bore into Nat's.

You bastard, Nat thought. *You would like nothing better*. But aloud he said, "I am telling you the truth. You have got to believe me!" The panic in his voice was real enough.

Zawahiri shouted again over the noise from outside, "We shall see! Take him into my bathroom! Make him talk! Take it one finger at a time. I want to know the truth, if it is the last thing I ever know!"

Another loud explosion overhead, followed by a series of smaller ones, made further conversation impossible. . . not that it mattered. Nat had the distinct feeling that the time for talk was over.

His arms were gripped from both sides; Adam turned to the bathroom door, and Zawahiri walked towards his desk. It was now or never. Nat transferred his weight to his left leg and threw a heel kick where he hoped it would find a knee. He heard the crunch of broken bone and a cry of pain from the man on his right, who let his arm free. Nat spun around, bending his arm, and sent his elbow into the side of the other guard's throat. He went down like a felled tree. Nat came full circle and saw Adam turning around and raising his sword. His contorted face bore an expression of surprise and rage.

He roared as he rushed towards Nat with the sword raised over his head. Nat did not move. *Use your opponent's momentum to your own advantage*. The CIA's close-combat instructor's words echoed in his brain. Suddenly, it seemed to be happening in slow motion.

Nat could see the veins on Adam's neck pulsating; he switched from holding the sword in both hands to holding it in his right. He was knock-kneed and pigeon-toed. Nat shot forwards and sideways, leaving his left leg in Adam's way. He flew past Nat, who turned to see his assailant crash into the entrance door. The door stopped him from falling. He turned around, blood rushing from a gash in his forehead, lifted the knife in both hands, uttered a guttural sound like a wounded animal, and rushed again at Nat, who started to prepare for the onslaught. Suddenly, he felt arms gripping him from behind, like a steel band had been placed across his chest.

Zawahiri! Nat had forgotten the man was there! Big mistake! Gavin would be disappointed. This was the end! Nat went limp and lifted his feet off the floor so that Zawahiri took his full weight and staggered forwards towards the raised blade, which reflected in the light from the naked bulb in the ceiling.

It is strange how much time you have to think before you're about to die. Sonja would cry, but then she would pick herself up and carry on, raising their children. He felt sorry that he would not see them grow up but glad that they would grow up in a world which he had helped make better.

There was a flash of bright light and a shockwave, as if he was stepping into another dimension. It did not hurt. Dying this way was not painful.

Nat felt a rush of relief, and then. . . nothing.

Chapter 68

Heaven was bright and cool with cloudlike, undefined contours, much like he had imagined it to be. He thought he could see the form of a person with golden hair, but the image was too blurred. Was he going to find out what God looked like? He strained his eyes to see better, but the scene in front of him dissolved like a mirage in a desert. He gave up. He would try again later, when he didn't feel so tired.

She had a beautiful smile. She was blond, blue-eyed, and dressed in white, but it was not Sonja, and just as well, although he was looking forward to her joining him up here one day.

"Hello, Mr. Jameson. How are you feeling?"

Feeling? He looked down, saw his own hands, wiggled his fingers, and felt the cool softness of the sheet. He could feel! He was not dead! A rush of relief flowed through his body like a warm river. "I feel...I feel fine, really fine." It came out more as a question than an answer. He started to laugh, but the laughter turned into tears, tears of happiness, tears of gratitude. "I'm so sorry."

"No, no, you have no need to be." She put a comforting hand on his shoulder. "You have been through a lot, and we are all very proud of you."

We? All very proud of you? Who was she? Where was he?

She beat him to asking the questions. "There is somebody waiting outside who will fill you in on everything. He is very anxious to see you as soon as possible. Do you think you're up for it?"

Nat nodded and looked around the room. It was obviously a hospital room, but where in the world was it? "What is your name?"

"Helen." She was halfway across the room, heading for the door, but turned around and smiled at him. "Shall I?" She gestured towards the door. He nodded and she opened it. "He will see you now."

She stepped aside, and in walked a man, who Nat had only met face to face once. Tom was grinning from ear to ear. "You son of a gun! You did it! Congratulations! The results of Operation Endgame exceeded all our expectations." They shook hands, and Nat flinched.

"Ouch! That right shoulder of mine is a bit tender."

Tom laughed. "You have a few bruises and a slight concussion from the stun grenade, but that is all. We thought you were dead. The SEALS found you in a pool of blood. We thought it was yours, but it was Zawahiri's. His skull was almost split in two. They certainly had us fooled about him dying in a drone strike. Must have been a look-alike sacrificed for the Cause. What happened in there?"

Nat told him, and Tom listened without interrupting. "I thought I was dead too," Nat concluded.

"No wonder! You did fantastically well; Gavin will be proud of you."

"I doubt that I would be here talking to you now had he not given me that crash course in close combat."

"Sure sounds like it. Listen, I'll be brief; there is somebody else who wants to talk to you—your wife. She knows you're fine, but I need to put you in the picture before you speak to her." Tom sat down on a chair next to the bed. He coughed and cleared his throat. "We got them all. They fought bravely to the bitter end. You are the only survivor. We lost two SEALS and have one damaged helicopter. We got a mother lode of intel, and—"

"What about the bomb?" Nat broke in.

"Yeah, Jesus Christ! Looks like we got there in the nick of time, doesn't it?"

"They were going to detonate it in Tel Aviv on the fourteenth of May next year, on the seventy-fifth anniversary of the creation of Israel." Nat's words hung in the air like black smoke.

"Bastards! Dead bastards now, thanks to you." Tom looked at his watch. "Anyway, it's on its way to Langley as we speak, together with everything else we found in the compound. It's an intel treasure trove. You'll be seeing arrests taking place all around the world in the coming weeks and months. We have a hundred people at Langley sifting through the info. It's going to take a few months to go through it all." Tom took out a handkerchief and blew his nose before he continued. "Anyway, there's been a change of plans. Based on how this thing panned out, we no longer think that you and your family need to go into hiding—that is, unless you feel you want to come forward and take the bows and get the credit you deserve. The fact of the matter is that anybody who saw you in the compound, or on the way to the compound, is dead, including the pilots who brought you and Omar, your escort."

"But that leaves Imam Badawi and Mahoud, the barber from Manchester." Nat frowned as he propped himself up on his good elbow.

Tom hesitated before answering. "Actually, no, it doesn't. Imam Badawi was hit by a car when he left the mosque yesterday evening—hit and run—poor fellow, and the barber from Manchester was found dead in his bathtub, also yesterday evening—massive heart attack."

Nat swallowed hard. "But that is murder!"

Tom shook his head. "No, just tying up loose ends and making sure that you and your family are going to be safe."

Nat let it sink in and realised that Tom was right. This way, there would be no need for changed identities and special protection, no need to worry that someday maybe somebody would come after them to exact revenge. "You are right, Tom. I can go back to life as usual...I mean, I can continue in my job, and nobody, other than those who were in on the plot, will be any the wiser."

"That's right, Nat. The downside is just that the rest of the world will never know what you did, will never know of your ingenious plot which dismantled al-Qaeda, and will therefore never give you the credit that you so richly deserve."

"That's not important. All of us who played our part will have the satisfaction of knowing that we made a difference, and that is good enough for me," Nat added. He needed to speak to Sonja, speak to her right now. That was the most important thing.

"Look, Tom, I need to speak to Sonja. Where are we, and when can I go home?"

"You're in Al Hada Hospital, near Taif Air Base, in Saudi Arabia, and we'll fly you out this morning if the doctors give you the all clear, and you'll be back in London around noon local time. The sooner the better, since you are only supposed to be home with a cold. This is your first day here. Your deputy is bound to call you when he reads the papers this morning. Lucky for us, we are two hours ahead of London, and…" He looked at his watch. "…it is only six thirty here, so we have a couple of hours before he reads the good news." Tom pulled something out of his pocket and held it up. "When he calls you, you will answer on this. Sonja knows that your home phone will be forwarded to this one from 7:00 a.m. her time. This will work even if you're in midair over the ocean when he calls. You will have a nice chat about events, and you'll tell him that you'll be back in the office tomorrow, come hell or high water. Put some coughing and sputtering in for good measure."

Tom placed the phone, which just looked like a slightly bulkier cell phone, on Nat's bedside table. "And until we switch it over, you can call her now with this. The line is secure; nobody can listen in." He handed it to Nat. "I'll wait outside."

Nat dialled her number; his hands were trembling. It was only five in the morning in London, but Sonja picked up on the second ring.

She was wide awake. "Nat, is that you?"

"Yes, darling, none other."

"Oh, Nat, it is so good to hear your voice. Are you all right?"

"Yes, I'm fine, just a bit bruised, that's all."

"Thank God. Thank you, God!" She started to cry softly. "When will we see you?"

"Sooner than you think, darling. How are the children?"

"They're fine. Just waiting for Dad to come home from his business trip, that's all."

"Tom says they'll fly me out this morning if the doctors agree. He says I could be home by noon your time. The sooner I get home the better it will be. We'll be together; the office will continue to believe I've been out with a cold, and Tom says we'll be able to continue our lives as if nothing happened. I'll explain later."

"Hurry home, darling. I love you!"

Click.

She had hung up, again, before he had a chance to say goodbye.

The doctor who examined Nat found him fit to travel and gave him some tablets to take in case he developed a headache. Nat complained that his ears were ringing, and the doctor assured him that this would gradually go away over the next week or so but advised him to get a hearing test in a month's time, to determine whether there was any permanent hearing damage.

Tom reappeared, and Nat gave him the thumbs-up. "I'm good to go."

One hour later, Nat settled back in the soft leather seat of a Gulfstream G5. He was the only passenger. Before leaving, Nat had expressed concern that Helen, his nurse, might know who he was.

Tom told him not to worry. "She is one of us, and so are the crew on the plane that is taking you home. Don't worry, we are not going to screw this up."

Nat had dosed off when the phone rang. He fumbled it out of his jacket pocket. "Hello, Jameson residence." His voice had the roughness of sleep.

"Wow. You sound rough, still. Have you seen the paper this morning?" Anthony Burville's voice was charged with excitement.

Nat confessed that he had not. "Our delivery man has a cold, too, I think."

"Big news, Nat; good news. They raided al-Qaeda's headquarters last night. All their top brass, including al-Zawahiri who we thought we'd killed, are dead... found them in the bushes in Somalia... High-tech hideaway with its own hidden airstrip. Four teams of Navy SEALS parachuted in, followed by four helicopters. Nobody survived. No al-Qaeda survived, that is."

Nat coughed. "Fantastic! That is terrific news! What a great finish to the year!" Nat coughed and sputtered some more. "I'll turn on the TV and get it there. Hold the fort one more day, Tony. I'll be in first thing in the morning."

"No problem, but you are missing the celebrations. We are all in a party mood here—champagne all round, at lunchtime."

"Thanks, Tony; we can celebrate some more tomorrow. Everything else going OK?"

"Not to worry, boss. All is fine here. We miss you, that's all. Get well!"

"Thanks, Tony; I'll see you tomorrow morning." Nat hung up and sank back in the leather seat. He decided to do a little celebrating himself and asked Betty if she could bring him a mimosa with his scrambled egg and bacon breakfast.

He had finished breakfast and was on his second coffee when the phone rang again. Burville again? Nat dreaded another conversation with him.

He pressed the button and put the phone to his ear. "Hello, Jame—"

"I know who you are, son. Congratulations! Well done!" President Adam's booming voice resonated in Nat's ringing ear.

"Thank you, sir. I'm glad you approve."

"Ha, ha, ha! Approve? Damn right I do. If I could, I would give you a knighthood. As it is, Langley tells me I can't acknowledge your spectacular effort to anyone. . . for your and your family's own safety, they tell me." He paused.

"It was teamwork, Mr. President. We all did our bit."

"Yeah, but you went to the snake pit, and you smoked the snakes out. I hate the idea that there is nothing I can do to reward you for what you have done. There must be something I can do without compromising our little secret?"

Nat's eyes roamed around the cabin, trying to think of something to say, when it struck him. "There is something you could do for me, Mr. President."

The president listened intently, and when Nat finished his request, the president laughed heartily and said, "Well, son, consider it done; just give me the dates. It will be my pleasure. And one more thing—I want you to come to Washington in the new year so you can give me your whole story, blow by blow, and before you come, please practice calling me Ted. Merry Christmas!"

CHAPTER 69

It was quarter to one London time when the limousine stopped in front of the redbrick townhouse in Cadogan Gardens. Nat stepped out of the car and was on the stair landing when the front door flew open, and Sonja came running out and threw herself in his arms. He held her tight and savoured the moment. Words were unnecessary. She laughed and cried at the same time, and he kissed her salty tears. She pulled him inside, and Darwin joined the celebrations, jumping up and down against Nat's leg and spinning around his own axis. The special importance of this reunion was not lost on him. They both looked down at him and laughed.

Life could start again—back to normal, a *better* normal.

Sonja would pick the children up from school at 3:00 p.m. as usual, and he would come with her and give them a surprise. They would quiz him about his business trip, then they would do their homework and have a bath before dinner around the oak table in the kitchen. They would ask to stay up a bit longer. *And tonight,* Nat thought, *we will let them.*

Preparations for the Christmas holiday had been less hectic than usual, as they would arrive at a fully decorated chalet in

Zermatt with a real Christmas tree. Nat and Gregory had made a sturdy polystyrene box for the Gingerbread House, complete with a handle, and it was Greg's carry-on.

And now they were on their way to the airport in the Bentley, with George at the wheel. It was a first for them all, except for Nat, and Greg was impressed with the TV screen and the CD player.

It was Sonja who first noticed that something was not quite right and addressed George. "Where are you taking us, George? This is not the shortest route to Heathrow."

"It is the route the ambassador told me to take, madame." George had a hint of a smile on his face in the mirror.

Five minutes later, an airport came into view, much smaller than Heathrow. George pulled up in front of a low building, and two porters appeared immediately and brought their luggage inside.

"Welcome to Harrod's Aviation." A smiling young lady stepped out from her reception desk and came out and shook their hands.

Sonja gave Nat a long look, smiled, and shook her head.

Greg, meanwhile, ran past the reception desk and through a very plush lounge, at the end of which was an all-glass wall. "Dad, Dad, look at all the private jets! Wow!" His face was plastered to the glass. "Look, they're loading our luggage into the one over there!" He ran back to the reception counter, where the receptionist had just handed back their passports.

"You are all set to go. Let me escort you to your aircraft."

On their way out to board the plane, Sonja leaned closer to Nat and said, "How did this come about? Delusions of grandeur?"

Nat gave her a big grin and squeezed her arm. "No, but I said to Greg at the start of all this, when Jim and I flew private, that maybe we could all do it someday. When the president asked me if there was something I would like, since my involvement in Endgame must forever remain a secret, this struck me as a good substitute for fame and glory. I warned your parents about the change in travel plans, and they'll follow the day after tomorrow."

Greg had run ahead and was shaking hands with the captain and the co-pilot before running up the short flight of steps.

"My hero with the warm heart." Sonja leaned into him and kissed his cheek.

Epilogue

In the weeks and months following the "Raid on al-Qaeda's Bosaso Headquarters," as the press had labelled the event (the compound had been found on an elevated plain fifty kilometres south of Somalia's largest port city: Bosaso on the southern coast of the Gulf of Aden), al-Qaeda cells were rolled up on all five continents, and plans for hundreds of terrorist attacks were discovered and prevented. The United States provided reinforcements to the EUNAVFOR (European Union's Naval Force), and together they put an end to piracy along the Somali coast.

Slowly, the scattered remnants of al-Qaeda were starved of funding and were unable to regroup and rebuild, and when President Adams came to Europe the following year, he dealt a final blow to Muslim extremism when he proposed that financial support to Israel and the Palestinians should be suspended until both sides held a referendum asking two simple questions:

Do you want a two-state solution, where Jews and Arabs live separately in their own countries? Mark "X" in this box

Do you want a single state in which Jews and Palestinians live together? Mark "X" in this box

Politicians on both sides resisted for nearly twelve months but in the end had to give way to national and international public pressure.

The referendum was held, and to everyone's surprise, except the people who voted, *75 percent of them voted in favour of a single state.*

The politicians were stunned. The world was stunned. All the fighting and bloodshed had been such a terrible waste.

The new state, comprising all Jewish and Palestinian lands, was named New Palestine, and the capital was Jerusalem, where Jews and Arabs could share their respective holy sites. A country was created where Jews and Arabs could live and prosper together in peace—a country *by* the people and *for* the people.

Since returning to his job as ambassador to the Court of St. James, Nat had worked tirelessly to improve US relations with China, Russia, and Iran, who had changed their outlook on the West after New Palestine stepped forward and unilaterally scrapped its, by international standards, modest nuclear capability and challenged all other nuclear powers to follow suit.

There were mumblings in diplomatic circles that Ambassador Jameson was the president's favourite, judging by his regular visits to the Oval Office and Camp David. Nobody could understand why.

After all, what had he done that was so special?

Printed in Great Britain
by Amazon

53902309R00326